Crossings

CROSSINGS

Women on the Santa Fe Trail

Frances Levine

University Press of Kansas

© 2024 by the University Press of Kansas
All rights reserved

Published by the University Press of Kansas (Lawrence, Kansas 66045), which was organized by the Kansas Board of Regents and is operated and funded by Emporia State University, Fort Hays State University, Kansas State University, Pittsburg State University, the University of Kansas, and Wichita State University

Library of Congress Cataloging-in-Publication Data

Names: Levine, Frances, author.
Title: Crossings : women on the Santa Fe Trail / Frances Levine.
Description: Lawrence, Kansas : University Press of Kansas, 2024. | Includes bibliographical references.
Identifiers: LCCN 2024007629 (print) | LCCN 2024007630 (ebook) | ISBN 9780700637812 (cloth) | ISBN 9780700637829 (ebook)
Subjects: LCSH: Women—Santa Fe National Historic Trail—Biography. | Women—Santa Fe National Historic Trail—History. | Santa Fe National Historic Trail—History. | Santa Fe (N.M.)—History. | Saint Louis (Mo.)—History. | New Mexico—Commerce—United States. | United States—Commerce—New Mexico. | United States—Territorial expansion. | BISAC: HISTORY / United States / State & Local / Southwest (AZ, NM, OK, TX) | HISTORY / United States / 19th Century
Classification: LCC HQ1438.S54 L48 2024 (print) | LCC HQ1438.S54 (ebook) | DDC 978/.0209252—dc23/eng/20240730
LC record available at https://lccn.loc.gov/2024007629.
LC ebook record available at https://lccn.loc.gov/2024007630.

British Library Cataloguing-in-Publication Data is available.

Printed in the United States of America

10 9 8 7 6 5 4 3 2 1

The paper used in this publication is acid free and meets the minimum requirements of the American National Standard for Permanence of Paper for Printed Library Materials Z39.48–1992.

*In loving memory of my brother,
Philip Cyril Levine
(1946–2020)*

CONTENTS

Preface ix

Acknowledgments xiii

Introduction 1

1. Bartering Women: Captives, Commodities, and Traders 26

2. On the Trail of Carmel Benavides Robidoux 48

3. Schoolgirls on the Trail: Adaline, Marian, and Francisca 69

4. Seeking Health on the Santa Fe Trail 97

5. Unequal Companions: African American Women on the Santa Fe Trail 118

6. The End of the Trail 143

Conclusion: The Legacy of the Santa Fe Trail 173

Notes 185

Bibliography 225

Index 241

PREFACE

In the winter of 2014 I changed jobs and moved from Santa Fe, New Mexico, to St. Louis, Missouri. I joked that I simply put my car in reverse and traveled eastward on the Santa Fe Trail, the route that had joined these places two centuries ago. Early in my career I worked as an archaeologist and ethnohistorian, studying historical sites and evidence of cultural change. I had excavated or studied artifacts from several archaeological sites in and around Santa Fe that contained deposits from the Santa Fe Trail era and before the arrival of the railroad (which led to even more changes in technology and demographics). For New Mexicans, the Santa Fe Trail had a profound impact on the variety and quantity of goods available. This is apparent in archaeological deposits that document economies at the household level.[1]

After moving from New Mexico to Missouri, I began to understand the direct connections between the families and businesses at both ends of the trail. Focusing on women's experiences on the Santa Fe Trail allowed me to explore the complexity and depth of the links between the Southwest and the American heartland. I was able to see the evolution of women's roles in interregional travel and intercultural exchanges. Women were central to the western experience and, told through their own words, the story of the Santa Fe Trail is much more than the march of Manifest Destiny and the rise of commercial enterprises.

Working in museums in Santa Fe and St. Louis has given me access to artifacts and archival collections that document some of the material changes that occurred, as well as women's perspectives on the history of the Santa Fe Trail. Museum collections generally house photographic and painted portraits of women and items of clothing and jewelry they wore for special events. Such items are presumed to have been made, sewn, and embroidered by women or used by women in domestic settings. As often as not, these items are unattributed unless they belonged to or were donated by a prominent family. Admittedly, museum collections tend to reflect the taste and contents of elite households, but I reasoned that, coupled with archival collections, they could illuminate how the Santa Fe trade more broadly affected families and communities in New Mexico and Missouri.

Two centuries after this trade officially opened, numerous accounts and recollections of women who traveled the Santa Fe Trail have been published. Some are new sources recently donated to archival collections; others are older sources that are being reexamined to analyze how women's roles in the trade were ignored or erased from earlier publications. Several authors have published lists of women who accompanied American soldiers serving in military forts or women who came later as the wives of New Mexico's territorial officials. Still other lists contain the names of young girls from elite New Mexican families who were sent to St. Louis for schooling. Early territorial census records, specifically those dating from 1846 to 1879—between the assertion of American control and just before the arrival of the railroad in New Mexico—list young women whose birthplaces in the eastern United States or Europe indicate that they traveled at least partway on the trail. These lists do not illuminate the women's experiences as they crossed the country; nor do they impart any deeper understanding of the significance of the Santa Fe trade. They do, however, indicate opportunities for an analysis of the roles, agency, and experiences of women who traversed the Santa Fe Trail. The lists tend to focus on women who traveled west, gesturing toward Euro-American women's role in settling the West. But several of the women I write about traveled from west to east, from New Mexico to Missouri, and some made the trip more than once in both directions. This offered the opportunity to examine the experiences of women who participated in cultural exchanges that went both ways.[2]

The research and writing of a book can take surprising turns and lead to revelations that are quite different from those envisioned at the beginning of the process. I knew the Santa Fe Trail was well documented in English-language materials, but I found an abundance of relevant materials in many venues. Collections at the Missouri Historical Society, St. Louis Mercantile Library, Missouri Botanical Garden, State Historical Society of Missouri, and St. Louis Art Museum added to my understanding of the scale and scope of connections between St. Louis and Santa Fe. They illustrated my argument that St. Louis is central to understanding the history of the Santa Fe Trail. Many of the names tied to the history of French, German, other Euro-American, and Jewish families in New Mexico were associated with enterprises and families from St. Louis and elsewhere in Missouri. The Santa Fe Trail was key to understanding how resources extracted in the Southwest and West led to fame and fortune for people and industries in St. Louis. It was illuminating to find a link between people from New Mexico and St. Louis, as well to the broader history of trade with Chihuahua, Mexico. The opportunity to visit historic sites, towns, trail segments, and even the graves of women and men associated with the Santa Fe Trail connected the history at both ends of the trail in a meaningful way for me. But there was still the question of why the stories of the trail mattered and how women's roles in the trade and the trail might lead to greater understanding.

In some ways, I was inspired to write this book about women on the Santa Fe Trail by historian Virginia Scharff's essays in *Twenty Thousand Roads*.[3] Scharff examines the motivations and participation of women in westward expansion as they traveled on wagon trails, railroads, and highways—endeavors that have largely been documented by men's actions and activities. Scharff approaches this history from what she calls an oblique angle on the shifting image of the West, arguing that women demonstrated their own agency and destinies through movement and travel. I selected women from different eras to examine how the country and the context of the trail changed over time. I selected not only women who traveled east to west to settle the American frontier but also those who traveled from the Southwest—largely from the Hispanic communities of northern New Mexico—to the East, taking part in the processes of cultural blending and cultural divisions occasioned by the Santa Fe trade.

I consider some of the women who moved from Mexican and Native American settlements east to the French communities of the confluence region (where the Missouri and Mississippi Rivers meet), as well as women who moved from the United States into and in some cases onto lands appropriated from Hispanic and Indigenous communities. While exploring the motivations and examining the reflections of these women who traveled the trail between St. Louis and Santa Fe, I try to set their stories within the broader history of interregional encounters. My goal is not to prove a single theory. Rather, I examine the many reasons women traveled the Santa Fe Trail. These women were not safe from the dangers nor immune to the lure and adventure of travel. I searched for women from different cultural and economic backgrounds who traveled the trail for a variety of reasons. I wanted to share perspectives beyond those of homesteaders or emigrants and look past the stereotypes of women as reluctant travelers.

I primarily limited my subjects to women who traveled to, from, or through St. Louis or other towns in Missouri. As a result, several women who made the journey from Kansas, Colorado, or Oklahoma to New Mexico and took other routes that fed into the trail did not make it into this study. In some cases, fathers, husbands, brothers, and partners were the only sources documenting the women's experiences on the trail. I focus on women who crossed the continent from 1760 to the late 1870s. By arranging the women's stories chronologically, I consider the successive layers of history and cultural encounters between people traveling from St. Louis to Santa Fe—and often back again—as well as the events, contexts, and commerce that brought them together.

ACKNOWLEDGMENTS

Crossings took more years to write than it probably should have. Several of the women included in this book have been the focus of my research and writing over many years of my academic and museum careers. In some ways, though, my move to St. Louis in 2014 made it a stronger book, once I came to understand how important the confluence of the Missouri and Mississippi Rivers was in shaping the Santa Fe trade. My research was enriched by working at the Missouri Historical Society (MHS) in some of the same spaces as previous trail researchers and by the opportunity to use collections donated by families with deep ties to the Santa Fe Trail.

I relied on the skills of reference librarians, museum curators, and trail aficionados to answer questions and help me sort out the sequence of events in the trail's long history. Friends and family listened to me tell these stories, repetitively, and maybe they pondered why these particular women occupied so much of my time.

One unexpected benefit of the extended time it took to complete this project was the opportunity to meet the descendants of several of the women I have written about. Mary Outten, who has lived at both ends of the trail, is a descendant of Francisca López de Kimball. Mary graciously loaned me documents, books, and photographs, and we spent hours talking about and visiting sites in and around Florissant, Missouri, an area associated with the Kimball and Douglas family histories. I missed the lovely dinners and casual gatherings during the pandemic years (2020–22), but I know there will be more in the future.

Mary introduced me to Amanda Gesiorski, the helpful archivist at the Visitation Academy in St. Louis. I appreciate the special efforts by Susan Nalezyty, former school archivist and historian at the Georgetown Visitation Preparatory School. During the pandemic shutdown, Dr. Nalezyty researched Fanny López's attendance at Visitation's Washington, DC, campus.

The internet carried far and wide some of the shorter articles I have written about these women. That is how several other descendants learned about my research or heard me speak in online formats. Diana Landry lives in Illinois now, but she was raised in Fort Lupton, Colorado, and made frequent visits to her family in Vallecitos and Española, New Mexico. She is a descendant of María Rosa Villalpando through her maternal line. When she read a piece I wrote in the MHS publication *Gateway* in 2019, she emailed me, and meeting her was like connecting with a dear friend. She, in turn, introduced me to her distant cousin Adele (Dellie) Flanigan Johnson, who is a direct descendant through María Rosa's daughter Hèléne Salé dit Lajoie Leroux. Dellie introduced me to Mark Redohl, who is a descendant of María Rosa and Jean Baptiste's son Lambert. We all spent a wonderful day together visiting the Old Cathedral of St. Louis and searching for additional materials about their family history. It was amazing to spend time exchanging records and talking about this remarkable story with the descendants of María Rosa's children. Thanks to Dellie's efforts, María Rosa's family has been recognized as one of the original families of St. Louis by the St. Louis Genealogical Society. My thanks to Mary Ellen Vanderlinden for her help in locating the graves and burial records for the Leroux and Primm families, descendants of Hèléne Salé dit Lajoie Leroux, at Calvary and Bellefontaine Cemeteries. I was privileged to be with the family for the fall 2022 dedication of a new gravestone for Hèléne at Calvary Cemetery in St. Louis. Dellie and her brother Ted Flanigan met community members of Los Ranchos in fall 2023 and explored their intertwined family histories in New Mexico and St. Louis. It was thrilling to hear about their visit.

Robert Stollsteimer from Montrose, Colorado, contacted me after reading something I had written about his great-grandmother Carmel Benavides Robidoux. Robert graciously shared the family history he wrote, and we spoke on the phone several times. I so appreciate his enthusiasm for history and his honesty in speaking about the painful stories we all have in our family histories.

Daniel Kosharek and I worked together in New Mexico when I was director of the Palace of the Governors, New Mexico History Museum, and he was curator of the photo archives. It was quite a surprise to learn several years later, while researching Carmel Benavides Robidoux, that Daniel is a descendant of Antoine Robidoux. I can see the resemblance now in their photographs and profiles.

I had the pleasure of meeting Peggy Stelloh and Kristin Cantrell of Dallas, Texas, who are the great-nieces of Stella Drumm Atkinson. Stella was the librarian at MHS from 1913 to 1943. Her annotated version of Susan Shelby Magoffin's Santa Fe Trail diary written during the fateful summer of 1846 remains one of the most famous women's trail journals. I was touched that her nieces were interested in my research and by the respect they have for their late great-aunt.

Thank you to my colleagues in New Mexico who helped me bridge the two ends of the trail and do my research remotely—literally and virtually. Henrietta "Hank" Christmas is an extraordinary and generous genealogical researcher. I am always amazed at the connections she makes and her knowledge of the links among families through the centuries. Dr. Rick Hendricks and Robert Martinez both served as New Mexico state historians. They answered many questions and helped me be a more careful researcher. Any mistakes are my own.

Dr. Enrique Lamadrid is the muse to much of New Mexico's folklore and music. Our long friendship has spanned many projects. His voluminous scholarly work nurtured my interest in the *Inditas*, or songs of captivity in New Mexico. Many of them were recorded by renowned ethnomusicologist John Donald Robb, and through his late daughter Priscilla "Pris" Robb McDonnell, who was an active member of MHS, we were connected to history at both ends of the trail.

Also, thanks to Enrique for introducing me to Francisco "El Comanche" Gonzales of Los Ranchos, who has led the Comanche dances at Ranchos de Taos for a long time. He was pleased to learn the details of María Rosa Villalpando's history in St. Louis. She and others who were captured and never returned are remembered through the songs of captivity and rescue performed in Ranchos every year. I look forward to seeing the Comanche dance again, but now through a new lens of history. Jerry Gurulé collaborated with Enrique and me on a project in New Mexico involving first contact documents. I appreciate his enthusiastic participation in this book, especially his prompt emails and his transcription and translation of documents relating to María Rosa's abduction and her relationship with Jean Baptiste Salé dit Lajoie.

Kate Kingsbury's story has been told by several authors, but Dr. Alysia Abbott's study of the Odd Fellows Cemetery added a new perspective questioning Kate's final resting place. Finding John Kingsbury's letter in the MHS archives and his order for a tombstone to be erected in Santa Fe provided poignant details of Kate's short and tragic life.

Many former colleagues at the Palace of the Governors, New Mexico History Museum, aided in this research or reviewed and collaborated on pieces that appeared in *El Palacio*, the journal of the Museum of New Mexico. Thanks particularly to Hannah Abelbeck, curator of photographs and archival collections, and photo archivist Caitlyn Carl for their assistance with images. Hannah is an astute researcher and was helpful in finding appropriate photographs. Patricia Hewitt, who has since moved back to her beloved Boston area, supported my research in the earliest stages of the book, as did Tomas Jaehn. I am grateful to both of them.

Parts of several chapters originally appeared in *Gateway* or in *El Palacio*.[1] Thanks to former *El Palacio* publisher Shelley Thompson, who invited me to write for the journal, and to the editors I enjoyed working with there: Candace Walsh and Charlotte Jusinski. Kate Nelson, former managing editor and award-winning feature writer for *New Mexico Magazine*, will always be my sounding board for ideas about history. She gets my geekiness and love of history no matter where we find it—on the road, in the corners of antique shops, and in the letters and memoirs written by those who came before, leaving us clues to the past. She was my first editor at *El Palacio* and my collaborator on many exhibition scripts in New Mexico.

At MHS, Chris Gordon, director of library and collections, is a terrific guide to the history of the region and the bird species of the confluence. Thanks to Chris for taking me to Samuel and Susan Magoffin's property in Kirkwood, Missouri, where she likely spent her last days. Chris also guided me to more resources in the MHS collections than I was able to use in this study. Brothers Bill and Peter Vatterott shared some of their deep background research on the Magoffin lands and proposed another location in Kirkwood where Susan might have spent her last days. Their generosity and research skills are amazing.

Thanks to the MHS library staff who located items for me, helped me transition to the online collections while the library was closed during the pandemic, retrieved interlibrary loans, dropped off books, and were more than just politely interested in this work: Randy Blomquist, Jaime Bourassa, Kelly Brown, Emily Jaycox, Molly Kodner, Magdalene Linck, Dennis Northcott, and Jason Stratman. Lauren Mitchell is the attentive editor of museum publications. She performed the surgical editing that made my *Gateway* articles about the trail connect to both New Mexico and Missouri readers. Hattie Felton and Adam MacPhàrlain led me to wonderful items in the MHS collections to support these stories and many more that I could have included.

The MHS Leadership Team comprises outstanding museum professionals, and working with them always produces creative and engaging history. They taught me to be a better museum professional. Thanks to Karen Goering, who often loaned me works and then found additional materials for this ongoing project. Katie Van Allen encouraged me to keep writing even when administrative duties called. Jody Sowell, a terrific and creative storyteller—not a fibber—has a wonderful ability to craft engaging exhibitions. Mark Sundlov brings sound thinking to our work and is responsible for our connection to the veterans community. Christina Renz brought order to the chaos in the finance department. My successive assistants Anne-Marie Thurman, Mary Birkenmeier, Sharon Wilcutt, and Tamaki Stratman protected the few hours of writing I was able to do each week, and Charles Moreland and Kris Scott kept the trains of many committee meetings from crashing. Thanks to the Board of Trustees and Subdistrict for their trust in me and support for our entire team. There are many others to thank, and I hope they know how much I treasured and benefited from working with our MHS team from 2014 until July 1, 2022. I enjoyed a brief seventy-seven days of retirement and then joined the St. Louis Kaplan Feldman Holocaust Museum as interim director. The opening team there included Helen Turner, Amy Lutz, Lory Copper Naylor, Becky Donovan, Jillian Howell, Haley Stodart, Brayden Swathwood, Zach Turner, and Diana Matthis. Only their dedication to telling the Holocaust history coaxed me back into the game.

Colleagues at other St. Louis institutions graciously read chapters or referred me to other materials. Thanks to Bob Moore, formerly of Gateway National Park; John Hoover and Julie Dunn Morton at the St. Louis Mercantile Library; Amy Torbert at the St. Louis Art Museum; and staff at the library of the Missouri Botanical Garden. Many other scholars are cited in the notes, and I am grateful for their work, which provided me with such important guides to the region.

I cannot remember when I first met Mike Olsen, eminent scholar of the Santa Fe Trail, but our friendship has spanned decades. I appreciate the work that Mike, Joanne VanCoevern, and a dedicated group of volunteers have done to preserve the physical evidence of trail ruts, crossings, and other landmarks along the length of the Santa Fe Trail. I am grateful as well for the trail history I learned as a member of the National Santa Fe Trail Association and the support received from team members of the National Park Service Long Distance Trails Program. Dorris Keeven-Franke taught me so much about Germans in Missouri and the role of St. Charles in the Santa Fe Trail.

When I moved to Missouri, one of my first outings was to Arrow Rock and the area around Franklin. Since then, Kathy Borgman's friendly voice and warm hospitality have enhanced many stays in the area. My thanks to Dr. Tom Hall and Margaret Hall for their gracious reception in Arrow Rock and all they have shared about their deep love of its history. Rich and Deb Lawson, at Arrow Rock Trading Co., have tempted me with many treasures, and Rich showed me the crossing and trail segments on their land. Thanks to Steve Byers, Friends of Arrow Rock, and the many people whose love of the Santa Fe Trail makes Arrow Rock a charming place to visit.

At the University Press of Kansas, I had the good fortune to work again with Bethany Mowry, the original acquisitions editor, and then David Congdon, who shaped the book and stood by me through a few years of writing and pandemic-related struggles. The review comments provided by Dr. Rick Hendricks, Dr. Susan Lee Johnson, Dr. Virginia "Gingy" Scharff, and anonymous reviewers have made this a stronger book, but I accept all errors and omissions as my own.

What would I do without the copyediting skills of Mary June-el Piper? I know that all I produce would look and sound disjointed without her touch. She is the goddess of the keyboard and my dear friend and colleague for more years than either of us will admit.

I have an awesome posse of women friends who support me in life. We grew closer during the pandemic years, and I am grateful for walks in the neighborhood and Forest Park, for the exchanges of delicious recipes, and for all the gifts of laughter and solace, books and treats that got us through so much. FaceTime and tweets, Zoom happy hours, and notes and cards made the bad times bearable. Their thoughtfulness filled me, sustained me, and brought me to a resting point during very difficult years, and they continue to love me—as messy and emotional as I can be. Thank you Patricia Aguirre, Yemi Akande-Bartsch, Page Allen, Joan Briccetti, Marie Casey, Betsy Cohen, Anna Crosslin, Kathy Greminger, Kris Kleindeinst, Helen Kornblum, Marylen Mann, Lisa McLaughlin, Karry Meshberg, Sandra Moore, Jane Sauer, Cherie Scheick, Ann Scott, Laura Shaughnessy, Ginny Sloan, Ellen Soule, Carla Van West, Eileen Wells, and Jeannie Wood. And I can't leave out my "brothers" Tim Carson, Mike Delello, Bob Denlow, Josef Díaz, Joe Feldman, Joe Gallagher, Patrick Gallagher, Vic Johnson, Jim Kemp, Malcolm Purdy, Andrés Siegel, Michael Slawin, Frank Steeves, and Mark Utterback, who called and sent cards or notes to lift me up when grief nearly crushed me and who keep me laughing and loving. A special thanks to Wayne Crosslin for his help in preparing photos for publication, for reminding me that fewer but larger images look better, and for encouraging me to use my knowledge of women in history to write other works as well. Thanks to BigMacc coaches who trained me for strength, endurance, and resilience in ways beyond the physical sphere—Ahmand Johnson, Ben Sojka, and Chelle Habecker.

Thank you to Tom Merlan, who corrects my persistent misuse of commas and tries to understand my handwriting and my winding path away from the home we built together so long ago. Anna Merlan and Steve Merlan have been especially attentive to my needs during these strange years. I love and respect them so much. Carolyn Williams Brandi and Grace Lucero Valdez became and remain dear family members by choice. Linda Grant, my sister-in-law who is my sister dearest, has accompanied me on quite a journey through the years, with so many lessons yet to learn.

The notes and bibliography pay tribute to the centuries of scholars who have written about the Santa Fe Trail—the routes and sights and history of the trail connecting Santa Fe and St. Louis, where East met West and the French and Euro-American communities met Native American tribes and the Spanish-speaking residents of the Southwest. Knowing about the travelers who crossed the continent—in both directions—puts a different perspective on American history. Thank you for stimulating my interest and answering my queries.

Introduction

With the stroke of a congressional pen on August 10, 1821, ninety-five-year-old María Rosa Villalpando Salé dit Lajoie became a US citizen in the newest state in the Union. She was not born in Missouri and was not French, but she had lived in St. Louis since 1768 as the wife of one of the village's French-born founders. She had been born nearly one thousand miles west of St. Louis in the mountains of northern New Mexico. How she came to travel that distance and witness Missouri's new political affiliation was a demonstration of extraordinary resilience. She was one of many women and children abducted from northern New Mexico by Comanches in the eighteenth and nineteenth centuries. They are still remembered during annual feast days in New Mexico's Hispanic villages and documented in the state's historical literature. María Rosa's story is steeped in New Mexican folklore, but it has resonance too in the history of the Santa Fe Trail and the economies that connected Mexico, New Mexico, and Missouri with the western expansion of the United States.[2]

New Mexican folk culture has a rich tradition of oral histories, performances, and songs that commemorate the alternating cycles of trade and raids between Plains Indians and New Mexicans. The literature and oral histories center on themes of captivity and redemption, as well as the role of women in cross-cultural encounters. These folk performances are more than mere dramatic productions. They are the performative manifestation of identity and of the inheritance of intercultural exchange and cultural hybridity that is often ignored in the tourism slogan that reduces New Mexicans to three broadly glossed cultures: Indian, Hispanic, and Anglo.[1] In the songs and performances, community members lament the men, women, and children who were taken captive, and they celebrate those who were ransomed or escaped and returned to their New Mexican homes.[2]

María Rosa was captured by Comanches during a raid on the Villalpando family compound in Ranchos de Taos, New Mexico, in August 1760. Her mother was killed, her infant son was separated from her, and she was carried off with a number of other captives. Over the next year, Spanish authorities tried to ransom and redeem the captives, but María Rosa was not among those returned. Subsequently, she was traded to the Pawnee and then purchased by the man who later became her husband. Jean Baptiste Salé dit Lajoie was a fur trader from the nascent French settlement of St. Louis. He brought María Rosa to St. Louis, along with the son she had with a Comanche man and another son born to Lajoie and María Rosa in the Pawnee camp. In St. Louis, María Rosa made the transition from being a captive to being a Creole citizen of this alternately Spanish- and French-controlled colony and ultimately a citizen of the United States. While Missouri celebrated statehood, Mexico was nearing the end of its quest for independence from Spain. With that new sovereignty came free trade between Mexico and the westward-expanding United States.

There were enormous political changes across North America and in Mexico in 1821. Treaties and compromises penned by politicians asserted US claims to tribal lands and affirmed decisions that would have long-term consequences for people of color in North America. The issue of whether states would enter the Union as slaveholding or free drove Congress to craft the Missouri Compromise in 1820 to balance sectional interests. Maine became the twenty-third state on March 15, 1820, as a free state. Missouri, which had been annexed to the United States as a result of the Louisiana Purchase in 1803, was admitted as the twenty-fourth state on August 10, 1821, as a slave state.

Less than a month after Missouri was granted statehood, the Mexican people would learn that they were free of Spanish rule. Mexico had fiercely sought independence beginning in 1810. It finally won that fight when Spain withdrew its hold on August 21, 1821. The Republic of Mexico and the United States thus became tenuous neighbors, opening new trading opportunities between Missouri, which was then the far west of the United States, and New Mexico, the northernmost territory of Mexico. On September 11, 1821, the last Spanish governor of New Mexico, Facundo Melgares, recognized Mexican rule over the former Spanish colony. Melgares knew firsthand about the United States' keen pursuit of Mexican resources and markets, having previously dealt with American intrusions into Spanish territory. In 1804 Spanish authorities had sent military parties to apprehend Lewis and Clark during their explorations of the Missouri River. Three years later, Melgares was detailed to accompany Zebulon Pike's party from Santa Fe to a hearing in Chihuahua to decide the fate of that illegal expedition into Spanish territory. Despite their service to opposing governments, Pike and Melgares maintained a cordial relationship that would benefit the first traders who arrived from Missouri in the fall of 1821.[3]

In the waning months of Melgares's administration of New Mexico, a small group of Missouri men, led by William Becknell, entered Mexican territory. Missourians, beset by a banking collapse in 1819, looked to their neighbors in New Mexico and Mexico for debt relief. There were opportunities for adventurers, bankers, merchants, and traders in Santa Fe and Taos and in the larger markets in the Mexican interior. Economic recovery and perhaps even wealth lay within reach on the beaver-rich streams and in the ready markets there. Some French trappers from Missouri had already engaged in trade with Native peoples, and traders and trappers from Missouri River towns were on their way west as news of Mexican independence reached Santa Fe and Taos in the early fall of 1821. The Becknell party arrived in Santa Fe in mid-November 1821.

Almost certainly among the people who assembled in Santa Fe Plaza to witness the arrival of the Missouri traders was nine-year-old Carmel Benavides. Her family lived on the eastern edge of the plaza, so she could hardly have missed the excitement as the traders were escorted to the governor's palace a short distance away, where Melgares welcomed them. Soon after Becknell's return to Missouri with legendary profits, more Americans entered the Santa Fe trade.

On January 6, 1822, New Mexicans celebrated Mexican independence in Santa Fe Plaza. The elaborate scene was described by Thomas James, another Missouri trader who had arrived in New Mexico shortly after Becknell. James described a carnival atmosphere, while Melgares officially reported a scene of formal decorum. Carmel must have witnessed the raising of the Mexican flag over the plaza, and she was surely among the children who ran freely and enjoyed the festivities that lasted five days.[4]

The aging María Rosa, living in St. Louis, and the young Carmel, living in Santa Fe, would both become part of the history of the Santa Fe Trail. Through their family connections at both ends of the trail, their stories illustrate the changing political, cultural, and economic relationships among, Indigenous, French, and Hispanic communities in the United States and northern Mexico that emerged from the Santa Fe trade in the late eighteenth and nineteenth centuries.

Positioning the Santa Fe Trail

This book has several goals. Foremost is to compile the stories of women in Santa Fe and St. Louis, two important cities at each end of the trail, who were involved in or affected by the Santa Fe trade. The second goal is to extend the trail's geographic position farther east to the confluence of the Mississippi and Missouri Rivers (map 1). The third goal is to underscore how the trail forged relationships among the diverse peoples and cultures that encountered one another on the trail and in the extensive networks of commerce it enabled. Although the book does not provide a central theory of how cultures change, it examines the changes wrought by the social and political contexts of interregional trade. The trail was established during the expansion of US control of North America, the birth of the Mexican nation on the southern border, the subjugation of Indigenous peoples, and the rising tide of sectional politics. This heady mix of circumstances and political motives affected trail travelers and trade. By focusing on the women who traveled across the continent during a century of great political and social change, this book offers different perspectives on the Santa Fe Trail and how it affected families and communities in both the United States and Mexico.

Much of the literature on the Santa Fe Trail emphasizes its strategic importance as a route of international commerce or as a route for the US military conquest of Mexico. The history of the trail has more to offer readers beyond tactical appraisals when individual stories—particularly the stories of women—are the focus. By shifting attention away from commercial and military enterprises that excluded women, we can examine different motivations for and consequences of western expansion. There were many reasons women traveled west or east on the Santa Fe Trail at different points in time. Native American, Hispanic, African American, and Euro-American women from many immigrant groups were integral to the great western exploration and settlement of North America, but in many cases, their stories must be gleaned from sources other than their own words. In part because the Santa Fe Trail was not specifically an emigrant trail, women were often left out of the earliest writings about it.

Roads have many functions, serving as links or boundaries between geographic regions. Roads can expand opportunities by connecting people and places, but they can also limit interactions by restricting or purposefully channeling the flow of information and goods. The Santa Fe Trail was the setting for many intercultural encounters, yet it was also the consequential architect of those interactions. The trail moved more than people; it carried their ideas and ideals, their political and moral stances, and their dreams and

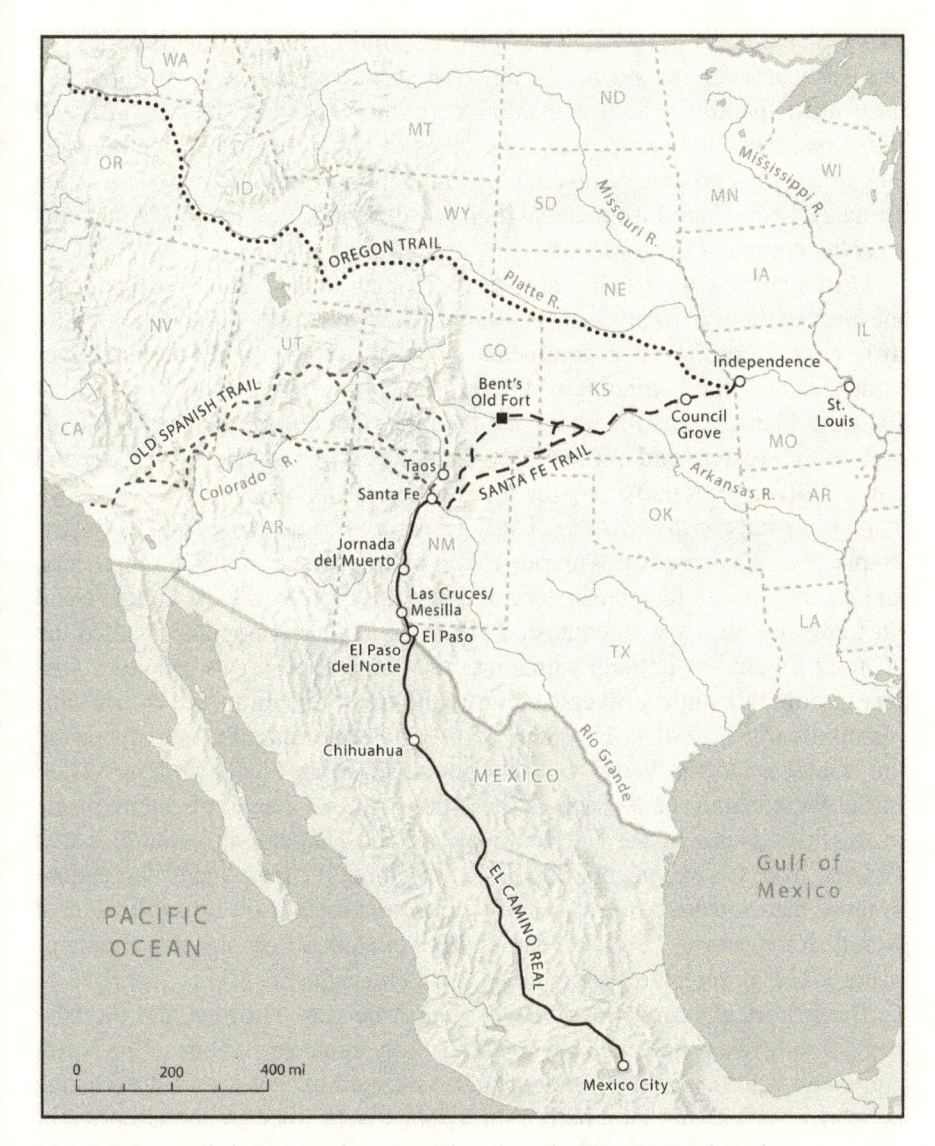

Map 1. Many trails led east and west, north and south. From St. Louis and Independence, Missouri, goods were shipped west to Santa Fe, New Mexico. From there, trails west to California and the Pacific Northwest and south to Mexico created a vast network for global exchange and expanding settlements. Women played many roles on these trails. (Erin Greb Cartography, 2023)

views of a place's potential. The Santa Fe Trail increased opportunities for the westward-moving people of the United States and the northward- and eastward-expanding Mexican frontier, but at the same time, the trail restricted the movements and appropriated the lands of Native and Hispanic peoples. The overarching theme of this book is the opportunities and experiences the Santa Fe Trail offered women and their families of different cultures and eras over the course of the trail's use.

More than one thousand miles separate Santa Fe and St. Louis, spanning the heart of the North American continent. The two ends of the trail link vastly different regions. The lush confluence of the Mississippi and Missouri River drainages near the beginning of the trail in Missouri gives way to the Great Plains in Kansas and Oklahoma and then the high desert and Rocky Mountains at the western end of the trail in Santa Fe and Taos. The geographic and cultural diversity found along the trail undergirds its history.

At both ends of the Santa Fe Trail, its history has been depicted as the triumphant expansion of the American West by trappers, traders, entrepreneurs, and the military. In fact, the history of the trail is more complex; Santa Fe and St. Louis are places with contested histories. Santa Fe, popularly called the "City Different," is imbued with a mythical reputation for its tricultural history, grouping its many diverse cultures and traditions into three overly simplified identities: Indian, Hispanic, and Anglo-American. St. Louis is called the "Gateway to the West," but that phrase does not identify whose vision of the West began there. Each of these designations disregards many of the inequalities found in the Native American and Hispanic communities that evolved from US expansion. Popular myths about the American West endure in those places, where the voices of women and men of diverse cultures and with different stories to tell have often been excluded from the chronicling of history. This book addresses some of those omissions.

The historical connections between the American Midwest and the Hispanic Southwest run deep. They are not simply adjacent regions of the North American continent; their relationship was forged in centuries-old exchange networks that existed long before these lands were ruled by the US government. Native peoples of both regions had vast networks through which they traded the unique products of the lands and rivers in their respective regions. European explorers quickly found that those networks could be profitable for them as well; they did not provide the vast treasures of gold they might have wished for, but other goods could be extracted from the lands and labors of Native peoples. In Mexico and New Mexico, exchange networks among Hispanic communities, Pueblo Indians, and other Indigenous peoples were at the core of widespread trade during the colonial period. Trade partnerships also stimulated Missouri tribes and traders who ventured into the mountainous West even before the Santa Fe trade was formally recognized.

St. Louis is seldom thought of as being situated on the Santa Fe Trail, and in a strictly literal sense, that is true. The strategic importance of St. Louis has often been overlooked in trail scholarship as historians and writers focused on the activities at the trailheads and annual gathering places in western Missouri and eastern Kansas. The eastern terminus of the Santa Fe Trail is usually located at Independence or St. Joseph in far western Missouri—the beginning of the trail's vast overland stretch west across the plains of Kansas and Oklahoma to the southern Rocky Mountains. Other places, such as Franklin and Boone's Lick, Missouri, along the banks of the Missouri River, have also been cited as the beginning of the Santa Fe Trail. That is where William Becknell made his first crossing toward Santa Fe in 1821. The charming historic town of Arrow Rock, Missouri, on the west bank of the wide Missouri River, is another contender for the beginning of the Santa Fe Trail. There is no denying the importance of any of these towns as supply points and regular gathering places for the annual trade caravans. In the 1820s the Franklin area was second only to St. Louis in population and commercial importance. In short, the Santa Fe Trail had many points of embarkation, depending on the era, the mode of travel, and where any particular traveler began the journey, but many threads in the history of the trade are tied to St. Louis.

The wharves and riverboats on the Mississippi and Missouri Rivers in the St. Louis area were strategic to the global reach of the Santa Fe trade (figure I.1). Francis Parkman Jr., writing about his travels across the continent in 1846, observed numerous steamboats on the levee in St. Louis carrying passengers, freight wagons, horses, mules, and a wide range of equipment heading up the Missouri River to western trailheads at Independence for what he termed "the great western movement."[5] Without the robust economy and market networks served by St. Louis, the distribution of textiles, furs, commodities, and sundries would have been limited, affecting the scope and prosperity of participants in the Santa Fe trade. Nineteenth-century daguerreotypes and prints show the wharves along the Mississippi and Missouri Rivers piled high with furniture, barrels, crates, and boxes, illustrating the quantity and variety of goods flowing through the confluence region (figure I.2). Textiles and luxury items shipped from Europe, New England, and New York and housewares and hardware from Philadelphia joined produce and products—and, regrettably, enslaved people—from New Orleans and ports in the South to be transported upriver to the trailheads in western Missouri. St. Louis wagon makers J. Murphy & Sons, Espenschied Wagon Co., Luedinghaus Wagon

Fig. I.1. John Caspar Wild, *St. Louis Waterfront*, 1840, color lithograph. Steamboats, carts, and crowds near the red brick customs house welcomed travelers and merchants to multicultural St. Louis. (N30052, Missouri Historical Society, St. Louis)

Fig. I.2. Thomas Easterly, daguerreotype of the St. Louis waterfront, 1853. Wagons were loaded in St. Louis for western commerce. (N17007, Missouri Historical Society, St. Louis)

Fig. I.3. Advertisement for J. Murphy Wagon Manufacturer, St. Louis City Directory, 1859. (N00211, Missouri Historical Society, St. Louis)

Co., Linstroth Wagon Co., and others manufactured the conveyances that plied the Santa Fe Trail throughout its history (figure I.3).[6]

The confluence of the Mississippi and the Missouri Rivers fed the nation's interior waterways and served as a commercial catchment, supplying goods to the Santa Fe trade. St. Louis's banking capital, manufacturing and shipping businesses, and military patrols mounted from the US Army's Jefferson Barracks were essential to the Santa Fe trade. Those waterways and trails served the western advance of multiethnic populations from the region, connecting them with the cultural mix of Indigenous and Hispanic peoples from Mexico and New Mexico.

The terms *frontier* and *wilderness* were often used in contemporaneous accounts of trail travelers, and they persist in some popular writing about the seemingly open country crossed by the western trails. In part, those terms were an attempt to describe the landscape of the prairies and plains as vacant and therefore available for appropriation. In many cases, this depiction was false and ignored the presence of Indigenous people who were legitimate occupants or seasonal users of the land through which the western trails passed. The terms *frontier* and *wilderness* are vestiges of romantic and largely ethnocentric constructs that failed to consider Indigenous and Hispanic settlers who were—and in many cases still are—living on the lands crossed by historic trails that were then annexed by the United States and deemed the American West.[7]

Stephen Aron views the confluence region as the virtual heart of the United States, a social crucible where ideas and people from north and south, east and west met to produce a unique and socially complex mixture. He argues that *confluence* is a more meaningful way of describing the cultural changes and mergers that occurred, rather than the limits and boundaries between peoples of different cultures envisioned by *frontier*. More recently, Walter Johnson placed St. Louis at the center of the often violent and exploitative racial dynamics of mercantile capitalism that accompanied westward expansion. These tensions are important elements of the trail's historical context and the centuries of history written about the land and economies of the country.[8]

Ned Blackhawk writes that while St. Louis's claim as the "gateway" to the West might be hyperbolic, there is no denying that traders from St. Louis and St. Joseph, Missouri, introduced seismic changes in the lives of Native peoples. This included the Missouri and Osage peoples in St. Louis; Pueblo, Navajo, and Apache communities in New Mexico; and many of the tribes along the length of the trail and in the fur trapping and trading centers of the West. Native peoples' connection to lands they had occupied since time immemorial was legally extinguished by the colonizing actions of Spain and the United States, but even today, some tribes continue to assert traditional ties to ancestral places in public ceremonies and through legal actions seeking to reclaim land. Commerce between and among Indigenous people and Hispanic settlers—both men and women—was an integral part of the interregional economy that preceded the Santa Fe trade, but it functioned on different social terms. Blackhawk reframes American history, acknowledging that trade, diplomacy, and violent interactions were the triad of cultural encounters in the American West. He recognizes that Missouri traders, with their greater access to manufactured goods, replaced Chihuahua traders. He argues that Ute leaders invited some of the early Missouri traders to extend their networks to serve Indigenous peoples, who tried to retain their place in the region's changing economy. But Ute participation in the Santa Fe trade did not survive the US military dominance and Indian policies of the 1840s.

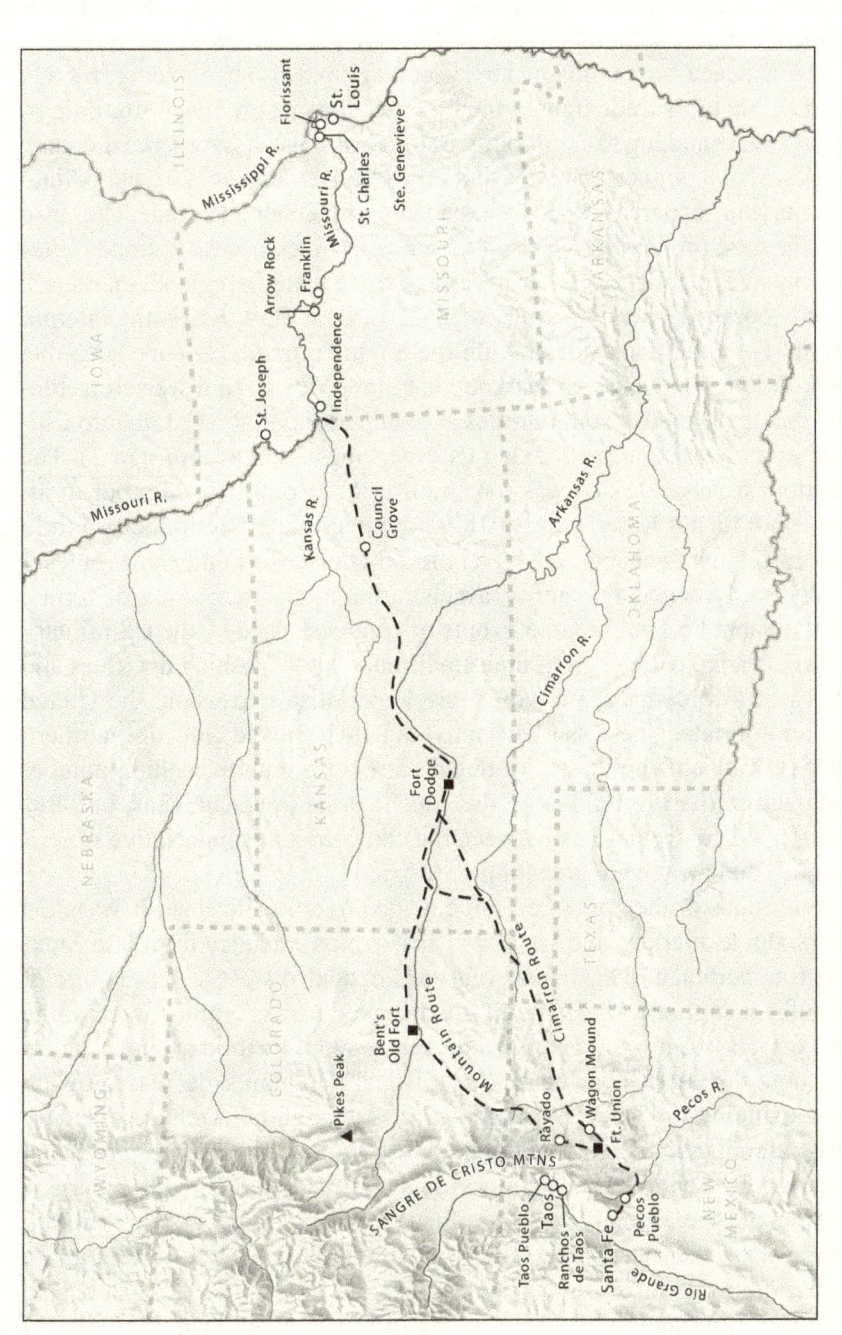

Map 2. Santa Fe Trail. St. Louis was the point of embarkation for many people who traveled west on the Santa Fe Trail between 1821 and the early 1870s. (Erin Greb Cartography, 2023)

In reviewing Blackhawk's work, Ana María Alonso observes that in the interactions between colonial powers and Native peoples throughout northern New Spain, peace was maintained by diplomacy and also by violence in some cases. The Santa Fe trade transformed the meaning of *exchange* from diplomacy and peacemaking to commodity transactions that did not serve the same ends. Blackhawk argues that Utes and other Native peoples were pulled into the "American" economy with the expansion of the Santa Fe trade. Utes also used their own forms of power and violence to block access to trade routes and to enslave members of other tribes and trade them in regional markets.[9]

Max Moorhead's seminal study of the Santa Fe Trail details the international market conditions surrounding the Santa Fe trade. He concludes that the link among the Missouri markets, the New Mexico and western settlements, and the Mexican communities along the Camino Real south into Chihuahua and as far south as Mexico City was most significant (map 2). The population of New Mexico was too small to offer profits to Missouri traders for more than a few years. By 1824, the real profits lay farther south in Mexico, although Santa Fe was, for a time, still the nexus of the trade routes.[10]

By the mid-nineteenth century, a generation after the opening of formal trade, the Santa Fe Trail became a route of conquest, used by the US military to remove Native peoples from their traditional lands. Pushing doctrines and practices of a forceful, some would say imperialist, expansion, the United States appropriated these Native lands and then moved into the northern frontier of Mexico's holdings. Mounted patrols from an expanding number of forts and military installations accompanied the trade caravans, but they never stopped confrontations between the caravans and some Native American groups and the sovereign nation of Mexico.

The terminus of the Santa Fe Trail changed over its life span. It stretched farther south as markets and business partnerships extended deep into Mexico, and it shortened over time as railroads extended west to serve more of the continent (figure I.4). As the railroad snaked across North America, the Santa Fe Trail lost its commercial and even some of its military importance. Throughout the late 1860s, the trail's logistical importance decreased owing to the expanding rail lines, but it gained a certain allure, fueling adventure stories and romantic literature about the West. Women became more frequent travelers to the Southwest and California as railroads shortened the journey. Native people were removed or confined to reservations, and the military presence made the routes safer. By 1875, travel from St. Louis to Santa Fe was possible in a steam-driven railroad car that newspaper ads pitched to women as a safer and more secure mode of travel. More than 785 miles of the journey could be accomplished by rail. The old trail ruts were becoming

Fig. I.4. Elsberg and Amberg wagon train in front of the Palace of the Governors, Santa Fe, October 1861. (11254, Palace of the Governors Photo Archives [NMHM/DCA])

a literary pathway to a place captured in the writings of the new settlers. The trail now led to a legendary and somewhat imaginary Southwest, a mixture of ancient cultures and new identities set in a magnificent landscape.

Changing Cultures, Communities, and Families

The commercial enterprises that undergirded the Santa Fe Trail created opportunities for people from French, Native American, Euro-American, African American, and Hispanic backgrounds to form new multiethnic communities and families of mixed descent. Historian David C. Beyreis aptly notes that in the nineteenth century, belonging to an extended family such as the Bents or the Robidoux in Missouri or the Baca or Ortiz families in New Mexico gave individuals the basis of their identity and place in society.[11]

Family members who engaged in the Santa Fe trade and the annexation of the Southwest, Mexico, and California are central to western history, but only recently has the influence of those events on family structures and communities been seriously considered. Historian Anne Hyde writes compellingly about eighteenth- and nineteenth-century intercultural families that blended Native American, French, Hispanic, Euro-American, and African American members. She attributes the failure to recognize such families to an erasure of individuals of mixed descent, or those who might be considered multiracial or even multicultural.[12] Ideals of "racial purity," the promotion of elite bloodlines, and racism certainly underlie this expurgation. Also at play was the pursuit of an ethnocentric and Eurocentric American historiography. The myth of the national melting pot characterized Americans as culturally and racially neutralized through a voluntary mixing, blending, and blurring of genetic diversity. In addition, until recently, there was a failure to focus on families in general, and on families of mixed cultural and national origins in particular, as being integral to and worthy of analysis in scholarly history.

St. Louis has a special place in the historical scholarship on cross-cultural marriages and families of mixed French, Spanish, Native American, and African American descent and the westward expansion of the United States. Some of the earliest Euro-American fur traders who came to New Mexico were from the French colonies along the Mississippi and Missouri Rivers. French Catholic fur traders and missionaries from Canada and the northern border expanded their trade networks south along the Missouri and Mississippi Rivers into the area of Cahokia and Kaskaskia, Illinois, between 1699 and 1703. This area was called Upper Louisiana in 1717, when it was placed under the French administration serving New Orleans.[13] In the process of expanding their trade, the French established a Creole culture through intermarriage or alliances with Native women and their trade with the numerous Indigenous groups. Ethnohistorian Fred Fausz characterizes the French as the most expansive and culturally tolerant of the European colonizers, stating that "French-Americans experienced more frequent, consistent, mutually productive and physically intimate relations with a greater variety of Indians over a longer span of time than any other European colonizers."[14]

The end of the French and Indian War in 1763 brought British Protestants to the east bank of the Mississippi in Illinois, pushing Spanish Catholics as well as French and French Creole immigrants to the west bank settlements in Ste. Genevieve, Missouri, and then, after 1764, upstream to St. Louis. The French contribution to western expansion is especially important to a consideration of the Santa Fe Trail because many of the earliest parties to reach the Rocky Mountains were from French settlements in the confluence area. French Creole men made early forays into wide-ranging fur trapping and trading grounds, much to the consternation of Spanish officials, who considered them interlopers.

Scholars of French colonial history studying the upper Missouri River have emphasized the relations between French fur traders and Indigenous and African American women. Tanis Thorne's seminal work examines the relationship between Frenchmen and Indigenous women from the Kansas, Osage, Ponca, and Omaha tribes, arguing that the fur trade created interdependencies that generated cross-cultural marriages and extended kinship networks. Thorne claims that, because of the emphasis on "American masculinity, adventure, independence and individualism" in studies of the fur trade, the roles of women, families, and kinship networks are often overlooked, and the social consequences of cross-cultural marriage is "incompletely" understood.[15] She explores the ancestry of several prominent St. Louis families—the Papins, the Bents, and the Robidoux—whose sons sometimes took Native women as partners even though they simultaneously maintained families in St. Louis. These families with multiple lines of descent supplied the furs and hides for the expansive global trade emanating from St. Louis.

Jay Gitlin, Robert Michael Morrissey, and Peter J. Kastor reexamine the French history of St. Louis, drawing attention to the importance of cross-cultural families or families of mixed descent in the city's colonial history. The French communities and families of the confluence area were "more heterogenous and more cosmopolitan." Families in colonial St. Louis were Creole, and their mixed European and Indigenous ancestry gave them some ascendency in the early years of western expansion. French hegemony extended over a vast portion of North America, yet it has often been ignored in American history. Gitlin, Morrissey, and Kastor attribute this erasure to several themes. For instance, much of American history has a decided east-to-west focus and a biased narrative of American exceptionalism. They also argue that Anglo-Saxon characterizations of masculinity dismissed French society in part because of its Creole cast and British dominance of the French by the end of 1763.[16] Yet this mixture of cultures gave French traders entree to wider trade networks. Black women also married into the Creole families of colonial St. Louis, although biographies of specific Black Creole women have only recently been considered in historical scholarship. Andrew Wegmann's analysis of Black women in the Creole society of New Orleans and St. Louis examines several women who were part of communities of mixed descent. He argues that their place in society was separate from that of the enslaved and free people of color depicted in southern historical literature.[17]

Recognizing that interregional trade was initiated by members of communities of mixed descent, rather than an imaginary amalgamation of individuals

Fig. I.5. Fringed buckskin coat with red and blue quill embroidery made by Native American or *métis* women for the fur trade, circa 1840s or 1850s. The coat is thought to have belonged to a member of the Chouteau family in St. Louis. (1906-013-0002, Missouri Historical Society, St. Louis)

of "American" ancestry, casts a different light on both the trade and the traders. Their mixed-descent families and intercultural marriages were among the social factors that allowed them to navigate the customs, the mores, and in some cases the languages of trade. Native American woman—as commercial partners and wives—were crucial to the economics of the fur trade, which was central to the impetus for westward expansion. As companions and wives to mountain men and traders, they processed furs and hides and sewed and embroidered garments and other goods, contributing enormous labor and value. Goods made from processed hides, including moccasins, clothing, and bags, were prized even in cosmopolitan St. Louis. Patricia Cleary documents the multicultural history of St. Louis families based on their wills and even the clothing preserved in museum collections. The clothing itself is symbolic of the city's Creole society, being made from fabrics imported from France or combined with finely tanned hides and quill-embroidered garments made by Native artisans. The clothing documents the trade and the aesthetics of

St. Louis's upper class, illustrating the merger of Indigenous and imported European material culture (figure I.5).[18]

Even more social complexity is evident in the extended family connections, commercial networks, and political alliances forged from the commerce of the Santa Fe Trail. Margaret Jacobs, in a review of the historiography of women in western American history, instructs scholars to "get out of the rut" and expand our knowledge of the cultural encounters and power relationships in different colonial settings.[19] The trail brought people of diverse European backgrounds to a region that was considered (and in some respects remains) culturally distinct from other parts of the United States. In the Four Corners of the American Southwest and in much of the West and California, the reminders of consecutive conquests are still evident. Spanish conquest still weighs heavily on Indigenous tribes, as evidenced by its retelling in rituals and oral traditions. Western expansion by the United States, incidents of violence, and the appropriation of land and rights remain imprinted on Indigenous and Hispanic communities.

Long ago, Patricia Limerick articulated in her seminal work *The Legacy of Conquest* the more destructive encounters and changes resulting from interregional contact and conquest that were lost in the telling of triumphalist history. The Santa Fe Trail is not simply a line on a map connecting historic places. It was an essential conduit of the cultural encounters between expanding US settlements and sovereign neighboring territories and tribal lands. In early histories of the West, the very acts of conquest and colonization facilitated by the Santa Fe Trail are glossed over or relegated to stories of grand adventure. The stories of the women in this book are set against this background of conquest, colonialism, commerce, and the larger social consequences of the rapidly expanding United States.

Sourcing and Telling Their Stories

The bibliography and historiography of the Santa Fe Trail encompass an enormous body of literature published over two centuries, but researching the lives of particular women remains difficult. The vast distances individuals traveled in the eighteenth and nineteenth centuries, linking different parts of the country and different families, are often surprising. This travel also means that people were not always present in communities when official records such as census documents and property maps were made. Their absence in these records limits our understanding of their roles and activities in specific communities, especially women. Except for elite and well-educated women who kept diaries, wrote letters, or were directly involved in commerce or social enterprises, the vast majority of women in the eighteenth and nineteenth centuries are largely missing from history.

Finding biographical details and, rarer still, autobiographical accounts of Hispanic, French, African American, and Native American women who participated in the fur trade and the larger interregional trade in the nineteenth century holds many challenges. I consulted women's trail journals and memoirs and other examples of their own writings, when they exist, as well as the extant documentation of their lives. I describe and analyze the contexts of their individual experiences, freed from the myths and archetypes of women that were once a prevalent part of western American history and folklore. The women I write about cannot be reduced to stereotypes. In most cases, they were not reluctant travelers or "gentle tamers" or sunbonnet-wearing pioneers of the West. They traveled for a variety of reasons. Several of the women wrote about the challenges they faced, articulating their specific responses to those challenges.[20] They survived grueling crossings, enduring the same hardships and discomforts men faced on the trail. Many women travelers were enthralled by the beauty of the country and the spirit of adventure their westward journeys offered. Their own words and recollections reframe some of the long-held stereotypes about women's hesitant participation in crossing the historic western trails.

At least some of the impressions of how women fared in their travels come from images in art, literature, and film. In 1909 Missouri chapters of the Daughters of the American Revolution (DAR) began marking the Santa Fe Trail with boulders or granite monuments inscribed with the names of historic stops along the route. The project expanded, and additional markers were placed along the Santa Fe Trail and other historic roads and trails in the 1920s. A much larger undertaking was planned by the DAR and funded by Congress in 1927 to commemorate pioneering women on historic trails from coast to coast. Between July 4, 1928, and April 29, 1929, the National Society of the Daughters of the American Revolution erected twelve imposing stone monuments across the country, representing their ideal of the women who traveled the historic trails. These immense figures were molded in a warm pink stone material called algonite, made from crushed marble, Missouri granite, stone, cement, and lead ore. Wearing a flowing dress and a sunbonnet, the woman depicted in the statue holds a rifle in her right hand and a child in her left arm, with a little boy clutching her billowing skirt as he walks beside her. To the DAR's commemorative committee, she symbolized the determination of the young nation as she marched from ocean to ocean. Like so many commemorative statues, she was not based on any particular woman but was fashioned as a white woman, with some attention paid to historical accuracy in her clothing and a balance of strength and determination with motherhood.[21] Some of the literature of the Santa Fe Trail was born of the same symbolism and idealization—projections of what could be when Manifest Destiny was imposed on the people and places west of the Mississippi River.

The images of men who traveled the Santa Fe Trail have also been subjected to exaggeration. They include the famous and the anonymous. These men are remembered in history sometimes by name and sometimes by their romantic or heroic adventures as fur trappers and Indian traders, freighters and frontiersmen, soldiers and generals, statesmen and writers. Some of the earliest trail literature consists of the journals of men who crossed the continent in search of adventure and those with an eye toward lucrative business ventures.[22] Two works by women are often cited as classics of trail history: Susan Shelby Magoffin's *Down the Old Santa Fe Trail into Mexico* and Marian Sloan Russell's *Land of Enchantment*.[23] These two women were certainly among the early Euro-American travelers on the trail, and their accounts are particularly important because they were based on their own diaries or recollections of their journeys. I relied heavily on Magoffin's trail diary and Russell's memoirs. For the most part, however, few women who traveled the trail are remembered by name, and those identified by broad professional classifications are often dismissed with a single mention of their domestic roles. They included the maids, cooks, prostitutes, laundresses, teachers, nannies, nurses, and nuns who accompanied the settling of the American West and the schools and settlements that followed. Much of women's history has been told by those whose experiences were considered unworthy of celebration in popular culture or scholarly studies until recently. When the only records of their experiences were the official documents of their lives, or when only the bare facts of their transit were known, I used other sources to illustrate the time and context of their journeys.

The trail literature documents the history of cultural encounters across the continent in the nineteenth century. Some are firsthand accounts; others are edited versions that offer different vantage points on the expansion of Euro-American settlement as travelers moved west from the middle of the continent to meet eastbound travelers from the Spanish Southwest. Westbound travelers came from many different cultures, but all were either immigrants from the expanding United States or colonists from English-, French-, or German-speaking communities of the midcontinent. Some westbound travelers were African American servants or enslaved, and I made an effort to bring them into focus, pulling them out of the depths of footnotes or casual remarks. Those who traveled east from the Mexican borderlands to the United States had different experiences, depending on when they traveled. After about 1838, New Mexican and Mexican traders began to visit Independence, St. Louis, Philadelphia, and New York to purchase manufactured goods to take west on the Santa Fe Trail; then the trade extended into Mexico, where a larger population made the trip more lucrative. Susan Calafate Boyle notes that although Mexican traders were "cautious entrepreneurs," they did not want to cede potential markets exclusively to Missouri traders.[24]

The historical and cultural backgrounds of all travelers informed their point of view about the potential of the new land, the resources, and the people they met, influencing the meaning of their experiences on the trail. All these travelers crossed the lands of Native peoples, yet precious little remains of the voices or words of these diverse Indigenous individuals. The trail traversed the traditional lands of at least ten Native nations, including the Osage, Pawnee, Comanche, Kansa or Kaw, Kiowa, Plains Apache, Ute, Jicarilla Apache, and Pecos Pueblo. Travelers encountered people of others Native nations, such as the Cheyenne, Arapaho, and Shawnee, at different military and commercial centers built along the trail, but any records that exist lack ethnographic detail. If Native peoples are recorded in trail history at all, it is often through the lens of fearful interactions, amused stereotypes, or, at worst, racist caricatures. Travelers seldom reflect on the stark reality of Euro-American incursions on Native land and resources or Native peoples' reduced circumstances and removal from their homelands. Author James Riding In reviews the many reasons why contemporaneous publications contain so little information about Native peoples, despite the Santa Fe Trail's route across their traditional lands and the presence of Native peoples at the forts along the way. He attributes this omission to failures in perception, to the stereotypes pervading nineteenth-century encounters between Euro-Americans and Native people, and to the persistence of a "false narrative" that "Indians" were the aggressors during Euro-American expansion.[25]

All historical writing is a refracted view of the past, dependent on the source documents available and the research process employed. Writing women's history is similar to making a quilt out of small bits of fabric or gluing the pieces of a broken vessel together. In many ways, writing about women on the trail is like interpreting archaeological remains—looking for indirect evidence of women's lives and roles. There is seldom one single source that tells the full story of any person's life—woman or man—in a coherent sequence. The sources are often incomplete, even when women kept diaries or wrote their own accounts. Several of the women made multiple crossings, adding to the depth of their observations about how the country had changed and dispelling the myth of women being averse to the risks of travel on the trail.

In some cases, however, there are no first-person accounts—no diaries or letters—so I depended on the words of fellow travelers or their families and on other accounts and records.

Property records and census records, as well as birth, marriage, and death records, were particularly useful for identifying where women lived. Court records and property maps showed women's ownership of real estate and businesses. Museums' textile collections and domestic artifacts illustrated the lives and material culture of the women in their homes and communities and sometimes even in their trail camps. Photographs, letters, diaries, clothing, mementos, and genealogical materials made many of the women's stories more tangible. Newspaper accounts, memoirs, and biographies contained powerful stories and in some cases preserved the voice and tone of the women narrating their own crossings. They were among the agents of cultural and political change who made a new American West from the expansive northern frontier of Mexico.

Chapter Overviews

Crossings takes its title from several contemporaneous descriptions of the vast open spaces encountered by travelers heading west. For them, setting out on the Santa Fe Trail was like taking a sea voyage, and for some, it was the first time they escaped the cities of Europe and the eastern United States. They experienced immense vistas, encountered unfamiliar animals and trees, slept under clear starry skies, and breathed clean air. Most travelers met people of different cultures and had new experiences that challenged or widened their worldviews. Others stayed focused on the task at hand, whether the goal was making a profit, "civilizing" the people they met, or domesticating the landscape according to their own value systems. *Crossings* is also a reference to the new cross-cultural experiences travelers often mentioned in their trail journals.

The chapters are roughly in chronological order, covering the late eighteenth century to the last half of the nineteenth century. That period was framed by political and economic changes for families and communities at both ends of the Santa Fe Trail. The chapters examine different themes and the various motivations that led women to embark on their crossings. The chronological organization shows how women's participation in the trade changed over time. In the early chapters, covering the experiences of Native American and Hispanic women, there are few contemporaneous accounts by these women. Importantly, however, several of their stories remove some of the romantic tropes of the fur trade and illustrate the violence accompanying the commerce between Native people and European settlers. After the Santa Fe Trail transitioned from a road of commerce to a road of emigrants and military excursions, there are many more contemporaneous accounts by women. Some of these accounts, recorded in their own words, reflect the tensions roiling the country in the mid-nineteenth century and the choices and experiences the Santa Fe Trail offered them.

Chapter 1 covers in some detail the story of María Rosa Villalpando: her capture by the Comanche, her exchange from the Comanche to the Pawnee and then to French traders, and her life as a member of the new French Creole settlement of St. Louis. Her captivity and exchange occurred at a time when women and children were trafficked, along with livestock and furs, among Native tribes and with Spanish and French colonists throughout the intermountain West and along the interior rivers. Although this took place before the Santa Fe Trail was named, her story was known to Santa Fe traders as well as to residents of both New Mexico and St. Louis. What makes her life story so remarkable is that the raid in which she was kidnapped from the vicinity of Taos, New Mexico, was well documented by historians and is still recalled among folklorists. Her capture was certainly dramatic, but so was her resilience as a member of the Creole community in St. Louis. That part of her story has not been fully explored, and it is told here based on primary documents and genealogical details and set against some of the harrowing stories of other women who were captives or rescued by Santa Fe Trail traders.

Soon after trade between the northern frontier of Mexico and the new state of Missouri was established in 1821, fur traders and other adventurers who participated in the Santa Fe trade established relationships with Hispanic merchants in New Mexico or with Hispanic women. Some of these cross-cultural marriages and relationships extended the kinship networks of centuries-old Hispanic families with deep roots in Spanish and Mexican history. Several such alliances were between New Mexican women and men from French colonial families of the confluence region. In all cases, however, these relationships were advantageous to foreigners, who then had access to hunting, trapping, and land-use rights that pertained only to New Mexicans. Chapter 2 examines the relationship of Antoine Robidoux and Carmel Benavides in this era of expanding and changing Indigenous, French, Spanish, and Euro-American communities.

As American and New Mexican families formed alliances in business and in marriage, some looked east to Missouri for educational opportunities for their sons and daughters. Chapter 3 traces the experiences of three young girls—Adaline Carson, Marian Sloan Russell, and Francisca López—all of whom traveled the Santa Fe Trail after the death of a parent. Adaline was the daughter of famous scout Christopher "Kit" Carson and his Arapaho wife Waa-nibe. Born in 1837, Adaline "Prairie Flower" Carson moved east from Bent's Fort, Colorado, to Kit Carson's family home near Franklin, Missouri, in 1842. Her crossings from New Mexico to Missouri and back to the West explore the larger issue of where children of mixed descent fit in communities during this period of territorial expansion and Native subjugation. Marian Sloan Russell's memoir describes several crossings she made with her mother and brother beginning in 1852. Though she recalls the adventures she had, the memoir also reveals the great instability and sectional stirrings as slavery was debated. Francisca López's father brought her to Missouri after her mother's death in 1848. Her charming letters show her increasing command of English and her rise to prominence in St. Louis society through marriage. The contrast among the lives of Adaline, Marian, and Francisca illustrates the paths of women and children from different cultural and economic circumstances who traveled the Santa Fe Trail in the late 1840s and early 1850s.

The tragic story of Kate Kingsbury is told in chapter 4. She accompanied her husband John to New Mexico in 1854, hoping to restore her fragile health. Kate suffered from tuberculosis, a common ailment in the crowded urban centers of the mid-nineteenth century. Although Kate's husband and family provided her with every treatment available at the time, she did not survive. Her story unfolds against the background of the trading empire established by her husband, her brother William S. Messervy, and his trading partner James Josiah Webb. Correspondence among the partners captures the mood of the fragile economy, the tensions over market saturation, and the challenges of supply chains as competition and the threat of civil war increased. Importantly, their correspondence also expresses their concerns over Kate's health. Kate's state of mind has not been documented, as no diary, letter, or other written record by her has been found. However, as an educated woman, she certainly would have been privy to deliberations as the family weighed her treatment options in this era of limited medical knowledge. Her final thoughts were recorded by her sister, as she described Kate's last moments on a moonlit night on the Santa Fe Trail in what can only be called a beautiful death.

Chapter 5 explores the relationship between Susan Magoffin and her enslaved maid Jane, as described in Susan's diary during their crossing. Jane's experiences and Susan's record of their travels together during a pivotal moment in US history offer only a glimpse of the war over territorial expansion that brought them to New Mexico. When the Army of the West seized New Mexico as a possession of the United States in the summer of 1846, several women from Missouri arrived with the caravans. The American *entrada* played out over a matter of weeks in a series of scripted encounters that asserted American control of northern Mexico and its antecedent Spanish borderlands. Magoffin christened herself the first American woman to cross the continent. In her diary entry for August 31, 1846, she expanded on her self-styled fame, noting that she had arrived under the auspices of the "star-spangled banner" and speculating that she "seemed disposed to be the first [woman] under any circumstances that ever crossed the Plains."[26] Her place in the history of the Santa Fe Trail is secure, in that hers was the first woman's diary to document, nearly daily, her experiences traveling from Independence, Missouri, to Santa Fe, but her claim of being the first woman to cross the plains invited closer analysis. In addition, Jane's experiences and Susan's record of their travels together offer a compelling comparison of how an enslaved woman experienced the trail west and the unequal positions of women and men of color in this period.

The Civil War disrupted the movement of families to the West, but several women who lived at western military posts provide poignant views of a country split by the issue of slavery. Lydia Spencer Lane provides much of that perspective in chapter 6. Other women who came west during the Civil War brought strands of activism that challenged the emergence of statehood proponents in New Mexico and on the western edge of the United States. Julia Anna Archibald Holmes, who is also introduced in chapter 6, was a suffragist whose passion for equality extended not just to women's rights; she was also an abolitionist who used her writings and political aptitude to advocate for the freedom of the enslaved.

Chapter 6 also traces the history of the trail's last years as it changed from a road of military conquest to a pathway leading to an enchanting, mythical place, as captured in the writings of new settlers in the Southwest. Florence "Flora" Langerman Spiegelberg, bride of German Jewish merchant Willie Spiegelberg, kept a diary of her journey from St. Louis to Santa Fe in 1875. On the final leg of their trip—from West Las Animas, Colorado, to Santa Fe—they traveled for six days and nights on a stage. That relatively short journey was not without drama. Susan Wallace, wife of New Mexico governor Lew Wallace, also traveled partway to Santa Fe by train and then completed the last stretch by stagecoach. Flora Spiegelberg and Susan Wallace were accomplished authors and activists, yet neither of them refers to the other in their observations about Santa Fe. They seem to be preserving the illusion that they alone witnessed these changing times in the land of enchantment created by their words.

The conclusion of *Crossings* examines how the perspectives on women who traveled in either direction on the Santa Fe Trail from 1760 to the late

1870s reframe our understanding of the trail's influence on the construction of the American West. By embracing broader perspectives on the processes of cultural exchange and the expansion of the United States seen through the experiences of women over that century, perhaps we can better understand the inherent power imbalances and exploitation of land and labor resulting from the trail. Many of the family bonds and cross-cultural friendships documented in the literature of the trail are also the origins of diverse communities in the West. The power relations of the past live on in many places, and the limited opportunities and inequality for women and minorities are still with us. The women who were our founding mothers and sisters included women of mixed race who partnered with men of diverse origins. *Crossings* embraces the cultural complexity brought about by encounters on the Santa Fe Trail and reflects on the lasting effects of intercultural contact, colonialism, and episodes of conquest on the land, on our memories, and in our communities.

1

Bartering Women
Captives, Commodities, and Traders

The Santa Fe Trail was not the first route of interregional or intercultural trade in the American West. Trading for goods and trafficking in humans occurred among Native peoples and with Europeans in a variety of settings across the centuries and in changing geopolitical contexts. Women, taken as captives by Comanches and other Plains Indian groups in raids on New Mexican settlements, were trafficked intertribally or bartered in hostage exchanges with the Spanish government. Women taken from European settlements were also enslaved by tribes or taken as sexual partners. They were, literally, commodities. On occasion, this trade gave birth to intercultural families who became mediators of cultural exchange. Women also supplied the labor to process hides and manufacture goods, making them invaluable partners in the fur trade that anchored eighteenth- and nineteenth-century commerce.

Historian Juliana Barr examines the relations between various Plains Indian groups and Europeans in seventeenth- and eighteenth-century Texas. Captives were taken when Spanish diplomacy failed to secure peace or when trade networks failed and Native factions broke with previous trade partners.[1] Her study has special relevance to the story of María Rosa Villalpando, who was abducted from Ranchos de Taos, New Mexico, in August 1760 during a Comanche raid. Eight years later, fur traders who hunted between the Missouri River and the settlements of the St. Louis region notified Spanish authorities that two sisters and a child born to one of them while held by the Comanches were now living in a Pawnee encampment. Jean Baptiste Salé dit Lajoie, a founding member of the French settlement of St. Louis, purchased one of the women and her child and brought them to St. Louis. There is no doubt, based on subsequent documents, that this was María Rosa. She would live in St. Louis until her death in 1830, and her deft use of the courts and commerce in St. Louis hints at the skills she possessed and how she managed to survive captivity.

In this chapter, I expand the documented history and reduce the romantic speculation surrounding María Rosa's abduction. I also examine her life in Creole St. Louis during a formative period when it transitioned from a French fur-trading outpost to a major US port. The chapter concludes by contrasting María Rosa's story of resilience with the brutality experienced by other women captured in raids on frontier settlements and then rescued by traders. Captive narratives are a well-known historical genre and have formed the basis of folklore, fiction, and film. Several biographies depict the reality of life as a captive, and based on these sources, it is possible to imagine—though obviously imperfectly—what María Rosa experienced. Her story is set against this background of changing relations among Native people and French and Spanish settlements and the rise of American control of trade and the continent over more than sixty years.

Josiah Gregg Introduces María Rosa to Readers

Josiah Gregg's *Commerce of the Prairies*, published in 1844 after a nine-year career as a Santa Fe Trail trader (1831–40), is widely recognized by scholars in many fields for its detailed descriptions of the geography and botany of the Southwest and northern Mexico. Gregg was a keen observer and recorder of the logistics of travel, as well as the tactics and diplomacy of international trade. Gregg's ear was well tuned to local history and the cultural traditions of the people and communities he encountered along the trail. Perhaps because he began his journey on the overland trail in western Missouri, Gregg dismisses the notion of St. Louis as a starting point of the trade. He points instead to places farther west, where caravans gathered to embark on the Santa Fe Trail.

The caravan Gregg joined in 1834 ventured into Chihuahua, Mexico, where he spent several years as a merchant and a collector of botanical specimens.[2] Gregg became fluent in Spanish, and early editions of his published journal contain a glossary of terms to assist North American readers. His language ability is important because it gave him insights into the cultures and the political landscape surrounding the trade in both countries.[3]

Gregg linked St. Louis and New Mexico in an incident that occurred before the Santa Fe Trail became a regular transcontinental route. He briefly relates the story of a Comanche raid at the *rancho* of an early settler he identifies as Pando. Gregg recounts that Pando's unnamed daughter was captured in the raid, but in fact, her name and history are well documented: she was María Rosa Villalpando, captured by Comanches in a raid on the settlement of Ranchos de Taos in the northern Río Grande Valley in August 1760.[4] Gregg embellishes the story, adding romantic flourishes and a trope that characterized the accounts of many captives in nineteenth-century American literature.[5] He blames María Rosa for the raid on the settlement, claiming it was in retaliation for her refusal to marry a Comanche chief, a union supposedly arranged by her father when she was a child. Through a series of trades or purchases, she was eventually brought to St. Louis after nearly a decade in captivity and became a well-connected member of the Creole community. Gregg reports, "There are many people yet living who remember with what affecting pathos the old lady was wont to tell her tale of woe."[6]

Like many folklore interpretations of history, Gregg's version telescopes events, mixing history and romance. In an analysis of the dynamics of the relationship between the Plains Indians and New Mexicans, James Brooks explores the larger meaning of María Rosa's captivity. He examines her intrinsic value as a commodity of exchange and the advantages that even a forced kinship generated between New Mexicans and their Plains Indian trade partners. He places the alternating cycles of trading and raiding in the larger context of the political economy of these two regions in the mid-eighteenth century.[7] Because the topic was peripheral to his main analysis, Brooks spends little time examining how María Rosa adapted to life in St. Louis. By taking a more in-depth look at her life, I show the agency she exerted and the context of her social evolution from captive to Creole. Her captivity among the Comanches and Pawnees ended before the beginning of the Santa Fe trade. She lived to see the French, Spanish, and US flags raised over the midcontinent, along with the mixture of customs, traditions, and laws that defined the expanding boundaries of the United States and the changes resulting from those encounters. Her acceptance into the Creole community of St. Louis contrasts with several other captivity narratives about Euro-American and Hispanic women that continued to be part of the Santa Fe Trail literature into the nineteenth century.

The Eighteenth-Century Taos Frontier

María Rosa Villalpando's story began six decades before the opening of the Santa Fe trade and centered on the boisterous exchanges taking place during the intercultural trade fairs held at Taos Pueblo. The beautiful Taos Valley is situated along the front range of the Sangre de Cristo Mountains, where

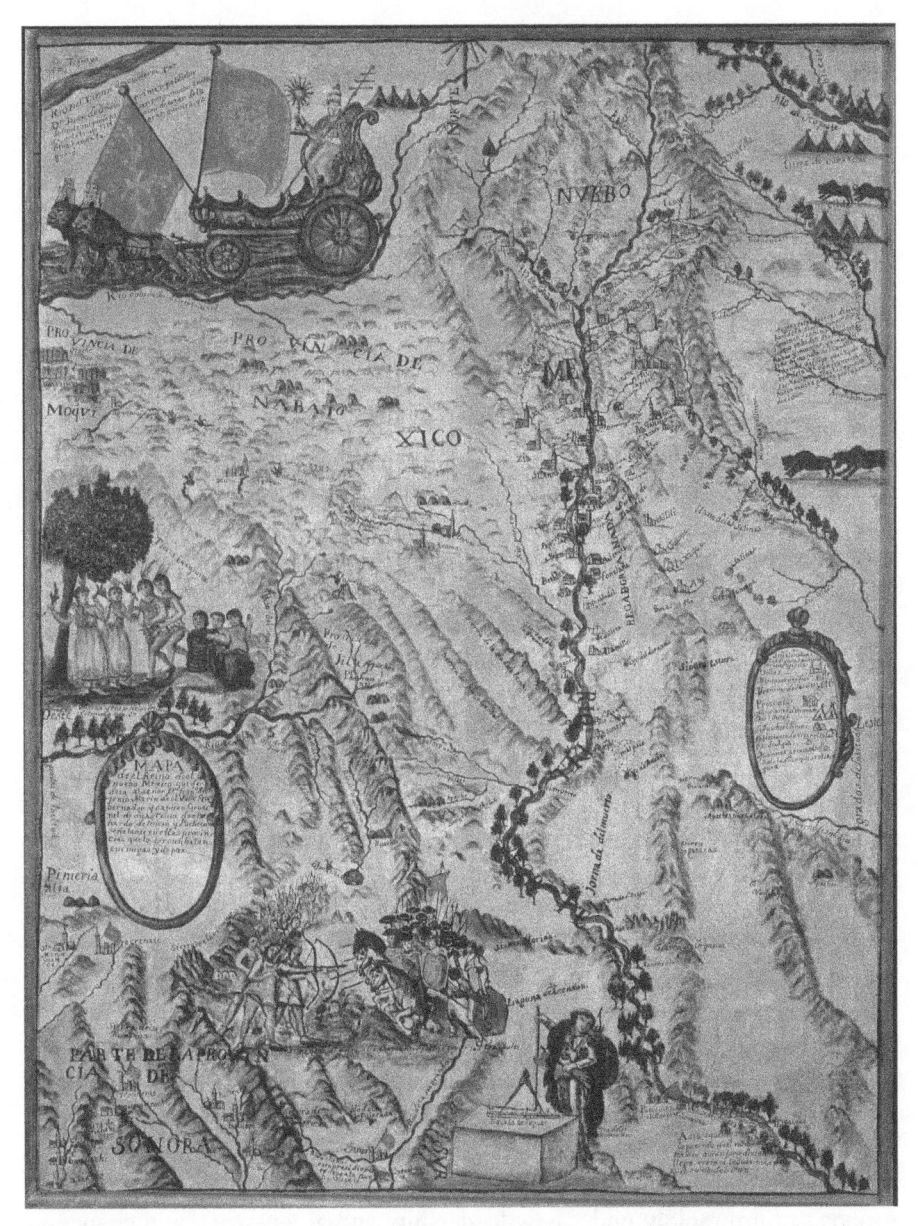

Fig. 1.1. Map of New Mexico by Bernardo Miera y Pacheco, 1760, showing dispersed Spanish colonial settlements along the Rio Grande and Comanche encampments east of Taos. (*Mapa de el reino de el nuebo Mexico*, from the collections of Mapoteca Manuel Orozco y Berra, Servicio de Información Agroalimentaria y Pesquera, Mexico City)

the escarpment of the Río Grande Valley etches a deep canyon. That gorge marked the northern and western extent of Hispanic settlements in the mid-eighteenth century (figure 1.1). Ranchos de Taos, where the raid on the Villalpando compound occurred, is located about four miles south of the Spanish colonial settlement of Taos and about seven miles south of the Tiwa-speaking Taos Pueblo Indian community. Ranchos de Taos has a complex multicultural history.

Throughout the eighteenth and nineteenth centuries, the communities of the valley were at the crossroads of diverse cultures, a place where Plains and Pueblo Indians, French fur trappers, and Spanish settlers gathered to trade. Comanches first appeared at the Taos trade fairs in 1706, as they extended their range and moved south into the Spanish frontier. These fairs, which operated under different economic systems, were in many ways precursors to the Santa Fe trade, although they benefited Native American groups more directly than the later trail trade did. The trade fairs brought Native and European trappers and traders from the Mississippi and Missouri Rivers to New Mexico and the Rocky Mountains, introducing them to the potential profits of trade with the Spanish Southwest and Mexico. Trade fairs at Taos Pueblo were stimulated by several New Mexican governors, sustained by New Mexico's Spanish settlers, and abhorred by officials of the Catholic Church. In the early eighteenth century the fairs were part of alternating cycles of warfare and tenuous peacemaking that characterized the relationship between the Pueblo Indian and Hispanic settlers in the Taos area and the Plains Indian groups that ranged into the Sangre de Cristo Mountains of southern Colorado and northern New Mexico.

From their strategic location, Comanche bands dominated the southern High Plains and exchanged goods with traders from all points of the compass, intensifying the competition for allies among French, Spanish, and British settlers and governments.[8] Establishing intercultural trading partnerships was an essential characteristic and public expression of Comanche leadership qualities. As the Comanches adopted horses as a means of transportation, their trade partnerships expanded geographically. Horses became a form of mobile wealth and an objective of Comanche raids on Pueblo, Spanish, and later American settlements. The considerable fluidity of Comanche social organization allowed groups to form rapidly under new leadership, and group size could change in response to trade, subsistence, and geographic opportunities. Captives taken in raids gave Comanches human capital that they used in several ways. Captives might be held for ransom or they might be adopted to replenish tribes depleted by disease and warfare. In some cases, the adoption of captives enabled Comanches to form kinship links with strategic trade partners.[9]

For about three decades between the late 1740s and the late 1770s, allied Comanche and Ute forces attacked northern New Mexico, including the Taos area, more than one hundred times. Some Spanish colonial governors pursued the Comanches and Utes with retaliatory force; other governors withheld access to trade fairs to punish offenders. Slave raids and commerce in captives were part of the frontier violence that occurred in colonial New Mexico and French colonial Missouri, as well as among Native groups. Women and children were more likely to be taken than men, and in some cases they were "adopted" into Hispanic and French families in an attempt to legitimize the practice. Men were seldom taken captive; they were more likely to be killed in the heat of battle and during raids. In a few cases, men were traded to mining camps in the interior of Mexico. Whether captives were bartered for diplomatic exchange or trafficked among the Utes and Comanches, violence served the ends of both Native and European trade partners. Blackhawk observes that "trade fairs were the 'epicenters' of the colonial and Indian slave trading networks," concluding that "the introduction of enslaved people brought violence into the domestic and intimate sphere of both Indian and Spanish households and communities."[10] This was also true in St. Louis, where the violence surrounding the human trafficking of enslaved Indian women and children and Black slaves was introduced into French colonists' communities and homes.

The raid on the Villalpando compound in Ranchos de Taos ended a fragile peace that had been brokered between Comanche bands and Governor Tomás Vélez Cachupín during his first term in office (1749–54). Several bands of Comanches attacked Ranchos de Taos on August 4, 1760, allegedly in response to a dance ceremony performed at Taos Pueblo that used the scalps of Comanches.[11] Although they are not named in the official report, María Rosa's husband and mother were killed during this ferocious battle, and she was among the women captured. Bishop Pedro Tamarón describes the fury of the attack:

> They [the Comanches] diverted, or provoked, them [the settlers] from a very large house, the greatest in all the valley, belonging to a settler called Villalpando, who luckily for him, had left that day on business. But when they saw so many Comanches coming, many women and men of that settlement took refuge in this house as the strongest. And, trusting in the fact that it had four towers and in the large supply of muskets, powder, and balls, they say that they fired on the Comanches. The latter were infuriated by this to such a horrible degree that they broke into different parts of the house, killed all the men and some of the women, who also fought. And the wife of the owner of the house, seeing that they were breaking down the outside door, went to defend it with a lance, and they killed

her fighting. Fifty-six women and children were carried off, and a large number of horses which the owner of the house was keeping there. Forty-nine bodies of dead Comanches were counted and other trickles of blood were seen.[12]

New Mexico governor Francisco Antonio Marín del Valle and one thousand Spanish and allied Native troops pursued the Comanches involved in the raid at Ranchos de Taos. They reportedly covered some 200 leagues, or about 520 miles, in forty days until their food gave out. Their Apache auxiliaries were dispirited and starving, and the troops returned to New Mexico.[13]

In the year after María Rosa's capture, Fray Pedro Serrano reported on conditions in this far northern frontier to the viceroy in Mexico City. He described the shocking social conditions, immorality, and lax religious practices in New Mexico. He was appalled by the utter debauchery and frenzy that accompanied the trade fairs at Taos Pueblo. New Mexican officials—from the governor to local military officers—were the worst offenders and also the main beneficiaries of the trade. Governors brought ironware—farm implements, axes and knives, horse tack—and other commodities to exchange with the Plains Indians for finely tanned deer hides, buffalo hides, and other goods. As Fray Pedro noted, "saddest" were the Indian men, women, and children exchanged like so much chattel. Women and girls as young as ten were among the most prized commodities and also the most outrageously victimized. Fray Pedro was pained by the obscene treatment they were subjected to—public rapes that he described as "hellish ceremonies."[14] These women were then considered ready to be sold to other men. The trade fairs also became venues for the ransom and return of men, women, and children taken in previous raids. The Spanish term *rescate* (rescue) was often used to refer to the trade fairs.

In the winter of 1761 Comanche leader Onacama and ten others traveled to Taos, accompanied by seven captives—either all women or a group of three women and four children. Interim New Mexico governor Manuel de Portillo Urrisola and a small party of soldiers arrived at the Comanche camp not far from Taos Pueblo and refused to allow the Comanches to proceed to the trade fair, where they had planned to present the seven captives as a peace offering. Portillo demanded that all the captives taken in 1760 be returned before the Comanches would be admitted to the fair. When negotiations broke down, Spanish and allied Ute forces attacked the encampment, allegedly killing some four hundred Comanche men. The Utes ran off with more than one thousand horses and mules and captured three hundred Comanche women and children. Portillo considered this a victory, and in a letter to Bishop Tamarón relating the "glorious" details of the battle, he criticized Governor Vélez

Cachupín (who returned for a second term in 1762) for what he assumed would be the governor's response to the battle.[15] Surely Vélez would have used diplomacy rather than force to win the release of the captives and secure the peace once again.

When Vélez returned to New Mexico in January 1762, he used his understanding of Comanche diplomacy to negotiate for peace. Again using Comanche women as emissaries, he promised to restore the previous amity with generous terms for the Taos trade and the return of captives.[16] Vélez sealed this peace when he brought thirty-one Comanche women and children to a council with visiting Comanche leaders and allowed them to select relatives to be returned to the tribe. The restoration of trade relations between the Spanish and Comanche leaders represented what historian Richard White refers to as a negotiation for a "middle ground."[17] The parties' more neutral positions were brought about by a process of mediation, mutual invention, and shared production, whereby Native peoples and governing authorities reached a kind of equilibrium and restored the trade valued by both sides.

María Rosa was not among the unnamed women and children returned to New Mexico in either 1761 or 1762. Why she never returned to Taos might be as much about her adaptation to captivity or her usefulness to her captors as it was about what happened to her while captive and how her life changed after she arrived in St. Louis.

Life as a Captive

In many ways, María Rosa's fate was a notable exception to the lives of others affected by the raids and battles that took place between 1760 and 1762, but evidently she never saw New Mexico again. Likely she heard occasional reports from fur trappers and traders who traveled between New Mexico and Plains Indian settlements and those who traveled to the Missouri and Mississippi River Valleys. María Rosa was a married woman of about twenty years of age and the mother of at least one son when she was kidnapped from her parents' home. Though her mother and her husband were killed in the attack, her infant son, José Julián Jáquez, miraculously survived and was not captured.

We can only speculate how María Rosa was treated during her years in captivity. The stories of other women and children held captive by the Comanches may offer some clues, but many of those people were captured during the nineteenth century, when US Army troops, settlers, and buffalo hunters added to the complex political economy unfolding on the southern

High Plains.[18] She was likely taken to Comanche camps along the Arkansas River north and east of Taos, where French fur traders from the Louisiana and Illinois frontiers also ventured.[19] Following the pitched battle of the raid and the frenzied pursuit afterward, she likely wondered whether she would be adopted into the tribe or ravaged and killed, and perhaps even her captors did not know at the time. She would have endured a mournful period of indoctrination, but her status as a slave or an adopted member of the camp might have changed over time. She became pregnant and gave birth to a son during her captivity, and although she later brought him with her to St. Louis, she never recognized him as her legitimate heir. She would have observed that both Spanish governors and Comanche leaders used women as emissaries of peace. Perhaps she even found herself useful during some of the ensuing peace talks and trade negotiations, although this is sheer conjecture. Her path from captive to Creole citizen of St. Louis, however, is fairly well documented.

In a letter dated June 26, 1768, unnamed traders reported to authorities in St. Louis that a "Spanish woman" and her "sister" were living among the Pawnee. According to the traders, the Comanches had enslaved the Spanish woman some eight years ago and, under duress, made her the "wife" of the "principal chief," with whom she had a son who was now three or four years old. She and the child had then been sold to the Pawnee, who in turn sold them to a French trader. Although the document does not name either Jean Baptiste Salé dit Lajoie or María Rosa, there is no doubt that this letter documents their relationship.[20] The letter covers the span of time that Jean Baptiste and María Rosa met in the Pawnee camp and some of the specifics of her years in captivity. He paid 300 francs to acquire her and the child, indicating that the trafficking of captive women and children was part of the eighteenth-century French and Native American trade. The letter does not mention that the French trader and the "Spanish woman" were expecting a child of their own, although that may not have been apparent yet. According to the traders, the woman's half-Comanche child would be brought to St. Louis and given a Christian baptism and instruction. Authorities directed the traders to bring the ransomed woman and child to St. Louis "without fail" by June of the following year or sooner. During this period, the French policy toward Indigenous and *métis* captives was moving away from enslavement and closer to protection. The letter states that the Spanish woman left her enslaved sister behind, and the traders were going to attempt to buy her as well.[21]

Joining the Creole Community in St. Louis

Jean Baptiste Salé dit Lajoie was born in about 1741 in Saintous, France.[22] He would have been about twenty-three when he arrived in St. Louis and about twenty-six when he met María Rosa.[23] He had been one of the men recruited by Pierre de Laclède Liguest and Auguste Chouteau, who came to St. Louis in 1764 from the Illinois settlements. He served as a *voyageur*—a boatman and fur trader—with Laclède and Chouteau. He also established himself as a trader and baker in St. Louis—profitable ventures in the settlement then known as *Pain Court* for its shortage of bread.[24] Lajoie's name appears on three maps of St. Louis made during a 1767 survey of the new settlement by French cartographer Guy Dufossat, under the direction of the controlling Spanish government (figure 1.2). A creek bearing the name and a plot of ground labeled "Prairie de la Joie" are both located north of the settlement.[25]

Jean Baptiste and María Rosa settled on the northwest corner of block 57 on one of the original lots distributed among members of the founding party. Lajoie had purchased the land in about 1767 from another settler and built a stone house and garden and enclosed the plot.[26] Their house, described in later legal documents as measuring twenty-five by twenty feet, was built in the French style of vertical posts set on a stone foundation.[27] María Rosa joined a community that would have shared some similarities with Taos. Both were frontier towns with people of many cultures, including mixed-descent Native American and European populations engaged in intertribal and intercultural commerce based on the fur trade. María Rosa would have found a community with a strong Catholic faith and governed by the Spanish, although St. Louis had a predominantly French population.[28] Among the five hundred settlers living in St. Louis in 1770, there was a mix of French and French Canadian citizens, *métis* individuals (those of mixed European and Native American ancestry), and enslaved people of Native American and African heritage. She would have met other women whose children had different fathers and were of mixed ancestry, whether publicly acknowledged or not (figures 1.3 and 1.4). The settlement was a compact village, and the surrounding landscape contained more than twenty archaeological mounds, evidence of the Mississippian people whose homelands were located in this confluence area from about AD 800 to 1200, as well as their tribal descendants. Native peoples of the Illinois, Missouri, and Osage nations were vital trade partners who controlled natural resources and hunting grounds that provided them with trade goods to exchange with the French settlers in St. Louis.[29]

On July 3, 1770, María Rosa and Jean Baptiste entered into a marriage

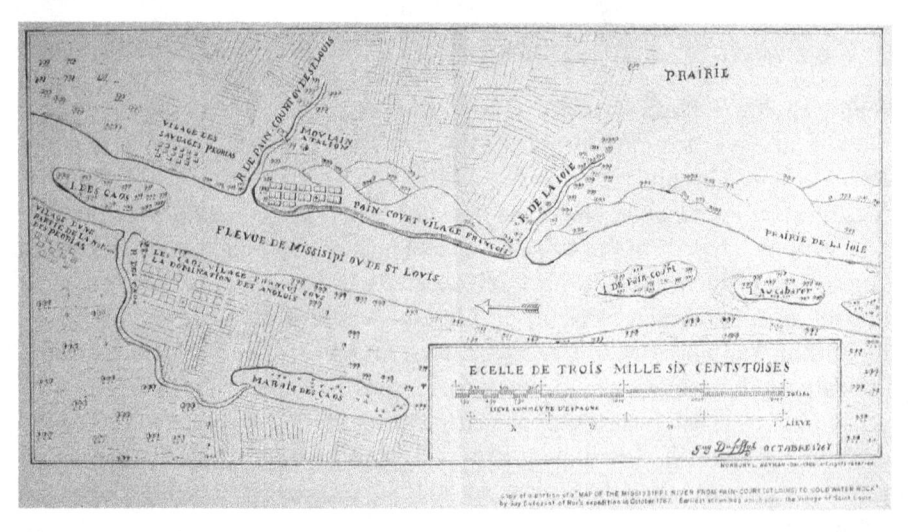

Fig. 1.2. Map of the Mississippi River from Pain-Court (St. Louis) to Cold Water Rock, 1767. Guy Dufossat, a French cartographer, mapped the early St. Louis settlement (showing Lajoie's fields) under the direction of the Spanish army and the governor of Upper Louisiana, Antonio de Ulloa. (Norbury Wayman Collection, St. Louis Mercantile Library, University of Missouri–St. Louis)

contract containing certain prenuptial conditions, and they were apparently married that same day in the first church built in St. Louis—really just a simple cabin—that had been dedicated on June 24, 1770.[30] Their marriage contract was quite specific about their obligations to the two children in their household, the property they shared, and what they would bequeath to their children. Twenty-month-old Lambert was identified as their legitimate child, but Antoine, born to María Rosa when she was a captive among the "savages," had no claim on their estate. They acknowledged, however, their obligation to nourish and educate him. Lambert was baptized in the same church on July 4, the day after their marriage. The record of his baptism notes that he had been born on November 12, 1768, which may indicate that María Rosa and Jean Baptiste were already living in St. Louis by that time.[31] It is possible that they were living in St. Louis on November 19, 1769, when Spanish lieutenant governor Pedro Piernas arrived to administer the oath of allegiance to the Spanish Crown.[32]

The timing of this marriage contract is noteworthy because Piernas was charged with enumerating the Native American men, women, and children enslaved in Ste. Genevieve and St. Louis. The enumeration completed on July 8, 1770, shows Jean Baptiste as the owner of an Indian boy and girl,

Fig. 1.3. Anna Maria von Phul, *Woman, Child and a Dog in French Colonial St. Louis*, 1818, graphite, ink, and watercolor on paper. Von Phul spent the summer of 1818 visiting her family in St. Louis and painting scenes of French colonial life. (Missouri Historical Society, St. Louis)

each thirteen years of age and not baptized. Their tribal affiliations are not indicated on the census, and Antoine, who was half Native, is not listed.

Lajoie was enterprising and acquired several pieces of property in St. Louis in the 1780s. On the St. Louis census recorded December 31, 1791, for the Spanish government in Havana, "Juan Bap Salé" is listed as the head of a

Fig. 1.4. Anna Maria von Phul, watercolor on paper, 1818. A Native American woman, likely of the Osage tribe, is shown wearing a blanket and earrings, indicating the type of goods French and American traders used in their exchanges with the Osage. (1953-158-0026, Missouri Historical Society, St. Louis)

household of five people and three enslaved people.[33] The names of the other household members are not given, but the ages indicate that this was Jean Baptiste and María Rosa, their two adolescent sons Antoine and Lambert, and their daughter Hèléne. Three slaves are listed—two men described as *pardo* or mixed race without indicating whether they were of Black or Indigenous heritage, and one woman identified as *negro* or Black. It is not possible to determine whether these are the same people listed on the 1770 census, however. The 1791 census contains a detailed list of the furs and hides traded in St. Louis and Ste. Genevieve in 1791. It includes a quantity of deer hides, buffalo hides, bear skins, and ermine, otter, and beaver furs, showing the fur trade's continuing importance to the region's economy.

At some point in 1792, when he was about fifty, Lajoie returned to France and took his son Lambert with him, leaving María Rosa and the other children behind. Their daughter Hèléne married into a well-connected family in St. Louis around the same time.[34] This was evidently not the first time Jean Baptiste had traveled to France with goods to trade, but he did not return to St. Louis after this particular trip. Why he stayed in Bordeaux may never be known, but during a subsequent lawsuit over the title to the house and property, neighbors testified that Lajoie had left St. Louis in the company of a woman named Madame Barrere. She accompanied him as far as New Orleans, where she joined her sister before she too returned to France. María Rosa considered herself abandoned by her husband, but she was not without resources. Lajoie claimed in a later affidavit that although he had no intention of returning to her, he had left her and the children with considerable resources and the power of attorney to dispose of and inherit the property in St. Louis. Certified copies of statements he sent from Bordeaux in December 1817 list the property and goods, including a store, supplies, boat rigging, one hundred pistols, wines, credits, and furs, which he valued at between 60,000 and 90,000 francs. Lajoie claimed to be nearly impoverished, though he was living on property he had acquired when he returned to France. He implored María Rosa to be friendly, charitable, and grateful for all he had given her and not reduce him to public indigence. He ended his letter to María Rosa by wishing her health and happy days.[35]

In the early 1800s María Rosa had already begun a series of legal actions to distribute her real estate and other property, which included two young children of enslaved Black women in her household.[36] The legal instruments by which she transferred the enslaved girls laid out her claim to the children. The documents reveal that she bought each of their mothers by public sale and deed, with the understanding that their children would also belong to her—a rather disturbing assertion from a woman who had once been enslaved herself. Though she names the enslaved children, she does not identify their mothers. Her legal documents assert her right of ownership and her right to transfer that ownership to her granddaughters:

> I declare I bestow and make a pure, perfect and irrevocable donation, in law termed *inter vivos*, to my granddaughter and godchild, Carolina Salée, daughter of my aforesaid son Lambert Salée, of a negress named Estera, two years old, belonging to me, having raised her and purchased her mother by public deed and executed in this government, on condition that should God spare her and

she should have children, the first shall belong in full property to my said son Lambert Salée, her [Carolina's] father, and if she has others, they shall be for my said granddaughter, to whom I give the above named slave free from all tribute, mortgage, dominion, or bond, special or general, and from this day forward and forever, I abandon and renounce all right, dominion and possession, title, cause and action over said slave.[37]

María Rosa gave another enslaved child to her minor granddaughter María Leroux. That child was identified in legal documents as a "negress" named Josepha, six years old, who was placed in trust to Hèléne.[38] The timing coincided with the end of French and Spanish rule, as María Rosa distributed the property just before the United States asserted control over the region in March 1804. Under French and Spanish law, she had the right to exert authority over the distribution of her property—rights that women would lose under American rule. María Rosa, however, learned how to use the American court system as well. In 1806, as next of kin of her deceased son Antoine (who was not her legitimate heir, according to her 1770 marriage contract), she sued for payments owed to him.[39] "Marie Rose Vidalpando," identified as the widow of Jean Salé dit Lajoie, is listed as having property valued at $800 on the 1805 enumeration of St. Louis property owners.

María Rosa may have been surprised in 1802 to receive a visit from the son she was separated from and had perhaps assumed killed during the 1760 raid on Ranchos de Taos. José Julián Jáquez, who had been living with family members near San Juan Pueblo in New Mexico, appeared in St. Louis to claim his right to his maternal inheritance.[40] How he learned his mother was still alive is not known, but he likely heard about her from fur traders or from participants in the 1792–93 Vial expedition, whose members had wintered in St. Louis.[41] María Rosa acknowledged José Julián as her legitimate son, but that did not entitle him to any part of her estate. José Julián brought legal action against Hèléne, which resulted in him forfeiting any claim to his mother's future estate for the sum of $200. He apparently did not return to New Mexico immediately because in 1809 he was summoned by the governor on behalf of his wife, whom he had left behind. Even in the last years of her life, María Rosa remained a fierce protector of herself and her property. She was ninety years old when she brought charges against a dray driver, claiming that on May 1, 1823, he had beaten her with a heavy rope about her shoulders and person.[42]

María Rosa arrived in St. Louis as a recently freed captive, but given the social status of women in eighteenth-century French Creole communities, she was able to exert personal and property rights through the legal system. In a

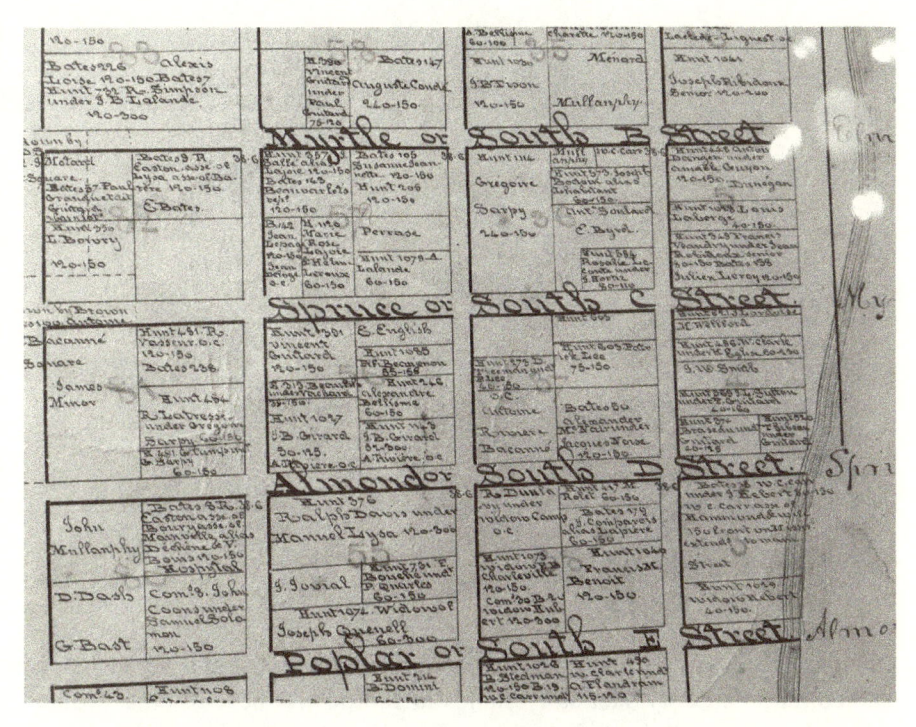

Fig. 1.5. Property owners in St. Louis, 1823, including the Lajoie and Leroux properties in block 57. (Missouri Historical Society, St. Louis)

case study from Ste. Genevieve, located some fifty miles south of St. Louis on the Mississippi River, Susan Boyle found compelling evidence that women enjoyed wide authority to establish and manage commercial enterprises, buy and sell property, and hold title to real and movable property inherited from their families of origin as well as their spouses.[43] The US commandant of the Upper Louisiana Military District noted in 1812 that women in the territory seemed to have great influence over their husbands and enjoyed more authority and respect in their marriages because of premarital contracts that set the terms of property rights and inheritance.

María Rosa died on July 27, 1830, at the home of her daughter Hèléne on Elm Street, between Fourth and Fifth Streets, not far from where she had first settled (figures 1.5 and 1.6). She was buried the following day in the cemetery of the Old Cathedral of St. Louis. Her passing is marked in a brief obituary noting that she was well over one hundred years old—surely an unusual feat to live to such an advanced age at the time. Although her exact age is not known with certainty, the story of her captivity and her adaptation to Creole

Fig. 1.6. Portrait of Marie Hèléne Salé dit Lajoie Leroux (1773–1859), daughter of María Rosa, by Emile Herzinger, 1863, wash drawing based on an 1859 daguerreotype. (XO5824, Missouri Historical Society, St. Louis)

life over the formative years of colonial St. Louis demonstrates her resilience and cultural dexterity. Her story stands in contrast to those of other women whose lives in captivity did not end with such a demonstration of their own agency.

Rescued on the Santa Fe Trail

Contrasting María Rosa's story with the narratives of women taken captive in the early decades of the nineteenth century reveals the persistent fears that accompanied western expansion. A wider perspective on the role of women is attained when captivity narratives are placed within the changing political economy of the midcontinent between 1760 and the mid-nineteenth century. This span of time encompasses immense social and political change in Indigenous communities as well. When María Rosa joined the Comanches in 1760, their economy and social organization were in the midst of momentous change. Over more than a century, from the 1740s to the 1860s, the Comanches made the transition from being primarily hunters and gatherers to having a mixed economy, expanding their embrace of pastoralism and raising horses and other livestock. The Comanches were flexibly organized bands under pressure to change from both external sources and internal needs. They had to balance hunting and pastoralism, market production and subsistence, local needs and the availability of grass to feed their growing herds. Horses were not only the basis of their economy; they were also the source of social prestige.

Much of the midcontinent relied on the horses and mules the Comanches captured from wild herds, bred, or stole from Texas, New Mexico, and Mexico. As bands lost members through disease and warfare, they took human captives and in some cases incorporated them into the band, thereby adding laborers to the economy as well as mates and mothers. Extra women in a household meant that more furs could be processed and hides tanned. Captive women could join Comanche women in gathering food and making items for trade, while additional children—taken in raids or born of captives—meant there were more potential herders and stock tenders.[44] Comanche leaders continued to use trade fairs and diplomatic trade with the governments in New Mexico, Texas, and Mexico as sources of valuable trade goods or as places to raid for the spoils of war. Women captured in the raids were used by all sides as intermediaries and negotiators.

The Santa Fe Trail increased wagon traffic across the landscape but did not necessarily contribute to intercultural interactions or exchange networks. Fear was a common emotion expressed in many of the diaries and narratives of the trail—travelers had to contend with the parching sun; the search for grass, water, and shelter; and the constant threat of Indian attacks. These fears were fueled by the history of violent encounters as wagons carrying goods crossed Native lands. The route of the trade caravans from the docks of the Mississippi River to the plazas of New Mexico and Mexico traversed lands formerly occupied by numerous Native American nations. According to Josiah Gregg, in the first years of the Santa Fe trade, several trade expeditions were able to use barter and livestock to avoid conflict with Comanche, Arapaho, Pawnee, and other southern Plains tribes they encountered. By 1829, US military escorts accompanied caravans, but that did not guarantee that conflicts were avoided or violence was averted.[45]

The caravans that traveled from New Mexico to Missouri in August 1838 carried three women who had survived capture and torture on the Texas–New Mexico frontier two years earlier. Sarah Ann Horn, Caroline Harris, and Rachel Plummer had all been abducted by Comanches. On April 4, 1836, Comanches attacked one of the south Texas frontier communities founded by land speculator Dr. John Beales and named after his wife, Dolores (which means "sorrows" in Spanish). Located near the current city of Laredo, the small frontier outpost was attacked by a party of fifty to sixty Comanches, who took Sarah Ann Horn (Mrs. John Horn) and Caroline Harris (Mrs. Richard Harris) from the settlement, along with their children.[46] In all, eleven men, two women, and three children—Sarah's sons John and Joseph Horn and the infant daughter of Richard and Caroline Harris—were at the settlement at the time of the attack. Nine of the men were killed, and all the women and children were abducted. Mrs. Harris witnessed the murder and mutilation of her husband and then saw her infant daughter being bashed to death the following day. The Dolores attack occurred during a particularly volatile time in Texas history, when Texans, Mexicans, Americans, and the surrounding Native tribes were all aligned with different political and economic goals.

The following month, on May 19, 1836, Rachel Parker Plummer was taken in a raid by Comanches, Kiowas, and their allies on the Parker compound in central Texas. Also abducted was Rachel's son James Pratt Parker, her cousin Cynthia Ann Parker, Cynthia Ann's brother John, and their aunt Elizabeth Kellogg. Cynthia Ann's story is well known even to contemporary readers and has been fictionalized in film and romance novels. From the age of ten or eleven, Cynthia Ann lived with the Comanche. She became the wife of Peta Nocona and was the mother of famed Comanche leader Quanah Parker, as well as another son and a daughter. Although Cynthia Ann's family brought her back to Texas after she had spent twenty-five years living as a Comanche, she never adapted to the way of life her family tried to impose on her.[47] Rachel Plummer was held for twenty-one months before being rescued by *comancheros* (traders) from New Mexico, then transported to Missouri on the Santa Fe Trail under the protective watch of William and Mary Donoho. The Donohos had been traders and inn operators in Santa Fe since 1833, but they left New Mexico after a popular uprising led to the bloody massacre of the Mexican governor there. Plummer was returned to her family in 1838 through the concerted efforts of her father, who also managed to rescue her son (his grandson) James Pratt Plummer. Rachel died in March 1839, before James was returned, perhaps as a result of injuries, or perhaps following the birth of a child she had with her husband after her return to Texas.

All three women—Horn, Harris, and Plummer—penned or contributed to narratives of their ordeals.[48] The physical and psychological abuse they suffered may offer a glimpse into the treatment María Rosa endured. Horn and Harris acknowledge the succor provided by *comancheros*, who bought them from different bands of Comanches in the summer of 1837 and brought them to New Mexico for care. It took many months for their families to be notified of their rescue, and during that time, Horn and Harris were moved from one New Mexico settlement to another. They were not always treated well, and they were even exploited by those seeking to profit from their rescue until they were placed with the family of William and Mary Donoho.

Caroline Harris was reportedly in the worst psychological and physical condition, having been beaten and burned by the Comanche woman who enslaved her. Sarah Horn credited her survival to the skills she learned while held by the Comanches, such as processing hides and making moccasins, garments, and jerky.[49] While still in New Mexico, Sarah Horn learned the fate of her sons—one was dead from exposure, and the other could not be found. Neither Horn nor Harris survived long after they returned to their families. Horn settled near New Franklin, Missouri, and died in Pulaski County, Missouri, in 1839. Mrs. Harris never returned to Texas but stayed near Boonville, Missouri, where she died shortly after the return crossing. Each of the women described the depraved cruelty and near starvation they endured in captivity; on the return journey, they feared another attack as they followed the trail back through the same country. Each was fortified by faith and by the hope of being restored to their families and their frontier communities. Their narratives make María Rosa's journey from captivity to the Creole society of St. Louis all the more remarkable.

The Legacy of Captive Narratives

María Rosa's story has become more widely known as the literature and history of western expansion have been reframed to consider the experiences of women and people of color. Tales of captivity encompass song, dance, storytelling, and religious ceremony and have a long tradition in New Mexico, where capture by nomadic tribes was a real threat throughout history. In many New Mexican communities, folk traditions keep the history of tragic loss, captivity, and redemption alive, as well as the history of peacemaking and cross-cultural kinship.[50] Comanche, Apache, Navajo, and other Native groups are represented in the annual cycle of traditional Hispanic dances, depending on the history of the region. In Ranchos de Taos there is a strong performative culture, and captive tales are reenacted on saints' days and New Year's Day. The dances are public recognition of the mixture, or *mestizaje*, of identities that resulted from cross-cultural marriages or, in some cases, rape as a form of retribution and cultural dominance between warring cultures and communities in which women were trafficked.

On New Year's Day, dance troupes of Ranchos de Taos, Talpa, and other New Mexican villages honor the feast of Saint Emmanuel, combining a mass at the village church with elements of their Comanche heritage. They dress in buckskins and dance to a sustained drumbeat as they visit homes in the community where those named for the saint reside (figure 1.7). The daylong cycle of dance and song combines and in some cases telescopes decades of

Fig. 1.7. La Comanchita, dancer from Los Ranchos de Taos, New Mexico, where the annual performance honors the women, men, and children captured by Comanches and other Plains Indian tribes. (Used with permission of the photographer, Miguel Gandert)

Comanche relations with the communities of the Taos Valley. Though her name may not be spoken during this annual dance cycle, María Rosa and other captive men, women, and children are certainly remembered. The music and oral traditions honor the captives and the children of mixed ancestry who were born in captivity.

María Rosa was not the first woman to be captured by Comanches or other Plains Indians, and she was not the last. Readers' fascination with captivity narratives acknowledges the psychological damage these raids imposed on New Mexico, Texas, and other frontier settlements along the Santa Fe Trail. Captive narratives, folk songs, and lurid illustrations are some of the earliest forms of this North American literary genre.[51] For more than a century, firsthand accounts and retellings made captivity stories both relevant and pervasive. María Rosa's survival and adaptation to Creole culture in St. Louis run counter to many captive narratives. It was probably a combination of her resilience, her linguistic skills, and perhaps her diplomacy or tenacity that contributed to her survival. Did she fare better than other captives who endured horrendous abuse at the hands of the Comanches? Or did she too suffer the injuries reported by other women? What price did she command when her Comanche captors bartered her to the Pawnee before Lajoie paid 300 francs for her and her child?

Josiah Gregg described María Rosa as a woman who was eager to tell her tale of woe to anyone who would listen. In the decade after María Rosa's death, Sarah Ann Horn, Caroline Harris, and Rachel Plummer would narrate their own woeful stories. Each of them was captured, bartered from one group to another, battered by some of their captors, and betrayed by others claiming to be their rescuers. María Rosa's survival and her adaptation to Creole life in St. Louis have a larger context. Hers is an extraordinary story of strength and determination. Certainly, part of that is attributable to her own constitution, which allowed her to live to such an advanced age. María Rosa's adaptation to life in St. Louis, as evidenced by her long life and the success of her children and grandchildren, stands in contrast to the experiences of Mrs. Horn, Mrs. Harris, and Mrs. Plummer. María Rosa may have had fears about returning to Taos, if she could have done so, given that this was where her husband and mother had been murdered. While Native women were captured and enslaved in New Mexican families, María Rosa would have been returning to a New Mexico where the colonial *casta* system may have had a difficult time reincorporating her. Brooks's analysis of captivity and kinship among elite New Mexicans argues that Spanish colonial attitudes and values of *calidad* (character and virtue) and class could have been a barrier to her reentry if she was thought to be dishonored by her captivity.[52] The women captured in the nineteenth century who were returned to Euro-American communities suffered reintegration issues and often died soon after their return.

Another aspect of María Rosa's endurance may have been the receptive nature of St. Louis's Creole society. There, the mixture of French, Spanish, and Native American cultures allowed the seemingly open acceptance of cultural and biological relations. How her own *métis* son Antoine, fathered by a Comanche man, manifested his identity and how he managed to navigate St. Louis society are open questions. María Rosa and Jean Baptiste denied him the opportunity for adoption when they presented his half-brother Lambert for baptism in July 1770, continuing his marginalized legal and familial status.

The status of African American people who were held as property cannot be ignored. María Rosa enslaved and exploited women in her own household. She may have entered the trade network as a captive herself, but she emerged and asserted ownership rights over women as her human property within the complexities of St. Louis's changing legal system. That did not prevent countersuits and claims on her estate by her heirs, but in each case, the strength of her claims included recognition of her rights, and her voice was often powerfully present in the recollections of her family and neighbors. Her historical legacy was created from conditions that transcended the sorrows of her life and the romanticism that shrouded earlier narratives of her captivity.

2

On the Trail of Carmel Benavides Robidoux

The trade fairs that brought Apaches, Comanches, Kiowas, and other Plains Indians to New Mexico also brought French trappers and traders from the upper Mississippi and Missouri Rivers seeking goods for international trade. In the decade before the Louisiana Purchase, French trappers and traders tentatively expanded their range south and west into the Rocky Mountains, even though they were legally barred from New Mexico because it was a colony of Spain. Given the ill-defined borders of Spanish holdings, a few French trappers and traders entered Taos and Santa Fe accidentally or perhaps confident that they could arrange their release if they were arrested.[1] Jean Baptiste Salé dit Lajoie did not travel to New Mexico; he purchased the Taos-born María Rosa through those same trade networks that connected French trappers and traders with Indigenous tribes across the continent. This chapter examines the history of the Santa Fe Trail through the lens of a cross-cultural marriage between a New Mexican–born woman and her French partner. Unlike Jean Baptiste's acquisition of María Rosa, Antoine Robidoux did not purchase María Carmen de la Cruz Benavides (known as Carmel Benavides Robidoux after her marriage). They met in Santa Fe at the beginning of the legal trade between Missouri and New Mexico. Carmel and Antoine's relationship was one of many cross-cultural marriages, liaisons, and business partnerships between New Mexicans and *los extranjeros* that developed in the earliest years of the Santa Fe trade.[2]

Following Mexico's independence from Spain in 1821, trade between New Mexico and French settlements on the Mississippi and Missouri Rivers became legal (figure 2.1). Although the earliest traders to reach New Mexico were often identified as Americans, many were from Missouri, which had only recently become part of the United States. Within the first decade of

Fig. 2.1. Copy of an 1844 lithograph showing the arrival of a caravan in Santa Fe. (40511, Palace of the Governors Photo Archives [NMHM/DCA])

the trade, several French and American traders chose Hispanic women as domestic partners and wives, which granted them access to important social and commercial networks. By the 1830s, through these family and social networks, Missouri merchants joined New Mexican and Mexican traders to serve larger and more lucrative markets, extending the Santa Fe–St. Louis trade into Chihuahua and farther south. French traders were especially well positioned to take advantage of the new markets in New Mexico and Mexico through their contacts with Indigenous trade networks along the interior rivers of the continent.[3]

Antoine Robidoux and several of his five brothers entered New Mexico to trap and trade furs with tribes in the southern Rockies and then pushed west into the Gunnison River basin of western Colorado and the Green River drainage, now part of Utah. He held permits issued by the Mexican government, but he also built successful alliances with Ute bands. His relationship with Carmel, along with his brother Louis's marriage to another New Mexican woman, offered them access to trapping areas restricted to New Mexicans and Hispanic families, granting them strategic advantages in the Santa Fe trade. Through the Robidoux family's web of business and social connections, the resources they harvested during western expeditions were brought to St. Louis and shipped far and wide. The Robidoux family—six brothers and their wives and children—were intertwined in business and family networks that anchored their lives across the changing economic and political landscape of Missouri and the West.

The advantages of Carmel and Antoine's relationship is evident in the access he gained to New Mexican hunting grounds and her association with the Robidoux family's vast trading and commercial networks. But for Carmel, the primary benefits of her marriage were perhaps less tangible, as this chapter explores.

Seeking Carmel in the Historical Record

As in many situations involving contact between different cultures, women played an important role in linking the diverse people traveling the Santa Fe Trail.[4] Women acted as culture brokers, negotiating the cross-cultural customs and mores and in some cases the languages of trade. Native American woman were crucial partners in the economics of the fur trade, which was central to the impetus for westward expansion. Women processed furs and hides, contributing enormous labor and value. They were also consorts and wives to mountain men and traders, many of whom came from the French colonies of the midcontinent. The advantages women derived from these relationships depended on many factors—time, location, and the men with whom they were aligned. Many of these relationships gave rise to families that, like the Robidoux, spanned the continent and extended trade networks internationally into Mexico and Canada. Those expansive opportunities, however, did not assure women a place in the historical record.

Unlike María Rosa, Carmel did not leave a trail of documents in either New Mexico or Missouri. She was present, however, at different points in the history of both places, sometimes with Antoine and sometimes without him. Carmel traveled the trail from Santa Fe to St. Louis and back again multiple times.[5] The various ways her name was recorded in official documents make it hard to trace her movements with any certainty. She is listed as Carmel Benavides or Carmen Benavides, as Carmel Robidoux or Carmen Robidoux, and even as a woman identified as A. Robidoux. Secondary accounts and unsubstantiated sources report that she may have made as many as five trips on the trail between 1828 and 1888, when she died in southern Colorado. Several key documents place her in Santa Fe until the early 1840s and then in various locations in Missouri until 1860, when she returned to Santa Fe. Based on the church record of her birth, her standing as an adoptive mother or godmother to others, and her listing in census records at both ends of the

Fig. 2.2. Undated portrait of Antoine Robidoux (1794–1860). (007803, Palace of the Governors Photo Archives [NMHM/DCA])

trail, it is possible to trace the rough timeline of her life as she traveled across the continent.

Several books have been written about Antoine Robidoux and his extended family (figure 2.2). The spelling of his name was idiosyncratic, depending on its rendering by French, Spanish, English, or German speakers in written documents. He was Antonio in Spanish records, Antoine in French, and Anthony in English, making research a challenge. The spelling of the family name also varied; he was referred to as Antonio Rubidu or Robidio in New Mexican documents. He and his five brothers traded over a vast region of the upper Missouri and extended their fur-trapping and Indian trade empire into the Rocky Mountains, the Great Basin, and as far as California. On occasion, the record is unclear as to which of the six brothers is being described. Yet Antoine expressed himself in letters, reports, and newspaper articles that were published both during and after his lifetime. Finding Carmel—understanding when she lived in Missouri or New Mexico, how she came to be there, and what she might have known about the situations in either place—meant examining the historical records of Antoine's trade and travels and then determining whether she was residing in the same place at the same time.

Despite residing in the multilingual Spanish, French, English, and Native American center of the continent, Carmel apparently was not literate in any of those languages. She must have spoken and understood several European languages, however. She may have been passingly familiar with words in the Ute language, given Antoine's long association with the Ute tribes of the Great Basin, but that is mere speculation. She was godmother to a Ute child that Antoine and she presented for baptism in a Santa Fe church in 1841, and she lived her last years at the Ute agency in Colorado, in the household of her granddaughter and grandson-in-law, who was the US Indian agent there.[6] She signed with an *X* on an English-language deed when she sold her centuries-old ancestral home in New Mexico in 1879. So far, no one has found an image, letter, diary entry, or public statement that captures Carmel's thoughts or emotions. We can only imagine how she navigated the changing social milieu of Santa Fe, St. Louis, and other places along the trail. Whether apocryphal or not, one of Antoine Robidoux's biographers (admittedly prone to exaggeration) describes Carmel as an excellent horsewoman, skillful and agile, graceful and beautiful.

Carmel and Antoine were life partners from 1828, when they met in Santa Fe, to 1860, when he died in St. Joseph, Missouri. Their thirty-two-year relationship spanned an era of rapid and dramatic political and cultural changes at both ends of the Santa Fe Trail. Antoine Robidoux's words and deeds were chronicled by himself, his admirers, and his competitors. Even without a single document in Carmel's own words, her place in his life is preserved. His affection for her, whom he referred to as "Carmeletta," was recorded in his final days and reflected in his last will and testament, where he calls her his dear wife. After Antoine's death, Carmel returned to her birthplace and the home she still owned, despite having spent almost twenty years away from New Mexico. By then, Santa Fe was no longer part of Mexico. Her husband had helped deliver the territory to the United States, having served as translator for the Army of the West. At the end of her life, true to her adventurous nature, Carmel was living on the edge of the Ute frontier in southern Colorado.

Extranjeros entre Nosotros *(Foreigners among Us)*

Carmel was born in Santa Fe in 1811 to a prominent New Mexican family with deep roots in the region's Spanish colonial history. It was a year that would be remembered all over the world when a comet streaked across the sky, leaving a trace thousands of miles wide and an even longer tail. The comet's light lasted most of that year and into the next. The great Shawnee leader and orator Tecumseh saw the comet as a potent sign and called for intertribal unity against the westward spread of the United States. He warned his followers of the greed and avarice of the white man, reportedly saying: "Nothing will satisfy them but the whole of our hunting grounds; from the rising to the setting sun."[7] At the many gatherings where he preached this message, Tecumseh urged Native peoples to return to their traditions and revitalize their cultures before it was too late.

In Mexico, the quest for liberty was ignited by the oratory of Father Miguel Hidalgo y Costilla, a Catholic priest from the village of Dolores in the state of Guanajuato. Hidalgo's *Grito de Dolores,* delivered on September 16, 1810, powered Mexican independence, as Mexicans fought against Spain's weakening support and increasing taxation of the colony. Hidalgo was shot by firing squad on July 30, 1811, but his followers persevered until independence was achieved in 1821. In Missouri, a massive earthquake on December 15, 1811, rocked the Mississippi River so convulsively it was said to flow backward for months. The quake's epicenter was near New Madrid in southern Missouri, but the aftershocks—both literal and figurative—were felt widely for the next year.

Missouri was not the only place where the natural environment seemed to convulse; across the country, intense climatic events were unfolding—floods, stifling heat, disease. Even animals reacted to the strange phenomena. As the War of 1812 enveloped the country, Missouri and Illinois were swept into the fray as the British and allied Native peoples sought to control the destiny and political alignment of the land disturbed by the earthquake.[8] Eighteen-year-old Antoine and several of his brothers enlisted as volunteers in the St. Louis Artillerists, but the family was already heavily committed to the fur trade and trade with Native peoples unhampered by British regulations. It was, after all, one of the reasons their grandfather Joseph Robidoux had migrated from Canada, via the Great Lakes, to the growing settlements around St. Louis in the early 1770s.[9]

Antoine was raised in the Florissant area, immediately west of the confluence of the Mississippi and Missouri Rivers. It was one of the settlements that branched off from St. Louis in the late eighteenth century as settlers were attracted to the fertile bottomlands and the strategic location of the confluence. To this day, Florissant retains its colonial street grid emanating from the Church of St. Ferdinand. Following the War of 1812, several fur-trading companies based in the St. Louis region looked west for new opportunities in the lands annexed through the Louisiana Purchase, taking them to the edge of the Spanish-controlled Southwest. But it was not until Mexico won its independence from Spain that trade opportunities flourished.[10]

Santa Fe was a town of about five thousand people when the first Missouri traders ventured west on the trail. The Santa Fe Trail itself ended in the central plaza, not far from the rambling home on Calle del Granero, or Granary Street, where Carmel was raised and where generations of her maternal family had lived. The street ran east of the Palace of the Governors on the north side of Santa Fe Plaza. The house was part of a colonial property with a distinguished lineage: Diego Arias de Quiros received the land east of the palace for meritorious service to Governor Diego de Vargas during the Spanish reconquest of New Mexico in 1693. The property was sold after his death in the mid-eighteenth century. On the 1766 map of Santa Fe, the house appears to be a single structure at the center of a square compound, with adjacent fields east of it. The house was evidently expanded and passed down over several generations to Carmel's maternal grandmother, Ana Gertrudis Ortiz, and then to her daughter (Carmel's mother), María Guadalupe Baca. María Guadalupe left the house to Carmel and her two siblings. It was common for colonial homes to be deeded in their component parts—the roof to one child, the windows to another, and the doors to another still—so the property they inherited was valuable only in its entirety, though owned by several individuals. Carmel inherited the westernmost end of the colonial building and held title to it even after she left New Mexico.[11]

In the decades preceding Carmel's birth, a long-lasting peace was negotiated with Comanche bands that had been targeting New Mexican towns. The 1786 treaty was the result of a series of discussions between the governor of New Mexico, Juan Bautista de Anza, and several Comanche leaders that took place at the Palace of the Governors and at Pecos Pueblo, southeast of Santa Fe. The treaty's terms were dependent on annuities granted to several bands of Comanches in exchange for the safety and security of the Spanish settlements along the eastern border of the territory. It was a fragile peace, as incursions and hostilities continued between New Mexicans and neighboring Apache, Navajo, Comanche, and Ute bands.

Smallpox had decimated New Mexican Native and Hispanic communities in 1790–91. So in the last decade of the eighteenth century, even as its empire was waning, Spain undertook an impressive public health initiative to inoculate the population. Live smallpox vaccines were transported from Mexico City up the Camino Real to New Mexico, carried in the scars on the arms of several inoculated Indian children. By 1808, New Mexicans had been inoculated against smallpox, curtailing the threat of a widespread pandemic.[12] The combination of the Comanche treaty and the smallpox vaccination effort contributed to a decade of relative peace in New Mexico, although Spanish support for its distant colonies was stretched thin.

Carmel was born during this period into a family with resources and important connections among the elite of the small colony. A short block northeast of the family home was the church where she was baptized as a two-day-old infant on November 22, 1811. Her parents were identified in Santa Fe church records as María Guadalupe Baca and José Pablo Benavides. The Baca family was prominent, as its ancestors had led the settlement of New Mexico during the Spanish colonial period.

The year after Carmel was born, her maternal uncle by marriage, prominent merchant Pedro Bautista Pino, presented a detailed report on conditions in New Mexico to the court in Cadiz, Spain. Although Pino was part of a wealthy extended family, he was not selected for this distinction based on merit. He was the winner of a literal drawing of straws to determine who would go to Spain. Winning the draw also meant that he had to pay all his own expenses—no small sum in the nineteenth century. He had served as one of two *alcaldes* (mayors) of Santa Fe in 1803, but he was not appointed to successive terms or even to a second term in office. The two mayors served different districts in the city and were charged with hearing administrative as well as legal proceedings.[13] There are several historical *dichos* (folk sayings) about Pino's accomplishments. One says he merely went to Spain and came back; the other says he went and came back with a fancy coach. Either way, his visit to Spain supplied none of New Mexico's many needs.

Nevertheless, Pino's report on the economy of New Mexico remains an important source of information about the late Spanish colonial period just before the opening of the Santa Fe trade. He noted the lack of sufficient markets, the absence of schools, and the need for more support for the church. He described the military's chronic shortages of arms and soldiers and the depredations of nomadic tribes. His list of needs was compelling, but he would return largely empty-handed because Spain was stretched beyond its capacity. It was bold of him to even present the Spanish government with a list stated in such stark terms rather than the formal, ornate language of the Spanish court. He speculated that the United States could easily conquer this weak outpost.[14] Within a decade, the Americans would indeed take over the markets and, in less than forty years, the governance of New Mexico. Little did Pino know that even his niece, who was an infant at the time, would be won over by a Frenchman whose own community had only recently become part of the United States following the Louisiana Purchase.

In St. Louis, a near contemporaneous letter details an attempt by Frenchmen from Mississippi and Missouri River towns to extend their hunting and trading range into the Arkansas River Valley on lands that were part of the Louisiana Purchase. Spain contested this attempt, as evidenced by the exchanges between St. Louisan Jules DeMun and the governor of New Mexico. DeMun's journal of his unauthorized expedition to the area in 1815 and an

1817 letter seeking redress for items confiscated in New Mexico document the issue of who owned the Arkansas River territory. They raise questions about whether DeMun was an informal emissary of New Mexico's governor who was truly seeking to establish trade, or whether he was simply hoping to obtain a more favorable outcome in the quest for the return of his merchandise.[15] DeMun, Auguste P. Chouteau, and twenty-four of their men were held in the "dungeons" of Santa Fe for forty-eight days in the spring and summer of 1817 for trapping on streams in the disputed territory. When they returned to St. Louis in the fall, DeMun wrote to Missouri governor William Clark seeking remuneration for his losses, which, he claimed, had taken him and his men to the "brink of ruin." His letter of November 25, 1817, pleaded with Governor Clark to grant them permission to proceed to the headwaters of the Arkansas and Platte Rivers, which New Mexico authorities had denied them. Clearly, DeMun knew that the area was claimed by both the United States and Spain, and he was seeking expeditious access to that area and a license from authorities in either country to trade and trap on those waters.[16] DeMun's letter does more than beseech the governor for compensation for the furs, horses, and other goods the Spanish governor had confiscated. His letter assesses the area's resources and the atmosphere in Santa Fe for establishing diplomatic ties with Missouri.

DeMun explained that he had been in the Arkansas River area trading for furs when he learned that several Missouri men had risked wintering in New Mexico in 1816–17. He found the men at Taos, where they had been welcomed, so he journeyed to Santa Fe to meet the newest governor and notify him that he and other Missouri men were in the territory. He characterized "Don Alberto"—Governor Alberto Maynez—as "an old gentleman of good information, who possesses, in a great degree, the good manners and politeness peculiar to his nation."[17] DeMun petitioned the governor to allow the men to trap beavers, which were abundant on the streams between Taos and Santa Fe. Although the governor lacked the authority to allow this, he offered to write to the authorities in Mexico on DeMun's behalf. DeMun seemed to assume that this was an invitation to return to Santa Fe to check on the status of his request. In DeMun's letter to Clark, he went further and presented the idea that Maynez was amenable to trade with Missouri. He likely overstated Maynez's position when he reported: "I must not omit to say that the Governor did not seem a moment to doubt that we had a right to frequent the east side of the mountains, and there to trade or to catch beaver if we could."[18]

The Missouri party that had spent the winter of 1816–17 on the Arkansas River reported their unpleasant interactions with the New Mexican governor to Clark. But DeMun assumed that because the New Mexican authorities knew the Missourians were in the area awaiting permission from a higher authority in Mexico, they could spend the winter trapping, trading, and caching furs for their eventual return to St. Louis. In early March DeMun went to Taos, hoping to hear that the permits had been granted. Instead, New Mexican troops arrested DeMun and the rest of his party and seized their caches of fur and other goods. The party reached Santa Fe on June 1, 1817, and was greeted by an enraged governor, who stated, according to DeMun, that if he had pursued the Missourians himself, he would have killed them. DeMun further enraged the governor (whom he calls the president) by asserting that the Arkansas River was not Spanish domain and that the Louisiana Purchase gave them the right to harvest from those lands:

> The president denied that our Government had a right to grant such a license, and entered into such a rage that it prevented his speaking, contenting himself with striking his fist several times on the table, saying, gentlemen, we must have this man shot. At such conduct of the president I did not think much of my life, for all the other members were terrified in his presence, and unwilling to resist him; on the contrary, do anything to please him.[19]

There were exaggerated claims on both sides as the governor accused the party of building a fort on Spanish lands and amassing thousands of troops for an assault on New Mexico. The final insult to the DeMun-Chouteau party was that they were assembled in front of witnesses, including Pedro Bautista Pino, and forced to kneel and kiss the decree that banished them from New Mexico with only their "worst" horse and none of their stored furs. DeMun's appeal to Governor Clark seemed to signal a desire not only to recover his losses but also to paint a picture of the ready markets in the far reaches of the territory that Clark himself had explored. Authorized trade between Missouri's frontier settlements and those in Mexico was imminent.

Mexico's independence from Spain emerged slowly from the activism of Father Miguel Hidalgo. General Agustín de Iturbide was recognized as the president of Mexico in September 1821, although news of its impending independence had been circulating for several months. New Mexico's last governor appointed by Spanish authorities, Facundo Melgares, dutifully reported to his superiors in Mexico that the transfer of power was observed with decorum: "The pen cannot express the growing pleasure and great patriotism aroused in Santa Fe on this occasion, for both the ears of the tender young as well as those of doddering ancients devoted themselves fully to listening to the discourses that praised our Liberator [Iturbide] and the campaign. . . .

Fig. 2.3. James Abert, *Ciudad de Santa Fe*, 1846, lithograph. (Pictures of American Cities photo #22, 111-SC-89562, National Archives, Washington, DC)

The rejoicing grew steadily, as more persons read sonnets, tercets and other poetic works."[20]

In contrast, Santa Fe Trail trader Thomas James described a raucous scene in Santa Fe Plaza as independence was celebrated on January 6, 1822 (figure 2.3). James took credit for instructing Melgares to raise the Mexican flag and did the honors himself, at the behest of the governor:

> As the flag went up, the cannon fired and men and women from all quarters of the city came running, some half-dressed, to the public square, which soon filled with the population of the city. The people of the surrounding country also came in, and for five days the square was covered with Spaniards and Indians from every part of the province. During this whole time the city exhibited a scene of universal carousing and revelry. All classes abandoned themselves to the most reckless dissipation and profligacy. . . . Men, women and children crowded every part of the city, and the carousal was kept up equally night and day. . . . Tables for gambling surrounded the square and continually occupied the attention of crowds. Dice and faro banks were all the time in constant play.[21]

Carmel had just turned ten years old when this revelry—or decorous ceremony—unfolded. Surely she witnessed the moment. The next year, Antoine Robidoux and his brothers came to New Mexico to trap and trade, acting on the potential glimpsed by DeMun and Chouteau. Unlike previous

Missourians, they came with a license to trade recognized by both Mexican and US authorities and a permit allowing them to cross New Mexico to trade with several Indian tribes as well. A new day had dawned, joining the two nations in trade and opening new opportunities that would have historical, if unintended, consequences for Native peoples in the region and for Mexico and the United States as well. Once the Robidoux brothers entered the Santa Fe trade, they began to extend their trapping and trading farther west into the Great Basin. They were not the first trappers to go there, but historian Ned Blackhawk considers the trading posts established by Antoine Robidoux to be among the most successful.[22]

The Robidoux brothers' initial success in the Great Basin coincided with a worsening relationship between the New Mexican government and the Utes. Ute bands had made peace with the Spanish government when they served as allies during its long fight to attain a lasting peace with the Comanches in 1786. The Spanish-Ute relationship was reinforced by regular trade exchanges and by the Utes' safe passage to Santa Fe. That alliance was tested after Mexican independence failed to deliver on the terms of the earlier Spanish peace accords. Thomas James recorded an eloquent and forthright speech delivered in Spanish at the Palace of the Governors by Ute chief Lechat. Lechat and fifty members of the tribe came to Santa Fe expressly to invite the Missourians to come to the Great Basin and trade with the Utes. In his direct and unflinching speech, Lechat described the Ute country in terms that must have been irresistible to the newly arrived fur trappers and traders but belittling and embarrassing to their New Mexican hosts:

> You are American, we are told, and you have come from your country afar off to trade with the Spaniards. We want your trade. Come to our country with your goods. Come and trade with the Utahs. We have horses, mules and sheep, more than we want. We heard you wanted beaver skins. The beavers in our country are eating up our corn, all our rivers are full of them. Their dams back up the water in the rivers all along their courses from the mountains to the big water. Come over among us and you shall have as many beaver skins [as] you want . . . (then pointing to the Spaniards, in the most contemptuous manner and with a scornful look) he said, What can you get from these? They have nothing but a few poor horses and mules, a little *puncha* [tobacco] and a little *tola* [cornmeal porridge] not fit for anybody to use. They are poor . . . too poor for you to trade with.[23]

Benefits of a Cross-Cultural Marriage

Antoine Robidoux was the third of six sons and two daughters born to Joseph Robidoux and his wife, Catherine Rolet. Born on September 22, 1794, Antoine was raised in the Florissant area of north St. Louis, where Creole culture grew from Spanish and French roots. Joseph Robidoux and his six sons—Joseph, Francois, Antoine, Isadore, Louis, and Michel—were prominent fur traders in the eighteenth and nineteenth centuries. Their names were intertwined with those of other Frenchmen who trapped and traded with Native peoples across a wide swath of the intermountain West, from St. Louis northwest to the Black Hills of the Dakotas and then west to the Rocky Mountains and into the Great Basin.

The push out of Missouri and upper Louisiana was in many cases a response to the stresses of a growing frontier and the near economic collapse that came with the bank failures of 1819. The pull of new markets in the Southwest was surely on the minds of merchants and profiteers. Antoine was among the early French fur traders to settle in Taos and then Santa Fe. He established a base for his extended family's trapping and trading businesses with Native peoples over a large part of the American West.

Some of the Robidoux brothers may have been involved in New Mexico as early as 1822 or 1823, according to their obituaries and the recollections of others involved in the fur trade. Antoine was spending so little time in Missouri that the *St. Louis Enquirer* published a notice on April 27, 1822, concerning his accumulating mail, which no doubt included several notices of trespass suits, debt calls, and breach of promise suits filed by creditors.[24] Antoine received a permit and a pass from Mexican authorities in Santa Fe to cross New Mexico to Indian country on February 19, 1824.[25] For the next two years, he and brothers Michel and Isadore and occasionally Louis traded with the Great Basin tribes for hides and furs that they sold in Missouri.

By 1826, the Robidoux brothers were well established in Taos and Santa Fe. Louis had already taken Guadalupe Garcia as his common-law wife, opening up other family networks. The brothers' liaisons with Carmel and Guadalupe, daughters of prestigious families, gave them enormous advantages in business and local politics.[26] On July 16, 1829, Antoine and Louis appeared before the local Mexican administrator seeking naturalization as Mexican citizens, claiming they were residents of Santa Fe and had been married there.[27] There were many advantages to naturalization, including lower taxes on goods imported from the United States for sale in New Mexico and less chance of having their furs confiscated in the shifting political climate of New Mexico.[28] That did not protect Antoine from other losses, however, and in 1829 he filed suit against three of his neighbors, accusing them of robbing his home. They were found guilty and ordered to return the goods to Robidoux.[29]

The attraction between young Frenchmen and New Mexican women was probably not based solely on materialistic calculations. In an analysis of marriages between *nuevomexicanas* (New Mexican women) and immigrant men between 1850 and 1900, Amanda Taylor-Montoya found a low incidence of such unions; New Mexican women largely preserved their endogamous marriage practices.[30] Here again, the Frenchmen who arrived in the early years of the Santa Fe trade had a cultural advantage as potential marriage partners. The Missouri French and French American traders who entered New Mexico in the early 1820s would have encountered women whose traditions and legal status did not differ markedly from those of women in the French settlements of the Mississippi and Missouri River communities. New Mexican women under Spanish and Mexican rule retained title to their personal and real property and to their wages. They retained their maiden names after marriage, adding the husband's name but often continuing to use the name of their family of origin. As more Euro-Americans entered the trade, they encountered women of French and Spanish heritage with many more property and individual rights than American women had.[31] New Mexican and French households were often multicultural and multiracial. Many of the French and French American traders were themselves members of culturally and racially mixed families. In the Southwest, with its mixture of Spanish, multiracial Mexican, and Native American populations, many American writers found these mixtures exotic, but for others, it led to prejudice against and disdain for New Mexican women.

Matt Field, a journalist for the *New Orleans Picayune*, described Louis Robidoux's home in Santa Fe, which he visited in 1839. Field was impressed by the simple, clean furnishings, the style of the furniture, and the elegant woven blankets. He did not express the same enthusiasm for the wall decorations of "rude images of saints" and broken bits of mirrors or bright pictures. He noted that these "ostentatious" displays were removed when a "resident American prevails over the taste of his Spanish wife."[32]

Through his marriage to Carmel, Antoine had ties to elite families with prominent, even illustrious, ancestors dating back to the Spanish colonial settlers. In New Mexico, these deep roots and webs of kinship gave Antoine entree into trade networks that extended to Mexico and settlements in California as well. His status as a naturalized Mexican citizen also offered him relief from tariffs and opportunities to trap on streams in the Mexican territory that were not open to noncitizens. Having been raised in the French-Spanish

Creole culture of the Missouri River frontier, the couple might have shared many traditions as well as the Catholic faith.

For Carmel, this association gave her an elite position in the region's changing economy and social structure as French traders took on more important social and governmental roles in New Mexico. This allowed Carmel to travel the Santa Fe Trail bound for Missouri before doing so was common among New Mexican women. There, at the eastern end of the trail, she found herself in a robust family that claimed distinction, as well as notoriety, on this multicultural frontier. She joined the extended Robidoux family of French, Native American, and racially mixed women who were the brothers' wives or companions.[33]

Between Here and There

Tracing the specific wagon trains and expeditions shared by Antoine and Carmel proved daunting, in part because women were not named in many narratives, but also because the brothers were often referred to only by their last name, making it difficult to determine who was where and at what time. Santa Fe historian Mary Jean Cook concludes that Carmel made six crossings of the Santa Fe Trail between the time she took up with Antoine in 1828 and his death in 1860. This may be overestimating the number of times Carmel accompanied Antoine and underestimating Antoine's crossings. Even with the wealth of documents and passing references to Antoine in the literature of the trail and the fur trade, tracing his journeys on the trail is problematic. Historian David Weber concludes, "the comings and goings of Robidoux parties during the 1820s and 1830s are perplexing, and perhaps they always will be."[34]

Antoine was active in local affairs and was elected head of the town council, or *ayuntamiento*, of Santa Fe in 1830. He would remain in New Mexico through the turmoil of the growing dissatisfaction with Mexican rule, which led to a local uprising in 1837. However, he evidently did not give up trading and trapping expeditions during this time. He inscribed his name and a short but inscrutable message in French on the cliffs of Westwater Canyon along the Green River in eastern Utah on November 13, 1837. Historians have longed tried to determine where he was bound on that particular journey.[35]

In the early 1840s Carmel and Antoine were sometimes together in Santa Fe; at other times, he was in Missouri or elsewhere while she remained in Santa Fe. They both witnessed the marriage of a household servant in Santa Fe in September 1840. Antoine was back in Missouri by late fall, but Carmel might not have been with him. She charged a purchase to an account with a mercantile firm in Santa Fe in July 1841, and she was listed in Santa Fe in the 1841 census.[36] At the end of the year, on December 13, Antoine presented a twelve-year-old Ute girl for baptism at the church in Santa Fe. She was given the name María Carmel, and Carmel served as godmother. This raises many intriguing questions about how Antoine acquired the child. Was she an enslaved servant who was baptized and brought into their household as a member of the family, as was the custom in New Mexico? Was she actually Ute, or was she one of the children taken by the Utes from other tribes and traded to New Mexicans? Was she recently acquired while Antoine was trading in Ute country earlier that year, or did he have a longer association with her family of origin?

The Great Basin trade centers were strained in the early 1840s by declining beaver prices and overhunting. Utes faced increasing pressure from emigrants, and by 1844, their relations with New Mexico turned violent. Antoine's fortunes changed rapidly between 1841 and 1843 because of livestock losses and the collapse of the fur trade in the Great Basin. In December 1841 he and partner Manuel Alvarez lost hundreds of head of livestock and two men on the trail along Cottonwood Creek near Council Groves, Kansas. Some sources claim that Carmel was with him during this dramatic event, but she is not mentioned in any reports of the incident. Antoine continued to engage in the fur trade and the trade in Native slaves, among other ventures. He became a promoter of California settlement, writing glowing tracts that encouraged Missourians to journey west. His brother Louis left New Mexico and took up a claim in California, where he found the land and climate more favorable. Louis wrote to a business associate in Santa Fe, "The land in California is not ungrateful like the land of New Mexico." Likely he was speaking both literally and figuratively. The brothers were having problems in Santa Fe; Louis had been jailed for public drunkenness, and Antoine continued to experience business setbacks.[37] Antoine left New Mexico in 1844, following a Ute raid on the Palace of the Governors that included a frightening assault on the governor's office. The raid was caused in part by the end of the profitable fur trade and the Utes' dissatisfaction with the annuities provided by the Mexican government. Robidoux, as a trader with long ties to the Ute fur trade in southern Colorado and the Great Basin, was sure to be implicated in equipping the Utes with guns, though not specifically for arming this insurgency.[38] Carmel and Antoine likely departed together for St. Joseph, Missouri, where his brother Joseph had developed a prosperous business supplying westbound travelers.

Antoine would not remain in Missouri for long. He soon began to cross the country in search of the next opportunity. In June 1846, as the drumbeat of Manifest Destiny and war gathered on the western front of Missouri, Colonel Stephen Watts Kearny, leading the US Army of the West, tapped Antoine to be his interpreter and to render other services. There was no man more skilled for the job. Antoine, referred to as Anthony in Kearny's letter, was called to join the troops gathering at Fort Leavenworth on June 12, 1846. Men serving with the Army of the West recalled Robidoux's exemplary service and knowledge of the road during their slow and often grueling march.

Antoine was called on to translate the oath of allegiance to the United States in plazas and from rooftops throughout New Mexico. Antoine's account of the taking of New Mexico was recorded in a letter he wrote that appeared in the *St. Joseph Gazette* on October 9, 1846. While he recounted the rumors that anticipated the New Mexican defense and Governor Manuel Armijo's craven defection, he said nothing about the reaction of family, friends, and former business associates to the conquest or to his own role in the American takeover.[39] Frustratingly, the record is silent on Carmel's reaction to the loss of the government that her extended family had served for centuries.

The descriptions of Antoine's skill as a guide, his bravery on the battlefield, and the miracle of his survival after being seriously wounded while serving with Kearny are as gripping as the details of his earlier life as a mountain man and trader.[40] Kearny took a small detachment from Santa Fe to continue west and claim California. That force included Kit Carson as scout, Antoine as interpreter, and a topographic engineering corps led by Lieutenant William Hemsley Emory. Antoine was gravely wounded at the Battle of San Pasqual on December 6–7, 1846. Kearny was also injured in the battle, as were many others. Lieutenant Emory's report of the battle between American and Mexican forces includes an expressive description of the how he attended to the injured Antoine. Emory initially believed Antoine's lance wound would prove fatal, but despite significant blood loss, Antoine was roused by the smell of coffee, and the story added to his legendary status. Emory's journal, which describes caring for the wounded and removing the dead from the battlefield, is a sobering narrative of the battle's aftermath. His account of Robidoux's grave condition and miraculous revival bears quoting:

> Don Antonio Robideaux [sic], a thin man of fifty-five years, slept next to me. The loss of blood from his wounds, added to the coldness of the night . . . made me think he would never see daylight, but I was mistaken. He woke me to ask did I not smell coffee, and expressed a belief that a cup of that beverage would save his life, and that nothing else would. Not knowing that there had been any coffee in camp for many days, I supposed a dream had carried him back to the cafes

of St. Louis and New Orleans, and it was with some surprise I found my cook heating a cup of coffee over a small fire of wild sage. One of the most agreeable little offices performed in my life, and I believe in the cook's, to whom the coffee belonged, was to pour this precious draught into the waning body of our friend Robideaux. His warmth returned, and with that the hopes of life.[41]

The Army of the West still had nearly thirty miles to march before it reached the coast at San Diego. The troops were attacked again, and some died of their wounds. Antoine, though rendered infirm, would live for many more years. He remained in California until his discharge at Monterey in the spring of 1847 and then endured a long sea passage. When he returned to Missouri, he began the process of applying for a military pension.[42] He supposedly remained in St. Joseph until 1855 and then visited New Mexico with his family. Antoine's case for infirmity pay dragged on, and on May 23, 1856, the US House of Representatives' Committee on Invalid Pensions recommended that he be compensated for his work as a Spanish-language interpreter and for the wounds sustained at the Battle of San Pasqual at the rate of $16.66 per month, beginning on December 1, 1855, and continuing until his death. The bill was passed by the Senate on August 22, 1856, and signed into law the next day by President Franklin Pierce.[43]

Carmel's travels during this period are not as well documented. However, on August 18, 1850, she was living in the home of Isadore and "Maltine" Barada in Washington Township, which was part of Joseph City in Buchanan County, Missouri. Interestingly, Carmel is listed simply as "A. Robidoux," a thirty-eight-year-old female born in Mexico. "Maltine" is likely Martine (née Martina Anaya), a cousin Carmel and Antoine had adopted in Santa Fe after the death of her parents. Also in the household were several other Barada children and young adults who listed their place of birth as Mexico.[44] Ten years later, on August 9, 1860, the census shows Carmel living in the Third Ward of the City of St. Joseph. Once again she is identified as A. Robidoux, age forty-eight, born in New Mexico. That household was much smaller, consisting of only a nine-year-old girl, A. Barady (Amanda Barada, the daughter of Martine and Isadore), born in Missouri, and M. Bither, a nineteen-year-old woman from Germany. According to their family history, Martine Barada died of cholera when Amanda was only one month old, leaving Carmel with another orphaned child to raise. Antoine is not listed in her household or in any other Robidoux household in St. Joseph, although according to his obituary in the *St. Joseph Gazette*, that is where he passed away on August 29, 1860. The obituary notes that Carmel was with him in the last weeks of life and refers to his importance in the United States:

He was possessed of a sprightly intellect and a spirit of adventure.

Mr. Robidoux was a very remarkable man. Tall, slender, athletic, and agile, he possessed the most graceful and pleasing manners, and an intellect of superior order. In every company he was affable, and highly pleasing. His conversation was always interesting and instructive, and he possessed many of those qualities which, if he remained in the States, would have raised him to positions of distinction.

[During his last two weeks] he was taken with violent hemorrhage of the lungs, which completely prostrated him, and from the effects of which he never recovered. He was attended to by the best medical skills, and his wife and many friends were with him to the hour of his dissolution. He will be long remembered as a courteous, cultivated, agreeable gentleman, whose life was one of great activity and public usefulness, and whose death will long be lamented.

Carmel was the executor of Antoine's estate. After his death, Carmel made her own crossing from Missouri to Santa Fe, accompanied by her adopted granddaughter Amanda Barada. While crossing Kansas, their wagon train was reportedly attacked by Comanches. Because I could not find the specific dates of their crossing, it was difficult to corroborate this event. Presumably, Carmel and Amanda returned to the Baca family compound on Granary Street.

Santa Fe had changed a great deal since Carmel migrated to Missouri in the mid-1840s. She had been born in the waning years of Spanish colonial rule to a family that could trace their New Mexico roots back for centuries. Her family retained its prominence during the Mexican period, and through her association with Antoine Robidoux, she linked the Baca and Benavides family to a French Creole family that extended from Canada to Mexico, from St. Louis to California, through their vast trade network and multicultural family ties. By the time she returned to Santa Fe, New Mexico was a territory of the United States, and the nation was struggling to remain united. How did Carmel feel when she saw the Confederate flag briefly raised over the Palace of the Governors in the late winter of 1862, when Texas troops once again tried to extend their reach across the Rio Grande? Carmel and Amanda stayed in Santa Fe, where fifteen-year-old Amanda married a German immigrant, Christian Frederick Stollsteimer. He was a shopkeeper who expanded his business interests north to Colorado and traded with the Utes living in the area of their agency at Ignacio, Colorado. The fate of Carmel's Ute goddaughter baptized in Santa Fe in 1841, who would have been in her late thirties or early forties by this time, is not known. When the July 16, 1870, census of Conejos in the Colorado Territory was prepared, Carmel was living with the

Stollsteimers and their two young children, who had been born in Colorado, and a sixteen-year-old woman from New Mexico. On this census, Carmel listed her name as Carmel Robidoux, age fifty-nine, born in New Mexico. In 1879 Carmel sold her property in Santa Fe to former New Mexico governor L. Bradford Prince. The house was described as having seven rooms containing sixty-one vigas. Prince enlarged and modified the building and then resold the property. In 1942 it was owned by Martha Field and her children. During World War II the property housed the recruitment office of the secret Manhattan Project.[45]

Carmel lived the remainder of her life in Conejos County as a pioneer. She was often identified only as the widow of Antoine and was never interviewed about her extraordinary life and times. Her story was preserved in a family history written by her great-grandson Robert S. Stollsteimer and shared with me.[46] She died on January 29, 1888, and was buried in Greenmount Cemetery in Durango, Colorado, far from Antoine. But even in life, they were often at opposite ends of the trail.

Many Crossings in Life

Carmel Benavides Robidoux's life story encompasses numerous events taking place in New Mexico and Missouri in the nineteenth century, many of which were occasioned by the opening of the Santa Fe Trail. Changes in the Spanish and French colonies, the emergence of Mexico as an independent republic, and the US annexation of the Southwest led to shifting political boundaries, economic opportunities, and cultural identities. Antoine's and Carmel's lives were shaped by these events and opportunities. Robidoux and his family are well represented in French, Spanish, Mexican, and American archives for their roles in the fur trade, local governments, and the momentous events that shaped the American West. The details of Carmel's life are harder to illuminate. We are left with just a shadow of her life story based on the remembrances or projections of others.

Despite everything we cannot ascertain about her thoughts and choices, we know that Carmel bridged many cultures. She was born in colonial New Spain, witnessed the birth of the Mexican republic, and experienced the loss of her Mexican citizenship with the forced US annexation of New Mexico. She lived among many cultures, first as a citizen of New Mexico, with its many cultural contributors—Spanish, Mexican, Pueblo, Navajo, Apache, and Ute—and then in Missouri, with its mix of Natives and Europeans of many nations. If Antoine's will can be considered a final statement about their relationship, he obviously loved her and entrusted her with his possessions. We do not know whether they were married in a civil ceremony or if theirs was a common-law union, but it made no apparent difference in their long-term relationship. Why didn't they marry in a church, given that both were raised in the Catholic faith? Or was there simply no record of their marriage in the extant records of the Archdiocese of Santa Fe? What motivated Antoine to change his citizenship and alliances throughout his life? Was he simply an opportunist, or was he morally and politically flexible, realigning with the dominant culture wherever he lived? How he is remembered may depend on which era of his life one focuses on. Robert Willoughby, biographer of the brothers Robidoux, concludes that they were Americans by accident who exploited Native women. He judges their loose morals and scheming business practices, their drinking and gambling, but he also absolves them, attributing these characteristics to the adventures of legendary frontiersmen. That absolution does not excuse the violence and exploitation that accompanied westward expansion. It places them in the canon of folklore and forgives the very behaviors that must be confronted in telling the history of the West. How should we remember Carmel? Her story has been overshadowed by the exploits of the Robidoux brothers, but she lived an independent life in New Mexico, Missouri, and Colorado. She traveled the Santa Fe Trail between New Mexico and Missouri, sometimes with Antoine, but they did not return to Santa Fe together after the American conquest of Mexico. When she did return to Santa Fe after his death, she did not stay for long in her ancestral family home. Perhaps she preferred the company of her granddaughter's family in southern Colorado. Or perhaps she did not remain because she was no longer comfortable among her extended family in Santa Fe or in the changing political and social environment that emerged in New Mexico prior to the Civil War. It was a world that Robidoux had helped deliver into the hands of the American military.

3

SCHOOLGIRLS ON THE TRAIL
Adaline, Marian, and Francisca

By the mid-nineteenth century, the Santa Fe Trail was central to the American acculturation, education, and indoctrination of children of elite New Mexican families. In response to the growing US influence in the Southwest, some New Mexicans sent their sons and daughters to Missouri for schooling. It was a time of shifting political alliances, sectional turmoil, and increased US aggression toward Mexico. The push for an "American" education lasted until just before the Civil War. This chapter explores the life experiences of three women who traveled the Santa Fe Trail as young children after losing a parent. Adaline Carson and Francisca López were brought to Missouri by their fathers, hoping to find better care and educational opportunities for their daughters. Marian Sloan and her brother William made several crossings during their childhood as their single mother, Eliza, sought a better life in the West.

Each girl came from a distinct cultural background and had access to different resources. Adaline Carson, daughter of the legendary frontier explorer Kit Carson, was brought to her father's family home in Missouri after the death of her Northern Arapaho mother, Waa-nibe, in 1842. Her life illustrates the difficulties experienced by a child of mixed ancestry and with a notably peripatetic father. Francisca "Fanny" López and her three brothers were brought to St. Louis in 1850, two years after the death of their mother. Their father, a prosperous merchant with business interests along the trail and extending into Mexico and California, wanted his children to be educated with other elite New Mexican and Missouri families. Marian Sloan made her first crossing of the Santa Fe Trail with her mother and older brother in 1852. Marian and William were educated at both ends of the Santa Fe Trail and on the trail itself as they made numerous crossings. Although happiness was elusive for their restless mother, the siblings treasured the memories of their adventures on the trail.

Adaline's life was narrated largely through the same romantic trope of the American West that influenced stories of her father. Much of her history was related by authors whose views of Kit Carson changed with the prevailing interpretations of the West. Over the generations, his domestic life has been scrutinized or fantasized by fiction writers, scriptwriters, genealogists, and historians. In contrast, Fanny's life was captured in business records, wills, school reports, and an occasional letter in her own hand as she adjusted to her new life in St. Louis. Much of that documentation was written by her father or by the series of men hired by him or appointed by the courts as trustees of the López estate. Marian's memories of her crossings were recorded later in life as she looked back on what she recalled as grand adventures. Each girl moved from New Mexico to Missouri, or from Missouri to New Mexico, during volatile times, sent on the journey by her surviving parent, who had to assess the opportunities available. Together, their stories illustrate some of the dynamic changes in communities and families in the tendentious and fraught cultural fabric of the mid-nineteenth century. The stories of Adaline, Marian, and Francisca are parallel experiences that illustrate, in various ways, the clashes wrought by US expansionism, polarized political views, and the vicissitudes of the times.

Educating Children in a New Country

Several wealthy and politically connected families, many of them associated with the Santa Fe and Chihuahua trade, began to send their children to Mexico or St. Louis for formal education in the 1830s and 1840s. The absence of public education in New Mexico had long been an issue, and New Mexicans had repeatedly pleaded with previous Spanish and Mexican authorities to fund education. Pedro Baptista Pino's 1812 report to the Spanish court on conditions in New Mexico decried the lack of funds for public services. In particular, he cited the near absence of teachers:

> The province does not count, nor has it ever counted upon to date, the kinds of public facilities enjoyed by other Spanish provinces. So backward are things in that regard that some people cannot even put a name to what they lack. The state of primary education, for example, is reduced to this: only those who can contribute to the hiring of a schoolmaster are able to have their children taught. In the

capital itself [Santa Fe], it has not been possible to fund a teacher for the general instruction of the community.[1]

Pino continued to detail the "distress" caused by the lack of higher education—no doctors, no surgeons, no pharmacists, and not a single literary scholar. There were no craft guilds and no apprentices, and only recently had New Mexico received better-quality looms for the local production of wool and cotton blankets.

Albino Pérez, appointed governor of New Mexico in 1835 by Mexican dictator Antonio López de Santa Anna, was despised almost from the moment of his arrival. In an early assessment of the deficiencies in the province, Pérez directed his harshest criticism to the lack of education and prescribed the establishment of a public school system financed by students' parents. He then went further, recommending that parents be fined if their children between the ages of five and twelve did not attend school.[2] Rebellion against the many taxes he sought to impose not only to establish schools but also to finance his government led to open revolt throughout northern New Mexico. Pérez was assassinated and mutilated by a mob in early August 1837.

Bishop Jean-Baptiste Lamy, the first administrator of the new Catholic diocese in the recently annexed US territory, brought the concept of formal, religion-based education to New Mexico when he arrived in 1851. Four members of the Sisters of Loretto, who traveled the Santa Fe Trail from the mother house in Kentucky, opened their first school in Santa Fe in November 1852.[3] The Christian Brothers began their Colegio de San Miguel in 1859. Lamy continued to argue against a system of public education separate from the Catholic Church, and it was not until 1891 that the New Mexico legislature enacted a public school system.[4]

The lag in establishing formal schools in New Mexico meant that families of means sent their children to Mexico or St. Louis for schooling. In St. Louis, most boys attended St. Louis University, but a few families sent their sons to Christian Brothers Academy. Some New Mexican families sent their daughters to Visitation Academy or Sacred Heart Academy in St. Louis. Doyle Daves analyzed the records from these schools and found that fifteen boys and three girls were sent to St. Louis from New Mexico in the 1840s, twenty-two boys in the 1850s, and forty-eight boys in the 1860s; at the height of this practice in the 1870s, thirty-two boys and twenty-two girls were sent to St. Louis for schooling.[5] These records do not always list the ages of the students or how long they remained at the school. It appears that boys were sent to St. Louis between the ages of eight and sixteen, although a few older teens went as well. The girls were slightly older—the majority between eleven and sixteen—although a few younger girls were sent to live at convent schools in St. Louis after the deaths of their mothers.

Daves's analysis shows that the children of elite families benefited from a St. Louis education. During the sixty years that New Mexico was a US territory, eight men who served as delegates to Congress had attended St. Louis University. Members of the Chaves, Otero, Luna, Romero, and Perea families—all active in the Santa Fe trade—were also politically active. All these families sent sons to St. Louis, where presumably they were introduced to the elites of that city and acquired the knowledge they would need after they returned to New Mexico. In addition to their own educational attainments, the advantages for women included marriage to men from other educated and prestigious families.

Fanny López's family and guardians had the means to ensure that she received a formal education at a residential convent school. Adaline Carson and Marian Sloan were not from elite families, so the schooling they received was quite different. Marian and Fanny penned accounts of their schooling in a memoir and letters, respectively. Adaline left no writings about her experiences, but that does not mean her life went unrecorded or escaped historical interpretation and fictionalization. Her story has been incorporated into many treatments of Kit Carson's life and legend.

Adaline "Prairie Flower" Carson

Kit Carson has been the subject of many biographies that provide conflicting accounts of his life, his feats of courage, and even his purported thoughts. His autobiography is frustratingly vague, in part because he was not literate and was characteristically a man of terse but polite communications, not prone to emotionally charged or voluble rhetoric. Harvey Lewis Carter tried to pin down the details of Carson's travels and life in the annotations he added to Carson's memoir.[6] Some historians and writers considered Carson a western American hero, the epitome of a nineteenth-century frontiersman. In more nuanced histories, especially those told from Native American perspectives, he is portrayed as a merciless killer of Native peoples and not heroic at all. Despite all these writings and revisions, very little personal information is available in Carson's own words, and even less is known about his wives and their children. Marc Simmons, a historian with an immense body of work on the Southwest and West, focuses on Carson's family life in his biography. Simmons weighs conflicting accounts of Carson's life in a number of other biographies and occasionally dismisses those authors' speculations and offers his own. This is especially noticeable when he imagines the conversations that might have occurred between Kit Carson and his second wife, Making Out Road, whose bad-tempered behavior has been noted by several authors. Susan Lee Johnson examines in great detail the historiography surrounding Carson, as well as the methods and motivations of two biographers who have written extensively about him: Bernice Fowler Blackwelder, an intriguing mix of singer, writer, and likely CIA agent, and Quantrille Day McClung, a librarian and genealogist. These two women were dedicated scholars and correspondents who shared a passion for sleuthing the details of Carson's family history and public life. Johnson analyzes how their research and writing were influenced by their own lives as well as the prevailing social and historiological influences of the times in which they wrote.[7] Johnson, Blackwelder, and McClung all faced the problem of interpreting Carson in the absence of his own thoughts and words and under the weight of so much speculation and outright hyperbole written about him. He had intimate relationships with Native American and Hispanic women and fathered ten children with two of them. His many biographers and even his own descendants disagree about the details of his life. The life story of Adaline, his first child, is also elusive and full of contradictions.

Adaline's mother was Carson's first wife, the Northern Arapaho woman known as Waa-nibe, or Singing Grass (figures 3.1 and 3.2).[8] Waa-nibe and Adaline are not well documented in official records, but they are among the anchors in writings about Carson's domestic life and character. Simmons approaches Carson as a man of his times, imperfect in retrospect but given to extraordinary feats in demonstrating his loyalty to US expansionist causes. Simmons narrates the most widely accepted beginning of the relationship between Waa-nibe and Carson at the Green River rendezvous in the summer of 1835. They had two daughters and lived at Bent's Fort on the trail and in Taos, but their time together was short. Waa-nibe died in 1839, perhaps following the birth of their second daughter. Carson then began a brief relationship with a Cheyenne woman named Making Out Road.[9]

McClung dismisses the question of whether Carson married Making Out Road because, from her point of view as a genealogist, it was irrelevant since they had no children together. According to some accounts of Carson's life, Making Out Road "divorced" him "by putting his belongings outside the tipi," demonstrating Native women's power in their households and relationships.[10] Carson's actions and travel are somewhat obscure until the spring of 1842, when he took Adaline to live with his family in Missouri. He left his younger daughter with his close friends, the Charles Bent

Fig. 3.1. Fictional rendering of Kit Carson's Arapaho wife Waa-nibe. Lithograph from E. G. Cattermole's *Famous Frontiersmen, Pioneers, and Scouts*, 1926. (GRA 00545, Missouri Historical Society, St. Louis)

family, in Taos. Only the roughest outlines of Adaline's life are known with any certainty, yet she lived to adulthood and was even with her father during some well-documented events. So how did she disappear from the historical record?

CARSON'S LIFE: REAL AND SURREAL

Born and raised on the frontier, Kit Carson moved with his family from Kentucky to the Missouri River town of Franklin in 1811. When his father died in 1818, his mother apprenticed him to a saddle maker. By 1826, he had jumped his bond and joined several of his brothers on the western trails. He worked in Taos, sometimes as a camp cook and a trapper. No doubt his saddlery skills were valued as well. In 1829 he embarked on his first overland trip to California and distinguished himself for his trail sense. Trappers and fur traders fed the mercantile systems of the Santa Fe Trail, partly through their relationships with Native Americans. Seasonal residence in Native encampments, partnerships with Native leaders, and true kinship ties through marriage or domestic relationships with Native women underpinned the fur trade. Many fur traders

Fig. 3.2. Imagined portrait of Kit Carson and Waa-nibe's daughter Adaline "Prairie Flower." Lithograph from E. G. Cattermole's *Famous Frontiersmen, Pioneers, and Scouts*, 1926. (GRA 00544, Missouri Historical Society, St. Louis)

were sponsored by French Canadian, French American, or American companies that shipped their products from St. Louis. Carson proved adept at living in and among different cultures.

In August 1835 Carson attended the Green River rendezvous in Wyoming. Rendezvous, temporary seasonal encampments of traders and Native peoples, took place in different areas close to rivers and hunting grounds in the Rocky Mountains, the Great Basin, and the upper Missouri River basin. The Green River rendezvous met at the confluence of the Green River and Horse Creek in Wyoming, near Fort Bonneville, for about five years from 1835 to 1840, when beavers were plentiful. But the rendezvous was more than a market; it was also a social gathering where alcohol fueled competitions and demonstrations of prowess.

Having just completed the annual beaver hunt, trappers, hunters, and several thousand Native peoples of different tribes were camped along the banks of the Green River when an incident occurred that gave rise to Kit Carson's reputation as a loyal patriot, someone who could handle volatile situations, and a man who could win the affection of desirable women.[11] Carson and a French trapper referred to as Shunar (likely Joseph Chouinard of St. Louis) were involved in a duel. They might have known each other previously, as they had both been employed by Pratt, Chouteau & Company in Missouri. Chouinard, known for his brawling and drinking, apparently went on an alcohol-fueled rampage, hurling insults at the Americans. Carson challenged him to a duel (whether because of the insults or perhaps because of the two men's competition for the affections of a Native woman), despite his much smaller frame and lighter fighting weight. Both men armed themselves, and in the event, a rifle ball grazed the left side of Carson's head. Whether Chouinard was killed or only wounded has been debated for generations among western writers.[12]

Whatever the instigating cause or the outcome of the duel, Carson emerged from the rendezvous with Waa-nibe as his wife. He was about twenty-five, and she was described in various accounts—whether factual or fictional—as young and beautiful, an "Arapaho belle." Her mother was from the Atsena or Gros Ventre tribe, and her father was Arapaho. In one of the few quotes in which Carson describes her, he noted, "I never came in from hunting that she did not have the warm water ready for my feet."[13]

By marrying Waa-nibe, Carson followed the path of other trappers and traders, establishing kinship ties that led to hunting privileges and trading advantages in tribal trade networks. But what did Waa-nibe get out of the marriage? Simmons perhaps overstates the benefits when he assumes that she was the recipient of the generosity and undivided attention accruing to a wife in a monogamous household. He also assumes that a wife would escape the drudgery of preparing hides and the cruelty and beatings of an "Indian" husband. But this may not have been the case if trappers expected their Native wives to continue to bear the burdens of labor. It also assumes that trappers and traders did not have multiple wives, as Native men did, to increase their profits from hide production.[14]

Native American women played an important role in the fur trade, not simply as the labor force for hide preparation but also as the producers and purveyors of other goods. In fact, many of the items traded at rendezvous were made and exchanged among women, including processed hides, dried meat, and beaded and quill-embellished clothing. In addition, as the sexual partners of French, Canadian, and American trappers, traders, and commercial hunters, Native women literally gave birth to new cultural communities. Communities on the western American frontier were often forged by these liaisons. Women gained status by participating in trade relationships, but these interracial and cross-cultural relationships could benefit both partners.[15] The children of these unions, those of *metís* or mixed descent, did not necessarily fit into either Native American or frontier communities. For many, prejudice followed them all their lives and complicated their legal rights on both sides of their heritage. The term *metís*, specifically as used in Canada and increasingly in the upper Midwest, refers to a mixed French and Indigenous heritage. It is similar to the term *mestizo*, used in the Southwest to refer to mixed Spanish and Indigenous ancestry. Eighteenth-century Missouri and Illinois settlements were culturally and racially mixed communities consisting of French-speaking Creoles, Canadians, *metís* individuals, French-born men involved with Native American women, enslaved Native and Black people, and free Blacks and Native peoples of many tribes.[16]

FINDING A HOME FOR ADALINE

What happened after the 1835 rendezvous is unclear. Did Waa-nibe leave the rendezvous with Carson in September 1835? Did she spend the fall of 1835 with him as he hunted and trapped in Montana's Yellowstone and Big Horn River regions? Was she living with him at a trading post established near Fort Hall on the Big Snake River during the winter of 1835–36? They were apparently at Fort Hall in the spring and early summer of 1837, and they might have stayed there for several reasons: the hunting season had gone poorly, smallpox was spreading across the country, and a financial depression had seized the markets. Simmons calculates that Adaline was born sometime during the spring or summer of 1837. She may have been born or spent her early life at the Arapaho encampment at Green River, where Waa-nibe could have been attended by her female relatives and friends. There are more questions than documented answers about the Carson family's life at this time. Surely, though, baby Adaline was named in honor of Kit's niece and childhood playmate, the daughter of his elder brother William.[17] What Waa-nibe called her infant daughter was not recorded, but some authors claim she was called Prairie Flower, though it is unknown whether this is speculation or the translation of an Arapaho name.[18]

Carson moved around a fair amount in the next two years—to southwestern Colorado and then to Wyoming for the winter hunt in 1838–39. His and

Waa-nibe's second daughter was born in 1839, but her name and the circumstances of her birth have been lost to history. Waa-nibe died around the same time, and Simmons suggests that she perished from puerperal fever, a common cause of death after childbirth at the time.[19]

Carson returned to the Green River rendezvous in 1840 and then headed to the Uintah region and Fort Robidoux in the Great Basin. He was surely acquainted with several of the Robidoux brothers who lived in Franklin, Missouri, and in Taos. At the end of another disappointing beaver harvest, Carson and other mountain men headed to Bent's Fort, located north of the Arkansas River in Colorado. There he met Making Out Road, a Cheyenne woman remembered in western lore, if not in fact, as beautiful and strong-willed. Carson evidently left his daughters with her when his hunting and trading expeditions took him to Taos and elsewhere. In Taos, Carson was involved in other relationships, first with a member of the extended Luna family and then with the young woman who would become his third and last wife: María Josefa Jaramillo, the younger sister of María Ignacia Bent, Charles Bent's wife. Josefa was famously described by mountain man Lewis Garrard as a beauty of the "haughty, heart-breaking kind—such as would lead a man with the glance of the eye, to risk his life for one smile."[20] Josefa was not yet fifteen and Carson was thirty-three when they married in January 1843.[21] Carson had already made other domestic arrangements for his two daughters.

THE TRAIL EAST—RECONNECTING TO MISSOURI

By spring 1842, Carson was heading east in a Santa Fe Trail caravan led by Charles Bent. He left his younger half-Arapaho daughter with the Bent family in Taos and took Adaline with him. They spent five weeks on the trail, and Adaline, who was four or five years old, surely needed someone to mind her—likely another woman whose name and role have been lost to history. After reaching the Bents' outpost at Westport, Missouri, just east of what is now Kansas City, Carson and Adaline found lodging at Daniel Yoacham's tavern. Yoacham's daughter Susannah recalled that Adaline was dressed in buckskin and seemed socialized to Native ways, even eating roots and shoots from the garden. While Carson traveled to St. Louis to collect wages owed him by Bent, St. Vrain and Company and then proceeded to reconnect with his family in Franklin, Adaline was outfitted with the finest dresses available in Westport. It had been sixteen years since Carson had seen his family, and much had changed. His mother had died the previous year, and the town of Franklin itself had been destroyed by floods and moved to higher ground.

While in Franklin, he was clearly assessing the best way to provide for Adaline's care and education.

The decision to leave Adaline could not have been easy. Carson knew the drawbacks of being illiterate himself and was likely familiar with the lack of educational resources in New Mexico. He also knew that his Missouri family might not approve of his half-Native daughters, although mixed-descent children were not uncommon in St. Louis if not explicitly acknowledged in more rural Missouri communities. He had likely heard of other New Mexicans sending their children to schools in St. Louis. Members of the Otero, Perea, Chavez, and Gutierrez families, and Charles Bent himself, sent their sons to St. Louis for schooling in the 1840s. Rose Philippine Duchesne, a sister of the Society of the Sacred Heart of Jesus, had opened a school for Native American girls as early as 1825 near Florissant, Missouri.

There is much speculation about where Adaline went to school. According to Carson family history, she first went to live with Kit's younger sister, Mary Anne Carson Rubey, and then spent six years on a farm between Glasgow and Fayette, Missouri, with Mrs. Leander Amick, the daughter of Kit's sister Elizabeth. She may have attended the Rock Springs School west of Fayette and then Howard High School, although no school records listing the names of students survive. Other authors claim that she went to a convent school in St. Louis for at least part of the time she spent in Missouri. The details of when and where she was educated have proved as elusive as the details of her birth.[22]

The trip back to Missouri changed the course of Carson's life and made him a hero to some. A chance meeting with John C. Frémont while both were traveling up the Missouri River on the steamboat *Rowena* transformed Carson from hunter and trapper to trailblazer. Frémont, the husband of Jessie Benton and son-in-law of Missouri senator Thomas Hart Benton, was headed west for his first exploration of the upper Missouri and Columbia Rivers. Carson's historical reputation was certainly influenced by this chance meeting and by Jessie Benton Frémont's admiration and her writings, which promoted both her husband's and Carson's exploits. Carson's knowledge of the geography of the Great Basin and Rocky Mountains, his kinship with Native Americans, and his skills as a mountain man were vital to the explorations. His skills complemented Frémont's determination and near-reckless stamina and Senator Benton's fervent desire to see American settlement of the Oregon Territory. Carson was with Frémont on his 1842 expedition to the Great Basin, his 1843–44 expedition to the Oregon Territory and California, and a third expedition to California in 1845–46. Carson also served as guide to the Army of the West in 1846 and to Frémont on one last mission carrying dispatches to Washington, DC, in the spring of 1847.[23] In Washington, Jessie Frémont introduced him to President James K. Polk, who was allied with Senator Benton in asserting the United States' right to expand into western territories, though they might have disagreed on methods and means. Polk rewarded Carson for his service to the country with a US Army officer's commission in the regiment of Mounted Volunteer Riflemen. Carson endured a celebratory dinner at the White House, where he impressed Mrs. Polk with his table manners but was obviously uncomfortable in Washington society.[24]

Carson was in a hurry to get back to New Mexico, where the Bent family was still recovering from the shocking murder of Charles Bent in January 1847 at his home in Taos during an uprising against the American conquest of the region. Carson evidently maintained a relationship with Adaline and his extended family in Missouri as well. He visited them in the Glasgow area in June 1847 as he traveled back to New Mexico from Washington and then again just over a year later.[25]

Carson settled into domestic life with Josefa Jaramillo in the early 1850s, and Adaline joined his family in New Mexico for a time. He was living in Rayado, New Mexico, on the Maxwell Land Grant. In 1851, when Adaline was about fifteen years old, Carson moved her back to the Taos area. At seventeen, Adaline married forty-five-year-old Louis (Louy) W. Simmons, a trapper and courier who had worked for the Bents and Carson in New Mexico.[26]

Adaline and Louy joined Carson and a group of backers and Missouri relatives when he assembled a sheep drive and settlement venture to California in 1853, energized in part by the draw of the goldfields. Carson had seen the promise of California's fertile valleys and temperate climate during his first trek there many years earlier. Adaline would live the rest of her life there, but there are few documents to ascertain her path. It seems that she parted from Simmons and took up with a man named George Stilts. That is the surname inscribed on a monument erected to her near Mono Lake, California, where she died in 1861. Whether her father learned of her passing before his own death in 1868 is not recorded. Such was the end of a child born on the edge of the frontier to a man who never had much to say about her or his own life. He was attentive to Adaline's needs and provided for her, but whether she became part of his life and his burgeoning family with Josefa is not clear. During her short life, Adaline moved across cultural and geographic space without leaving much trace in the historical records. She lived among a wide range of people—in an Arapaho camp with her mother's people; at Bent's Fort during the height of the fur trade and the Santa Fe Trail; in Taos, where Pueblo, Apache, Navajo, Ute, and Hispanic people created a society with porous social boundaries; then back to her father's original home in Missouri on the edge of the American frontier. Ultimately, Adaline found a home on the far western frontier of an expanding United States. She never recorded what it meant to be part Arapaho and the daughter of the legendary Kit Carson. What did she learn from her famous father and from her own time living in various frontier settlements? How did she feel about American troops advancing westward, conquering her Northern Arapaho relatives? How did she learn about and react to the brutal murder of Charles Bent in the Taos household where she and her younger sister stayed from time to time? How did she identify herself in this period of sweeping political and social changes in the West? We are left with many questions and few answers.

"Maid" Marian Sloan Russell: Veteran of the Trail

The most vivid recollection of a childhood crossing is that of Marian Sloan Russell, who dictated a memoir to her daughter-in-law in her later years. She was seven years old when she made her first trip on the trail in the spring of 1852, a journey that she would repeat four times as a child and again when she married a soldier stationed in New Mexico.[27] Her beautiful prose captures the adventures she and her older brother William experienced. Her mother's memory of that first trip may not have been as romantic, and Marian may have been unaware of her mother's sorrow as she moved her children in search of a home.

Marian Sloan was born in Peoria, Illinois, in 1845, the younger child of Eliza St. Clair and Dr. William James Sloan. Marian remembered little about her father, who was an army surgeon. She recalled an image of him in an old daguerreotype that hung in their home. She believed her father had been killed at the Battle of Monterey, which would have been in July 1846. Evidently, that was the story her mother told her, but Dr. Sloan did not die in battle, and her mother's reasons for saying he was dead are not recorded.[28] Eliza moved Marian and William to St. Louis, and Marian recalled some vivid details of their home from "the shadowy background of infancy." She thought the garden in back of their house was "a wild unexplored jungle" and the attic a place of infinite adventures. She remembered getting lost in the street and being rescued by an "old negro" who was tolling a bell and shouting a wide appeal for "little Marian Sloan" to be found.[29]

Eliza remarried in September 1848, when Marian was three years old, to a man Marian refers to only as Mr. Mahoney. His name was Jeremiah Mahoney, and he served as a soldier during the Mexican-American War. Marian recalled Mahoney as a handsome and kind man who sang Irish ballads as he played the banjo and was knowledgeable about Indian people.[30] The family moved to Fort Snelling, near St. Paul, Minnesota, when Mahoney was appointed an ordinance sergeant in the Sixth Infantry in 1849, during the last decade of the fort's history.[31] Though Marian was quite young when they took a "stern-wheeler" (which she thought looked like a sawmill) upriver to their new home, she remembered the high cliffs, the murky water, and the vines hanging from the tall trees along the Mississippi. The Mahoneys arrived in the area as the fur trade was starting to decline, and the American removal and reservation systems signaled the end of relative independence and prosperity for the northern Native tribes. Marian recalled "Sioux and Chippewa" encampments outside the fort, but during the Mahoney family's time at Fort Snelling, the Siouan-speaking Eastern Dakota and the Ojibwe were served by the Indian agency there.[32]

Marian's memoir has Mr. Mahoney dramatically shuttering the fort for good with the turn of a key, but Fort Snelling was not officially closed until 1858. Perhaps she remembered him locking up the fort at the end of the day. Marian recalled her mother's grief when she learned that Mahoney had been killed in an "ambush by Indians" while on a scouting expedition.[33] This memory is questionable as well, as Jeremiah Mahoney continued to serve at Fort Snelling until at least 1858. Nevertheless, Marian recalled that Eliza and the children left Fort Snelling at the end of the school year in 1850, although the 1850 census of the fort shows them as residents at the end of September.[34] Eliza Mahoney, as she continues to be identified in official records, then spent two years in Kansas City, waiting for the children's Sloan grandfather to return from the California goldfields and help with their own move to California. Sadly, their grandfather and two of his sons died in the widespread cholera epidemic, so Eliza Sloan Mahoney, perhaps twice widowed and now without the support of her first husband's family, had to plan for their future.

In spring 1852 Eliza moved the family to Fort Leavenworth, Kansas, where they would join a wagon train headed for California. She would have read about opportunities in the West and heard stories of California from returning Santa Fe traders. The family traveled with the wagon train of Francis Xavier Aubry, a famous wagon master in whom Eliza found an "ardent admirer" and the children found a sympathetic and attentive friend.[35] Eliza was able to book reduced-price passage on a government-owned wagon by agreeing to cook for two army officers from Fort Union.

They spent two months on the trail, and although Marian does not specify when they left or when they arrived, her descriptions of the land, the rain, and the lavender, red, and yellow wildflowers indicate that it was spring or early summer. Cholera was still buffeting the country, but through the eyes of a child, it was an enchanting trip as some five hundred wagons headed west to New Mexico and beyond:

> I remember so clearly the beauty of the earth, and how, as we bore westward, the deer and the antelope bounded away from us. There were miles and miles of buffalo grass, blue lagoons and blood-red sunsets, and once in a while, a little sod house on the lonely prairie....
> It was strange about the prairies at dawn, they were all sepia and silver; at noon they were like molten metal, and in the evening they flared into unbelievable beauty—long streamers of red and gold were flung out across them. The sky had an unearthly radiance. Sunset on the prairie! It was haunting, unearthly and lovely.[36]

That same spring, the first schoolteachers from the Sisters of Loretto in Kentucky also traveled on the Santa Fe Trail. If Marian met any of them, she did not mention it in her memoir. She did recall the threat of Indian attacks and the constant search for water, shade from the sun, and shelter from intense thunderstorms. At night, the circled wagons provided a playground for the children, and campfires afforded the adults a chance to rest, visit, sing, and tell stories of other crossings and their hopes for what lay ahead. Eliza dreamed of reaching California, where surely good fortune awaited them.

When they reached New Mexico, Aubry counseled Eliza and the children that it was a lawless place, but it also had a special power—something in the air—that revived the sick, healed their hearts, and let them live their dreams. Eliza never made it to California. Her meager savings were stolen in Albuquerque, and she was forced to find employment there. She kept a boardinghouse until spring 1854, when she moved her family to a house on the northwest corner of Santa Fe Plaza. They stayed in Santa Fe until August 1856, taking in US military boarders.

New Mexico offered Marian and her brother Will a different type of education. They learned about adobe architecture, New Mexican foodways, and the history of the region, and they learned to speak Spanish. Marian was enrolled in the school operated by the Sisters of Loretto (figure 3.3). She was one of five American girls and ninety-five Hispanic girls, and Marian was the only non-Catholic.[37] The sisters taught them reading, writing, arithmetic, and what Marian described as the more difficult lessons of contemplation, self-reliance, and compassion. She recalled the patience and control it took to create the stitched and beaded sample books they made at school. Will attended the school associated with San Miguel Church but not the Colegio de San Miguel, which had not yet been founded. Both Marian

Fig. 3.3. William James Hinchey, *On the Arkansas–Southern Bank*, March 23, 1855, graphite sketch. Sister of Loretto Roberta Brown (née Harriet) with her New Mexican companion as they head back to St. Louis and ultimately Kentucky after she left the order. Hinchey's daily diary identified Sister Roberta. (Bequest of Katherine Jane Hinchey Cochran, 94:1995, St. Louis Art Museum)

and Will were "little heretics," she claimed, as their faith was not the fervent Catholicism being taught in New Mexico.

In an eloquent passage, Marian described New Mexico and pondered the transformations brought about by Euro-American immigration:

> This was a land of vast spaces and long silences, a desert land of red bluffs and brilliant flowering cactus. The hot sun poured down. This land belonged to the very old Gods. They came on summer evenings, unseen, to rest their eyes and their hearts on the milky opal and smoky blue of the desert. For this was a land of enchantment, where Gods walked in the cool of the evening. What did the Gods think of the wagon trains that came creeping like serpents, of the red men who watched with bitter eyes that vast immigration?[38]

The family left New Mexico in August 1856, returning to the house they owned at Fort Leavenworth. Marian was eleven and Will was thirteen when they recrossed the country. Marian described a number of disturbing events during this crossing, including a menacing visit by some Apache men as they camped near Walnut Creek in Kansas. Then there was the piteous woman who pleaded, to no avail, for refuge from her abusive husband when the wagon train stopped at a watering hole on the prairie. In another graphic memory, Marian recalled happening upon a cabin containing the scalped and mutilated bodies of two white trappers. The eastward journey was not filled with the wonder of their first trip to New Mexico. Eliza may have had other reasons for leaving New Mexico. Dr. Sloan, who was still alive, had evidently been detailed to Santa Fe in August 1856 as the chief medical officer of the Military Department of New Mexico. Perhaps Eliza knew this and left New Mexico for that reason.[39]

Their time in Kansas, from the fall of 1856 until 1860, provided little respite, as the country was torn by factions. Border warfare and political struggles increased the tensions between Missouri and Kansas. On the trip east, their wagon train halted for more than two weeks at Diamond Springs, sixteen miles southwest of Council Groves, Kansas, while the leaders considered the safest way through the danger and how to avoid the "border ruffians," as the midcontinent was divided by the rise of pro- and anti-slavery factions. Marian recalled evenings spent playing a piano they found in an abandoned stone building, listening to a man play the fiddle, and reciting lessons they had learned at school in New Mexico. Eliza grew impatient with the indecision of the men leading the wagon train, so she walked the sixteen miles to Council Groves, accompanied by Marian, to assess the situation herself.

By November, the family was back in Fort Leavenworth, and Marian was enrolled in the Presbyterian Young Ladies Seminary. Despite her Presbyterian teachers' efforts to balance Marian's Catholic education, the teachings of the Sisters of Loretto remained strong. Marian's writings and drawings were filled with images of adobe churches, virgins, and angels as she dreamed about being back in New Mexico. Will did not attend school in Fort Leavenworth. To help the family financially, he was employed at the local newspaper. With the encouragement of the paper's owner, he became immersed in the teachings that would lead to his life in the ministry.[40]

When Marian was fifteen and Will seventeen, Eliza decided to return to New Mexico. Perhaps it was coincidental, but Dr. Sloan had returned to Missouri in October 1860. As they journeyed west, Will and Eliza revisited some of the same camps and recalled their two earlier trips—one east to west, the other west to east. To Marian, the Native people seemed less threatening, the border ruffians who had menaced their eastward journey in 1856 were gone, and the buffalo roamed the prairies as plentiful as ever. The family was glad to be back in Santa Fe. Marian recalled:

> I think I was never so glad to return to any place as I was to Santa Fe that autumn of 1860. I brought with me many eastern ways and a rather nice wardrobe. At first I showed off a bit, but failing to impress either the students or sisters, I forgot all about it and settled down into my uniforms and the school routine as if I had not been four years an easterner.[41]

This time, they settled quickly into life in Santa Fe, speaking the language, eating the spicy New Mexican cuisine, and visiting with neighbors. Marian noted that the gossip among her schoolmates was different from that in the East. Here, they talked about relations between the Navajos and the Santa Feans, speculating that the "strangers" in town dressed in Mexican costumes were guerrillas from farther south. Will's education resumed at the school near San Miguel, but outside the classroom, he was learning about the economy of the Southwest. He joined a caravan with their neighbor and friend Kit Carson to gather salt from the ancient salt lakes in south-central New Mexico, a trip that made a deep impression on him. Ever restless, Eliza took them all back to Kansas at the end of the year; this time, they settled in Kansas City.[42] Eliza figured Kansas City was the best place for Marian to be if she hoped to marry well. When Marian spurned her first suitor, she joined Eliza on another trip across the trail—their fifth.

This trip in 1862 was Marian's last. She was married in February 1865 to Lieutenant Richard Russell (figure 3.4), whom she had met at Fort Union, where Eliza was employed as a cook. Marian and Richard lived at the fort, which was temporarily being commanded by her old friend Kit Carson, whom she had met as a child in Santa Fe. The couple subsequently moved to other New Mexican posts—Camp Nichols and then Fort Bascom—and finally to southern Colorado, where Richard mustered out. There, Richard and Marian established a homestead on land that was part of the contested Maxwell Land Grant. Eliza settled for a time in Fort Hays, Kansas, where she was listed on the 1870 census as operating a boardinghouse.[43]

Eliza helped Richard and Marian get settled in Colorado and then moved farther west, joining William in California. Marian and Richard's family grew to include nine children. When she got word of Eliza's death in California in about 1883, Marian recalled her mother's spirit and strength: "Eliza St. Clair Sloan was like a beautiful Bird of Paradise. She flew best against the wind. Always she kept her brave face to the wind. Always she loved to follow new trails."[44] Five years after Eliza's death, Marian's beloved husband Richard was shot in the conflict that developed when the new British owners of the Maxwell Land Grant ejected settlers from their homes. That land would become embroiled in lawsuits over boundaries and rights that are still being litigated.[45]

Fig. 3.4. Portrait of Marian Sloan Russell (1845–1937) and Richard D. Russell (1839–88) from a photograph taken in Santa Fe, New Mexico, circa 1867, soon after their wedding. (OG PAMU.60, Palace of the Governors Photo Archives [NMHM/DCA])

Richard had been in a tenuous position, seeking to negotiate a peaceful end to the conflict between the settlers and the Maxwell owners and their agents. He and Marian had already sold their improvements and were planning to head back to New Mexico, but Richard delayed their departure in the hope of resolving the conflict. He was shot on the porch of the local hotel while waiting for a gunfight between the factions to end. Marian sat beside him for five days as medical help was prevented from reaching his bedside.[46]

After Richard's death, Marian continued to try to perfect the title to their land, but in 1895 she lost when the Supreme Court recognized the Maxwell Company's title.[47] She had already moved to Trinidad, Colorado, where she lived until her own death in 1936, after being struck by a car. But before she died, eighty-nine-year-old Marian was able to make one last visit to the places she loved in Santa Fe, Fort Union, and along the Santa Fe Trail in New Mexico. So many of the places were gone, some of the adobe buildings and trails returned to dust, but what a treasure she left for readers in her finely drawn memoir.

Francisca López de Kimball: A Family in Motion

In 1850 eight-year-old Francisca López arrived in St. Louis from New Mexico. She would never go back. At the end of her life at age sixty-six, she was eulogized as the doyenne of an important St. Louis family.

As Francisca's father was arranging to bring her and her three brothers to Missouri, Adaline Carson was preparing to leave Missouri to rejoin her father and stepmother in Taos, and Eliza Mahoney had paused in Kansas City with William and Marian to plan their move west. It might seem unusual for Francisca's father to bring his children east when so many others were heading west to California, but the López family's circumstances were different. They were a family of privilege. Even so, Francisca did not have an easy childhood, as her school years in St. Louis demonstrate.

Dámaso López was an enterprising merchant whose deep roots extended from Mexico back to Gordexola in Vizcaya, the Basque region of northeastern Spain.[48] He was the sixth child of eight and the fourth of five sons in a part of the world with a long-standing practice of primogeniture. As a result, younger sons from the Basque region were among the settlers of many Spanish colonies throughout the world. Dámaso and his older brother Lorenzo chose Mexico, arriving sometime before 1818. They were running a merchant business in Chihuahua by that time, when Dámaso was about twenty-five and Lorenzo six years older. In 1820 some New Mexican traders owed the brothers 10,000 pesos for goods they had purchased, so Dámaso traveled to New Mexico to sue them for payment.[49] That was perhaps the first time he traveled up the Camino Real de Tierra Adentro from Chihuahua to New Mexico.

Dámaso arrived in New Mexico just before Mexico won its independence from Spain in 1821. It was a propitious time for Chihuahua merchants, as the economy favored those familiar with the supply chains that developed as Mexico eased trade restrictions along the Camino Real. Dámaso was resourceful and actively engaged in a wide variety of activities, including mining, freighting, merchandising, real estate development, livestock raising, and trading in New Mexico, Mexico, and ultimately California. In the early 1830s he became an inspector and then a partner in a gold mine southeast of Santa Fe with the Ortiz family (the same merchants whose debt first brought him to New Mexico). When local politicians invoked a Mexican-era decree banishing those of Spanish birth to the frontier, Dámaso lost his interest in the gold mine and moved to the frontier settlement of Abiquiú. Around this time he married María del Carmen Seferina Ruiz de Esparza, whose family had ties to Durango, Mexico.[50] Dámaso partnered with Manuel Alvarez in a successful mercantile and livestock venture in about 1833. Alvarez had emigrated from Spain to New Orleans and then moved to New York. He ultimately settled in Santa Fe, where he was the US consul to New Mexico, although he was never granted formal authority for that position. Alvarez had a close personal and business relationship with Dámaso that lasted all their lives and connected them to a wide sphere of other merchant families.[51] It was probably their combination of skills—Alvarez the skillful diplomat, and López the astute businessman—that formed the basis of their lasting partnership.

Three of María Carmen and Dámaso's sons were baptized or buried as infants in Abiquiú, New Mexico. Their first child, Jesus María, referred to as a *párvulo* (young child), was buried in Abiquiú on March 27, 1835. José Trinidad was born in Abiquiú and baptized six days later on December 12, 1836. José Melaquides was born in Abiquiú in November 1838 and baptized in Santa Fe on December 19, 1838. His godparents were New Mexico governor Manuel Armijo and his wife, María Trinidad Gabaldon, indicating that Dámaso and María Carmen had already found a place in Santa Fe society. Francisca was born on October 21, 1841, but the location is unclear. According to a family history recorded by Francisca, she was born in Chihuahua, Mexico, before the family moved to Santa Fe. But the family had been in New Mexico for quite a while by then, and there is no record of her birth in either New Mexico or Mexico. New Mexico was still part of Mexico at the time, so Abiquiú could have been considered Mexico in the telling of the family history. That was a particularly disruptive period, especially the Texans' raid on New Mexico, and record keeping may not have been the highest priority. Some evidence that lends credence to Francisca's birthplace being Abiquiú is found in a letter Dámaso wrote in August 1840 from that settlement to his "countryman and friend" (*paysano y amigo*) Manuel Alvarez, stating that he had been so busy with his liquor still and livestock that he was unable to visit his friend in Santa Fe. He asks Alvarez to tell him the political news, particularly what he knows about the Texans.[52]

In 1842 Dámaso served as godparent in Abiquiú to two Native children he had bought from the Utes, perhaps taken in a raid from Navajo settlements. Dámaso then undertook a sheep drive to California in 1843 that proved profitable to him and his partner. The last child of María Carmen and Dámaso, José Francisco, was born on February 16, 1844, and baptized the following day in the village of San Miguel del Vado, on the Pecos River in eastern New Mexico.[53] The village was located at a strategic ford of the river and was the site of a customs house on the Santa Fe Trail. Abiquiú and San Miguel del Vado were well known for serving the Spanish Trail to California and the Santa Fe Trail, respectively. Dámaso acquired land and real estate in several villages in New Mexico but did not necessarily live in these places. The family apparently continued to live in Abiquiú, but through business dealings, an extended family network, and their standing as godparents, the López family was connected to other families throughout New Mexico.[54]

The López family likely witnessed the American takeover of New Mexico by the Army of the West in the summer of 1846. As Stephen Watts Kearny read the oath of allegiance in every village, the mood was somber. Kearny promised, on behalf of the United States, to make life better; to end the threat posed by Texas on New Mexico's eastern border; to tame the Navajo, Ute, and Apache raids on the settlements; and to protect those who submitted to the rule of military law. The American occupation of New Mexico was advantageous for some Santa Fe traders, but Alvarez and López's close relationship to the conquered New Mexico governor would not shield their business interests. And nothing the United States had to offer would protect the López family from the sadness caused by María Carmen's death in 1847 or 1848. Although it seems that Dámaso married Carmen Leyba sometime in the late 1840s, that chronology has not been substantiated with documents. At this time, New Mexico was still roiling from the American occupation and the rise of many factions that eventually led to the assassination of Charles Bent, the first military governor appointed by the United States.[55] The high taxes on trade goods and the growing political unrest were reasons enough for Alvarez and López to look for new business opportunities.

In the spring of 1850 Dámaso took his four children east on the Santa Fe Trail. Writing from Independence on May 17, 1850, he informed Alvarez in Santa Fe that he and the children had arrived safely at the eastern end of the trail.[56] The family stayed in the Independence area with Dr. David Waldo, a longtime business acquaintance. Waldo was a member of a wealthy St. Louis family and, in addition to being a medical doctor, was a successful entrepreneur in Santa Fe Trail endeavors. Following the American conquest, New Mexican students enrolled in St. Louis schools at a steady pace. The two youngest López boys— José Melaquides, about ten years old, and José Francisco, about five years old—were enrolled at Chapel Hill Academy near Lexington in Lafayette County, Missouri, about thirty-five miles northeast of Independence. The academy, which had only been open for about a year when the López brothers arrived, was operated by the Presbyterian Church, which recognized in 1851 that Chapel Hill was a worthy place to foster "friends of the church."[57] The older children went to school in St. Louis. José Trinidad, then about fourteen or fifteen, was enrolled at St. Louis University, and Francisca attended Visitation Academy. Both were Catholic schools located about two hundred miles east of where the younger boys were schooled. With the rise of the American legal infrastructure, local political machinations, and discrimination against Hispanics, Alvarez and López were facing business difficulties, including having trouble collecting debts. "Bad luck and hard times" became a common justification when debtors failed to pay. Alvarez and López turned their attention to growing opportunities in California.[58]

SCHOOLED IN LIFE'S TRAGEDIES

Why Dámaso López enrolled his children in different schools is not explained, but he selected schools where other elite New Mexican and Missouri families sent their children. Francisca was certainly not the youngest New Mexican girl to enroll in school in St. Louis, but she was among the few girls who came east on the trail in the 1850s. When Francisca arrived at Visitation Academy, one other child with ties to New Mexico and to Missouri's Santa Fe Trail traders was already enrolled: Donaciana Waldo. The expenses for both girls were paid on June 1, 1850, listed in sequential entries in the school's ledger of student accounts.[59] This suggests that they arrived on the same day and likely traveled there together, as the López family was staying with the Waldo family in Independence. Dámaso paid $144.75 for Francisca's board and English instruction through July 15, 1851; this covered bedding, music lessons, and board during vacations, as well as $2 for tables and chamber furnishings.

Fig. 3.5. Graphic detail from the prospectus of the Menard Young Ladies' Academy of the Visitation, Kaskaskia, Illinois, 1840–42. (Visitation Academy Archives, St. Louis)

Dr. Waldo paid school expenses for his daughter Donaciana through February 8, 1851.

Visitation Academy in St. Louis was the new name and new location of what had previously been the Menard Young Ladies' Academy of the Visitation, established in Kaskaskia, Illinois, in 1833 (figure 3.5). The school moved to St. Louis in 1844. The academy's 1840 prospectus captured its physical setting, lofty goals, and plan of instruction:

> The situation of their newly finished Academy is near the village of Kaskaskia, commanding on one side a full view of the beautiful river of the same name, as it winds its course beneath a ridge of lofty hills, and on the other overlooking a considerable portion of the Village. The lot, consisting of twenty-two acres, borders upon the river, is handsomely laid off into a garden, orchard &c, and affords an agreeable place of recreation to the boarders. The site is not only picturesque, but, at the same time one of the healthiest in the Union, the air being pure and salubrious, the water wholesome and agreeable, and the course of exercise such as must contribute to the preservation of health and strength.
>
> The general course of Instruction embraces the English and French Languages, Reading, Writing, plain and ornamental, Orthography, Grammar and Composition, Sacred and Profane History, Ancient and Modern Chronology, Mythology,

Poetry and Rhetoric, Arithmetic, Geography, the use of the Maps and Globes, and the Principles of Natural Philosophy, Chymistry [sic] and Astronomy; besides plain and ornamental Needle-work, Tapestry, Lace and Bead-work, &c.

The fine Arts, such as Music, Drawing, Painting, Dancing, &c., form extra charges.

The prospectus also discussed the competitive atmosphere of the academy, which issued monthly reports detailing the proficiency and conduct of every student, in what was described as "the spirit of emulation." Although the Sisters of the Visitation was a Catholic order, there was no insistence on faith. There was, however, a strict set of expected behaviors: "Regularity, neatness, cheerfulness, and decorum of manners and deportment are objects incessantly inculcated, and specially attended to, by the Ladies who preside over the Institution; and every effort is made by them to form and improve the hearts of their pupils, and to implant in them a solid esteem and love of virtue, but without exercising any undue influence over their religious opinions."[60]

In a letter to her father on April 22, 1852, Francisca wrote in beautiful penmanship and perfectly charming English: "I think a great deal about you, my dear Father, and especially when I am going to bed at night. I always say a little prayer for you and my little brothers too. I wish I could see you so much and I do hate to think we are so far apart." She wrote about preparing for her upcoming first Holy Communion, using words no doubt suggested by her teacher. She asked her father to pray for her to "receive her God worthily." But she also expressed her own childlike pride in her progress and her love of music and her other studies. She closed the letter by saying that her hand was aching because she had written so much and asked him not to forget "your little Francisca" (figure 3.6).[61]

It is likely that Dámaso López never received that letter. By the fall of 1851 he was already making his way from New Mexico to California with more than forty-six hundred sheep to supply the near-insatiable needs of the gold miners and settlers. He had made an earlier trip there in 1843–44 and knew the rigors and dangers of winter snow, the lack of grass in spring, the blazing summer sun, and always the threat of Indian attacks. He and Alvarez faced fierce competition from other sheep men, some of whom also came from New Mexico. López paused in Sonoita, Arizona, for several months but left there in late July or August. Crossing the Colorado River was a major undertaking and a considerable expense, since it required taking John Frederick Jaeger's ferry at Fort Yuma, and his fees were steep. Once across, López might have started to calculate his potential profits, but they would never be realized. Dámaso López died on the trail on August 20, 1852, at Carricita, near Warner's Ranch.

Fig. 3.6. Undated portrait of Francisca López (1841–1907), likely when she was about ten years old. (Used with the permission of Mary Outten, López family files)

The *Los Angeles Star* reported his death—possibly of sunstroke—on August 26 and noted that his four children were in school in St. Louis. The notice of his death refers to López's prominence and important friends and contains a veiled threat against anyone who might try to defraud his children of their rights. How and when the children learned of his death is less clear, but on October 22, 1852, his obituary appeared in the *Missouri Daily Republican*.[62]

Manuel Alvarez did not learn of his partner's death for several months, at which point he turned to Francis X. Aubry, skilled trail master and friend of Eliza Mahoney, for help in settling Dámaso's business affairs and disposing of the sheep in California. Alvarez became the guardian of the López children on November 22, 1852.[63] Aubry capably completed his work, but it would take several years for Dámaso's estate to be settled. Francisca wrote a letter to Alvarez, addressing him as "My dear Guardian," in December 1853. In it she reported on her progress in English and music and mentioned her close bond with Donaciana Waldo, who made dresses for Francisca and was a source of comfort as well. Francisca longed to be reunited with her brothers, and she gently pleaded with Alvarez to visit her and bring her brothers with him. At this point in his life, Alvarez was an elder statesman and anxious to see his own family in Europe. He traveled there in 1855 and then returned to Santa Fe, perhaps after paying a visit to the López children in St. Louis. When Alvarez died on July 5, 1856, another of Dámaso's associates, Anastacio Sandoval in Santa Fe, was named executor and guardian of the children.[64] José Trinidad, the oldest son, returned to New Mexico and settled in the Mora Valley. He served in the New Mexico Volunteers in 1854–55 under the command of another Santa Fe trader, Ceran St. Vrain. In 1861, during a second enlistment, he served under Kit Carson at the Battle of Valverde. After the Civil War, he returned to Mora and, as an attorney, took up the long but ultimately successful defense of property titles held by his wife's family in the Boné Land Grant. José Francisco, the youngest of the López children, married Sandoval's daughter. José Melaquides returned to New Mexico and was living in Santa Fe and working as a printer by 1860.

During the 1858–59 school year, Francisca was one of nine young women from Missouri who attended Georgetown Academy of the Visitation in Washington, DC. She was accompanied by her close friend and classmate Pelagie Berthold.[65] Pelagie was a member of the multicultural Chouteau family, whose French and Native American ancestors were founders of St. Louis. Their home was the Berthold mansion, one of the many grand and beautiful residences in the thriving nineteenth-century city. There Francisca met her future husband, Pierre Benjamin Kimball, and she spent the year before her marriage living with the Bertholds. In the spring of 1860 Glasgow Brothers Trading Company billed Anastacio Sandoval for items that were part of Francisca's trousseau. The correspondence assured Sandoval that Francisca would soon be wed to *un caballero americano de buen character y buenas relaciones*, an endorsement of Kimball's character and good standing in the community. Also among the bills were those for purchases of clothing, fabrics, trimmings, embroidery on a gown, gloves, and a parasol from Ubsdell, Pierson and Company of St. Charles. She bought a bonnet and other items from the Rosenbaum and Thayer Company in St. Louis.[66] Francisca (now known as Fanny) and Benjamin (as he was known) were married on June 28, 1860; she was just shy of nineteen and he was twenty-two years old. They eventually had eleven children, building a highly successful family in the stable environment of St. Louis. Fanny died of blood poisoning from an unfortunate medical procedure on November 19, 1907, but her story transcends even this last tragedy.

Crossed Paths

It seems unlikely that Adaline, Marian, and Fanny ever met, but their life paths certainly crossed both literally and figuratively. How often did Kit Carson think about his own little Adaline as he walked across Santa Fe Plaza and saw Marian at play? Did Francis X. Aubry think about the Sloan children and their mother Eliza as he worked to settle the affairs and provide for the orphaned López children? Did José Trinidad and Kit Carson ever discuss the news from Fanny, who chose not to return to New Mexico? Adaline's, Marian's, and Fanny's lives were shaped by the cultural and political changes that accompanied the US expropriation of the continent.

The amount of formal education Adaline and Marian received is open to interpretation, but their life experiences and the learning that took place on the Santa Fe Trail were extensive. Adaline was certainly exposed to many different cultures. She might not have remembered much about her mother or her stepmother and their time in the Native American camps or rendezvous sites. She was only two or three years old when her mother died, and she was four or five when she went to live in Missouri. We do not know how she was treated in western Missouri as a child of mixed Native American ancestry. There is no record of her memories and experiences as a child of the American frontier and the daughter of a legendary frontiersman.

Marian provided the most vivid recollections of her travels on the trail, though much of her story was told through the rosy glow of childhood memories. Yet Marian was surrounded by loss and in some cases the violence that accompanied western expansion and the changing political and legal landscape of the West. She was led to believe that her father, Dr. William James Sloan, was killed in the Mexican-American War. Her stepfather, Jeremiah Mahoney, may or may not have been killed in an Indian attack while on military patrol. Her mother's admirer, Francis Xavier Aubry, was killed in a fight in Santa Fe, and her own husband was one of the victims of the Colfax County range wars. Frontier violence permeated her life, and although her memoir conveyed the rich textures, colors, and beauty of the desert landscape, it did not ignore those harsher elements of western American history.

Francisca's life was a mixture of privilege and loss. She was very young when her mother died, so it is hard to know what, if anything, she remembered of María Carmen. Then, just five years later, her beloved father died, followed by her guardian's death four years after that. Photographs show a beautiful girl and then a poised and lovely young woman, perhaps with just a hint of sadness in her eyes. She followed her father's advice to learn all that the nuns could teach her and her guardian's advice to stay in St. Louis. She found love and an extended family through her marriage, and at the eastern end of the trail, Fanny created a family of her own that continues to honor her journey through their deep embrace of the history of St. Louis and their family. In each case, Kit Carson, Eliza Mahoney, and Dámaso López had to choose how best to provide their children with security and opportunities in very challenging situations.

4

Seeking Health on the Santa Fe Trail

Travel on the Santa Fe Trail was not restricted to the hale and hearty. Some travelers made the strenuous journey in an effort to reclaim their health. Many of them—both men and women—noted in their diaries their increasingly robust constitution, attributing the improvement to the pure air and sunshine on the trail and the connection to nature they felt while sleeping under the stars. Others wrote about the discomfort of the trail and the challenges of their crossing, yet they still hoped the journey would improve their health. The trail from St. Louis to Santa Fe, and the return trip from the Southwest to the Midwest, was not without risk, danger, and even death on the prairie.

The story of Kate Messervy Kingsbury, who died on the Santa Fe Trail in June 1857, is especially poignant.[1] Kate crossed the trail three times between 1854 and 1857. As her husband, veteran trail merchant John M. Kingsbury, planned each trip from their home in Salem, Massachusetts, to supply houses in St. Louis and Santa Fe, he feared that one of those journeys might end her life. Kate suffered from consumption, as tuberculosis was called at the time. The disease struck many people in the crowded, often unsanitary cities of the nineteenth-century United States. One treatment employed well into the early twentieth century was travel to more healthful climates, where rest and fresh air, free of industrial pollution, provided much of the cure.

Nineteenth-Century Health, Environment, and Travel

The relationship between health and the physical environment—particularly the importance of clean air and water—remains a public health concern in our contemporary lives. The widespread effects of the COVID-19 pandemic offer some apt comparisons with the 1918 influenza epidemic, as well as other episodic diseases that were largely neutralized by vaccinations and modern medicine. Diseases such as tuberculosis, malaria, measles, and smallpox shaped many historical eras. Nineteenth-century travelers on the Santa Fe Trail became acutely aware of the benefits of clean air, pure water, and sanitary living conditions as they crossed the continent, many of them in search of healthier climates, better lands, and improved lives. Unfortunately, some of them contracted cholera along the way, as the trail itself became a vector for transmission.

Nineteenth-century travelers, writers, and medical and military officials elaborated on prevailing ideas about the relationship between health and geography. Conevery Bolton Valenčius analyzed how moving to a more favorable climate might improve the declining health of people like Kate Kingsbury. Although Kate's family was certainly concerned about her health, their decision to move her to New Mexico was also, in part, an economic decision, based on the mercantile business run by her husband, her brother William, and their partner James Josiah Webb in Santa Fe. Valenčius examined the early nineteenth-century correspondence of families settling on the rich bottomlands of the Missouri River Valley and found that they relied not on scientific parameters but on personal observations to correlate fertile soils with a heathy environment. Valenčius observed "an organic relationship between self and place that animated American Western settlement."[2] To be healthy in the nineteenth century meant that one's physical body was in balance with the land, water, and wind of the place where one lived. Josiah Gregg noted that the prairies were "celebrated for their sanative effects." He wrote, "Most chronic diseases, particularly liver complaints, dyspepsias and similar affections [sic], are often radically cured; owing no doubt to the peculiarities of diet, and the regular exercise incident to prairie life; as well as to the purity of the atmosphere of those elevated unembarrassed regions."[3]

Traveling by horseback or on foot, or even riding in a wagon, along with the work involved in making camp, offered opportunities to strengthen one's physical condition. Choosing a campsite was one of the many challenges of traveling the Santa Fe Trail, varying from season to season and depending on the availability of potable water and grass for the animals to feed on. US Army captain Randolph B. Marcy published a handbook for prairie travelers based on his own numerous crossings of the continent and reports from other military expeditions around the world. The manual described all manner of camp equipment to ensure sanitary and comfortable travel, as well as advice on the organization of caravans, handling of livestock, and proper clothing and provisions. Marcy quoted at length from a British military field report on the proper siting of encampments, cautioning that diseases flourished along watercourses, around swamps and ponds, and in areas cleared of native trees. The winds that blew along watercourses and in newly cleared areas were thought to carry disease, as was the moisture that rose from the ground. People crowded into canvas tents raised the air temperature and increased the ground moisture, creating very unhealthy conditions. Marcy's description of these unhealthy conditions mirrors the climate of the Mississippi Valley—cold and damp in the winter; hot, humid, and nearly tropical in the summer.[4]

New Mexico's altitude and climate, in contrast, were ideal for health seekers. The rigors of travel itself were part of the therapeutic prescription for those with tuberculosis. As early as the 1830s, vigorous exercise, outdoor labor, and exposure to fresh air were documented as an essential and rational approach to ameliorating, if not curing, pulmonary disease. Esmond R. Long, quoting others who had reported miraculous cures, believed that several factors—soil temperature, low humidity, thin air, and abundant sunshine—made New Mexico a favorable environment for tuberculosis patients.[5] As a woman of means, Kate Kingsbury would have been exempt from the work and strenuous exercise prescribed for healing. On the trail, activities such as equipping and making camp were often left to suppliers and caravan handlers who catered to travelers in St. Louis, St. Charles, and Independence.

James Ross Larkin, who traveled from St. Louis to Santa Fe in 1856–57, undertook the journey specifically to cure, or at least improve, his delicate health. Larkin came from a wealthy St. Louis family, and his trip was provisioned by cousins who owned the well-known Glasgow Brothers Trading Company. When Larkin began his journey in September 1856, he noted in his diary his many ailments and his concerns about the rigors of the trail.[6] His journal provides some insight into his thoughts as he monitored his constitution on the trip, something that is not available for Kate. He frequently remarked that his stomach was no worse than it might have been in St. Louis, but he was never without discomfort on the trail or in Santa Fe. Larkin carried a letter of introduction from his Glasgow cousins to John Kingsbury, assuring the payment of Larkin's debts at the Webb & Kingsbury store in Santa Fe, but there is no indication of a social relationship between them.[7] Larkin enjoyed the Santa Fe social life, attending military balls, literary circles, and local New Mexican fandangos, although he continued to experience stomach discomfort and other unspecified illnesses. His western journey was more a rite of passage and an adventure than a cure.

John Kingsbury likely hoped that Kate's move to New Mexico, or at least her crossing, would restore her health, as it had for others. William Watts Hart Davis crossed the country in 1853 to assume his duties as US attorney for the

New Mexico Territory. Davis's book about his two years in New Mexico, *El Gringo; or New Mexico and Her People*, reflects on the salubrious nature of his journey on the Santa Fe Trail, though he also records several nights of misery when the campsite flooded or the temperature plummeted. Davis may have exaggerated when he claimed there was comparatively little endemic illness in New Mexico, and he certainly never consulted the historical record, which would have shown seasonal influenza, cholera, and other maladies, some of which the trail travelers brought themselves. He touchingly captured his response to the wide-open spaces of the western prairie. He left Independence, Missouri, on November 1, 1853, and after about a week of travel, having covered some 150 miles, he wrote:

> To a person who has never been upon the great American prairies, a trip across them cannot be otherwise than interesting. Their appearance can hardly be imagined; to be appreciated they must be seen. . . . You appear to be standing in the midst of an immense ocean of dry land. And you strain the eye in vain for something to relieve the sameness around you. Out upon these great plains a person experiences different feelings than when confined within cities and forest, and surrounded with the appliances of civilized life. He appears to breathe deeper, and to increase in stature; the sky seems to be bluer and clearer, the air purer, and the sun to shine more brightly. The earth expands in size, and the vastness spread out on every side gives him a higher appreciation of the immensity of God's handiwork. The mind seems to become enlarged also, in beholding the greatness of Nature's works, and a man who is not insensible to such influences cannot fail to be made better and wiser by a trip across the prairies.[8]

Consumption: Nineteenth-Century Causes and Cures

Tuberculosis, known in nineteenth-century literature as consumption or by its more technical name, phthisis, was widespread throughout the world. An examination of the 1850 US census shows that infectious diseases accounted for 40 percent of the deaths that year. Acute diseases such as typhus, typhoid fever, smallpox, scarlet fever, measles, erysipelas (a bacterial infection), cholera, whooping cough, and diphtheria predominated, but consumption accounted for an additional 10 percent of the 1850 mortality rate.[9] Discussions of what caused the disease and how to cure it ranged from the scientific to the spurious to utter quackery. Antibiotics would eventually provide a cure, but nineteenth-century doctors and their patients experimented with cod liver oil, sugar vapor, inhaled iodine, and an inhalation made with creosote for short-term relief.

There were many theories about what caused consumption. Dr. Samuel Sheldon Fitch's 1853 treatise on respiratory diseases attributed the onset of the disease to modern lifestyles that were debilitating: "Consumption is a child of civilization; results chiefly from loss of symmetry, and from effeminacy, induced by too much clothing, too luxurious living, dissipation, too little exercise, and debilitating diseases and occupations, and poison in the blood."[10]

Professor C. B. Coventry, writing in the *St. Louis Medical Journal* in 1856, described the social conditions and stresses that gave rise to consumption. In examining some of the common ways the illness was thought to be contracted in the nineteenth century, he exposed the social pressures and expectations imposed on upper-class women—to be well educated, beautifully clothed (despite weather conditions), sheltered from physical exertion, fed too many sweets, and confined in small, crowded spaces:

> Permit me to give [a recipe] for producing consumption. Take a girl between the age of twelve and eighteen, who is growing rapidly, of delicate constitution; confine her six hours each day in a crowded school-room; let her have lessons to get out of school which will require from two to three hours of study, in addition to two hours' practice on the piano-forte; stimulate her to extra exertion by hope of a prize at the end of the term, or of excelling her classmates; let her sleep in a dark, close and small bedroom, with one or more persons; supply her plentifully with candy and sweet-meats, so as to destroy any little appetite she may have for wholesome and nourishing food; when out of school, confine her to a heated room, except occasionally going to church or to parties in thin stockings and shoes, and low dress, so as to expose the chest and neck to the cold—and you have all the requisites to produce disease. Should you not produce consumption, you will be likely to have disease of the brain, equally but more quickly fatal.[11]

It was not until 1882 that a German microbiologist identified the bacteria responsible for tuberculosis.

When rest and recuperation did not halt the disease, its progression was marked by specific symptoms. Dr. James Clark published a comprehensive consideration of the course of tuberculosis in 1835.[12] In its first stage, consumption could be diagnosed by a persistent cough and fatigue. Gradually, the patient might experience night sweats, chills, and some loss of muscle firmness brought on by fatigue after exertion (figure 4.1). There could be a seasonal aspect to the disease as well. If a patient first experienced symptoms in the spring, the onset of warmer weather and the opportunity for outdoor activities could slow or even arrest progression of the disease. If the patient

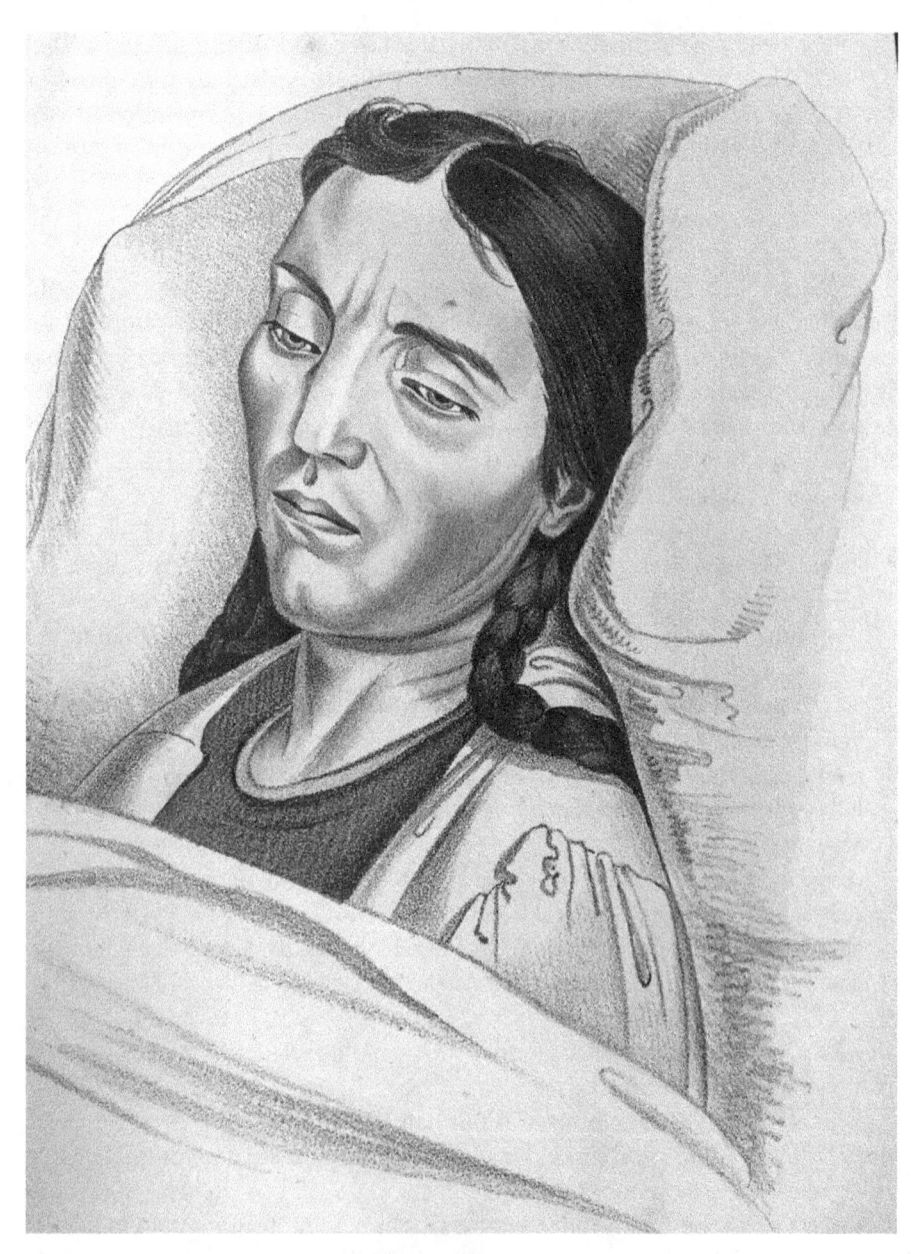

Fig. 4.1. Diagnostic sketch of a woman with consumption, 1842, by Dr. K. H. Baumgärtner, *Kranken-Physiognomik*, Stuttgart. (From the collection of the Becker Medical Library, Washington University, St. Louis)

contracted the disease in winter, Dr. Clark thought there was little chance it would subside.

The second stage of consumption was marked by a frothy, sometimes bloody, but always productive cough, as well as a pronounced rasp or crackling in the lungs. Bouts of fever and chills increased, and the patient began to experience pain in the chest and shoulders as the lungs "softened." Dr. Clark noted that in some people the symptoms persisted for months or even years, whereas others arrived "at the brink of the grave" within weeks. In the third stage, patients had frequent attacks of chills and fever, diarrhea, and prolonged coughing. By this stage, they also experienced a marked change in posture and body appearance as their shoulders rose and dropped forward, forming a concave upper chest and a stooped posture. Dr. Clark noted that patients had diminished physical and mental energy and might appear "skeletal." In their final days, patients became delirious, often violently so. Clark concluded with a rather telling summary of how consumption affected the patient's emotional state: "That inward struggle between hope and fear, which, whether avowed or not is generally felt by the patient in the latter stages—constitute a degree of suffering which, considering the protracted period of its duration, is seldom surpassed in any other disease."[13]

Bound for Santa Fe

Kate Messervy Kingsbury was a younger sister of William S. Messervy, a well-regarded merchant and New Mexico territorial politician (figure 4.2). He moved from Salem, Massachusetts, to St. Louis in 1834 and became a junior partner at James Josiah Webb's mercantile firm in 1839, opening a store for Webb in Santa Fe.[14] With suppliers in New England and St. Louis, Webb and Messervy followed a lucrative business practice that involved wholesaling fabrics, groceries, housewares, and hardware obtained in several manufacturing and market centers; aggregating the goods in St. Louis or Independence; and then transporting them across the heartland for the Santa Fe trade.

Bookkeeper John M. Kingsbury joined Webb and Messervy's firm in Boston in 1849 and was mentored by them. Kingsbury traveled between St. Louis and Santa Fe for the firm in 1851, and by 1854 he was a junior partner, handling its commercial transactions in Santa Fe. Webb, Messervy, and Kingsbury prospered in business, but they all suffered personal and economic losses that ultimately led them to abandon the Santa Fe trade. Messervy began to withdraw from the business after 1853, and he left New Mexico in 1854. Kingsbury's importance in the partnership increased after his marriage

Fig. 4.2. Copy of a daguerreotype of William S. Messervy (1812–86), brother of Kate Kingsbury and business partner of James Webb and John M. Kingsbury, circa 1849. (N088121, Palace of the Governors Photo Archives [NMHM/DCA])

to Messervy's sister Kate on December 21, 1853.[15] Kingsbury was the last of the partners to live in Santa Fe, spending most of his time there between 1853 and 1861.

When Kate married Kingsbury, she had already been diagnosed with the early symptoms of consumption. Although her brother and her husband feared she might not be strong enough to travel to Santa Fe, they also thought the journey offered the best hope for her recovery. Kate crossed the Santa Fe Trail three times, but she left no personal record of her feelings or fears. In correspondence between Kingsbury and Webb and with his brother-in-law Messervy, the progression of Kate's illness is discernible, and Kingsbury's emotional turmoil is evident as he balanced Kate's medical needs with his business responsibilities. At least part of the correspondence between Kate's husband and brother was preserved in their business records.

John Kingsbury was twenty-two years old when he first journeyed to New Mexico in 1851 as a clerk and bookkeeper for Messervy and Webb. He also served for a time as private secretary to William Carr Lane, the second territorial governor of New Mexico. Kingsbury was known as a careful bookkeeper with fine penmanship and good organizational and personal skills; he was "proficient with numbers as well as guns," according to the firm's biographers.[16] While Kingsbury attended to the trade, Messervy became involved in political affairs and stood to serve as a delegate to Congress from the newly recognized New Mexico Territory. Messervy's candidacy was rejected after a congressional committee hearing, so he was never seated in Washington. He served in Santa Fe as secretary of the territory and then as acting governor during the administration of David Meriwether (1853–55). When Messervy decided to leave the business, Kingsbury and Webb formed a new partnership.

Messervy continued to advise Kingsbury from afar, and it was through their family connections and lengthy correspondence that we learn about Kate's health and other personal details. Messervy was solicitous yet direct in both personal and business matters, as revealed in his correspondence with Kingsbury. His letters have a strong patriarchal tone, censuring Kate for what he sees as her failures as a wife and an upstanding Christian woman and criticizing her self-pity over her own illness and the unspecified deformity and illness of her only child. The letters Kingsbury wrote during his time in Santa Fe focus on the business climate and the difficulties he encountered in placing and receiving orders. His letters also express warm fraternal feelings for both Webb and Messervy. As Kate's condition worsened, Kingsbury's letters reflect his fears and his hopes, his frustration and his devotion.

Kingsbury and Webb returned to New England in the fall of 1853, both determined to find wives. They each married before the end of the year, and they kept up their correspondence, which was sometimes playful and sometimes serious as they tried to reassure each other of their continued success in the Santa Fe business. When Webb visited the Messervys in Salem in early October 1853, he wrote a long letter to Kingsbury, who was on a supply trip to St. Louis, mentioning that he had seen the "original" Kate, depicted in the photo John carried. William Messervy wrote to Webb as well, urging him to convince Kingsbury to resume his courtship of Kate and also to buy out Messervy's share of the Santa Fe business. Messervy was anxious to return to Salem and rejoin his own family. Kate's family described her as a genteel and fragile beauty, very devoted to her mother and sister in Salem. Kingsbury and Kate seemed uncertain about marrying, though it is not clear whether this was due to her illness, her family in Salem, or the dangers of living in New Mexico—all of which are mentioned in correspondence between Kingsbury and Webb. Webb writes:

> I spent but a short time in Salem, and had but little time to see the *gals*, but made the most of my time in talking with, and looking at, the original of the picture you value so highly. I talked much of New Mexico, and much of her going out there

provided you desired her to do so. I think she would go, but her sister and Mrs. Messervy have the greatest horror of that country, and the strongest attachments to home of any two persons I ever met. I told her (as I really thought and still think) she ought by all means to go there in preference to remaining in this country, even with pecuniary prospects equal. Her health is very delicate and I can but believe that the trip and a residence of a few years in that country would establish her health upon a strong constitution. I told her of the proposals I had made you and Mr. Messervy, that I was willing to take you in an equal partner, whether we continued the business, or he should withdraw from the concern. This I desire to do.[17]

On December 21, 1853, John Kingsbury and Kate Messervy were married in Salem. They honeymooned in New York, where they met up with James Webb and his new wife, Florilla "Lillie" Mansfield Slade.[18] Webb and Kingsbury used their respective honeymoons to buy supplies for the Santa Fe trade. They bought cloth and clothing, shoes and boots, alcohol, and hardware and sought markets to receive beaver pelts, wool, and minerals from New Mexico.

At the end of February 1854, there still seemed to be some question about when Webb and Kingsbury and their wives would return to New Mexico. Writing from Santa Fe, William Messervy chided his new brother-in-law for taking so long to make up his mind about his business offer and to decide whether Kate and her sister Eliza Ann would accompany him to New Mexico. He scolded his partners for their indecision, but he was also clearly pleased that they were returning to the West and that Kate was getting better:

> I was much pleased to learn that you and Kate had so fine a wedding and that Kate's health is improving. I have no doubt she will experience great benefit from her trip to this country, that is if she comes. I am most anxious about my sisters and am completely in the dark to know even where to write to them. You have managed this thing very badly. You should have made up your minds either to stay or come as long as the first of January....
>
> If my sisters are with you I must depend upon you and Mr. Webb to do the best you can to promote their comfort. Give Eliza Ann, if she is with you, all she wants. It is too late now for me to make arrangements....
>
> I wish you and Webb would think a little about what you are going to do when you get out here. You both remind me of two boys who have found birds' nests and think the whole world is in them. Would it not be well to give a thought as to where you are to live when you get out here—or do you intend to tumble in here with the whole crowd who come in at the same time with you.[19]

The surviving correspondence says little about the trip the two newly married couples made together on the Santa Fe Trail. None of the correspondence between Kate and Lillie has been preserved, leaving us with only the men's observations about their travels and Kate's health. Webb wrote to Kingsbury on March 7, 1854, urging him to set a date to begin the journey west, noting that they would need three weeks in Independence to gather the goods they had bought in New York, Philadelphia, and St. Louis. They began their journey in mid-March, and at the end of that month Messervy urged Webb to exercise caution, as bands of Jicarilla Apaches and Utahs (Utes) had increased their attacks on wagon trains and the US Army. Messervy wrote about a furious attack by Jicarilla Apaches on US troops near Taos. He described it as a massacre in which thirty-five of the sixty members of Company II of the dragoons were killed and seventeen injured. This is clearly based on an early report of the Battle of Cieneguilla, which took place on March 30, 1854. The battle led to a military tribunal at which the official report of Lieutenant John W. Davidson was accepted. That report was refuted, however, by participants in the battle. Historians now characterize Davidson's report as a cover-up for the loss of command, poor planning, and poor troop discipline.[20]

Messervy likely harbored some anxiety about the rescue of a woman recently ransomed from the Comanches. As secretary of the New Mexico Territory, Messervy either knew the details firsthand or had read news reports about the experiences of Jane Adeline Wilson. She had been rescued from the Comanches on the plains of Texas by a party of New Mexican and Pueblo Indian traders known as *comancheros* and brought to Santa Fe, where she related her harrowing story in December 1853.[21] Webb and Kingsbury likely learned about this rescue and the taking of other captives from news sources, but they were already in transit and sending goods ahead for consolidation in St. Louis.

Webb and Kingsbury shipped their items by rail from New York to Pittsburgh; from there, their goods continued on to St. Louis on the steamship *Granite State*. On April 11 the two men were in St. Louis, where they purchased wholesale groceries from Glasgow Brothers. They bought boxes of soaps, candies, condiments, cordage, sugar, tobacco, and whiskey, totaling just over $2,100. On April 17 they purchased an assortment of plates, glass lamp chimneys and globes, canisters, and housewares from E. A. & S. R. Filley on Main Street in St. Louis; that same day they also purchased a few chairs and tables, a camp bedstead, bolsters, cotton batting, pillows, and mattresses. Some of the items they no doubt used on the trail to make comfortable camps; others were likely intended to furnish their new homes in Santa Fe.[22] At the end of April, Messervy was anxiously awaiting the reunion with his partners and his sister. He wrote to Kingsbury that he would "give a dollar an hour if you and Webb were only here—it would take a great load off my shoulders."[23] The two couples arrived in Santa Fe in June 1854 to begin their new life.

The Santa Fe Experience

As the Webbs and Kingsburys established themselves in Santa Fe, William Messervy withdrew from business and politics. He resigned as secretary of the New Mexico Territory in July 1854 and sold his house, fronting Santa Fe Plaza and across from the Exchange Hotel, to the Webbs and Kingsburys.[24] Messervy returned to Salem but stayed in touch with both couples.

Santa Fe did not impress those who arrived in the nineteenth century. In his memoir of the time he spent there, W.W. H. Davis gives a detailed description of the architecture and settlement patterns, as well as the history and customs of the people. He muses that had the crossing of the thousand-mile trail not been so strenuous, the first sight of Santa Fe might have sent some travelers back to the East. Given that *El Gringo* was published in 1857, at the height of American claims on New Mexico and the Far West, it is a fairly well-crafted rendering of the Spanish and Mexican history of the area. Davis can be florid and fanciful, such as when he compares the adobe architecture in Santa Fe to "its namesake and prototype Timbuctoo."[25]

Webb, Messervy, Kingsbury, and Davis entered New Mexico as it was transitioning from military occupation to its new status as an administrative territory of the United States. They were joined by Bishop Jean Baptiste Lamy, who brought a French Catholic perspective and style to the church—a notable departure from centuries-old Hispanic practices and local traditions.

In the 1850s Santa Fe and the New Mexico Territory were divided by political allegiances, religious and family alignments, and feuds. It was a time of rising disagreements among the new territorial governing authorities, who had little experience with or understanding of local customs, politicians, and political processes. The military and the growing Euro-American population differed over how to deal with raids by nomadic Native groups. There was insufficient funding for the government, and the imposition of a new language, laws, and norms on the New Mexican population made solving problems difficult.

US Army surgeon Samuel G. DeCamp had established a hospital in an old adobe building north and west of Santa Fe's Palace of the Governors during the initial occupation in 1846. He also commandeered the hot springs near Las Vegas, New Mexico, to treat soldiers, teamsters, and citizens alike.

Reports from the front indicated that the hospital was kept in good order by the post doctor, nurses, and stewards, and it served the military and the community until 1875. Sanitary conditions in town were a concern to the post doctor, however, as "all manner" of refuse was left to pollute the soil and the air. Sometimes the only supplies available to deal with disease and injuries were soap and hot water, along with extra rations of food for the sick and wounded.[26] Merchants had the hard cash, but the territorial governors had to issue warrants to get them to support the new government.[27] The solvency of the territorial government and the stress it put on merchants are recurring themes in the Kingsbury and Webb correspondence. Their letters are filled with political intrigue and business details.

Davis became a trusted friend to the Webbs and Kingsburys. Kate and Lillie charmed him, especially that first summer when they brought him a heart-shaped cake.[28] Both women were pregnant, although none of the letters mentions their condition, given the mid-nineteenth century's limited discussion of pregnancy. Lillie Webb gave birth to a son on December 22, 1854, and Kate's son George was born in January 1855. What should have been a joyous event for the Kingsburys was not, although John's letter to his brother-in-law on the subject was evidently destroyed. On March 13 William responded to John's letter of February 1, 1855, and assured him that he had burned the earlier letter informing him of the birth of the Kingsburys' son, who was deformed in some way and might not survive. Messervy promised not to tell anyone about the birth of the child and offered counsel based on his own experience with a child who was not "perfect." He wrote that should the child survive, he was sure Kate and John would love him and, in their Christian kindness, provide whatever extra care was needed.[29] Kate's despair only deepened when the Webbs left Santa Fe in September 1855. By the next month, Kingsbury was concerned that Kate's health and stamina were being adversely affected by caring for their sick child.[30] He wrote of his concerns to his brother-in-law, and Messervy responded with a rather stern rebuke directed at his sister:

> She is the last person who ought to complain, and she should accept the condition of her little boy cheerfully and without a murmur. God placed him into your and her charge for a good and wise purpose, & it is her duty as a woman, as a mother & as a Christian to cheerfully—affectionately & pleasantly—without a murmur—to cherish & be proud of it—had it been my child, it would never have me an hours unhappiness. My rule is—"What we can't cure—we should cheerfully endure." Tell Kate, that as hard as she thinks her lot is—that there are but few who have been as highly blessed as herself.[31]

The news from Santa Fe in the winter of 1856 was not good: the market was very slow, and Indian raids had increased. At the end of April 1856, Kingsbury decided to send Kate and their son George to New England for the summer. They traveled with Davis as far as New York, where William met them and accompanied them to Salem, arriving on June 15, 1856. Kate must have been delighted to be reunited with her family, but that happiness would be short-lived. George died on July 29 of a gastrointestinal infection. John had already headed east to join them in Salem, and Davis was traveling in the opposite direction back to Santa Fe. He gave Kingsbury the news of his child's death at the middle crossing of the Arkansas River near Cimarron, Kansas.[32] John hastened to Massachusetts without finishing his buying and business negotiations in St. Louis. When he reached Kate in Salem, she was grieving and her health had worsened. He wrote to Webb in October 1856, expressing his own grief and pledging to return Kate to Santa Fe:

> I found Kate as my letters had indicated very sick. She is on her feet & able to move about the house but that is all. Her cough is very troublesome and has got a strong hold on her. I have had a long consultation with her physician but could get no encouragement from him. He thinks her lungs are past cure. All that remains for me is to get her back again to Santa Fe if possible.[33]

A Beautiful Death on the Santa Fe Trail

Kate and John moved into the Messervy homestead in Salem for the winter of 1856–57. Her sister Eliza Ann was with them, as well as one of their New Mexicans servants, Facunda. John wrote to Webb in Santa Fe and suggested that Lillie, who was in Connecticut, should visit, as it would cheer Kate, who was now often confined to bed. Kingsbury's letters vacillate between hope and despair. In November he wrote to Webb that Kate could not live long, but it was too soon to say whether she could withstand the trip to New Mexico. Messervy wrote to Webb at the same time, expressing doubt that Kate would ever return to Santa Fe. As the year ended, Kingsbury wrote to Webb, providing a long summation of Kate's condition and alternating between hope for her recovery and fear that she would die:

> Kate's health I am sorry to say, . . . is certainly no better. Her cough is still very troublesome, and in addition she is now confined to her bed with Rheumatism, this however, we hope is nothing permanent and may soon be relieved—but it is very unfortunate as it deprived her the privilege of taking fresh air, which is quite

important in keeping up her appetite—In losing her appetite she will of course lose what little strength she had gained. I felt at times quite encouraged, but now do not know what to hope for. I fear every change, & look with dread for the next. It is now two weeks since she was out, she is in as good spirits as can be expected, the weather is pleasant & cold for this season of the year, the cold does not appear to affect her unpleasantly.[34]

By January 1857, Kingsbury was determined to take Kate back to Santa Fe. Perhaps, given the prognosis of her doctors, he believed it was her only chance for recovery. The critical state of his wife's health was wearing John down, and he wrote Webb a long and emotional appraisal of the situation and his own anguish, as well as his worry about the business:

> Since my last letter the weather has been very changeable, extreme cold and then warm, which has been very trying for Katy. The last week she was again compelled to take to her bed, suffering severe pain in the chest and side—something like *pleurisy*. She is now just sitting up again. It has reduced her strength much. I have no encouragement from her Doctor or anyone else. She has already lived beyond their expectations. I am satisfied there is little hope for her here. I may be deseived [*sic*] but I cannot give up the hope that she may be able to start [the trip west] with me. The time is fast approaching and still it looks very dark. My mind is so harassed with anxiety for her that I am almost beside myself. I hope I shall have strength to do my duty. The disease is very flattering, and so far has been slow, and I think in spite of all opposition it will be a case of long & protracted termination. Her friends think different. They say if we start she will never reach St. Louis. If she remains there is but little hope of her getting through the summer. What am I to do? She is willing to start & wants to leave here, is very unwilling for me to leave her only for a single night. It is a very hard and trying case for me. I feel very anxious to go out with the goods and relieve you and still intend too [*sic*], but it may prove otherwise, a week's time may prostrate her so as to put it beyond a doubt and show me plainly what course to pursue. You may rest assured that I will not encroach upon your indulgence more than the necessities of the case will warrant.[35]

By mid-March, John, Kate, her sister Eliza Ann, and Facunda were all on their way to New Mexico. Messervy was with them in New York, and even he was hopeful that Kate would make it back to Santa Fe.[36]

They reached Westport Landing, on the Missouri River just north of Kansas City, Missouri, at the end of April but were delayed there by the lack of grass and the difficulty and expense of finding mules for their wagons. Kingsbury estimated that eight hundred wagons would reach Santa Fe as soon as grass was available. He had little choice but to use oxen to pull his wagons, and although those animals might be less likely to attract Indian raids, he was concerned that the slow pace would delay Kate's arrival in Santa Fe, where she could get the fresh air and rest she needed.[37] In separate correspondence, Messervy and Webb shared their fear that Kate would not make it to Santa Fe. Messervy asked Webb to see that Eliza Ann was well taken care of and safely returned to Salem should Kate die on the trail.[38]

As they approached the lower crossing of the Arkansas River east of Dodge City, Kansas, Kate's condition took a ruinous turn. Her breathing was labored, and she slipped into delirium, marking the last stage of consumption. Kate died there on June 5, 1857. Kingsbury had prepared for this eventuality, as he had packed a metal coffin in one of the wagons. John, Eliza Ann, and their close friends Mr. and Mrs. Tom Bowler accompanied Kate's body to Santa Fe, covering the 375 miles in a record eleven days. Her obituary described her last night:

> Mrs. Kingsbury was at no time improved in health on the whole route . . . she urged her husband and sister to take all care and preserve in trying to save her and then just after midnight she seem[ed] to realize the end was close.
>
> She said, "is it possible that I have come this far on my way and must now take leave of you all?" She then commended with perfect composure, and took leave of her sister and John. She wished to assure them that the course they had pursued was in every respect to her satisfaction, and asked forgiveness for every hasty expression, or unkind word that had passed her lips during her illness, her every wish had been complied with, and everything in the power of man had been done to promote her comfort.
>
> "And now," said she, "if my Heavenly Father has sent for me, I am ready to go. I leave myself in His hands, having the fullest confidence in His justice and mercy. Don't regret, or grieve over the step you have taken. I have taken leave of everything behind; I have got everything with me." "Oh," said she, "I am very tired and now let me go to sleep."
>
> Eliza Ann says that the whole scene of that night was the most overwhelmingly sublime that she has ever witnessed or imagined, transcending the power of man to describe. Not a cloud in the sky—not a breath of air swept over the plain—not a sound of man, beast or fowl to break the stillness of the night—all nature seemed hushed and subdued to silence by the sublimity of the scene. The moon shone in her most dazzling splendor, and the majesty and power of God seemed to pervade all nature. At 6 o'clock, all was over. . . .
>
> She died in the peaceful knowledge that her husband had made all the proper

arrangements for her body, and indeed he had. He pulled from one of the trains a crate labeled "private stores" and in it was a metallic coffin. Mrs. Bowler and Facunda laid out the body and by 9 o'clock they had completed their duties.[39]

Despite everyone's best efforts, Kate Kingsbury did not make it across the Santa Fe Trail a third time; she had reached the end of her endurance. Kate's obituary, based on her sister's account of those last hours, tells of a beautiful death under a moonlit sky, attended by the careful ministrations of family and friends. In keeping with her devout Christian beliefs, Kate had "resigned herself to the care of the Lord, and bid adieu to this world," trusting that heaven with all its glories awaited her.[40] She was laid to rest at the end of the Santa Fe Trail, beneath a headstone honoring her memory. John's instructions regarding the headstone were precise, although he hedged a little on Kate's age, making her a few years younger than records document (figure 4.3). It was to be a "neat white marble gravestone, with a base stone to set it in, [and] small footstone."[41] The inscription, in "distinct letters," was to read:

Mrs. Kate L. Kingsbury
Died June 5th, 1857
at the crossing of Arkansas River
Aged 30 years.
Blessed are the Dead which die in the Lord.

What John had envisioned as Kate's *final* resting place was not to be. She was buried in the Masons and Odd Fellows Cemetery, north of town and near the foot of the hill where Fort Marcy was located. However, in 1884 the cemetery was moved to a new location, southwest of town. Kate's remains were exhumed and her headstone was evidently moved to the new location sometime between 1890 and 1904, according to research by Alysia L. Abbott. Unfortunately, the portion of the cemetery where Kate now lies is unkempt, and the stone is deteriorating. It is not the eternal, beautiful rest John wanted for her.[42] John remained in Santa Fe until May 1861, when he finally sold the business and properties. He returned to Boston and resumed his life as a bookkeeper and accountant. He died in Roxbury, Massachusetts, on August 21, 1907.[43]

John Kingsbury brought Kate to Santa Fe in hopes that the climate of New Mexico would heal her, but he knew the odds were against it and her health was unlikely to be restored by geography alone. He was also motivated by his need to get back to New Mexico to attend to business, and he did not want to leave Kate behind any more than she wanted to stay in Massachusetts without

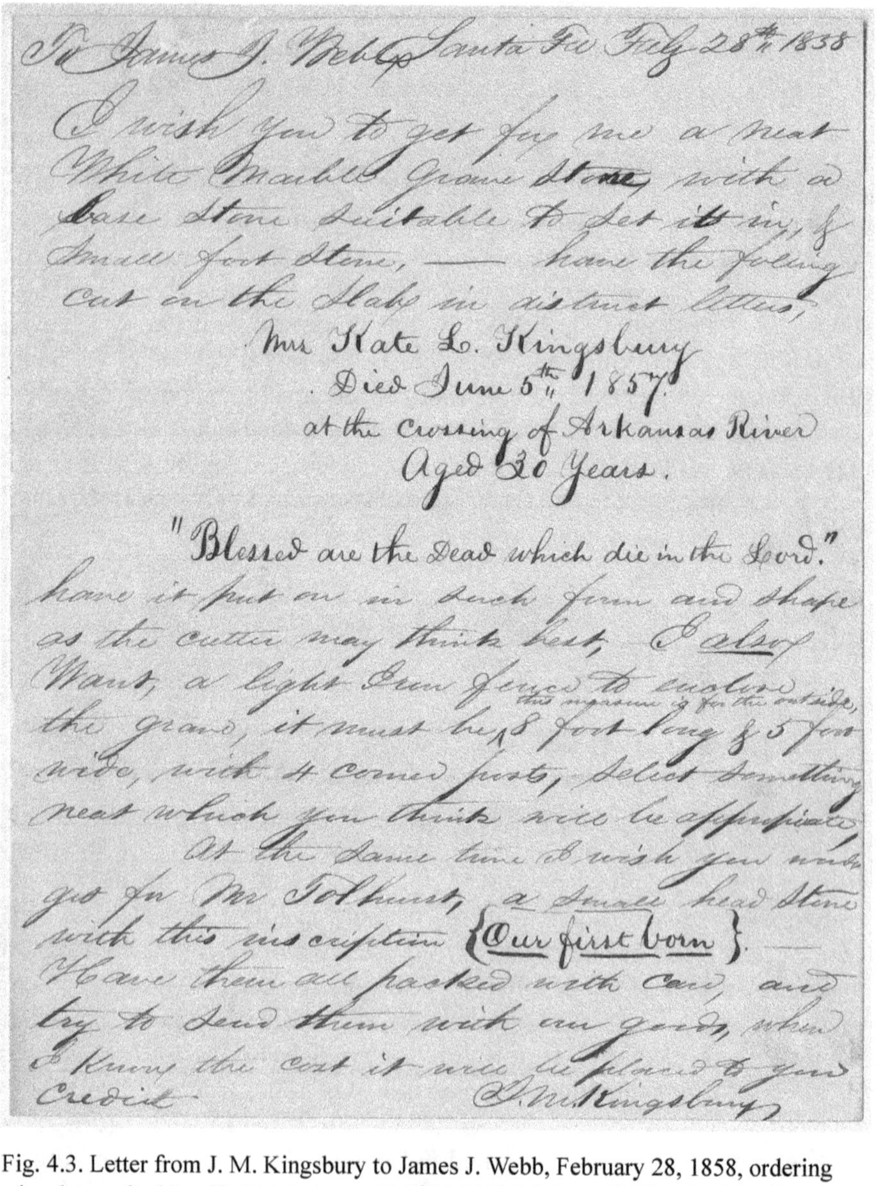

> To James J. Webb   Santa Fe Feby 28th 1858
>
> I wish you to get for me a neat White Marble Grave Stone with a base stone suitable to set it in, & small foot stone, — have the following cut on the slab in distinct letters,
>
>   Mrs Kate L. Kingsbury
>   Died June 5th, 1857.
>   at the Crossing of Arkansas River
>   Aged 20 Years.
>
> "Blessed are the Dead which die in the Lord." have it put on in such form and shape as the cutter may think best, I also want a light Iron fence to enclose the grave, it must be 8 foot long & 5 feet wide, with 4 corner posts, Select something neat which you think will be appropriate. At the same time I wish you would get for Mr Tolhurst, a small head stone with this inscription {Our first born}. — Have them all packed with care, and try to send them with our goods, when I know the cost it will be placed to your credit —
>
>   J. M. Kingsbury

Fig. 4.3. Letter from J. M. Kingsbury to James J. Webb, February 28, 1858, ordering a headstone for his wife Kate's grave. (A1724-00033, Missouri Historical Society, St. Louis)

Fig. 4.4. Gravestone of Kate Kingsbury, Odd Fellows Cemetery, Santa Fe, 2023. (Photo by Joy L. Poole)

her husband. The tensions of these deliberations are apparent in Kingsbury's correspondence with Webb and Messervy.

It is striking that the nineteenth-century medical protocols for treating tuberculosis prescribed rigorous physical activity and exposure to the elements. Men were likely to engage in these activities in trail caravans, but women of Kate's class and upbringing were not. Perhaps her doctors and her well-meaning family assumed that riding in a wagon in the open air would be enough to ameliorate her condition. But did they give any thought to the medical care available in New Mexico? Army doctors were certainly stationed at some of the forts along the Santa Fe Trail and at Fort Marcy in Santa Fe, but Kate would not have had the same type of medical care available in the East. Conversely, in the East she would not have had the benefits of the salubrious New Mexico climate. In making the decision to move Kate back to New Mexico, John may have realized that she would not be cured, but at least they would be together when she died. At the end stage of the disease, there was really very little health care professionals could offer her.

John did everything he could to make Kate comfortable and ensure a beautiful end to her suffering. Her sister and an attendant were there to serve her on the trail. Anticipating the worst, he brought a metal casket in the caravan and later ordered a fine tombstone engraved with a loving farewell (figure 4.4). He could not have known that the grave site he envisioned for her would not be her final resting place. At the end of 2021, Alysia Abbott reported in a short article the archaeological discovery of a metal casket, an associated coffin, and some human remains at the location of the cemetery. While this is not definitively Kate Kingsbury, it raises the question of where her final resting place might be. Once again, we are invited to query the fate of those who traveled the Santa Fe Trail seeking health, only to be claimed by death.

The impact of health seekers on New Mexico's history was enormous. It is hard to estimate how many travelers came to New Mexico in the mid-nineteenth century chasing a cure offered by the warm sun, dry climate, and high altitude. In the second half of the nineteenth century, with the advent of the railroad, health seekers steadily increased the population of New Mexico. An increase in trained medical personnel gave rise to industries focused on health and wellness, which brought even more Euro-Americans to the Southwest. The irony is that the increase in both residents and visitors meant increased exposure to tuberculosis among Hispanic and Native American health care and domestic workers. In the late nineteenth century the Bureau of Immigration touted New Mexico as a haven for those seeking health and wellness, and that reputation endures. Health seekers, in many ways, represented a new wave of conquest, arriving with their own ideas about health and their relationship to the land, to the Indigenous populations, and to one another. Some settled in New Mexico, while others stayed only as long as it took for their health to improve.[44]

5

Unequal Companions
African American Women on the Santa Fe Trail

Mexican independence not only opened trade between New Mexico and Missouri; more importantly, it guaranteed three fundamental rights to Mexican citizens: that Mexico would be politically autonomous from Spain, that Catholicism would be the country's religion, and that citizens of the new republic would have social equality. Social equality would, in essence, abolish the intricate *casta* system that classified people into a racial and social hierarchy based on their perceived quantum of blood.

This chapter traces the status of African Americans in the Southwest, with particular attention to how people of color were represented in the literature of the Santa Fe Trail. Black women and men played prominent roles in support of the trade, beyond the domestic spheres in which they are most frequently mentioned. The relationship between well-known trail diarist Susan Shelby Magoffin and her enslaved servant Jane highlights the unequal positions of power of this trail-traveling pair.

African American Women in New Spain and New Mexico

People of African descent were always a small proportion of the population of Mexico and New Mexico, but they were a prominent part of the historical narrative from the moment of first contact. In July 1539 the Black Moor Esteban, an enslaved member of the first non-Native expedition traveling north from Mexico, entered the Zuni pueblos in what is now west-central New Mexico. Esteban's arrival in advance of the *entrada* (entrance) of Fray Marcos de Niza and his party marks a major moment in Black history in Spain's North American possessions. It is also an event shrouded in stereotypes and race-based interpretations of Black men as lascivious or violent. Some sources depict Esteban as a swaggering Black man whose lustful behavior led to his murder by Zuni residents. In more nuanced interpretations, his entrance into the pueblo disrupted a ceremonial cycle, resulting in his killing.

Despite that inauspicious beginning, Black men and women remained part of colonial New Mexico, marrying into Spanish, Mexican, and Indigenous families and residing in their respective communities. Dedra McDonald traces the vacillations in Spanish law that characterized the rights of and prohibitions against people of African and mixed ancestry in the sixteenth and seventeenth centuries in New Spain.[1] Colonial decrees and laws limited Blacks to endogamous unions, required them to attend church, prescribed where they could live, and even prohibited Black women from wearing gold, pearls, and silk. By the end of the sixteenth century, Blacks, mestizos, and mulattos were required to pay tribute, indicating that the population was growing through more widespread intimate relations between Blacks and Indigenous peoples, as well as among the diverse mixed races (*castas*).

Enslaved Black men and women were part of the colonization enterprises that settled New Mexico in the late sixteenth and early seventeenth centuries. Among the colonists who accompanied Juan de Oñate to the first Spanish settlement was Francisco de Sosa Peñalosa, who brought three enslaved Black women and one enslaved mulatto man with him, as well as other servants of both genders who were *castas*. In 1600 Juan Guerra de Resa's retinue included several soldiers who brought presumably enslaved mulatto women and children with them. Isabel de Olvera, who came to New Mexico with the Guerrra de Resa party, demanded that the alcalde of Querétaro certify that she was a freeborn woman so that she could prove her status if she was threatened or challenged.[2]

Several enslaved African and mulatto women and men were brought north to the Spanish governor's home in Santa Fe from 1659 to 1662—a particularly rancorous time in New Mexico. In the summer of 1662 New Mexico governor Bernardo López de Mendizábal and his wife, Doña Teresa Aguilera y Roche, were among a small group of citizens arrested by local officials of the Holy Office of the Inquisition and charged with secretly practicing outlawed Jewish religious rituals. Inquisition officials in Santa Fe made an inventory of Doña Teresa's property at the time of her arrest. In addition to clothing and household items, the inventory listed a *mulatilla* named Clara, "who appeared to be 39 years old," and a *mulatillo* named Diego, a laborer aged seven or eight. Both had papers showing that they were enslaved.[3]

The evidence against the governor and his wife was supplied by clergy, neighbors, and their household staff living in the small, isolated Spanish colony in Santa Fe. The couple was transported down the Camino Real to the Inquisition prison in Mexico City. Doña Teresa met several times with her inquisitors before she was informed of the charges against her. On October 26, 1663, fourteen months after her arrest in the palace, the inquisitors presented forty-one articles containing the accusations against her, based on the testimony of twenty-six persons who were not identified to her. In addition to failing to attend to or fulfill various requirements to participate in church services, she was accused of bathing and changing clothes and linens on Friday nights—a possible sign of Jewish practices—and reading books in other languages and laughing over their contents. If she was found guilty of the charges, she faced torture or even death. In addition to condemning her for behaviors and habits that might be Jewish rituals, her neighbors and servants condemned her for her education, her worldly manner, and her personal hygiene.

The governor died in prison before he could testify in his own defense, but Doña Teresa was incarcerated for twenty months and testified more than a dozen times before being released with no verdict—she was neither convicted nor cleared. Doña Teresa's testimony revealed the depth of her distrust of the Black, mulatto, mestizo, and Native women who served in her household. She wrote to the court denouncing an unnamed enslaved Black woman, saying, "in case she should have testified, she is our enemy because she is a slave, as they all are enemies of their masters; and besides I punished her frequently for her insolence and idle chatter, carelessness and negligence and also gluttony." She also accused this slave of kissing another enslaved women and feigning pregnancy to avoid work. Clara and Diego attended Doña Teresa during her stay in prison, no doubt adding to the tensions between them. Doña Teresa ultimately sued the Inquisition, and several years after her death, the beneficiaries of her estate received compensation, and her confiscated property was returned.[4]

Blacks, mulattos, and other *castas* in New Mexico continued to serve New Mexican households and established intimate relationships among the Pueblo communities. Spanish authorities suspected several Black and mixed-race men of sowing the dissent that led to the Pueblo Revolt of 1680. The intimate alliances that allowed Blacks and mulattos to live with and have partners among the Pueblo and Hispanic communities also allowed them to unite in resisting the enslavement, taxation, and oppressive labor practices that led to rebellion against church and state in New Mexico.[5]

A series of eighteenth-century paintings produced in Mexico illustrates the complexity and some of the cultural stereotypes surrounding racial differences and social class. *Casta* paintings, produced by and for elite audiences, depicted the various social settings and racial characteristics of the *castas*. The paintings carried visual messages of the inherent disadvantages of intimate unions with the lower classes, particularly Black women. Paintings of Black and mulatto women showed them clothed in coarse fabrics or even rags, laboring in workshops or simple camp kitchens, or apparently engaged in fights with their partners. In contrast, those with a greater quantity of Spanish blood were shown in rooms decorated with European furnishings, clothed in fine embroidered fabrics and lace, and enjoying time with their partners and children in refined domestic settings.[6]

The application of *casta* terms varied from location to location in New Spain. In some places, more than fifty different terms were used to denote the blood quantum of mixed-race offspring. In the northern frontier of Mexico, the number of classifications was generally lower. The most complete colonial census of New Mexico was compiled in 1790.[7] An analysis of that document as well as sacramental records shows the different ways African ancestry was recorded and imprecisely tracked. In the El Paso area, which was then part of New Mexico, those of mixed African and Indigenous heritage might be referred to as *mulatto*, *coyote*, or *castizo*. Records in Santa Fe used the term *color quebrado*, which indicates, rather imprecisely, "broken color," or a person of mixed and indeterminate ancestry. As the eighteenth century ended, people of African descent were living in the villas or formal settlements of El Paso, Albuquerque, and Santa Fe, as well as in Pueblo Indian communities. However, they were not always enumerated with precision.

In his written report to the Spanish court in 1812, Pedro Bautista Pino asserted that New Mexico was unique among the Spanish provinces in having no African *castas* among its population. This was not true, but it demonstrated a European elitist, racist point of view that ignored centuries of intercultural encounters and the place of mestizos, Blacks, mulattos, and other *castas* in the history of northern Mexico and New Mexico. Pino's erasure of African descendants in New Mexico aspired to maintain the fiction of pure Spanish blood—*limpieza de sangre*. He was surely trying to impress the Spanish authorities by claiming that New Mexico had maintained the ideal of Spanish racial purity even on the far northern frontier.[8]

Laws promulgated soon after Mexican independence did not free enslaved people but took measured steps to end the importation of slaves. One law required owners to pay slaves and permit them to buy their freedom. Another law emancipated the offspring of enslaved mothers when the children reached age fourteen. Mexico's new government was split by factions and hampered by inadequate funding throughout the 1820s. But the ban on importing slaves stood, and in September 1829 slavery was abolished in Mexico.[9] As the Santa

Fe trade opened in Missouri, enslaved people who might have been protected in Mexico were impressed or joined westward trains. The question of whether the vast Mexican cession—the territories that eventually became the states of New Mexico, Arizona, Utah, Nevada, and California—would be slaveholding or free was a subtext through the mid to late nineteenth century.

No autobiography or detailed biography of an enslaved woman or free woman of color has been found in the vast trail literature. Acknowledgment of their presence is limited to brief mentions in texts and footnotes. Yet they were definitely there, intertwined in the lives and experiences of other men and women who traveled the trail, performing essential labor in camp and domestic life. Encounters with enslaved people were not rare, but they were often ignored or erased from narrators' stories as new landscapes and the more "exotic" cultures and customs of Native American and some Hispanic people captured their attention and were recorded in verbal and visual sketches.

African Americans—men as well as women—became more prevalent in the literature of the Santa Fe Trail after 1846 and the US takeover of the West. If we extend consideration of the trail to its beginning on the wharves and riverboats of the Mississippi and Missouri Rivers, African American men and women are more apparent. The men were wharf hands and haulers, wagon drivers and freighters, wranglers and livestock tenders, cooks and camp servants. African American women were laundresses, cooks, nannies, nurses, and household servants (figure 5.1). In some journals and ledgers of western military forts, African American women are recalled for their essential work, and even those brief references illustrate their role in the settlement of the West, despite the lack of recognition that may have typified their lives and times. In some communities located at strategic crossings and camps along trails, African American entrepreneurs built, supplied, and serviced wagon trains at trailheads. Hiram Young and his wife Matilda established a carpentry business in Independence, Missouri, in 1850. By the 1860s, the business had grown substantially, employing fifty to sixty men building wagons and yokes. At the time of his death in 1882, Young's estate was owed substantial sums for crops, cattle, and wagons appropriated by the US Army during the Civil War. Unfortunately, after a series of hearings, the case was dismissed in 1907, and the family received no compensation.[10]

Perhaps trail travelers were so accustomed to seeing Black men and women engaged in hard labor and domestic work that their presence on the trail did not constitute a special circumstance. The casual mention and dismissal of African American men and women in the literature of the trail are common, demonstrating the unexamined assumptions about African Americans in the history of this country. Two narratives written by enslaved women

Fig. 5.1. Aunt Sukey, circa 1860, identified as the eldest enslaved woman owned by the family of Robert B. Smith in Lafayette County, Missouri. (N25315, Missouri Historical Society, St. Louis)

who worked at least part of their lives as domestics in St. Louis illustrate the burdens and the cruelty they endured, as well as the arduous paths they pursued to secure their freedom. Elizabeth Keckley (1818–1907) and Lucy Ann Delany (1830–90) did not follow the Santa Fe Trail, but both left remarkable autobiographies of their experiences as enslaved girls and women and their almost unfathomable fortitude. Both persevered and obtained their freedom and, in some ways, prospered.[11] Where appropriate, I use these autobiographies to provide some insight into other women's experiences that were glossed over or reported only from the perspectives of their owners and, in some cases, their tormentors. Elizabeth Keckley's and Lucy Ann Delany's extraordinary lives and the documentation of their road to freedom stand in marked contrast to the lives of other women associated with the Santa Fe Trail who were brought to New Mexico as enslaved household and child-care workers.

Simply Jane

Susan Shelby Magoffin's 1846–47 journal is one of the best-known accounts of a woman's crossing of the trail. It contains several entries describing the experiences linking her and her enslaved maid Jane, whose presence might otherwise have been omitted from that moment in history. Jane accompanied Susan for much of the historic journey, but they were always unequal companions. Susan records some of their experiences together as the two women traveled with the advance parties of the US Army that conquered Mexico. Susan is conscious—even self-consciously appreciative—of her role as the wife of a prominent trader. But how Jane felt is seldom noted, except when her behavior is an affront to Susan's privilege and position. At some point, Jane is no longer mentioned in Susan's diary, and it is unclear whether she has been sold or Susan is just too preoccupied with her own fears and ill health to mention her. The biographical facts about Jane—her full name, where she was born, her family circumstances, and how she came to travel the Santa Fe Trail—are elusive. Everything we know about her comes from Susan's journal entries.

Susan Magoffin was the eighteen-year-old bride of Santa Fe Trail trader Samuel Magoffin (figure 5.2). Her marriage took her close to the front lines of a nascent war. Samuel's brother James was an experienced trader on the trail and is often credited for negotiating with—or accused of bribing—New Mexico governor Antonio Armijo to surrender New Mexico to the United States.

Fig. 5.2. Portrait of Susan Shelby Magoffin (1827–55) taken in St. Louis circa 1852–55. (N12846, Missouri Historical Society, St. Louis)

Susan's journal might have been dismissed as the romantic writings of a love-stricken bride had it not been for the circumstances under which it was written and the diligence of its editor, Stella Drumm.[12] Drumm has been called "an editor on a mission." At times she overpowers Susan's voice with "an avalanche of annotation," observes historian Virginia Scharff in a critical review of the editor's intentions.[13]

Drumm's annotations intentionally direct the reader away from Susan's diary to focus on the historic moment when Susan just happened to be present at the forced union of two nations. Drumm identifies the people and places Magoffin encountered on her journey. She links the people named in the journal to one another, tracing their genealogical and professional relationships, and she never misses the opportunity to insert commanding officers' orders to place Susan's journal in the context of the official conquest of the West. She situates Susan's journey in the gravitas of the times, not letting the young woman's alternating fear and frivolity or her self-conscious observations overshadow the objective of that fateful caravan of conquerors. Scharff notes that Drumm's focus on connecting webs of affinity and kinship and her detours into military history are invented historiographic traditions meant to set conquest in a national hagiography. It was Drumm's way of instilling authority into a work that had a distinctly feminine voice.

The trail took Susan Magoffin from the world she knew as the daughter of a wealthy, slave-owning family on a Kentucky plantation to unknown terrain—what Scharff aptly calls "suspect terrain": Mexico in 1846, when the United States was marching to the drumbeat of Manifest Destiny. Susan refers to herself as "the first American lady to cross the Plains." Howard Lamar's foreword to the republished diary is more precise, noting that she was likely "the first American white woman" to make such a memorable frontier journey.[14] Since 1926, when the diary was first published, other women's diaries and letters have shown that Magoffin was neither the first American woman nor the first white woman to cross the plains. Her diary, however, is the only known record of the events of the summer of 1846 by a woman who entered the Southwest within weeks of the Army of the West. At least two other women traveling with traders accompanied the caravan, and they too may have had servants who escaped the historical record. Eliza Michaud Leitensdorfer traveled from St. Louis with her husband, Thomas, and her sister-in-law Solidad Abreu, wife of Dr. Eugene Leitensdorfer. They joined the caravan in Independence at the same time as the Magoffins.[15]

Susan Magoffin matured quickly during the tense journey. She shifted her perspective from awestruck and naïve to more reflective as she came to comprehend the caravan's precarious situation. She was open to the freedom and experiences of the trail—climbing to the high points to take in the vast vistas and learning Spanish words, songs, and foodways. She was scandalized by the low necklines and ankle-baring fashions worn by the women in New Mexico and appalled by their makeup and cigarette smoking, but she found their hospitality and their curiosity about her entertaining. Susan turned philosophical as well, wondering why men went to war. She sometimes questioned her faith; at other times, she found solace in that same faith as she contemplated death from yellow fever or the swirling conspiracies that accompanied the US Army's entrance into northern Mexico. She was, at times, demure, even diffident, when she attracted attention—stares and whispers—because of her clothes and her mere presence in New Mexican villages. Her journal also illustrates her privileged position and her indifference to Jane's feelings, such as when she alludes to beating as the only way to deal with her slave's disobedience and drinking. Did she ever consider how fearful Jane might be as they advanced toward the front lines of the war in Mexico? Her opinions about the place of servants, her demeaning remarks, and her observations about Native American and Hispanic people bring us back to the journal and its author, rather than the meanings Drumm imposed on Magoffin's text.

Susan's shifting relationship with Jane seems to parallel the increasing tensions as the caravan moved closer and closer to the war in southern New Mexico. Susan's reaction to the many people of other cultures she met on the trail reflects the arrogance of Manifest Destiny. Susan describes the impressive retinue in which she traveled and often marvels at the comfort of her honeymoon lodgings on the trail. The Magoffins traveled with fourteen freight wagons, each drawn by six yokes of oxen; one baggage wagon with two yokes of oxen; one Dearborn wagon with two mules that carried Jane; Samuel and Susan's carriage with two mules; and two men on mules driving the loose stock, consisting of about two hundred oxen and several horses and mules. In all, they were accompanied by twenty men, three "tent servants" Susan describes as Mexicans, Jane, and Susan's dog Ring. She provides no information about Jane—neither her age nor her physical appearance. Even Susan realized that her surroundings and situation were extravagant, noting, "It is the life of a wandering princess, mine. When I do not wish to get out myself to pick flowers the Mexican servants riding on mules busy themselves picking them for me."[16]

The caravan traveling with the Magoffins totaled some forty-five wagons organized in three or four different camps—a virtual village. Susan describes it as "a strange compound of Americans, Mexicans, and negroes, horses, mules, and oxen."[17] Jane served many functions in this traveling community, if not always with the obedience Susan desired. Jane was Susan's companion and guardian on their walks and explorations, her servant, and her nurse when Susan was ill; she provided Susan with refuge in the literal storms they encountered on the trail between Independence and Bent's Fort. In a companionable moment, they made their way down the steep bank of Cottonwood Creek and Susan declared, "Women are venturesome creatures." Susan described snakes, mosquitos, and other bugs as "the only disagreeable parts of prairie life." Jane warned Susan when the mosquitos were especially vexing, but perhaps in a foreshadowing of her defiant attitude, she observed that if Susan kept her mouth closed, the mosquitoes would not fly in. When the Magoffins' wagon was irretrievably broken, Susan rode in Jane's carriage, and when the Magoffins' tent collapsed under a torrent of rain, Susan wrote

Fig. 5.3. Sepia ambrotype of H. E. Hayward (1857–1933) being held by his family's enslaved nurse Louisa, circa 1858. African American girls and young women often cared for the children of their owners. (N21596, Missouri Historical Society, St. Louis)

that Jane cheerfully welcomed her into her own bed.[18] But this good relationship would not bear up under the mounting tensions of the quickening war or the changes that came when they entered New Mexico and the road south to Mexico.

Throughout the month of July 1846, Susan was ill. On Thursday, July 30, her nineteenth birthday, she was particularly annoyed by the noise at Bent's Fort, the gambling, and the disagreements among the servants. She wrote: "José, our principal Mexican about the camp, and my maid Jane, have had a cat and dog difficulty, he says he can't stand it and she puts on airs, does her business when and how she pleases, leaving a part of it for *me* to do, and here we have it."[19] She did not write in her journal again until August 6, when she used dramatic and atypically direct language to describe her despair over miscarrying her first child. Susan compared her situation to the ease with which the Native woman in the room below gave birth and then walked to the river half an hour later to wash herself and the baby. She found this to be a "heathenish custom."[20] Had the Magoffins' child lived, no doubt child care would have been added to Jane's duties (figure 5.3).

They left Bent's Fort on August 7. Traveling became more difficult because of both the terrain and the increasingly worrisome news about the army's progress in securing New Mexico. Susan reported little about Jane's duties or fears during the next month as they traveled slowly west toward New Mexico.

Occupying Mexico and Losing Track of Jane

The Magoffins arrived in Santa Fe at the end of August 1846, two weeks after Brigadier General Stephen Watts Kearny read the act of possession in the plaza in Las Vegas, New Mexico, seizing all Mexican territory for the United States. The occupation and annexation of Mexico were part of the goal of Manifest Destiny—the right and inevitability of US expansion across the continent (figure 5.4). As Kearny read the act of possession, Antoine Robidoux translated it to the assembled crowds. Kearny made it clear that the United States would not harm any property—"not a pepper, nor an onion"— belonging to those who pledged their loyalty to the United States. But anyone who threatened sedition would be hanged.

In Santa Fe, the Magoffins were housed near the church, north of the plaza. All along the trail, Susan had practiced her Spanish, learning the names of objects and flowers, but she also learned to command the cooperation and compliance, if not the respect, of the Mexican servants:

> I've been teaching one of the Mexican servants his business how he is to do it, &c, and though we have considered him one of the numbskulls, I have found him both willing and apt in learning. The great virtue of these servants is their

ever pleasant faces; they never begin their work sullenly, and you may change it as often as you please or make them do it over, and over, and they continue in the same good humour, never mouthing and grumbling because they have too much to do, but remain perfectly submissive, and indeed it is a pleasure, when an underling is so faithful, to do them any little favour.[21]

While in Santa Fe, the Magoffins enjoyed the company of General Kearny, his fellow officers, elite Hispanic merchant families, and other local people. Susan found a group of female friends, visiting again with the Leitensdorfers, and her Hispanic neighbors called on her. "What a polite people these Mexicans are," she noted, "altho' they are looked upon as a half barbarous set by the generality of people."[22] She was amused by, if sometimes judgmental about, the local mores and fashions, including the pasty white, rouge-streaked makeup New Mexican women used.

Susan Magoffin describes in detail the dance she attended on September 23, 1846, in the Palace of the Governors. She records seeing "Doña Tules" there, with her false teeth and false hair but an imposing presence nonetheless. This was María Gertrudes Barceló, the flamboyant Santa Fe card dealer who controlled much of the gambling and the cash circulating in Santa Fe at the time of the American takeover. Susan describes her as a "stately dame of a certain age, the possessor of a portion of that shrewd sense and fascinating manner necessary to allure the wayward, inexperienced youth to the hall of final ruin."[23]

On October 5, 1846, the Magoffins left Santa Fe, following the army south. Susan had no regrets about leaving, although she had enjoyed having a home for several months. They made slow progress south and often stopped for weeks at a time while they received updates on the battles the American troops were fighting with Mexican forces. Samuel tried to sell the goods they had brought with them, but he was preoccupied with the fate of his brother James, who was traveling ahead with the troops south of the Rio Grande. William, Samuel's other brother, joined them in a house near San Gabriel, north of El Paso. Susan's troubles with Jane worsened, and by mid-December, they reached a pitch. Susan was suffering from a fever, and only the quinine pills prescribed by an army doctor seemed to help her. On December 16 she wrote in her diary: "Nothing hurts me more than to have a cross, ill-tempered servant about me. Jane is in a pet this morning [as she] has a little more work to do than usual." Jane talked back so rudely that Susan left the kitchen, telling herself that the best way to "treat the insolence is to rise above it, until such point that the rod is needed to correct the errant behavior."[24] Jane was drinking—Susan caught her dipping into a keg of brandy—and Susan hesitated

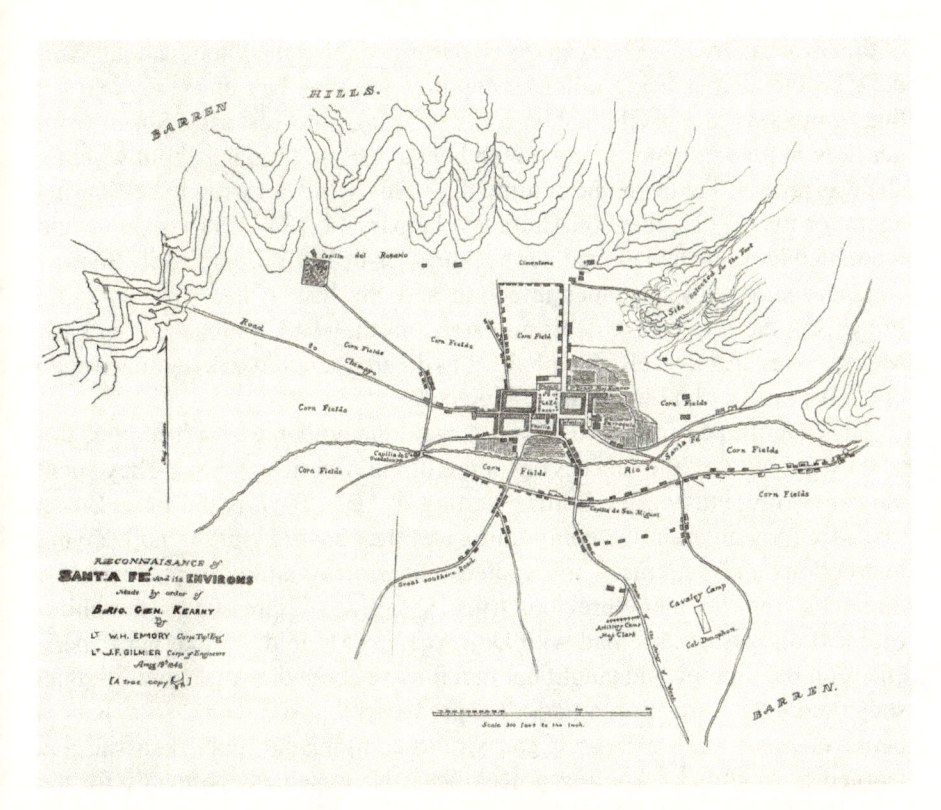

Fig. 5.4. Reconnaissance of Santa Fe and its environs by Lieutenants W. H. Emory and J. F. Gilmer, Corps of Topographical Engineers, August 19, 1846, as ordered by Brigadier General Kearny. (Historic Santa Fe Foundation, Santa Fe, NM)

to tell Samuel about this infraction, knowing that it was her place to train and discipline the domestic help—including her authority to beat Jane with impunity. Susan's diary records previous instances when she disciplined the domestic staff when they failed to meet her standards. In the South, where Susan was raised, women held their house slaves to exacting standards with threats of violence. Southern women may have been taught to be demure in the presence of men—the patriarchs of their homes and plantations—but they were also expected to manage their house slaves and demand their compliance.[25] This entry is the last reference to Jane in the diary. Did they leave her in San Gabriel? Did they sell her? We have no way of knowing what happened to her.

Susan's journal for the month of December 1846 is filled with anxious entries as they awaited word from El Paso about the location and intentions of the Mexican troops. She is anxious to learn whether the rumors about Samuel's brother James being killed or captured are true. Not until they learned that James was safe in Chihuahua could the Magoffins rest easy. Susan spent her time in prayer, making peace with her savior and thinking about whether she was prepared to die in the coming days. Susan did not write in her journal again for two weeks; then, on Thursday, January 14, 1847, she caught up and recounted how she had nursed her sick brother-in-law William while Samuel was also sick with a bladder infection and she herself had a fever. Little Francisco, the boy whose debts and freedom they had "purchased" in New Mexico, was sick as well. She pledged to do all she could to keep the orphan boy alive and not let him perish of neglect.[26]

The Magoffin outfit inched its way toward the border, where it stopped until they got word of the success or failure of the American troops. They spent almost two months on the border waiting to hear. To pass the time, Susan visited with women in the community, and they shared knitting and sewing instructions and patterns. They visited with Don Agapito, an old friend of Samuel's from his many previous trips. Susan was impressed by the philosophical discussions she had with Don Agapito. He told her that her experiences on the journey had taught her much more about the world and life than she could ever learn from a book. He predicted that she would soon have a better understanding of herself and would comprehend more than she had learned from all her schooling in Kentucky. He expressed sympathy for the troubles, dangers, and difficulties they had already faced and were yet to face before their journey ended.[27]

Don Agapito's words were prophetic. The Magoffins' worries mounted as they received conflicting reports about James's safety. Susan pondered her fate, wondering whether she would ever see her Kentucky family again. "Friends" warned that they were likely to be seized by Mexican loyalists or the Mexican army and murdered because they were Americans, and all their stores would be pillaged and their wagons burned. Samuel expressed anxiety about having brought Susan on the crossing. Finally, on March 10, 1847, they received word that the US Army was in possession of Chihuahua, and they made their way across the border. Susan's journal then became sporadic, and she notes that too much is happening for her to record it all. Their trials were not over, however. Susan contracted yellow fever and suffered the loss of a second child, a son.

On September 8, 1847, the Magoffins began the steamship passage from Camargo, Mexico, back to the United States. They stopped in New Orleans and then made their way back to Lexington, Kentucky, where their son James Wiley was born in 1849 and their daughter Jane, who inherited her mother's diary, was born in 1851. The family relocated to Kirkwood, Missouri, now part of the Greater St. Louis area, in 1852, where Samuel prospered in several businesses. Susan died at her home on October 26, 1855, soon after giving birth to another daughter. She was only twenty-seven years old. What became of her enslaved servant Jane is unknown, but at least for a time, her life was recorded in Susan Magoffin's journal, an important reference on a woman's life—in fact, two women's lives—on the Santa Fe Trail.

Charlotte Green at Bent's Fort

During the time the Magoffin party spent at Bent's Fort, Jane may have encountered another Black woman living there.[28] "Black Charlotte," the cook at Bent's Fort, was mentioned casually by several Santa Fe Trail travelers. She lived at the fort with her husband, Dick Green, and his brother Andrew. All three had been slaves of the Bent family in Missouri. Bent's Fort was not a US military fort; it was a trading post and supply point for Santa Fe Trail caravans. Four Bent brothers—William and Charles, who were experienced mountain men, and their teenage brothers George and Robert—set up the trading post in what is now southern Colorado in 1828. They located their first enterprise, called Fort William, along the Arkansas River within the winter hunting range of Cheyenne, Arapaho, Ute, Comanche, and Kiowa bands. By the time the post was completed in 1832, the Bents had established a major trading empire on the plains. William Bent married a Cheyenne woman named Owl Woman, and thanks to their extended kinship and trade relationships, the Bents held a decided advantage over trade in both directions on the trail.[29] The Bents navigated the social milieu of St. Louis, where they were raised, and the tribal networks that made their business possible. Their diplomacy allowed them to operate on the edges of competition among New Mexican, French American, and Euro-American interests. Bent's Fort was truly a crucible of frontier enterprise.

At Bent's Fort, Charlotte was allegedly as famous for her flapjacks and pumpkin pie as she was for her dancing. She was one of the few Black women named in any travelers' descriptions of the fort.[30] Some authors identify her as the person who cared for Kit Carson's daughters after the death of their mother Waa-nibe, although historian Marc Simmons labels this a "dogged legend" and suggests that this task probably fell to women of Waa-nibe's family and tribe.[31] This legend may persist because Charlotte is one of the few women, along with the wives of the Bent brothers and Carson himself, who are known by name. Charlotte's role in presiding over the kitchen at Bent's Fort was an important responsibility. Susan Magoffin mentions that there were several boarders at

Bent's Fort when they arrived in July 1846, noting that they dined at the fort and were comfortable in their quarters, but she makes no mention of the people who prepared their meals.[32]

How long Charlotte Green remained at the fort is not known with certainty. She may have been there since the Bent brothers established their first trading post at Fort William in 1832 or 1833. She was certainly there in 1835, when she is credited with serving a sumptuous meal to Colonel Henry Dodge, and she may have still been the cook in 1839, when *New Orleans Picayune* reporter Matthew C. Field told his readers about the hospitality the Bent brothers provided to trail travelers in their expansive and comfortable settlement.[33] Charlotte apparently remained there until sometime in 1847. The most extensive interaction between Charlotte and a Santa Fe Trail traveler was recorded by seventeen-year-old Lewis Garrard, who spent a portion of 1846 and 1847 seeking adventure on the trails, in the camps, and in the company of mountain men. Garrard's classic adventure narrative captures the colorful patois and lifestyle of the mountain men. He reached Bent's Fort after enduring a cold, snowy ride in late November 1846:

> My own, unenviable thoughts occupied me through the solitary day; and only when Paint was turned in the corral behind the fort to chew dry hay, and myself with numbed fingers, gradually thawing in the long, low dining room, drinking hot coffee, eating bread and butter and "State doins," and listening to Charlotte, the glib-tongued, sable fort cook retailing her stock of news and surmises, did I feel entirely free to throw off care.[34]

Charlotte, he notes, was one of the only "female, woman" at the fort, according to one Missouri teamster. Garrard himself calls her a "culinary divinity," and he acknowledges her as one of the Bent's Fort employees who made travelers comfortable. Garrard also describes the nightly dances at the fort and Charlotte's grace and presence on the dance floor, where she and a woman of French and Indian descent, the wife of the fort's carpenter, led the dancing:

> They nightly were led to the floor "to trip the light fantastic toe," swung rudely and gently in mazes of the contra dance, but such a medley of steps is seldom seen out of the mountains—the halting, irregular march of the war dance, the slipping gallopade, the boisterous pitching of the Missouri backwoodsman and the more nice gyrations of the Frenchmen—for all, irrespective of rank, age and *color*, went pellmell into the excitement. . . . It was a most complete democratic demonstration. And then the airs assumed by the fair ones—more particularly

Charlotte, who took pattern from real life in the States; she acted her part to perfection. The grand center of attraction, the belle of the evening, she treated the suitors for the "pleasure of the next set" with becoming ease and suavity of manner. She knew her worth, and managed; accordingly, and when the favored gallant stood by her side waiting for the rudely scraped tune from a screaking violin, satisfaction, joy, and triumph over his rivals were pictured on his radiant face.[35]

Garrard was at Bent's Fort again in the spring of 1847 as he made his way back home to Cincinnati. There he met English traveler George Augustus Frederick Ruxton, whose publications about his travels among the tribes and mountain men of the West include only a short description of Bent's Fort. Ruxton's writings are vivid, if not florid, depictions of the lives of mountain men.[36] He also describes the conditions of women taken in Native American raids on New Mexican settlements and traded among Native peoples and sometimes acquired by American and French mountain men. He marvels at the capacity of Native American women to work and the way that captives—men and women, Hispanic people, and African Americans—were degraded by their captivity and enslavement.

According to William Gwaltney's research on African Americans on the Santa Fe Trail, the Bent family gave Dick and Charlotte Green their freedom in 1847, in recognition of Dick's heroic acts defending the Americans during the battles leading up to the siege of Taos, when Governor Charles Bent was killed by men resisting the US takeover of New Mexico.[37] Garrard specifically recalls that he encountered the Greens in the company of the Bent and St. Vrain wagon train—and Charlotte's warm smile of recognition—on May 23, 1847, as he was making his way east.[38] The remaining years of the Greens' lives are not easily traced. Dick Green was severely wounded in the battle at Embudo, New Mexico, on January 29, 1847.[39] Many of the Missouri volunteers returned to Missouri at the end of their service in the spring and summer of 1847. Perhaps the Greens were on their way back to St. Louis as free people of color when Garrard saw them for the last time, though they are not listed in freedom suits or in census records. Perhaps Charlotte is the Charlotte Green who appears in the June 1870 census of Charette Township, located in the heart of a German settlement in Warren County, Missouri. That Charlotte Green is identified as a Black domestic servant, age sixty, and born in Virginia. She was living on the family farm of Alfred and Alvina Hart and their six children. If this is the same woman, she would have been in her thirties when she lived at Bent's Fort and commanded the kitchen, the dance floor, and the respect of travelers who recalled her attentive hospitality.

CHAPTER 5

More Cooks, Laundresses, and Domestic Workers on the Trail

The kitchen at Bent's Fort was a hub of activity long after Charlotte left, but trail travelers seldom mention the names of the domestic workers there. Catherine Cary Bowen, who signed letters to her parents in Maine with her nickname Katie, traveled from Fort Leavenworth, Kansas, to Fort Union, New Mexico, in the summer of 1851. Her husband, Captain Isaac Bowen, was appointed to the commissary office of the Ninth Military Department at Fort Union. Katie's letters record the couple's sixty days on the Santa Fe Trail. In her effort to render a "faithful account" of their travels, she details their living arrangements, crediting Isaac with providing a well-appointed camp, and records her reactions to the new landscapes and Native peoples she met. When her Irish maid Mary left them in Fort Leavenworth to marry a soldier there, she casually mentions buying a young Black servant named Margaret, whose mother was a free woman in Louisville. Katie states that they intended to return the girl to her mother when they left New Mexico.[40] The Bowens enjoyed their time at Fort Union, but Margaret's reactions to the post, where she presumably met other Black residents, is not part of the record. Two years later, the Bowens were transferred to Albuquerque and then to New Orleans in 1858, where they both died of yellow fever, along with one of their children. Margaret's story seems to begin and end with her purchase. Did the Bowens return Margaret to New Mexico, as they intended? On that promise, the record is silent.

James Ross Larkin, who traveled the trail from Westport, Missouri, in a caravan with William Bent a decade after the Magoffins, devoted several pages of his journal to a description of Bent's Fort. He arrived at the fort on October 13, 1856, after several days of hard travel in the rain. He noted the Cheyenne and Kiowa camp near the fort and the use of dressed hides as a medium of exchange between the fort traders and the Native peoples. The fort had fifteen rooms arranged around a central courtyard, including storerooms, sleeping quarters, a kitchen, and a dining room. Larkin, from a wealthy St. Louis family, was in poor health when he decided to travel the Santa Fe Trail in the hope that a western journey might help. After spending several days at the fort, he described his reaction to the situation there: "I was rather homesick & gloomy after arriving here—not fancying the state of affairs, mode of living, condition of society &c, but as I could not well better it, I managed to keep in a tolerable humour. . . . The fare is very plain—generally Dried Buffalo Meat boiled with Mexican corn, Coffee, Sugar, Biscuit & Butter—nothing very dangerous in that for dyspeptics."[41] He says nothing about who prepared and served his food or who kept his quarters. He spent most of his time observing how Native people lived and interacted with the fort's traders. If there were Black domestic workers or wranglers at the fort, they either escaped his notice or were not mentioned in his journal.

After the establishment of military posts in the West, Black buffalo soldiers of the Ninth and Tenth US Cavalry were stationed at many of the forts that protected Santa Fe Trail travelers. Several examples illustrate the dismissive reporting about the presence of Black women serving as domestic workers at these posts. Hezekiah Brake documents his 1858–59 trip from St. Louis, up the Missouri River to Independence, and across the plains to a ranch near Fort Union, New Mexico, where he worked as a dairyman. Brake does not name the "old Negress" who gave him roasted coffee, cakes, pickles, and sauerkraut to sustain him on his journey. Historian Marc Simmons identifies her as Sarah or "Aunt Sally Taylor," who was employed by Missouri trader Seth Hays in Council Grove, Kansas. How many thousands of other trail travelers enjoyed the food and hospitality provided by Aunt Sally and failed to notice or mention her?[42]

Other people traveled the trail with African American servants, sometimes for weeks, yet never mentioned their names. Ernestine Franke, an immigrant from Thuringia, Germany, left a short memoir of her 1864 crossing of the Santa Fe Trail. Ernestine met and married Franz Huning on March 5, 1864, in St. Louis. A month later, they left St. Louis for New Mexico. While they honeymooned on the trail in the spring of 1864, they enjoyed excellent cuisine served on china at a proper table and were entertained by the fortune-telling offered by the camp's "colored" cook, but Ernestine does not name the woman.[43] Although Ernestine's crossing occurred during the Civil War, she was preoccupied not by the war but by the potential for Indian attacks. On May 22 they passed Cedar Springs, Oklahoma, just short of the New Mexico border. Ernestine recorded that a wagon train had been attacked in the area by Indians the day before, but Franz's recollection was that Texans had committed the assault.[44] Huning, who would become one of the most prosperous Santa Fe Trail merchants in Albuquerque, made regular trips between New Mexico, Kansas City, and St. Louis.

Huning's crossing from St. Louis to Santa Fe in September 1867 was etched in his memory by the massacre of Ernestine's mother and younger brother on the trail. Huning met his mother-in-law and her son in Dayton, Ohio. From there, they took the train to Junction City, Kansas, where they joined the five wagons Huning had sent ahead with supplies for his New Mexico stores. Although there was some danger of an attack on such a small party, Huning was experienced and believed he could make it to Fort Zarah near Great Bend, Kansas, where he assumed he could engage troops to protect the party or join a larger group making a September crossing. As they left the fort, Huning recalled, they met a military expedition led by General Winfield Scott Hancock and cavalry commanded by General George Armstrong Custer, who was beginning a campaign against the Cheyenne and Kiowa after the bloody conflicts of the summer of 1867. Although the pageantry of the troops may have been impressive, it did not ensure Huning's party a peaceful crossing. According to Huning's memoir of the event, written in 1894 when he was sixty-seven years old, he was bitter about the soldiers' failure to provide protection and an escort for his wagons.[45]

At Plum Buttes near Chase, Kansas, a party of Cheyenne, Arapaho, and Kiowa attacked the small wagon train. Huning recalls that two wagons from the fort passed him as he made his way west but refused to help because their only job was to protect the settlements. Even long after the incident, Huning was angry when he recalled that the troops were transporting "Negro wenches" for a day of plum picking.[46] Captain Charles Christy, a civilian scout at Fort Zarah, wrote his memoir in 1908, some forty-one years after the event.[47] Christy and another civilian he identifies as a Mexican named Roma were the only people Huning found at the fort, where he went to seek assistance after the attack. Christy and Roma arrived at the scene of the massacre, where they witnessed the horror of wounded people, mutilated bodies, and strewn possessions. They gathered the wounded and the dead, enduring their own battle as they headed back to the fort. Christy drove the ambulance wagon while Roma exchanged fire with the "dog soldiers," or renegade members of various tribes, responsible for the attack.

Ernestine's mother and brother eventually died from their wounds, and Huning was left to share the details with his wife. He wrote to her on September 10, 12, and 13—about the attack, about the wounds suffered by her mother and brother, about an unnamed American woman who cared for them as they lingered between life and death, and about their burial at the fort. His letter dated September 13 at 6:00 a.m. reads in part: "Dear Ernestine, console yourself if you can. I cannot say 'do not cry' because I am crying too, but do not give up entirely to your sorrow. Since we have to give up the love of the departed, we will love all the more those who are left to us."[48]

In the aftermath of the Civil War, one of the most dangerous expanses of the continent was the region crossed by the Santa Fe Trail. Huning could not have chosen a more volatile time to attempt a crossing. The summer of 1867 saw an intensification of Native American and American hostilities. The US military was unable to defend merchant wagons, and the annuities meant to sustain the fragile peace with tribal nations were inadequate to meet the needs of Native peoples, whose lands and resources were being encroached on by a growing number of American settlers. The main branches of the Santa Fe Trail crossed country that was heavily in debt, still bitterly partisan, and unable to articulate a consistent policy for dealing with Native peoples. In August 1867 a congressional Indian Peace Commission met in St. Louis and concluded that the solution to the hostilities was to remove the Indians and establish reservations far from the trails and expanding rail lines. At the time of Huning's crossing, neither the military nor the tribal groups were inclined to compromise, and the small number of troops in the forts along the trail were unable to provide adequate defense and protection. Huning's memoir expresses his bitterness at the peace commissioners drinking beer at the fort rather than offering protection to his family. The Treaty of Medicine Lodge, signed with bands of the Comanche, Kiowa, Kiowa-Apache, Cheyenne, and Arapahoe in October 1867, would ultimately move the majority of the tribes away from the Santa Fe Trail.[49] The buffalo soldiers of the Tenth Cavalry were inadequate to garrison the several forts in Kansas. These troops suffered their own casualties from attacks on the forts and inadequate provisioning.[50] In any telling of the story, the army's refusal or inability to escort the wagons, Huning's attempt to cross this stretch of the Arkansas River with no protection, and the brutal killing of members of his party make this an unforgettable event in the history of the trail. It highlights the inadequate strength of the forces charged with protecting the heart of the nation and the unreasonable expectations of what they could do.

Seven months before this tragic event, sixteen-year-old José Librado Gurulé crossed from New Mexico to Kansas City as a trail hand in José Leandro Perea's outfit. (Perea, a prominent merchant and trader in sheep and wool, sent his sons to St. Louis University in the 1860s and 1870s.) Perea's trail bosses recruited several men and boys from Las Placitas, a mountain village east of Bernalillo, for the 1867 caravan. More than seventy years after this crossing, Gurulé dictated his oral history of that memorable time. His mind was still sharp as he described the clothing they wore, the eighteen-hour days spent running alongside wagons, and the meals that consisted of only an onion wrapped in a tortilla. The ten wagons they loaded for the crossing to *Los Estados* (the States) were carrying wool to the mills and markets served by the wharves of Kansas City and St. Louis. In Las Vegas, New Mexico, they joined other outfits until their caravan totaled about four hundred wagons. Gurulé recalled seeing people of different races and cultures along the trail in Kansas and Missouri—"Indian" men, women, and children near their crossing of the Arkansas River; a "Negro" minstrel band in Kansas City; and the Black women and soldiers at Fort Hays, Kansas, although he provided no details about the work they did or how he interacted with them.[51]

The Perea party spent three months on the trail and then made a quick turnaround, their wagons now loaded with copper kettles, hardware, and kitchenware. Gurulé was impressed by the endurance of the Black men hired to load their wagons. In addition, each member of the Perea wagon train had been outfitted with new clothes and shoes. Their westbound journey was beset with illness, as cholera claimed more than half the men in the Perea caravan. Gurulé recalled that the only treatment available was rest and corn whiskey. When they returned to New Mexico after eleven months, he was paid $8. At the dance celebrating their return, he displayed his store-bought suit of worsted wool. His memories of the sights, sounds, and people remained vivid long after the trip was over.

Historian Darlis Miller explored the roles of women on frontier military posts, where they were laundresses, domestics, foragers, cooks, and prostitutes. Black women are listed in military records as serving in domestic positions and were often held in low regard by post commanders. Black soldiers saw these women as necessary but a source of trouble as well. According to fort records, Black women were employed and brought to New Mexico by families of soldiers and officers who crossed the trail to serve at the outlier posts.[52] Although Miller tells the history of several women who lived on posts in New Mexico, one is particularly poignant and relevant to the issues women still face today. Emma Becks, a laundress, and Margaret Berry, a domestic servant, lived at Fort Union, the supply depot and active military post serving the Santa Fe Trail in northeastern New Mexico. They were among the sixty-two women living at or near the fort in the 1870s who served in various domestic roles.

Emma Becks died at Fort Union in 1879. She had been born in Georgia and was thirty-five years old at the time of her death. She was unmarried and was the domestic servant of assistant surgeon Carlos Carvallo. She had worked as an officer's servant for eight years and had been quartered along with other Black laundresses on the east side of the fort, adjacent to the jail and north of the hospital. An autopsy showed that her death was caused by a bungled abortion. Margaret Berry, another Black woman employed as a hospital matron at the post, testified that Emma had taken a mixture of "wild tansy steeped in whiskey" possibly mixed with borax, a powerful cleaning agent. She had also inserted a sharp needle or other instrument, puncturing the wall of her vagina and leading to blood loss and infection. Berry said Emma had done the same thing to abort another pregnancy the previous June. Surgeon Carvallo suspected Berry of being an accessory, and this was confirmed by her son-in-law, who claimed Berry had performed abortions on his wife "every time he made her pregnant." The man who impregnated Emma was never identified, nor was there any explanation of why Carvallo initially suspected Berry of being the abortionist.

Berry was accused of stealing Emma's clothing and causing disruptions in the laundresses' quarters and was expelled from Fort Union.[53]

Abortion was widespread among all classes of women in the nineteenth century. Among those in the lower economic classes, it was usually performed by a female family member or friend, not by a doctor. For many women, this was the only form of birth control available. Emma died, and Margaret was expelled from the fort. Did the soldier or officer who impregnated Emma bear any responsibility? Did he feel remorse for her death? Did he face the consequences of his actions? On these moral questions, the historical record is silent.

Race, Ethnicity, and Expansion of the American West

The years from 1846 to the late 1860s saw the last generation of heavy travel on the Santa Fe Trail. Merchants had opened the trail earlier, and the military presence on the trail advanced the American conquest of the West, tying St. Louis and the rest of Missouri to Santa Fe and beyond. The traffic on the trail did its part to both connect and divide the continent. Merchants transported goods from both ends of the trail to markets on the opposite end. Military expansion led to the advance of American settlement, and that growth led to the displacement of Native peoples. African American domestic workers and soldiers were part of the US conquest. They accounted for much of the workforce that packed and carried the loads and tended the households of the advancing frontier. New Mexico and the Far West were not the promised land for Black people. The population of Blacks and mulattos in New Mexico totaled thirty-nine in 1850 (twenty-three men and sixteen women) and more than doubled to eighty-five in 1860 (adding twenty-five men and twenty-one women). But Blacks would continue to endure discrimination and prejudice in New Mexico. In 1857 the territorial government restricted the movement of Blacks, confining them to areas where they already resided, largely on military posts. The question of which states carved out of the Mexican cession would remain free and which would be slaveholding persisted in the period following their annexation and complicated their admission to the Union. California entered as a free state in 1850, but New Mexico and Arizona would not enter until 1912, by which time the issue of slavery had long been decided by the Civil War.

George Ruxton's *Adventures in Mexico*, published in 1849, called on the United States to acknowledge the inhumanity of slavery and the practices of prejudice. He implored all his readers to speak out for abolition, knowing that the defenders of slavery were immovable:

> I feel that everyone, however humble, should raise his voice in condemnation of that disgraceful and inhuman institution, which in a civilized country and an enlightened age, condemns to a social death, and degrades (by law) to the level of the beasts of the field, our fellow men, subjecting them to a moral as well as physical slavery, and removing from them every possible advantage of intellectual culture or education, by which they might attain any position a grade higher than they now possess—the human beasts of burden of inhuman masters.[54]

Ruxton knew that his pleas would go unheeded and that the country would one day be convulsed by rebellion. He would not have been surprised by the Civil War, and maybe not even by the civil rights movement a century later. But what would he say today? Likely he would reiterate what he said in 1849 about the prejudice that accompanied slavery: "the plague spot remains; the foul cancer is eating its way, and only by its extirpation can the body it disfigures regain its healthfulness and beauty, and take its place in the scale of humanity and civilization."[55] The task of finding the names of those individuals enslaved as packers, freighters, and domestic workers is just beginning. There is so much more research to do to identify the African American women and men who participated in the settlement of the Southwest and the West and tell their stories. Those stories reside in the ledgers, correspondence, and court records of freedom suits and in the journals of life on military posts. African American history is found in the names and experiences of communities, graveyards, and churches; it is found in the family histories and local histories that constitute all our history.

6

The End of the Trail

From Commerce to Conquest

In the mid-nineteenth century the Santa Fe Trail shifted in strategic importance from a commercial road to a route of conquest after the United States declared war on Mexico. For President James K. Polk, the proximate cause was the alleged incursion of Mexican troops on lands claimed by Texas. By an extension of political reasoning, an attack on Texas was an assault against US interests. The justification was weak, but the US desire for continental expansion was strong. In the summer of 1846 the United States seized northern Mexico, which became the Southwest and Far West of the expanding nation. New Mexico was incorporated into the Ninth Military Department of the United States, headquartered in Missouri. The Mexican-American War generated profound changes for Mexican and New Mexican communities. Mexican citizens occupying this newly claimed American territory lost their political identity, their right to elect their own political representatives, and in some cases their lands and economic enterprises. Women lost rights as American property laws eclipsed the Spanish and Mexican recognition of women's right to own separate and inheritable property. In these years, the Santa Fe Trail crossed a socially volatile country. The Mexican-American War increased racism and discrimination against Mexican and Native peoples who were displaced by the expansion of American hegemony.

The route and tempo of the American conquest were documented in a series of letters penned from the front by Richard Smith Elliott, writing under the name John Brown. His letters were sent to the editors of the *Reveille* (figure 6.1), published in St. Louis, the point of origin for the majority of troops serving in this unjust war.[1] Elliott's letters began with the marshaling of volunteers in St. Louis in response to the patriotic fervor that overtook Missouri after President Polk declared war on Mexico on May 13, 1846. In a few short weeks,

Fig. 6.1. Masthead from the *St. Louis Weekly Reveille*, which carried news from the advancing Army of the West. Richard Smith Elliott, writing under the pen name John Brown, reflected on the war's effect on New Mexican citizens. (From the collections of the St. Louis Mercantile Library, University of Missouri–St. Louis)

one hundred volunteers called the Laclede Rangers, under the leadership of St. Louis lawyer Thomas Hudson and with Elliott himself as the first lieutenant, began marching to rally at Fort Leavenworth with Colonel Stephen Watts Kearny. A volunteer artillery company of German-speaking immigrants from St. Louis was organized under the command of Woldermar Fischer; they were known as Company B, Missouri Light Artillery Battalion. Company A, St. Louis Horse Artillery, was organized under the command of Richard Hanson Weightman.[2]

The Laclede Rangers left St. Louis on June 6 carrying a silk flag made by the women of the city but leaving behind the ceremonial swords the women had also presented to them. They traveled up the Missouri River on the steamboat *Pride of the West* to Fort Leavenworth, where they gathered with the assembling Army of the West and spent two weeks preparing for army life. On June 29 they began marching toward Santa Fe, with a stop at Bent's Fort. In all, Missouri would send more than 1,650 men to join the main corps of the Army of the West. Elliott was much impressed by Kearny's professional demeanor as he surveyed troops made up of volunteers from all walks of life. Elliott reported on July 29 that Kearny maintained his even disposition despite the untrained men under his command.[3]

In a dispatch to the *Reveille* written two days later, Elliott was pleased to report that some of the traders had their wives with them—women being a rare presence on the march west. Bent's Fort offered the Army of the West not only supplies and a strategic stopping place but also, Elliott noted, some indulgences and distractions to keep their minds off the seriousness of their mission:

> I understand that some of the traders' wives are up at Bent's Fort—I have heard the names of Mrs. Leitendoffer [sic] (or Magoffin, I forget which) mentioned as one of them. Not having yet been at the fort, I have not seen a lady since I left the borders of the State of Missouri. I believe the last ones I saw were two very pretty daughters of an Indian chief—a Shawnee—who visited our camp, near the State line, on the 1st of July, with the very innocent and enticing object of selling a bucket of sour milk, and a handkerchief of onions, which tended badly, I regret to say, to take off the romance of our interview with them. I have also been informed that they have ice at the Fort, and have been indulging in mint juleps, made with brown sugar and Taos whisky,—but men *will* indulge in luxuries occasionally. They also have had one or two balls up there, a little on the fandango order, have been otherwise amusing themselves vastly.[4]

Had Elliott gone to Bent's Fort, he might have learned that both Susan Shelby Magoffin and Solidad Abreu Leitensdorfer were there. He might have seen the fort's cook Charlotte Green dancing—other travelers reported that she led the fandangos. There was a significant gap in Elliott's dispatches between the time the Laclede Rangers left Bent's Fort and their arrival at Santa Fe on August 18. This is regrettable, as his dispatches might have captured, with his characteristic eye for detail, the mood of the crowd as Kearny and his translator Antoine Robidoux climbed to the roof of a low building in Las Vegas, New Mexico, to demand an oath of allegiance to the United States. There could be no doubt that the United States intended to take possession of the Mexican Territory. That was clear in the words Kearny spoke and Robidoux translated:

> Henceforth I absolve you from all allegiance to the Mexican government, and from all obedience to General Armijo. He is no longer your governor; I am your governor. I shall not expect you to take up arms and follow me, to fight your own people, who may oppose me; but I now tell you, that those who remain peaceably at home, attending to their crops and their herds, shall be protected by me, in their property, their persons, and their religion; and not a pepper, not an onion, shall be disturbed or taken by my troops, without pay, or by the consent of the owner. But listen! He who promises to be quiet, and is found in arms against me, I will hang![5]

Lieutenant W. H. Emory, serving with the US Topographical Engineers, recorded this version of Kearny's proclamation delivered in Las Vegas on August 15, 1846. A messenger had just delivered word of Kearny's promotion to brigadier general, and Emory noted "great sensation" at the news that General Armijo was no longer the governor of New Mexico.[6] Kearny repeated the orders in Tecolote, San Miguel, and Pecos, New Mexico's eastern frontier villages that had served Santa Fe Trail traders for the twenty-five years of the trail's existence.

August 1846 was the start of a momentous time on the trail. Missouri men—husbands, fathers, and companions of the women whose stories were told in earlier chapters—met one another on the march to Santa Fe. For some, it was not their first meeting, but it may have been the first time they were all crossing the Santa Fe Trail at the same time, united in a common purpose. Antoine Robidoux was acquainted with Kit Carson from their days as mountain men. He may have known that Carson's daughter Adaline was living in Franklin County, Missouri, where Robidoux had spent some years before moving to New Mexico. Robidoux and Carson likely knew both Samuel and James Magoffin, the husband and brother-in-law, respectively, of Susan Shelby Magoffin. They had all been prominent in the Santa Fe trade for many years. In early December 1846 Kearny, Carson, and Robidoux would be together at the ferocious Battle of San Pasqual. If these men had not met Dick Green, Charlotte's husband, at Bent's Fort, they would come to know him for his bravery during the 1847 Taos Revolt, where their fellow Missourian Charles Bent was murdered for his complicity with the American conquest. They would also come to know the feats of speed and bravado of Francis Xavier Aubry, the "ardent admirer" of Marian Sloan Russell's mother Eliza. They were brought together as the Santa Fe Trail transitioned from a commercial route to a crucial role in the conquest of Mexico and the expansion of the American West.

Elliott's communications were cautious expositions of the character of the men who fought in the early days of the Mexican War. Not until he wrote his memoirs in 1883 did Elliott reflect on the meaning and social cost of the war:

> The upshot was, that before the dispute was settled, millions on millions of wealth were wasted, thousands of good lives were sacrificed, unutterable distress brought to many homes, and a crop of veterans left to solicit in vain for pensions. ... We taught the successors of Montezuma the infallible maxim that justice and right are always on the side of the strongest armies. Abraham Lincoln, Thomas Corwin, and a few others in Congress regarded the war as cruel and unjust, but once begun it had to go on.[7]

At Bent's Fort, while she lay in bed recovering from a miscarriage, Susan Magoffin watched and listened to preparations for the army's advance on New Mexico. In her diary, she questioned why men would wage war when they were destined for higher callings. Susan and Samuel Magoffin arrived in Santa Fe some twelve days after Kearny's army and after her brother-in-law James had already departed for Chihuahua. If she ever encountered Richard Smith Elliott, she did not mention him by name, and he did not indicate that he knew the Magoffins in Santa Fe. Likely they were all preoccupied with settling in. Among those who served under Colonel Alexander Doniphan in the capture of Santa Fe, some credited the "generous and Christian conduct" of the American army for the peaceful surrender and, echoing the admonishments of Kearny, one man noted, "We took nothing, not even a melon, an ear of corn, a chicken, a goat or a sheep, from those poor people, for which we did not pay money."[8]

In New Mexico and California, the war transitioned to a military occupation under military law. The so-called Kearny Code, formally known as the Organic Law of the Territory of New Mexico, compiled and codified the laws of Mexico and the United States that would now govern New Mexico.

The Kearny Code granted civil authority to Charles Bent as governor of New Mexico and Donaciano Vigil as secretary. Kearny did not remain in New Mexico and assigned the drafting of the laws of the New Mexico Territory to Colonel Alexander Doniphan and other officers among the occupation forces. For the Polk administration, the code went too far in granting citizenship to New Mexicans, so that portion was stricken.

But all was not as quiet as it appeared, and a faction of New Mexicans living north and east of Santa Fe and centered around Taos rebelled against American rule in mid-January and early February 1847. Charles Bent was gruesomely murdered, as his Hispanic wife Ignacia Jaramillo Luna Bent, her sister Josefa Jaramillo Carson, and Ignacia's daughter Rumalda Luna Boggs escaped from the Bents' Taos home with the Bent and Carson children. As the wives of American traders, all three women had reason to fear the mob of Hispanic and Pueblo men who murdered Bent.[9] The Taos Revolt was put down by a US military siege of the church in Taos Pueblo. Vigil then served as acting governor under the direction of General Sterling Price, the US-designated military governor of New Mexico. The ruins of the church still stand near Taos Pueblo Plaza as a reminder of resistance to American rule.

Citizenship was granted to residents of the ceded territories under the Treaty of Guadalupe Hidalgo as proposed in 1848, but that important provision was omitted when the treaty was ratified in February 1850. New Mexico remained a territory governed by a series of men sent by presidents who did not always understand the people, their customs, the land, or the limitations of the available resources. New Mexico would face a long fight for statehood fueled by fear of and discrimination against the Catholic, Hispanic, and Native American citizens of the region. Not until January 6, 1912, was New Mexico admitted as the forty-seventh state. Although property rights under the Kearny Code and the Treaty of Guadalupe Hidalgo were protected in the broadest terms, New Mexico land-grant communities and women lost rights with the imposition of US laws and Euro-American customs.

View from Santa Fe Plaza

Richard Smith Elliott provides a stirring, emotional account of the advance of the Army of the West into Santa Fe and the anguished reaction as the American flag was raised over the Palace of the Governors, where Spain and then Mexico had governed for more than two centuries:

Our march into the city, ... was extremely warlike, with drawn sabers and daggers in every look. From around corners, men, with surly countenances and downcast looks, regarded us with watchfulness, if not terror, and black eyes looked through latticed windows at our column of cavaliers, some gleaming with pleasure, and others filled with tears. Strange, indeed, must have been the feelings of the citizens, when an invading Army was thus entering their home—themselves used only to look upon soldiers as plagues, sent to eat out their substance, burn, ravage and destroy—all the future of their destiny vague and uncertain—their new rulers strangers to their manners, language and habits, and, as they had been taught to believe, enemies to the only religion they had ever known. It was humiliating, too, to find their city thus entered, without a gun having been fired in its defence; and we thought that humbled, mortified pride, was indicated in the expression of more than one swarthy face. As the American flag was raised, and the cannon boomed its glorious national salute from the hill, the pent-up emotions of many of the women could be suppressed no longer, and a sigh of commiseration, even for causeless distress, escaped from many a manly breast, as the wail of grief arose above the din of our horses' tread, and reached our ears from the depth of the gloomy-looking buildings on every hand.[10]

How did New Mexicans assembled in the plaza feel when they heard Kearny demanding allegiance and submission to the United States, his words translated into Spanish by Robidoux, who had served as head of Santa Fe's town council in 1830? Were relatives of Robidoux's wife Carmel Benavides in the crowd? Robidoux was not alone in converting from Mexican citizen to American ally, but he was personally acquainted with the families and institutions that would be forever changed by American rule. He was also familiar with the local ways and means of navigating this complicated historical moment.

At the time of the American takeover, New Mexico had a population of about 160,000 people, one-third of them Pueblo Indians. Santa Fe had a population of about 6,000.[11] New Mexican women attracted a good deal of attention from the soldiers, given their long lack of female company, and the women's exotic style was new to American eyes. Among the attributes the men recorded in their trail and war journals were Hispanic women's dark eyes, dark hair, and the sway of their clothing and jewelry. Those images lingered in memoirs written years later. Men who traveled the trail had long enjoyed the company of New Mexican women at fandangos, where music, whiskey, and gambling fulfilled their many desires after months on the trail. Fandangos became both the solace for the soldiers separated from their families and the source of their misbehavior.

Missouri volunteer George Rutledge Gibson described his first visit to the palace and the room in which Kearny held his first ball. "The ballroom is a large, long room, with a dirt floor, and the panels of the interior doors [are] made of bull or buffalo hide, tanned and painted so as to resemble wood."[12]

The Americans' focus on the external appearance of New Mexico's Hispanic women obscures some of the important rights and powers they lost under US law. The American annexation brought social and legal changes that went much deeper than the women's makeup, their short skirts, and their smoking and dancing that so shocked Susan Magoffin. The social ease that American soldiers perceived as personal freedom was an accommodation to conquest. Doña Tules was described as a caricature in many of the early American reports from Santa Fe. She held formidable power and independence derived from her control of a monte wheel, a gaming table, and a saloon. Even the US military relied on loans of cash from Doña Tules's establishments to pay troops and furnish the war. Deena González, Anna Nogar, and Enrique Lamadrid have reframed the image of "La Tules." Rather than focusing on her physical features, cigarette smoking, and gambling skills, they describe her as a *mujerota*, meaning a strong, capable, enterprising women responding to colonization by the Americans.[13] Her strength and independence were based on law and customs as well, which were challenged by American ideas of women's place and property rights.

Importantly, women in New Mexico and in Spanish-speaking countries kept the name of their family of origin when they married, joining the husband's name to the wife's family name. This was more than a tradition or a ceremonial formality; it recognized that women held and controlled property and inheritances from their families of origin and were not entirely dependent on their husbands' fortunes. Many New Mexican women had their own means of support, such as farming, plastering adobe walls, spinning, sewing, and needlework. Women also had crucial medical skills, serving as midwives, healers, and producers of herbal remedies. In addition, New Mexican women produced and sold dried and baked goods, produce, meat, whiskey, and other trade goods under the *portal* (wide front porch) of the Palace of the Governors.

American writers often focused on the public contexts in which New Mexican women enjoyed social events—fiestas, dances, processions—that might include everyone from the governor to a shepherd.[14] Americans overlooked or were threatened by the powerful independence Hispanic and Indo-Hispanic (mestizo) women enjoyed in New Mexican society. In domestic spheres, women were integral to the New Mexican economy and to the flow of goods supporting the Santa Fe trade. Their property rights were threatened by litigation following American adjudication of land titles and property rights. Under American law, coverture gave husbands control of what had been their wives' separate property.[15]

By spring 1847, volunteers began to anticipate the end of their military service in New Mexico. Elliott captured New Mexicans' despair brought on by the military occupation and the dissolution of order among the troops. He was ready for the war to end, but he remained surprisingly sympathetic to New Mexicans' feelings:

> Nobody here fears anything of importance from the Mexicans, but it cannot be denied that they are highly discontented with our presence in the Province, and are heartily tired of us. This feeling of discontent will gain strength among the poorer classes [over] the course of a few months, as their supplies of provisions will be less than formerly, through the summer, owing to the increased consumption since we have been in the country. We have, it is true, paid them for all we have taken, except the grass which our stock have eaten; but the merchants already have the money; and though calico, muslin, trumpery rings, beads &c are in more profuse abundance than ever before, yet the consequence will be empty stomachs and aching hearts. I have no doubt, whatever, that if they were able, they would cut our throats with a hearty good will.[16]

As the troops left New Mexico, the palace became the seat of the territorial government. A series of appointed officials served at the palace, among them Dr. William Carr Lane, the first mayor of St. Louis in 1823. Lane served as governor of New Mexico for only about a year (1852–53). His term ended when the Whigs lost control of the US government to the Democrats, and he was replaced in Santa Fe. Even this brief time was marred by his unfamiliarity with the region and his scope of authority. He wrote to Colonel Edwin V. Sumner, military commander of New Mexico, that "never was an executive officer ever in a more pitiable plight than I was at this time. I was an utter stranger to my duties."[17] That could have been the honest assessment of several territorial officials. While the US administration of New Mexico pivoted with changes in national priorities, the population grew, and the intent and goals of those who ventured on the Santa Fe Trail changed.

Immigrants, Merchants, and Families

US authority did not immediately settle the issue of land titles or even the boundaries of the vast territory claimed by the Treaty of Guadalupe Hidalgo.

It would take several years of surveys and litigation to resolve those issues, and in some notable cases, titles remain contested to this day. But that did not stop mid-nineteenth-century immigration to New Mexico and travel through the territory to the goldfields of California.

Immigrants of many nations joined the army or served the Santa Fe trade, and many passed through St. Louis as the city's population grew remarkably from 16,400 in 1840 to 77,800 in 1849. With the influx of Irish and German immigrants, Protestants, and people of the Jewish faith, St. Louis changed from its previous incarnation as a French Catholic–dominated society.[18] More African Americans came to New Mexico with the army, serving as household labor and trail hands, though they were generally identified by only a first name or an occupation.

Julius Froebel, a revolutionary who had fled political unrest in Germany, traveled the Santa Fe Trail from 1852 to 1853. During his years of exile in North and Central America, his journals provide richly detailed observations of the landscapes, the logistics of travel, and the men who coordinated the caravans. He tended toward stereotypes based on religion and nationality, but he nonetheless concluded that men of diverse backgrounds performed their various trail tasks with skill. Anglo-Americans—whether Irish, Scottish, or English—were wagon masters and drivers of freight wagons but, Froebel observed, they were quick to use profanity and violence toward animals and other men, to no advantageous effect. In contrast, he described Mexican muleteers as skilled and compassionate animal handlers and marveled at their use of terms of endearment and songs to motivate the mules. Germans were too hotheaded, in his view, to drive the wagons or handle the animals. He found it surprising that so many German Jewish men were associated with the trade, which required "fearless courage rarely attributed to the Jewish nation."[19] He did not mention a specific role for African Americans in the trail hierarchy, though he surely encountered a number of them in his year of travel. He noted the division among Methodists—northern sects denying slaveholders admission to the church, while southern Methodists were pro slavery. He observed the rising tensions between Missouri and Kansas over the question of slavery. He described in some detail the demeanor and clothing of Comanche and Kiowa men he encountered along the trail and the passport documents the army issued to these men, identifying them as peaceful toward Americans. He noted that the women the Comanches and Kiowas offered for sale to the caravans were likely captives that they prostituted along the trail.[20]

Like many journals of the time, Froebel's failed to mention women in the caravans. Notably, during his 1852 crossing he did not mention fifteen-year-old Rebecca Mayer, newly married to veteran trader Henry Mayer and the only woman among a caravan of "50 men and 500 mules." Rebecca documented her impressions of the trail in a diary and in letters to her mother, and she mentions that Froebel was the bookkeeper of their wagon train. Her writings reflect her sense of adventure, her interest in the logistics of travel, and her admiration for the trail skills of her husband, who was twenty years older than Rebecca. Perhaps Froebel was referring to Henry when he expressed surprise at the "fearless courage" of the Jewish men in his caravan. Rebecca records several examples of her husband's strength while moving carriages and livestock, his fearlessness when they met some Native Americans at several points along the trail, and his skills as a hunter.[21]

German immigration to Missouri was a result of the push of political turmoil in Germany and the pull of opportunity and adventure in Missouri and the American West. Between 1820 and 1880 three million Germans left their homeland, becoming the largest immigrant group in the United States. Jewish people were part of the emigration from Germany, though it is difficult to determine religion simply by a person's name. By the late 1870s, the Union of American Hebrew Congregations estimated that there were 190,000 Jewish people in the United States, the majority of them from Germany.

St. Louis, as both a gateway to the West and a base of commerce feeding the Santa Fe Trail, attracted German and German Jewish merchants looking to fulfill their dream of quick riches in the West. Most of the men who joined the caravans from St. Louis or Independence were young men—some no more than eighteen years old—and looking forward to adventures in New Mexico and Mexico. One young German settler writing to his family offered a succinct opinion of New Mexico, noting, "Of course New Mexico is good only to earn money. It is a place, as everyone says, that God made last of all."[22] The Army of the West included a trade caravan composed of several young German Jewish men and others who were identified as Jewish by their fellow travelers but did not necessarily identify as Jewish.[23] William Patrick O'Brien noted that the speculative nature of the trade meant that Jewish merchants were accepted when mutual interest or self-interest produced economic benefits, but when such tangible benefits were absent, tolerance of Jewish merchants often vanished.[24]

St. Louis was more than a transit point for German and German Jewish merchants. From the docks of the Mississippi River they secured or furnished financing and supplies for the Santa Fe trade.[25] Dr. Eugene Leitensdorfer, whom some authors identify as Jewish, entered the Santa Fe trade in the 1830s. He married a New Mexican woman and apparently did not identify as Jewish, but his influence brought several German Jewish merchants into the trade. Perhaps the first Jewish woman to enter New Mexico was the wife of Louis Gold, a Polish immigrant who moved from Missouri in about 1850. He and his wife Mary presumably came to New Mexico to join Gold's uncle Joseph Hersch, who operated several businesses, including a gristmill that supplied the American forces with grain. Mary evidently left sometime after 1858 and went to New York, although several of the Gold children remained in New Mexico. Mary remarried and lived in New York until her death in 1894. Louis Gold established a relationship with Refugio Aguila, with whom he had three children in the late 1860s and 1870s. Louis identified as Jewish, at least as the Jewish community grew and there were opportunities to participate in Jewish holidays with other families.

Among the first and largest Jewish enterprises founded in New Mexico was that of the Spiegelberg brothers. Solomon Jacob Spiegelberg was the first to arrive and found employment in Santa Fe with Eugene Leitensdorfer by1846. Solomon was joined in quick succession by his brothers Levi in 1848 and Elias and Willi in 1850. Eventually, brothers Lehman and Emanuel also came to New Mexico. With their wide network of contacts and stores throughout New Mexico, the Spiegelbergs became competitors of James Josiah Webb and John M. Kingsbury, whose letters often commented on their rivalry for contracts, shipping priorities, or warehouse space. In his correspondence, Webb referred to the neighborhood where the Jewish merchants lived as Little Jerusalem, in a thinly veiled anti-Semitic reference. The Spiegelbergs were one of several prosperous and expansive German Jewish mercantile families who used their family connections to open stores serving the military and the growing communities of the Southwest. Levi Spiegelberg's wife, the beautiful Bertha "Betty" Seligman Spiegelberg, came to New Mexico in about 1860 and was evidently forbidden to leave the house unattended, for fear that an American soldier might kidnap her.

Florence "Flora" Langerman Spiegelberg (1857–1943) was the New York–born wife of Willi Spiegelberg (figure 6.2). They were part of a growing community of Jewish men and women who came west during the late nineteenth century and the final years of the Santa Fe trade. Willi, the youngest of the brothers, met his wife-to-be while visiting Germany. As an eighteen-year-old bride, Flora journeyed with him to Santa Fe in 1875. She was already something of a world traveler, having been born in New York in 1857 and taken as an infant through the Isthmus of Panama to her parents' home in San Francisco. Her family relocated to New York in 1866, and then her mother took the children to Nuremberg, Germany, after their father's death in 1869. It was there that Flora married Willi in 1874. After their European honeymoon, she recalled, they started for Santa Fe, traveling via St. Louis in primitive steam railroad cars to West Las Animas, Colorado, and then by stagecoach for six

Fig. 6.2. Undated, unattributed photograph of Flora Langerman Spiegelberg (1857–1943), a German Jewish woman who wrote about her experiences on the Santa Fe Trail as a young bride. Her husband, Willi Spiegelberg, was one of five brothers of a prominent merchant family. (Jewish Women's Archive, https://jwa.org/media/flora-langerman-spiegelberg)

days and six nights. In her diary and later writings, she reminisces about the trip and her life in this exotic and changing community.[26] If Flora was not formally identified with the suffrage movement, she was an ardent activist for families and public health. In Santa Fe, she and Willi welcomed two daughters and contributed to local cultural and civic life. In her memoir, Flora recalled her cultured discussions with Archbishop Lamy in his garden and her playful teasing of Governor Lew Wallace about the sure success of his book *Ben Hur*, written in the Palace of the Governors.[27] As much as they enjoyed life in Santa Fe, the lack of educational opportunities for their children and changes in the business climate led the Spiegelbergs back to New York.[28]

The business opportunities and urban amenities of New York convinced the Spiegelbergs to leave New Mexico in 1888, as did other merchants whose profitability on the trail ended with the coming of the railroads. Yet when Willi and Flora left, followed a year later by Lehman and his family, there was already a growing Jewish community in New Mexico. More women of eastern and European backgrounds came with the army as soldiers' wives and mothers and occasionally as military post workers. As the military offered protection to the southwestern frontier and the railroads made transportation easier, women were no longer a rarity.

The Army, Wives, and Mothers

A substantial body of published and archival material consisting of diaries, letters, and memoirs documents women's time on the trail or in military garrisons.[29] The works run the gamut from daily accounts of the hardships of the trail to memories of the adventures of their youth, but they all provide insight into the importance of families and women traveling alone in the expansion of US interests in the West.

The US military constructed roads and forts in New Mexico, leading to more secure settlements in the period after 1850. The interrelationship of the military, Indian agencies, and merchants created the basis for population growth. Military officers arrived with their families. Merchants married their eastern and European sweethearts and brought them to New Mexico. Some of these families were introduced in earlier chapters. The Messervy, Webb, Kingsbury, and Sloan families crossed the trail in the first decade of US control of the region. The Hunings and others came to New Mexico before and after the Civil War. An increasing number of women accompanied their spouses to New Mexico's military posts. Single women also joined wagon trains heading west to take up residence in the civilian settlements that grew up near the posts.

One of the first military families to enter New Mexico at the end of the Mexican War was that of Anna Maria De Camp Morris and her husband, Major Gouverneur Morris. Along with the families of several other officers, they arrived in New Mexico in the summer of 1850. Both Anna Maria and her husband came from wealthy founding families of New York and New Jersey. Anna Maria traveled with her servant, Louisa, who may have been African American, but she was also served by US troops whose trail duties now included setting up tents, hauling water, chopping wood, cooking, and tending camp for officers' families. One soldier remarked in 1878, "All that there is any need of saying in this case is that woman is humbug in a cavalry camp." He concluded that all the women passed their time giving orders to the men.[30]

The published portions of Anna Maria's diary cover mid-May to mid-July 1850, from the time they left Fort Leavenworth to their settlement in Santa Fe. She was an attentive observer of the privilege she enjoyed but was also aware of the difficult conditions on the trail. Arriving in Santa Fe, she noted, "I am not at all disappointed in the appearance of Santa Fe it is the most miserable squalid looking place I ever beheld except the Plaza there is nothing decent about it. . . . The houses are mud, the fences are mud, the churches & courts are mud, in fact it is *all* mud."[31] The Morrises remained in Santa Fe for three years during a time of revolving civilian leadership, changing territorial boundaries, and the sometimes uneasy integration of cultures. American military officers and their wives carried their social hierarchy with them and built their social lives around the forts. Town sites around some of the forts, like those surrounding Fort Union, often developed disreputable businesses that were the bane of fort administrators. As new American settlers took over the local government and imposed American laws on Hispanic and Native peoples, social displacement and discrimination took hold, even among the Hispanic elites who had held power for generations. For some elites, their loyalty to Mexico remained strong in the early years of American rule.[32]

Fort Union, an important supply post and Santa Fe Trail entry point, had more women than many posts, all of whom crossed the Santa Fe Trail from Missouri if not specifically from St. Louis. Catherine "Katie" Bowen, the wife of Captain Isaac Bowen, was one of four officers' wives who arrived at Fort Union in its earliest years. She enjoyed certain privileges owing to her husband's rank and their social position in the military hierarchy. She was fortunate to be at a post where there were other women of her social standing, including Charlotte Sibley, wife of Captain Ebenezer S. Sibley; Sophia W. Carleton, wife of Captain James H. Carleton; and the wife of Major Edmund B. Alexander. Some of the officers' households also included enslaved servants. Margaret, a young Black woman from Louisville, was with the Bowens. Hannah and Benjamin originally belonged to the Carletons, but they were turned over to territorial governor Lane when he assumed the office in 1852 to satisfy the Carletons' debts. Under the agreement, Governor Lane could sell the servants or rent their services, though their ultimate disposition is not known.[33] Katie Bowen's letters to her parents are enthusiastic about life at the fort, although it was not a plush posting. The officers' wives had time for writing, reading, sewing, and socializing.[34] This was not the case for wives of the enlisted men, who had fewer comforts on a frontier post.

Mary Gowan Clarke arrived at Fort Union in May 1852 with her husband, Charles Francis (Frank) Clarke, an enlisted man in the First Regiment of the US Dragoons. Both Frank and Mary were recent immigrants to Missouri. Frank had arrived from Suffolk, England, and first settled in Milwaukee before moving to St. Louis in 1849. The educated son of a minister, he had come to the United States seemingly on a whim, dreaming of easy riches. After some bad luck and poor business ventures in Milwaukee, he moved to St. Louis, where he was a civilian clerk at Jefferson Barracks, a military post. It was there he enlisted in the First Dragoons in 1849. Mary, an immigrant from Ireland, worked as a servant at Jefferson Barracks. In letters to his parents, Frank told them about Mary, a churchgoing girl he had been spending time with, and sought his parents' blessing on their intended marriage. He did not mention that Mary was Catholic or that she was a servant at Jefferson Barracks, nor did he provide details about how they spent their time together. But in a previous letter to his sister, written in June 1850, he described the beautiful landscape around the fort:

> I wish you could visit this place, you could not help admiring it, it is really very beautiful. The Barracks consist of eight large Blocks forming a hollow square, the parade ground in the centre & with the necessary Hospitals, Stables &c are built of stone, upon a promontory rising about 200 feet above & jutting into the river, the Mississippi, which although it is more than 1200 miles to its mouth, is at this place a mile & a half wide. The country around the Barracks is what is called here "Oak Openings" & resembles some of the Parks in the old country more than anything I know of, being thinly sprinkled with oak trees with a beautiful sod clear of Bush. It is now strawberry time and the ground is covered with wild strawberries. They are as large as the common kind in England but not as fine flavoured. The Town people here have their heads turned with strawberry picnic parties.[35]

Frank and Mary were married at the end of December 1850, and in the spring they moved to Fort Leavenworth. They were anxious to leave St. Louis behind, with its escalating tensions among different ethnic groups, unhealthy climate, and chronic housing shortage. Frank had seen the worst of conditions in the city when he arrived in the spring of 1849, in the aftermath of a devastating dock fire and a raging cholera epidemic.[36] Clarke was promoted from private to sergeant major, and as the scribe of regimental records, he seemed to be aware of conditions in the West, where his regiment would soon serve. On May 22, 1852, Frank, Mary, and their six-month-old son Charley joined a large military caravan of three hundred troops on the Santa Fe Trail headed to New Mexico. This was the same time and perhaps the same caravan in which Eliza Sloan and her children William and Marian crossed the country. The Clarkes' six-week journey was almost twice as long as Frank's ocean voyage from England to America. They reached Fort Union on June 30, 1852. Frank's letter to his father described the immense herds of buffalo on the trail, the condition of Fort Union, and the kit the soldiers carried. He spared his father the shocking details of the mail carriers killed in an attack by Jicarilla Apaches and Utes at Wagon Mound in 1850, and he reassured him that Mary and Charley rode in their own carriage pulled by two mules and fared well.[37]

Katie Bowen was already at Fort Union when the Clarkes arrived. She wrote to her mother of the caravan's arrival, describing how she had entertained the wives of the post surgeon and the paymaster, but she did not mention the enlisted men's wives. Frank may have been a member of the military party sent to warn Native American leaders—perhaps Kiowas and Comanches—not to harass wagons on the plains. Captain James H. Carleton led the expedition. Frank was part of the escort for William Carr Lane on his crossing from St. Louis to Santa Fe. Mary accompanied Frank to two smaller posts—Fort Massachusetts in southern Colorado and Cantonment Burgwin south of Taos, New Mexico. Both posts were situated in beautiful mountain settings, but Mary would not have had the company of other women or the help of servants or enlisted men there. She likely witnessed the somber return of troops to Cantonment Burgwin on March 30, 1854, after a fierce battle with Jicarilla Apaches.

The First US Dragoons, led by Lieutenant John W. Davidson, participated in the Battle of Cieneguilla, where twenty-three of its men were killed and twenty-two wounded. Davidson's failure of leadership and the ineffective and inappropriate tactics used by the dragoons were certainly to blame for the defeat. Davidson, however, managed to create a web of lies and intimidate witnesses who knew the truth about what had transpired. It is only through recent archaeological forensics and a reevaluation of testimony that the actual events have been untangled from fabrications about the battle.[38] Frank missed the fighting because he was delivering a dispatch to Santa Fe, but he surely heard details and saw the survivors. He wrote to his father in late May 1854 about the battle and the good news that he had been granted a furlough that would run until the end of his enlistment in 1855. He, Mary, Charley, and their newborn son spent two months on the Santa Fe Trail in the summer of 1854 as they made their way back to St. Louis in what Frank described as an arduous journey.[39] They did not remain in St. Louis but journeyed west again to make their home in the Kansas Territory.

Although traveling from post to post and living as an army wife did not suit everyone, Lydia Spencer Lane thrived on the adventures. She arrived in New Mexico in the summer of 1856 with her husband, William Bartlett Lane, a lieutenant in the Mounted Rifles. She and her husband began their wandering life together in May 1854, married to the army as much as to each other. In the sixteen years Lane served, he was transferred often, never spending more than six months at any post. Sometimes the Lanes had to move on in a matter of days, transferred from one army garrison to another as they journeyed west from Pennsylvania to Texas and then to remote posts in New Mexico, traveling by all manner and modes of transportation. In all, Lydia crossed the country seven times. They spent the first three months of their marriage at Jefferson Barracks near St. Louis (during a cholera epidemic), and Lydia never had warm feelings toward the town. To her, St. Louis was never more than a place to transfer from one boat to another. Later in life, Lydia observed that some wives were sorry when they found themselves continually uprooted by army life, but she was not. "I for one never regretted having done so," she said of marrying an officer, "and loved everything connected with the army; the officers—not always the wives, however,—the soldiers, mules, horses, wagon, tents, camps, every and anything, so I was in the army and part of it."[40]

Lydia's memoir, published in 1893, captured the mounting tensions as the country was divided in the 1860s between the interests of the North and the South, free states and slave-owning states. She and Lieutenant Lane were stationed at Fort Fillmore in southern New Mexico in the winter of 1861. She wrote about the widening divisions in the country, first manifesting as just an uneasy feeling and then as a deliberate act when soldiers deserted the US Army to serve with Confederate troops in Texas and the South. The tension was palpable between friends and even among family members, and she never forgot those soldiers who deserted the army, and sometimes their families, for the southern cause:

> There was an undercurrent of disquiet around us which was felt more than seen or heard, and there were plenty of men in the small towns, ready at a moment's notice, in case war was declared, to make a raid on Fort Fillmore, which, with its small garrison, could offer but little resistance. . . .
>
> The possibility of war between North and South was freely discussed at table, with considerable excitement, and so hotly at times the ladies were embarrassed considerably. There were advocates for both sides, while others were reticent as to their sentiments. We had so little fear that matters would ever terminate seriously, and war result, that we soon forgot the unpleasant episode. But those fiercely expressed opinions and angry words were not forgotten by all who were present, and bore fruit later on; some giving up everything, believing they owed it as a duty to their native States; while others fought, bled and died for the old flag.[41]

The rumor that Confederate troops were marching from Mesilla, New Mexico, up the Rio Grande to overtake the wagon train Lydia and her family were traveling in was seared in her memory. The family made it to Santa Fe without incident, and then she, the children, and her two African American servants—a nanny/nurse and a cook—headed across the plains to the east, away from whatever might happen on the southwestern war front. Lydia vividly remembered traveling with the dispirited soldiers of the Fifth and Seventh Infantry, transferring from wagon to boat to railroad car and finally reaching St. Louis. There, she signed a passport pledging allegiance to the Union and not to give "aid or comfort" to the enemy. She forgot to mention that her party included the Black nurse, and an enraged dock agent refused to let the nurse board the ferry because Lydia had failed to get a passport for her. Lydia refused to leave the nurse, and only through the intercession of an official of the ferry was the nurse allowed to board. The family traveled safely from St. Louis to Harrisburg, Pennsylvania, where they expected to receive news about Lieutenant Lane. Remarkably, Lane was waiting for them in Pennsylvania. He had hoped to take command of a unit and fight for the Union in the South, but instead he was assigned to muster volunteers in Pennsylvania. Back east, Lydia learned to, in her own words, "eradicate" kind feelings toward those friends who had joined the Confederate cause. She was loyal to the Union, but she never recorded how her Black household staff felt about the war, nor whether the nannies, nurses, cooks, and maids she employed were enslaved or free. She did not reveal her feelings at seeing all-Black troops in her travels. While she clearly questioned the motives of those who joined the Confederacy, she did not articulate a position on the status or rights of the African Americans in service to her household. She plainly stated her fear and distrust of Indigenous peoples, however, seeing them either as a threat to their safe passage from one post to another or as unwanted and uncouth visitors at army posts.

The Lanes remained in the East until after the Civil War, then returned to New Mexico in the summer of 1866. This was Lydia's fifth crossing. This time, she made the trip in the comfort of a buggy, while the rest of the family traveled in a wagon. As a veteran of the trail, she was amused by the outfits and the travails of the young army wives who were part of this group. The family made two more trips across the trail, in 1867 and 1869, taking routes through Kansas or Colorado that allowed them to board trains as railroad construction inched across the continent. New Mexico was a different place by then, and much of the change was tied to the expansion of military posts and a trail shortened by the railroad. Many more women were living on posts, and Santa Fe had been altered by the influx of US territorial officials, military families, and merchants.

According to historian Darlis Miller, by the early 1870s, women were living on almost all military posts throughout New Mexico and were officially recognized as servants, laundresses, or the wives of officers. All military posts had at least one resident officer's wife. In some cases, women living in communities adjacent to military posts found larger roles, but many were dismissed or characterized simply as camp followers or prostitutes. Miller's analysis shows a few instances in which the quartermaster hired a woman to supply the post with forage and foodstuffs, as well as compensating her for the use of corrals and property.[42]

Independent women, such as Eliza Mahoney, found a place working on wagon trains, in army kitchens and laundries, and in the army's supply chain. Ellen Koslowski and her husband Martin operated a ranch and supply post on the Santa Fe Trail half a mile southeast of Pecos Pueblo. He was a Polish immigrant who had come to New Mexico from Missouri with the US First Dragoons. The couple established the ranch when he completed his military service in 1858. The ranch was used as Union headquarters during the Battle of Glorieta Pass in March 1862. Martin Koslowski's license to trade with the army was revoked in 1877, and after the couple separated, the army transferred the license to Ellen for the use of her property. Martin was arrested for killing a man in 1878.[43]

The majority of women came from the East, and several penned journals and autobiographies that detailed life on military posts. Marian Russell is the only woman among this group of writers who crossed the trail several times and remained in the West. But the West was changing as railroad tracks were laid and as women's roles in society evolved.

Suffrage, Abolition, Activism, and Fashion on the Trail

Julia Anna Archibald Holmes represents a different type of female traveler in the late 1850s (figure 6.3). Her motivation for crossing the trail was adventure. In the popular literature of the Santa Fe Trail, Holmes is often remembered for two things: climbing Pike's Peak and wearing bloomers—long pants worn under a skirt. Her clothing allowed her considerable freedom of movement as she ascended Pike's Peak, but it was also sign of her allegiance to suffrage and her belief in the rights of women and freedom for the enslaved.

Pike's Peak is a landmark in southern Colorado, but this part of the Rocky Mountains was not always considered Colorado. It was named for Lieutenant Zebulon Montgomery Pike, the US envoy who explored this newly acquired portion of the Louisiana Purchase in 1806. He first saw the peak from a distance, and when he attempted an ascent, his party never made it to the summit. When Julia Holmes climbed the peak in 1858, this region of the Rockies was part of the Mexican cession and was still contained within the vaguely defined borders of New Mexico. Holmes's life was short—she died at age forty-eight—but her story is about so much more than the bloomers she wore or the peak she climbed. Her story marks the emergence of women's activism for equality for themselves and equitable and safe conditions for others.

Holmes literally wore her political positions, adopting a new fashion for women that included long bloomers visible under a skirt (figures 6.4 and 6.5).

Fig. 6.3. Undated, unattributed photograph of Julia Archibald Holmes (1838–87) that conveys her identity as a writer, not a "bloomer girl."

Fig. 6.4. Currier and Ives lithograph of the American reform outfit. (https://www.loc.gov/item/90711963/)

Fig. 6.5. Woman's tan plaid day dress, 1848–51. (Missouri Historical Society, St. Louis)

Her clothes made her something of a spectacle to some of her fellow travelers. She wrote her impressions of the three months she spent on the trail, traveling eleven hundred miles in an oxcart and on foot from Lawrence, Kansas, to the goldfields of Colorado and to Fort Union, New Mexico, in the summer of 1858. Her letters, published in a women's reform magazine called the *Sibyl*, were an eloquent and surprisingly contemporary voice advocating for women's independence.[44] She caused a stir on the trail with her fashion statement, which was part of the movement to free women from the constraints of their corsets and layers of clothing, allowing them to take part as equals with men in the social, educational, and political activities and labors of the day. The American outfit, or reform dress, drew attention:

> As I was cooking our dinner some of [the men] crowded around our wagon, gazing sometimes at the stove; but oftener on my dress, which did not surprise me, for, I presume, some of them had never seen just such a costume before. I wore a calico dress, reaching a little below the knee, pants of the same, Indian moccasins for my feet, and on my head a hat. However much it lacked in taste I found it to be beyond value in comfort and convenience, as it gave me freedom to roam at pleasure in search of flowers and other curiosities.[45]

But Julia's cause was much broader than freedom of dress. She expected to serve as a night guard on the trail and hoped to build her stamina by walking as much of the distance from Kansas to Colorado as her husband James and the other men did. Julia was disappointed to find that the only other woman in the caravan, likely Mrs. Robert Middleton, did not share the values of the reform movement and "confined herself the long days to feminine impotence in the hot covered wagon." On August 1, 1858, Julia, James, and several men from the Lawrence group began their ascent of Pike's Peak. Julia carried a seventeen-pound pack loaded with clothes, a quilt, and some writing materials, but more than half of this burden was the bread that would be the majority of their food during the week's exploration. James carried twice as much in his pack, including a book of Ralph Waldo Emerson's essays. The letters Julia penned from her campsite each night contain beautiful descriptions of the scenery and serenity she encountered on that historic trek. From their base camp at a place they named Snowdell, she wrote on August 4: "The beauty of this great picture is beyond my powers of description. . . . We think our location grandly romantic."[46] By August 10, they had returned from their climb and rejoined the wagons—some of them going back to Kansas and others, like those carrying James, Julia, and her brother Alfred, heading south to New Mexico.

Julia and James spent the winter of 1858–59 in the vicinity of Taos, where Julia accepted a position as teacher to the children of Santa Fe Trail merchant Peter Joseph. Then, sometime in 1859, she and James moved to Barclay's Fort, a trading post established by Alexander Barclay and Joseph Quinn Doyle, modeled after Bent's Fort and an important Santa Fe Trail stop close to Fort Union. Julia was hired to teach the children of the Doyle family, and Julia and James's first child, Ernesto Julio, was born at Fort Union. They moved to Santa Fe in the middle of July 1860 and could not have chosen a more volatile time to settle there.

Both James and Julia were ardent abolitionists, a cause that had brought each of their families to Kansas to settle that territory and ensure that it was admitted to the Union as a free state. They arrived in Santa Fe as the debate over New Mexico's status as a free or slave territory was intensifying, and James added to the volatility. When their son was about a year old, they took him to Lawrence to stay with Julia's family and then continued on to Washington, DC, where James was seeking an appointment in the territorial government. They arrived in the nation's capital within days of President Lincoln's call for volunteers to protect the city from Confederate troops. It was the same call to action James had answered in Kansas, and he joined a volunteer group called the Frontier Guard. His service lasted from April 18 to May 3, and he was rewarded by being named the territorial secretary of New Mexico, the official recordkeeper of the government in Santa Fe.[47] Both James and Julia knew, even before they left Washington, that his appointment would not be popular with the pro-slavery government faction in Santa Fe.

The February 3, 1859, Slave Code, more formally titled An Act to Provide for the Protection of Property in Slaves in This Territory, neither created nor legalized slavery in New Mexico. It was intended to protect slave owners' property rights over the enslaved, but the code went further in many ways. It prohibited marriages between "white persons and slaves, free negroes or mulattos." Slaves were prohibited from testifying against free white people in court cases, and they could not hire themselves out between sunset and sunrise. It specified the punishment for insolence toward a free white person—thirty-nine stripes upon the offender's bare back—and prescribed death for the rape of a white woman. Other sections dealt with the apprehension of fugitive slaves and the resolution of disputes between parties claiming the same person as property. This was a far-reaching act for a territory that included present-day New Mexico, Arizona, Colorado, and Nevada yet held fewer than fifty Black, free Black, or mulatto people.[48]

The greatest push for the Slave Code came from New Mexico's territorial representative to Congress, Miguel Antonio Otero Sr. Born into a prosperous

Hispanic family in New Mexico, he attended St. Louis University in 1841 and then received a law degree at Pingree College in New York. He was a powerhouse in and for New Mexico through his family connections and his eastern education. Otero's protection of slave owners' property rights was partly attributable to his marriage to Mary Josephine Blackwood from Charleston, South Carolina. He argued that supporting the South and protecting southerners' property would bring favor to New Mexico. This position was aligned with the western expansion of the railroads, which would ultimately serve the goals of those favoring statehood.

In the fall of 1861 the situation between James Holmes and the pro-slavery forces in Santa Fe was reaching a pitch. Julia reached out to George Luther Stearns of Medford, Massachusetts, who had been director of the New England Emigrant Aid Society and the organizer of abolition-oriented settlers in Kansas. In a letter dated October 26, 1861, she sought his advice in quashing the scandalous rumors being spread about James by the governor of New Mexico, Dr. Henry Connelly, and the superintendent of Indian affairs, James L. Collins. Julia told Stearns that Governor Connelly thought Holmes was responsible for the Senate's rejection of Connelly as a delegate, and Collins owned the only newspaper in New Mexico, which she described as "a miserable secession sheet which has hitherto drawn all its support from the government patronage but has never said one word in support of the government." As the secretary of New Mexico, James could award printing contracts to anyone he chose, facilitating his ability to bring another newspaper to the area. She concluded, "These two men so high in office are both secessionists at heart and both have labored with all their might to introduce into the legislature and cause to be passed the infamous slave code of 1858 & 9."[49]

Confederates marched into New Mexico from the south, taking Mesilla and Fort Fillmore and then winning the Battle of Valverde on February 21 and 22, 1862. Texas forces marched up the Rio Grande through Albuquerque and took control of Santa Fe's Palace of the Governors on March 10, 1862. Their win was short-lived, however. Colorado volunteers fighting for the Union reclaimed New Mexico in the Battle of Glorieta on March 26–28, aided by their famous maneuver of burning Confederate supply wagons in Apache Canyon, close to where Governor Armijo had fled the approaching Americans in the summer of 1846.

Another newspaper did appear in New Mexico, but the relationship between Holmes and the publisher only made his adversaries more uncomfortable. The publisher was Julia's uncle, aided by her sixteen-year-old brother Frederick. On June 12, 1862, Holmes placed a notice in the *Santa Fe Republican* offering a $20 reward for the return of a record book belonging to the executive of New Mexico, taken when the Texans fled south after occupying the Palace of the Governors. As tensions between the factions deepened, James was arrested on charges of aiding the enemy, apparently stemming from criticism published in the *Santa Fe Republican* about the design of the earthworks, or star fort, built at Fort Union. According to his detractors, Holmes had offered too much detail to the enemy about the fort's weak defenses. The *New York Times*, in a lengthy article about the situation in New Mexico, identified the pro-slavery faction as the perpetrators of a great injustice to Holmes. The *Times* article, published on August 4, 1862, noted that any information published about the fort was already known by defectors who had served in New Mexico and then joined the Texas forces. Further, the paper accused the pro-slavery faction of trying to censor the secretary after failing to remove him from office through their campaign of slander and appeals to President Lincoln himself.

James and Julia left New Mexico with their two sons, Julio and Charles, sometime after this. In 1863 James Holmes and Charles Luther Stearns took command of the Fourteenth and Seventeenth Regiments of the Tennessee Colored Troops. Julia lived with family in Alabama, and she was in Murfreesboro in 1864 when she learned that her dear brother Frederick had been wounded in battle in Missouri. She and James had two more children after the war: Phoebe, born in 1865, and June, born in 1867. The family moved to Washington, DC, where Julia's writing and publishing flourished, but her marriage dissolved.

It is hard to reconcile Julia's adventuresome life in Colorado and New Mexico and her fierce defense of abolition and women's rights with the marital conditions revealed in the divorce proceedings. James and Julia's marriage ended publicly and spectacularly, exposing the cruelty and abuse he inflicted on her. During their divorce trial, the ugly details of her humiliation and beatings were published in the *Daily National Republican* on October 13, 1871. Julia, identified as the proprietor of a woman's publishing office, was a capable writer and orator, but she was not allowed to speak at the trial. However, her deposition details three or four years of beatings and James's lecherous intent toward her sister. Julia also believed that James was living with another woman. Holmes responded to the charges with threats and a barrage of counterclaims against her family.

Julia continued to live in Washington after her divorce and was a recognized poet and author. She worked for the Department of Education and wrote about the conditions of child labor. She may have prepared some reports in Spanish, as she was fluent in the language. Julia and her mother, Jane Archibald, were active in the National American Woman Suffrage Association and attended the 1869 convention together, but neither would live long enough to cast a vote. Julia was a leader of women's rights, not simply the woman who wore the pants on the Pike's Peak expedition. She was at the forefront, but she was not alone in her activism. As railroads shortened the travel time across the country, women fighting for other causes journeyed west, and still others, born in New Mexico or immigrants to an adopted land, became the voice for one cause or another.

The Trail Passes into History and Legend

The first decade of American rule was a time of tremendous tension in New Mexico, as military law yielded to a civil government and finally to the terms of peace established by the Treaty of Guadalupe Hidalgo. Although the treaty ended the war, it did not settle the questions surrounding territorial boundaries or the rights of landholders, nor did it grant citizenship to residents of the ceded lands. Many of those questions lingered long after the occupying forces left, and some issues festered right up to the granting of statehood in 1912. New Mexican women married to Americans fared no better in securing their land and property rights. Statehood and security from Navajo, Apache, and Ute raids on the settlements, which the American conquest promised in vague terms, would be a long time coming. Native and Hispanic peoples lost their lands, and even their tentative alliance with Americans as they fought in Taos during the winter of 1847 would not last. The Santa Fe Trail would lose its importance as a commercial supply line.

As railroads began to advance across the country, creating wider networks for commercial access and supporting immigration to the West, the Santa Fe Trail lost its strategic importance. Planning and political lobbying for railroads began in Missouri in the 1830s. Some of the earliest boosters were familiar names promoting the resources and potential of the West. Senator Thomas Hart Benton and his daughter and son-in-law, Jessie Benton and John C. Frémont, championed a railroad from St. Louis to the Pacific. Just as St. Louis provided resources, goods, and markets to feed the Santa Fe Trail, city leaders rallied behind a railway across the state and on to the West Coast. The first train crossed west of the Mississippi River in December 1852, but early confidence was shaken when the Gasconade River railroad bridge collapsed on the train's first run to Jefferson City on November 1, 1855. Even after that disaster, several railway companies competed for support. Then, with the country straining under sectional fault lines, financial failures and the mayhem of the Civil War and its aftermath stalled railway construction in

Fig. 6.6. Advertisement for the St. Louis, Kansas City and Northern Short Line Railroad, 1873, featuring service to all points west and promising safe and comfortable travel for women. (PO116-00028-0001, Missouri Historical Society, St. Louis)

Missouri for more than a decade. By the mid-1870s, more than nine hundred miles of rail lines had been completed in Missouri, but St. Louis and Chicago were in steep competition for control of freight lines throughout the 1870s and 1880s.[50] Some merchants and their families still traveled the sections of the Santa Fe Trail that remained in use until 1880, when the Atchison, Topeka, and Santa Fe won the competition for a railway into New Mexico and opened a route through Raton Pass. The first train reached Las Vegas, New Mexico, on February 9, 1880, ushering in a new era of immigration and rapid cultural change.

Susan Elston Wallace (1830–1907), author and wife of New Mexico governor Lew Wallace, wrote about her arrival in New Mexico in 1878. She had traveled by train from Indiana to Trinidad, Colorado, and then by stage to Santa Fe. She cautioned that train travel was no guarantee of a smooth or uneventful ride (figure 6.6). While she marveled at the beautiful fall colors as they crossed the Mississippi River in St. Louis, she groaned in horror at the conditions of her sleeping compartment: bedbugs, crying children, and fussy and ill fellow travelers confined together for hours on end. The salubrious air, star-studded night skies, and immense buffalo herds would not delight these modern travelers. But like many of the writers and artists who came to New Mexico, Wallace was captivated by her experiences in New Mexico. She found Santa Fe "invested with indescribable romance," though some of it was projected through her allusions to classical literature and an overlay of ethnocentrism. Interestingly, Flora Spiegelberg and Susan Wallace, authors and scholars who lived in Santa Fe at the same time, did not mention each other in their respective writings. Surely they must have moved in the same social circles, and both were advocates and activists for causes that might have aligned their energies. Both were likely more interested in depicting the Indigenous and exotic elements of New Mexico than talking about women in their own milieu.[51]

Independent women would come from many places after the railroad started to serve New Mexico and the West. Progress, modernization, and even the imprint of a national identity would follow the rail lines west. The Progressive Era in New Mexico invited rapid architectural change as the railroads brought new building materials, and territorial politicians sought to project an acceptance of modernization as they fought for statehood. The Santa Fe Trail facilitated conquest, first by commerce and then by military might and US law. The railroads increased the pace of change, but the trail never faded from memory as artists, poets, writers, journalists, and historians used the allure of the Santa Fe Trail to invoke the past, sometimes in glorious colors and vivid memories.

Conclusion
The Legacy of the Santa Fe Trail

The Santa Fe Trail was a catalyst for change stemming from encounters among people of different cultures, races, and political beliefs. Some of these interactions were fueled by conflicts resulting from the rapid territorial expansion of the United States in the nineteenth century. Those encounters also generated new communities and opportunities. Traveling the route of the Santa Fe Trail today can still be a journey of discovery and an indication of the state of the nation. Road signs on modern interstates document political, cultural, and religious strains that divide the country or give voice to specific causes. Commercial billboards offer food for the journey, salve for the soul, and companionship for the lonely. American flags and political banners, some left over from the divisive 2020 presidential election, point to the remaining and, in some places, intensifying partisan divides. It is on the smaller "blue highways," the two-lane roads that take travelers on a slower path, that the history of the Santa Fe Trail is best experienced. Those routes still offer the wide prairie views that awed nineteenth-century travelers. Many of the original town centers, however, are deserted or have been transformed into art galleries or antique stores struggling to serve diminishing populations. In many of those towns there are still store signs painted on bricks that record the names of businesses and families that served trail travelers. Taking those back roads is slow going for me because I stop to read the historical markers, photograph the monuments, and try to discern the occasional trail ruts that cross fields and farms. It is in those places that I look for lessons from the past.

The history of the Santa Fe Trail is still remembered in many local communities along the more than one thousand miles connecting St. Louis with Santa Fe and Taos, New Mexico. The larger significance of western trails emerges not just in knowing and naming the points of departure at each end of the trail but by learning the larger economic and cultural contexts mediated by the trade. During several years of research and writing about the women whose lives I explore in this book, I developed a different level of understanding about the ways women participated in the trail and occasioned encounters between people and places. These cultural encounters involved more than Americans meeting Hispanic New Mexicans. Such broad classifications reduce the story too much, obscuring the complex mix of cultures among those who settled Missouri and the Southwest. Reframing the history of the Santa Fe Trail through the experiences of women from Native American, Black, French, Hispanic, Jewish, and other communities offers deeper perspectives on western expansion. The women I write about offered new assessments of events and exchanges that, at the beginning of my research, I thought I knew well.

The trail is now more than two hundred years old, but the lessons it provides are still relevant. The area at the confluence of the Mississippi and Missouri Rivers is crucial to understanding the global reach of its commerce. The vast drainage system that merges in St. Louis fed goods into and throughout the heart of the continent, making much of the overland trade feasible and sustaining the communities that grew up around it. The trade expanded enormously over the first generation of its existence, from Becknell's burros to annual caravans comprising hundreds of wagons and tons of goods. The scope and scale of the trade and the variety of goods crossing the trail were another part of my learning experience.

While excavating archaeological sites in New Mexico, I had seen and cataloged pieces of commercially produced glass and household goods that marked the changing economy generated by the Santa Fe trade. The inventories of wagons and the variety of goods enumerated on bills of lading illustrated the scale and significance of nineteenth-century commerce in regional and global economies. Seeing the actual material goods in museums and collections in Missouri clarified the point that the trade was pervasive, and the changes in New Mexico and points west and south were profound. The Steamboat Arabia Museum in Kansas City exhibits much of the 220 tons of cargo on that boat when it sank in the Missouri River in 1856. The quantity and variety of items it carried, bound for the western trails, are staggering. The availability of so much material culture had the potential to change individuals, artisans, households, and local markets in communities across the continent. Multiplied by the competition in the annual caravans that massed in western Missouri, the goods carried across the Santa Fe Trail influenced every aspect of household and community economies in New Mexico and the

West. It is similar to the way big-box stores have changed the landscape and economy of small towns across the United States in our times. The economic changes and settlement shifts taking place along the interstate highways have precedent in the history of commerce along the Santa Fe Trail.

Domestic life in New Mexico—the material culture of households—was altered by the variety and quantity of goods that had not existed when the territory was part of the vast Spanish empire. The artifacts and documents in museum collections led me back to several questions that motivated this research. How did the Santa Fe Trail affect the lives of women in Missouri, New Mexico, and Mexico? The hardware, tools, woven cloth, and home goods available for purchase in some cases led to changes in labor and production, as well as in the distribution of goods. Hand-wrought tools made by blacksmiths in New Mexico and Mexico, which collectors still admire, were exchanged for commercially produced hardware and tools imported on the trail. New Mexican, Mexican, and Native American weavers produced excellent woven goods that are still prized in museum collections, but the trail made commercially produced yard goods more plentiful and more economically priced, even if they were not as durable or as aesthetically pleasing. Pottery and tableware produced by Native American artisans, which is still used in Hispanic, Pueblo, and Apache homes and has filled museums and collectors' homes for generations, were replaced by crockery and tableware produced in the Midwest and the East or imported from Europe. The artisans who produced handcrafted items in New Mexico and Mexico were surely impacted by the economics of the Santa Fe Trail. In some cases, their labor became wage labor, and their profits were coveted by the newcomer merchants. The system of mercantile capitalism replaced the barter and exchange economy realized in response to New Mexico's distance from Spanish and Mexican markets. The mercantile economy replaced personal relationships with ledger books in many cases. It would take time—generations—before New Mexican and Native crafts would be valued as folk art and prized for their aesthetic qualities.

The Santa Fe Trail did not terminate in Santa Fe, as the push and pull of the trail brought commerce south into Mexico and west to California. The Santa Fe Trail was just one of the routes fed by Missouri caravans and steamboats carrying goods to California and the Northwest. The expansion of the Santa Fe trade into Mexico made handsome profits for Missouri traders, as well as for those families and business enterprises that grew out of marriages and alliances with Native and Hispanic artisans. Those profits and markets, in turn, stirred larger ambitions beyond simply selling merchandise carried by wagons on the trail, with far-reaching consequences. Merchants created an expanded land-based international commerce that carried goods farther and wider, fueling, in part, US aggression against Mexico.

The Louisiana Purchase was the opening salvo in the United States' expansion across North America. Trade among Native peoples and French and Spanish colonists of the interior West existed long before Lewis and Clark set off from the confluence region. On the lands that would become the American West, in regular or impromptu meetings, Europeans and Native peoples exchanged resources and information. The participants in these trade networks knew the land, the resources, and the mediums of exchange. Native men and women and French and Spanish trappers hunted and processed the hides and furs that drove the trade. But there was more to the trade than furs and hides, as the participants exchanged knowledge of the country's resources as well as sexual and marriage partners. In many cases, the domestic partners of the traders gave birth to children of mixed descent. Some of those children would find their place among the elite of St. Louis, such as the children of María Rosa Villalpando and Francisca López de Kimball. Adaline Carson did not find such a place, though perhaps she never sought it or wanted it. She did not settle with her mother's Arapaho community, her father's Missouri family, or his growing family of mixed Hispanic descent in Taos and southern Colorado.

The story of María Rosa Villalpando is an example of the human trafficking that was a part of that interregional commerce. She was brought to St. Louis by Jean Baptiste Salé dit Lajoie when it was a French colony with an uncertain future. She lived in St. Louis for more than sixty years, longer than she lived in New Mexico, where she was born. She saw the city develop from a French fur-trading post into a US state and a major supplier of goods to continental and international trade networks. Although historians and folklorists have written about her abduction from Ranchos de Taos in 1760, there was so much more to her story, preserved in documents of her life in Creole St. Louis. Josiah Gregg, who introduced María Rosa's story to many English-language readers, dismissed it as a "tale of woe." Gregg failed to record the trafficking that brought María Rosa and other enslaved women, children, and even some men to the intercultural and intercontinental trade. María Rosa's voice was not lost to history because she remained a powerful advocate for herself. Her intentions were strongly articulated through court proceedings and legal actions she initiated. She exerted her property rights, which included the children of her enslaved servants, showing that gender was no bar to participation in the slave trade. María Rosa's ability to exercise those rights was due to the legal privileges extended to women during the Spanish and French administration of Missouri.

María Rosa was more than resilient. She was assertive, strident, and even combative, based on the lawsuits she filed. And like several of the woman I write about, she sometimes resisted and exceeded the strict confines of community expectations. María Rosa's adaptation to life in Creole St. Louis is a counterpoint to the tragic captive stories that make up so much of American frontier literature. Captives continued to be a medium of exchange as traders from New Mexico and the United States ransomed them well into the mid-nineteenth century, and in some instances, traders played a role in returning those women and children to their families. María Rosa was able to build a life for herself in the changing economy of St. Louis through her access to land, capital, and enslaved labor and through extended family connections formed by her children's marriages into elite St. Louis families. Those resources and networks made her passage from captive to Creole possible. These were the same tools and means that made it possible for many men to succeed in the Santa Fe trade as well.

The Santa Fe Trail connected Mexico and the United States as the two governments sought to control their own borders. Both nations contained people of diverse backgrounds and cultures who had different reactions to the opportunities and changes the Santa Fe trade brought to both ends of the trail. French and American traders entered the trade after Mexico declared its independence from Spain in 1821. Within the first decade, several French and American traders had formed domestic partnerships with New Mexican women that granted them access to important social and commercial networks. Deena González terms the New Mexican women who aligned with the American traders "accommodators."[1] These marriages and social alliances between New Mexicans and the newcomers—whether of French or other European heritage—facilitated the conquest of New Mexico. The territorial era (1821–46) engendered social systems that eventually displaced New Mexicans and disadvantaged them in the economic and political spheres.

By the 1830s, Missouri merchants joined with New Mexican and Mexican traders to serve larger and more lucrative markets, extending the Santa Fe trade into Chihuahua and farther south and west to California. The relationships of Carmel Benavides and Antoine Robidoux, his brother Louis and Guadalupe Garcia, Kit Carson and Josefa Jaramillo, and Charles Bent and Josefa's sister María Ignacia all grew from the Missouri–New Mexico trade. The men expanded their opportunities by joining the kinship and commercial networks of Hispanic families. New Mexican women gained access to the expanded commercial networks as well, and they may have gained social capital as partners of the traders who supplanted Hispanic men in local institutions. Cross-cultural marriages and relationships were decidedly more advantageous to men, at least in the earliest years of the Santa Fe trade. González argues that the newcomers used Hispanic women as partners to "assist in the takeover."[2] While that may have been true in some cases, the marriages of Carmel and Antoine and Kit and Josefa lasted until the end of their lives. In his will, Antoine referred to Carmel as his beloved, indicating that theirs was more than a marriage of convenience or exploitation.

Much of the literature of the trail identifies the earliest traders as Americans, but some of the men who resided in New Mexico, such as the Robidoux brothers, were French citizens longer than they were Americans, becoming US citizens in 1821 when Missouri attained statehood. Their French cultural backgrounds may have made them more accepting of cross-cultural relationships, as such connections were common in the Mississippi and Missouri River communities frequented by French trappers and traders. Some of the French traders took Indian as well as European mates—sometimes simultaneously—though they may have lived in different settlements. Carmel Benavides Robidoux did not leave any documents in her own hand, but her relationship with Antoine was surely tested by the trail's evolution from a commercial road to a road of conquest. Robidoux's role in the American takeover of New Mexico, however, is preserved in official correspondence and in his own words. He was a dependable scout and translator for General Kearny and surely used his intimate knowledge of the country and the New Mexican people to the advantage of the Army of the West. Carmel likely had conflicting emotions about the events that brought the front lines of the US conquest to her doorstep in Santa Fe. Carmel retained her property in New Mexico, and after Antoine's death, that property provided the resources she needed to build a new life. Carmel sold her New Mexico home and moved to southern Colorado, on the outskirts of the Ute reservation. She lived the remainder of her life on the edges of the American frontier, but she left no explanation of why she did this. Was it because she no longer had a role in the social life of Euro-American–dominated Santa Fe? Did she prefer the more sparsely settled country of the Ute frontier? Or did she simply like or need to live with her granddaughter's family?

Carmel left no written account of how she reacted to Antoine's participation in the Mexican-American War, and few US military or political officials had much interest in New Mexicans' feelings about the invasion. Official reports and correspondence were filled with pretensions of moral and ethnic superiority and the assumption that the occupying forces were bringing the gifts of democracy, enlightenment, and greater prosperity to the culturally backward New Mexicans. Richard Smith Elliott, writing for the *Reveille* in St. Louis, chronicled the Army of the West's occupation of Santa Fe. His appraisal of the social costs of the war, the dissolution of order, and the deprivations New Mexicans faced after the American occupation captured the reality of the war in some detail. The Santa Fe Trail provided the physical route of conquest, but there was no easy victory for the Army of the West. Hispanic and Pueblo New Mexicans resisted US rule during the first year after annexation. In the end, Hispanic and Native peoples in New Mexico lost much of their ancestral land and were displaced from the power structures within their own communities as they were subjected to US occupation.

New Mexican and French colonial women traditionally held some important rights that women in the United States did not possess. The ability to retain control of inherited property and earned resources gave New Mexican, Mexican, and French women a degree of financial and legal agency that was not available to them under the less progressive US law. Gertrudis Barceló, "La Tules," was able to control the Americans she knew by taking advantage of her political and social alliances, her wealth, her business acumen, and the American army's dependence on her for capital.

Among the schoolgirls who came to St. Louis for an education, Francisca López was advised by a succession of legal guardians—all of them associates of her late father—to stay in St. Louis, or at least not to return to New Mexico. When she wed Benjamin Kimball, she brought considerable property of her own, inherited from her father, to the marriage, although those resources were managed by trustees who controlled access to the funds and paid her expenses. Adaline Carson seemingly did not find a place in either her mother's Arapaho culture or her father's western culture. One of the consequences of the new American-made West was that it did not always accommodate people of mixed ancestry. Marian Sloan Russell recalled her family's many trips across the country as grand adventures, but her mother's memories were tinged with the anxiety of providing for her children as a single mother. The violence that surrounded their crossings and settlement in New Mexico and Missouri is a reminder that brutality was present throughout the American expansion. Many of Marian's recollections are tinged with the memory of smoke from the homes and farms burned by vigilantes across Kansas and Missouri in the conflict over slavery. In the prelude to the Civil War, both Marian and Lydia Spencer Lane lived on military posts and witnessed men choosing to abandon their sworn duties to the nation and serve the Confederacy instead. In the aftermath of the Civil War, Marian witnessed violence at close range when landowners killed her husband in a range war. She referred to New Mexico as a "land of enchantment," but competition for land and scarce wages repeatedly drove her and her family away. They also returned on numerous occasions, always trying, but never succeeding, to make New

Mexico their home. Kate Kingsbury was also denied the health and healing she hoped to find in the salubrious climate of New Mexico.

Many of the histories of Americans who traveled the Santa Fe Trail—military families, government officials, and merchants—contain hints that more African Americans were involved in the successes and challenges of the trail than has been recognized. The status of indentured and enslaved servants in New Mexico and the trade in captives have corollaries in the country's history of slavery as well. Although Mexico and New Mexico outlawed slavery in 1829, the New Mexico Slave Code of 1858–59 revived the practice. This was a short-lived but cynical moment in which New Mexican politicians striving for statehood were willing to accept, once again, the idea that people could be property: that servants could be owned and sold and that they could not end their own indenture. The reckoning with slavery and white supremacy was foretold in several sources, most notably in the words of George Ruxton, a British traveler who clearly saw the stain slavery left on this country. His words still ring with the urgency of facing the consequences of slavery and its impact on the conscience of the nation. Julia Archibald and James Holmes wrote scathing editorials and letters, hoping to break the hold of the pro-slavery movement in New Mexico. Like so many women of her time and even later, Julia is remembered not for her activism for women's rights and abolition but most often for her attire. The railroad brought many women to New Mexico, sometimes with their husbands and families, but often on their own as writers, artists, and reformers. The land of enchantment was realized in many ways by the literature of Susan Wallace and Flora Spiegelberg and by the artists and anthropologists who made New Mexico their home in the late eighteenth and nineteenth centuries.

I have lived in Santa Fe and St. Louis, and I have often traveled between the two cities imagining how they were shaped by history and especially by the Santa Fe Trail. The history preserved in many of these places evokes the cultural encounters and events that shaped the West from Native lands and Spanish and French communities. Anglicized place names sometimes hint at previous residents and the layers of conquest and displacement that spread across the continent. Many places retain visible traces of the trail, and local museums preserve the histories of settlements that marked the trail. Some exhibits include short biographies of the people who traded or supplied the trail from the local area. In recent years, the signage in museum exhibits has become more inclusive, incorporating the stories of women, African American, and Hispanic participants in the trade and acknowledging that the trail crossed the lands of many Native American groups. The Santa Fe Trail Association's newsletter *Wagon Tracks* supports much of that local research and is an outlet for new interpretations as they become available. What has not changed, however, are the monuments along the trail that still present images of pioneering families as the norm. I recognize that many of these monuments, like the "madonnas" of the western trails, were erected long ago. Like many public sculptures, the statues of women representing the expansion of the American West are fraught with stereotypes. Unwittingly, these representations perpetuate the idea that white men and women settled the West. Those images exclude the women and men of diverse cultures from Hispanic, Black, and Native American communities and families who made history on the western trails.

The debate over monuments has intensified in this country, largely but not exclusively involving Confederate soldiers and slaveholders whose names or likenesses graced college campuses, town halls, and federal facilities. Throughout the United States, Confederate statues have been removed from public squares, but this new consciousness has not stopped reenactments on some Civil War battlefields. I am not necessarily advocating that the sculptures of the "madonnas" or wagon trains be removed, but I am suggesting that we can add context and details to the places where specific women played a role in history. It is not enough to remove a statue or to move it from a park or other outdoor setting into a museum. What does that removal accomplish if we do not discuss and confront the behaviors that result from the erasure and oversimplification of history? How do we build respect for a more nuanced recognition of US history if we do not interrogate the past and question long-held assumptions? Curators and public historians have rewritten exhibition labels, convened community members and scholars for discussions, and invited governing boards to join conversations about the many dimensions of the items in their collections. But this work is not done simply by changing labels or convening discussions; it requires broadening the participants who tell the stories of the past. History is not a static discipline constructed from facts that everyone accepts as received wisdom. Historical interpretation changes with broader and deeper examinations of the participants. Historical interpretation changes with the respectful listening to and telling of painful chapters and with the teaching of history as a discipline that benefits from multiple points of view. History can no longer be written in the voice of the victors; it must include the voices of many participants using a variety of media to examine how people, cultures, and events are represented in literature, paintings, sculptures, and music. Historical perspective needs to become a way of thinking about, documenting, and engaging with the past. History is not simply an act of memorization or memorialization of a single point of view. Many voices and reports of an event offer the opportunity to examine how actions and actors influence historical memory.

When I began this book, I never imagined that the world would grapple with a pandemic that seemed torn from the pages of centuries-old history. I did not expect that wars would erupt all over the world. I did not foresee the grief of families shattered by loss and the orphans facing uncertain futures as a result of disease and war. Particular years stand out for their historical weight and for the long-term effects of events that occurred. The 2020s will certainly be remembered for the global COVID-19 pandemic and its resultant social changes and economic pressures, for Russia's war against Ukraine, and for the brutal war between Israel and Hamas. In the United States and internationally, the divisive elections and political rhetoric of those years will surely be recorded in the history books. To better understand the COVID-19 pandemic, many people turned to history and the influenza pandemic of 1918. We consult history to find answers and draw parallels to earlier images of war-ravaged countries and the displacement of millions of people. History has been made relevant by the events of our own times. The past speaks to many with an eerie resonance in the words and deeds of those who lived more than a century ago. Their struggles and their capabilities, the difficulties their families endured, and the resilience that helped them rise from heartbreak, loss, displacement, and unimaginable hardship are bonds linking us to people of the past.

Women such as María Rosa Villalpando Salé dit Lajoie, Gertrudis Barceló, and Julia Archibald Holmes left their mark on history by living their lives on their own terms and by assuming social roles that challenged the norms of their times. Women from many cultures and communities were part of the social crucible that became the American West. But for too long, their stories were suppressed or dismissed, and their place in history was erased by narratives that favored white men.[3] The women I write about were, in some instances, the exception, but surely they were not the only women to take a stand, exert their rights, express their beliefs, and raise their voices to challenge the expectations of their communities. The leaders of this nation—all nineteenth-century men whose status offered them privilege—ignored or even erased cultural distinctions and women's participation in many of the intercultural and commercial endeavors that created the West and the Southwest. The predominantly Euro-American men who led the conquest of the West and the Southwest set their sights on the resources and opportunities that lay before them in their vision—or, more correctly, the mirage—of what the West could be. Women and members of diverse communities lived and worked alongside those men, sometimes as handmaidens to that goal of cultural and political dominance. Other women who settled the West and Southwest had their own stories to tell and their own visions of what the West might become. Their graves may mark their last physical place of rest, but I hope this book gives longer life to their stories.

NOTES

Preface

1. In New Mexico, sites predating the Santa Fe Trail are identified by local Native American–made ceramic sherds or small quantities of Spanish- or Mexican-made glazed earthenware called majolica. These imported items were rare, however, given the distances involved and the infrequency of trade with Spain and Mexico. In both Native and Hispanic New Mexican communities, women's labor was essential to the intertribal and intercultural economy. Women in both cultures made pottery, raised sheep to produce wool and weavings, and grew crops for food production in the domestic economies of their individual households and villages. In some Hispanic households, Native American men, women, and children were enslaved to provide this domestic labor. Archaeological sites postdating the Santa Fe trade contain much smaller percentages of Native American–made ceramics. Specific patterns of pottery sherds and other American and British manufactured items are markers of Santa Fe Trail–era sites. These items indicate that the people who lived in these households and communities had shifted from local exchange to the commercial markets created by the trail merchants. Several authors, including Heather B. Trigg, *From Household to Empire: Society and Economy in Early Colonial New Mexico* (Tucson: University of Arizona Press, 2005), and James F. Brooks, *Captives and Cousins: Slavery, Kinship and Community in the Southwest Borderlands* (Chapel Hill: University of North Carolina Press, 2002), describe the changes in New Mexican household economies before and after the Santa Fe trade began.

2. I am grateful to Doyle Daves, whose many publications in *Wagon Tracks: Santa Fe Trail Association Quarterly* provided the initial lists and summary statistics for the women whose stories are included in this volume. Marc Simmons compiled an early annotated bibliography of sources in "Women on the Santa Fe Trail: Diaries, Journals, Memoirs; an Annotated Bibliography," *New Mexico Historical Review* 61, 3 (July 1986): 233–243.

3. Virginia Scharff, *Twenty Thousand Roads: Women, Movement and the West* (Berkeley: University of California Press, 2003).

Acknowledgments

1. Thanks to *Gateway* and *El Palacio* for permission to use parts of my articles they published: "Introduction: William Carr Lane; First Mayor of St. Louis, Second Governor of the New Mexico Territory (article by William Carson)," *Gateway: The Magazine of the Missouri History Museum* 36 (2016): 9–12; "Stella Drumm, the Not-so-Quiet Librarian," *Gateway: The Magazine of the Missouri History Museum* 37, 2 (2017): 44–49; "From Captive to Creole: María Rosa Villalpando," *Gateway: The Magazine of the Missouri History Museum* 39, 2 (2019): 6–15; "Trading Places: Seeing the Santa Fe Trail from the Flip Side," *El Palacio* 122, 1 (2017): 56–63; "Desperately Seeking Carmel," *El Palacio* 124, 2 (2019): 52–59; "A Beautiful Death on the Santa Fe Trail," *El Palacio* 125, 1 (2020): 64–72. In some cases, I have taken the opportunity to refine my thinking and make corrections to what I previously wrote.

Introduction

1. These three terms reduce the diversity that characterized the cultures involved in western expansion. I use *Anglo-American* when that is the term used by the original authors. *Anglo* is still used in New Mexico to refer to anyone not of Native American or Hispanic ancestry, often regardless of that person's specific background. I use *Euro-American* in place of *Anglo-American* to signify the many countries and points of origin of western travelers and settlers.

2. In their collaborations, linguist Enrique R. Lamadrid and photographer Miguel Gandert have extensively documented the performances of Los Comanches in several communities of northern New Mexico. Enrique R. Lamadrid, with photos by Miguel Gandert, *Hermanitos Comanchitos: Indo-Hispano Rituals of Captivity and Redemption* (Albuquerque: University of New Mexico Press, 2003); Miguel Gandert and Enrique R. Lamadrid, *Nuevo Mexico Profundo: Rituals of the Indo-Hispano Homelands* (Santa Fe: Museum of New Mexico Press, 2000). Aulton E. "Bob" Roland explores the enduring history of Plácida Romero in *The Ballad of Plácida Romero: A Woman's Captivity & Redemption* (Santa Fe: Museum of New Mexico Press, 2022), centering her story in the landscape and memory of an Apache raid on central New Mexico in 1881.

3. David J. Weber, ed., "An Unforgettable Day: Facundo Melgares on Independence," *New Mexico Historical Review* 48, 1 (1973): 27–44.

4. Thomas James, *Three Years among the Indians and Mexicans* (1846), with notes and biographical sketches by Walter B. Douglas, 117–118, Kindle.

5. Francis Parkman Jr., "Across the Great Plains," in *In Their Own Words: Warriors and Pioneers*, ed. T. J. Stiles (New York: Perigee Books, 1996), 8–10.

6. David Sneed, "The Remarkable St. Louis Wagon Builders," *Wagon Tracks: Santa Fe Trail Association Quarterly* 32, 2 (2018): 10–11.

7. Patricia Nelson Limerick, *The Legacy of Conquest: The Unbroken Past of the*

American West (New York: W. W. Norton, 1987), contends that the term *frontier* was used in earlier historiography to indicate a time before white ascendency but avoid recognizing the conflicts and legacies of successive conquests of Native and Hispanic peoples in the western United States.

8. Stephen Aron, *American Confluence: The Missouri Frontier from Borderlands to Border State* (Bloomington: Indiana University Press, 2006), cautions against the ethnocentrism embraced by earlier historians in the idea of a frontier. Walter Johnson, in *The Broken Heart of America: St. Louis and the Violent History of the United States* (New York: Basic Books, 2020), positions St. Louis at the center of a violent history beginning with the removal of the Osage peoples from their ancestral lands and extending to the current history of violent confrontations between African Americans and police. In Johnson's polemical history of St. Louis, the Santa Fe Trail is part of the racialized capitalism that has defined the relationships among people of different races and cultures.

9. Ned Blackhawk is a historian and member of the Te-Moak tribe of the Western Shoshone. His seminal work examining the place of violence in the intercultural encounters of the Spanish colonial Southwest and the western expansion of the United States into the Great Basin is *Violence, Warfare, Terror and Colonialism in the Making of the United States* (Cambridge, MA: Harvard University Press, 2006). Blackhawk argues that Native peoples, specifically Utes and others whose homelands were within Mexico's borders, were given wider access to goods brought by Missouri traders. He calls those traders Americans, but they often included men from French and *métis* backgrounds. Ana María Alonso, "Reconsidering Violence: Warfare, Terror and Colonialism in the Making of the United States," *American Quarterly* 60, 4 (2008): 1089–1097.

10. Max L. Moorhead, *New Mexico's Royal Road: Trade and Travel on the Chihuahua Trail* (Norman: University of Oklahoma Press, 1958).

11. David C. Beyreis, "Business, Politics, and Power: The Transcontinental World of Bent, St. Vrain and Company, 1829–1849," *Wagon Tracks: Santa Fe Trail Association Quarterly* 36, 2 (2022): 17–23; David C. Beyreis, *Blood in the Borderlands: Conflict, Kinship and the Bent Family, 1821–1920* (Lincoln: University of Nebraska Press, 2020), 52.

12. Anne F. Hyde, *Empires, Nations and Families: A New History of the North American West, 1800–1860* (New York: Ecco Paperbacks, 2012), 19; Anne F. Hyde, *Born of Lakes and Plains: Mixed-Descent Peoples and the Making of the American West* (New York: W. W. Norton, 2022).

13. Carl J. Ekberg, *Stealing Indian Women: Native Slavery in the Illinois Country* (Urbana: University of Illinois Press, 2007), 3–6.

14. J. Frederick Fausz, *Founding St. Louis: First City of the New West* (Charleston, SC: History Press, 2011), 21. See also Fausz's chapter "The Capital of St. Louis: From Indian Trade to American Territory, 1764–1825," in *French St. Louis: Landscape, Contexts and Legacy*, ed. Jay Gitlin, Robert Michael Morrissey, and Peter J. Kastor (Lincoln: University of Nebraska Press, 2021), 67–91.

15. Tanis C. Thorne, *The Many Hands of My Relations: French and Indians on the Lower Missouri* (Columbia: University of Missouri Press, 1996), 4.

16. Gitlin, Morrissey, and Kastor, *French St. Louis*; Jay Gitlin, *The Bourgeois Frontier: French Towns, French Traders and American Expansion* (New Haven, CT: Yale University Press, 2010), 1–10.

17. Andrew N. Wegmann, "The Creole Frontier: Free People of Color in St. Louis and along the French Mississippi Corridor, 1800–1870," in Gitlin, Morrissey, and Kastor, *French St. Louis*, 157–184.

18. Patricia Cleary, "Fashioning Identities on the Frontier: Clothing, Culture and Choice in Early St. Louis," in Gitlin, Morrissey, and Kastor, *French St. Louis*, 93–128.

19. Margaret Jacobs, "What's Gender Got to Do with It?" *Western Historical Quarterly* 42, 3 (2011): 297–304; Margaret Jacobs, "Out of a Rut: Decolonizing Western Women's History," *Pacific Historical Review* 79, 4 (2010): 585–604.

20. In their seminal article "The Gentle Tamers Revisited: New Approaches to the History of Women in the American West," *Pacific Historical Review* 49, 2 (1980): 173–213, Joan M. Jensen and Darlis A. Miller review the historiography of women's perspectives and women's place in western American history.

21. The statues are in Springfield, Ohio; Wheeling, West Virginia; Council Grove, Kansas; Lexington, Missouri; Lamar, Colorado; Albuquerque, New Mexico; Springerville, Arizona; Vandalia, Illinois; Richmond, Indiana; Beallsville, Pennsylvania; Upland, California; and Bethesda, Maryland. Cynthia Culver Prescott, compiler of the website Pioneer Monuments in the American West, describes these figures and places them in the larger context of monuments depicting themes in western history. See also Cynthia Culver Prescott, *Pioneer Mothers Monuments: Creating Cultural Memory* (Norman: University of Oklahoma Press, 2019). The 2021 audit of US monuments conducted by the Monument Lab with support from the Andrew W. Mellon Foundation found that the overwhelming majority of statues are of men associated with the images and symbols of war. The Monument Lab Audit reported that "feminized bodies often appear in the sanctioned monument landscape as fictional, mythological, and allegorical figures" (17–18). Prescott and the Monument Lab Audit conclude that although monuments are not history per se, they have a role in perpetuating myths and aggrandizing war and conquest.

22. Josiah Gregg's *Commerce of the Prairies*, originally published in 1844, has generated a considerable body of critical literature parsing Gregg's adventures and observations. I used the 1954 edition edited by Max L. Moorhead (Norman: University of Oklahoma Press), which has been reprinted several times. *James Josiah Webb's Adventures in the Santa Fe Trade, 1844–1847*, ed. Ralph Bieber, was published in 1931 (Glendale, CA: A. H. Clark). For this research I used the 1995 Bison Book edition (Lincoln: University of Nebraska Press), with an introduction by Mark L. Gardner and retaining Bieber's annotations and edits. Both Gregg and Webb remain standard references of the early era of the commercial enterprises that brought American traders to the Southwest and northern Mexico.

23. Stella Drumm edited the diary of Susan Shelby Magoffin for the years 1846–47,

and it was first published by Yale University Press in 1926. Drumm was the librarian for the Missouri Historical Society in St. Louis from 1913 to 1943. When Yale reissued the book in 1962, Howard Lamar's foreword credited Drumm with research and annotations "so useful and valid after thirty-five years that her annotation stands unchanged" (xxxv). He also argued that while Magoffin's work could "never outrank" that of Josiah Gregg, her journal "deserves equal recognition" with James Josiah Webb's work (xii). The memoirs of Marian Russell were dictated to her daughter-in-law, Winnie (Mrs. Hal) McGuire Russell, edited by Garnet M. Brayer, and published by Branding Iron Press in Evanston, Illinois, in 1954. I used the 1993 edition by the University of New Mexico Press, with an afterword by trail scholar Marc Simmons. Simmons considers the Magoffin and Russell works the "two best accounts" among the disappointingly few by women.

24. Susan Calafate Boyle, *Los Capitalistas: Hispano Merchants and the Santa Fe Trade* (Albuquerque: University of New Mexico Press, 1997), 41–43, 61.

25. James Riding In, "American Indians and the Santa Fe Trail," *Wagon Tracks: Santa Fe Trail Association Quarterly* 35, 4 (2021): 17–24.

26. Stella Drumm, ed., *Down the Old Santa Fe Trail and into Mexico: The Diary of Susan Shelby Magoffin, 1846–1847* (New Haven, CT: Yale University Press, 1926; reissued 1962. Lincoln: Bison Books, University of Nebraska Press, 1982), 102–103.

1. BARTERING WOMEN: CAPTIVES, COMMODITIES, AND TRADERS

1. Juliana Barr, *Peace Came in the Form of a Woman: Indians and Spaniards in the Texas Borderlands* (Chapel Hill: University of North Carolina Press, 2007).

2. Gregg sent some of the plants he collected along the trail to Dr. George Engelmann in St. Louis. Those specimens, some identified for the first time and named for Gregg, now reside in the herbarium of the Missouri Botanical Garden, along with the correspondence between Gregg and Engelmann.

3. Editor Max L. Moorhead gives the broad outlines of Josiah Gregg's peripatetic life in Gregg, *Commerce of the Prairies*, xvii–xxix. Gregg was born in Overton County, Tennessee, on July 19, 1806, the youngest of four sons in a family that also included three daughters. The family moved to Illinois and then to Missouri by the time Josiah was six. By 1825, the family had moved farther west to Independence, where he was exposed to the burgeoning trade. Gregg studied surveying and then bookkeeping, which made him a valued trail employee on his first trip with the caravan of Jesse Sutton. Gregg's notes and letters became source materials for his post-trail career as a writer, botanist, and then medical practitioner or apothecary. See also Josiah Gregg, *Diary & Letters of Josiah Gregg . . . Excursions in Mexico & California, 1847–1850*, ed. Maurice Fulton (Norman: University of Oklahoma Press, 1944).

4. The story of María Rosa's captivity has been well documented by several authors. Charles Van Ravenswaay, *St. Louis: An Informal History of the City and Its People, 1764–1865*, ed. Candace O'Connor (St. Louis: Missouri Historical Society

Press, 1991), relates her alleged refusal to honor her father's promise to a Comanche chief, thereby making her both the cause and the victim of the Comanche raid on Ranchos de Taos. He broadly outlines her being "bartered to the Pawnees" and then sold to the French fur trader who brought her to St. Louis, and he traces her rise in society to her daughter's fortunate marriage to an aristocrat, thereby ensuring the high status of her descendants in St. Louis society. See also James F. Brooks, "'This Evil Extends Especially . . . to the Feminine Sex': Negotiating Captivity in the New Mexico Borderlands," *Feminist Studies* 22, 2 (Summer 1996): 279–309; Brooks, *Captives and Cousins*. Pekka Hämäläinen, *The Comanche Empire* (New Haven, CT: Yale University Press, 2008), explores the economic value, capricious treatment, and exploitation of women in the Plains trade, a topic with its own huge and growing bibliography. I have chosen to standardize María Rosa's name to the spelling in her Spanish baptismal record, adding the surname of her husband as listed in the records of her life in St. Louis. However, depending on whether it is a Spanish-, French-, or English-language document, her name may be given as María Rosa or Marie Rose. Her last name also has many variants, including del Videlpane, Vidalpando, Villarpando, Vial Pando, Panda, or Ponda; LaJoye or Lajoie; and Salée or Sallée. I am grateful to genealogist Henrietta Christmas for allowing me access to her research notes compiled over more than a decade of tracing María Rosa's family of origin and her Jáquez descendants.

5. John Neal Hoover, *Adventures and Sufferings: The American Indian Captivity Narrative through the Centuries*, 2nd rev. ed. (St. Louis: St. Louis Mercantile Library, 2002), contains an impressive checklist of the captive narratives found in the library's collections. Gregg likely read several of the captive narratives published during the years he traveled the trail, and importantly, he would have heard firsthand accounts of men and women who were captives or witnessed rescues.

6. Gregg, *Commerce of the Prairies*, 105. I tried to find contemporary accounts of people with whom María Rosa shared her "tale of woe," but I was unsuccessful. She was not listed or described in any contemporary newspapers or among letters exchanged with other women living in St. Louis at the time. Josiah Gregg's published correspondence provides no clues as to how María Rosa's story became known to him.

7. Brooks, "'This Evil Extends.'" Barr, *Peace Came in the Form of a Woman*, offers a fine study of captive women used by Comanches and other Plains Indian groups for diplomacy, in the creation of intercultural families, and as agents of culture change. Barr also looks at how male dominance in Plains cultures led to the use of sex and women's work as mediums of exchange. Barr's focus on history from the perspective of Indian values is an important departure from European ideas of dominance and colonial hierarchy.

8. Elizabeth A. H. John, *Storms Brewed in Other Men's Worlds* (College Station: Texas A&M Press, 1975); Elizabeth A. H. John, "Nurturing the Peace: Spanish and Comanche Cooperation in the Early Nineteenth Century," *New Mexico Historical Review* 59 (1984): 345–369.

9. Thomas Kavanagh concludes that the Kotsotekas, or Buffalo-Eater Comanches,

were the tribal division that maintained a trading relationship with New Mexico in 1786–1820. Thomas Kavanagh, *The Comanches: A History, 1706–1875* (Lincoln: University of Nebraska Press, 1999), 480. He also notes that the Kwahadas were a political organization "coalescing" or descending from the Kotsotekas circa 1860 and that they were traders in stolen cattle. Ibid., 481–482.

10. Blackhawk, *Violence, Warfare, Terror and Colonialism*, 46–47.

11. Rick Hendricks analyzes four accounts of the 1761 Spanish massacre of Comanches by the order of interim governor Manuel de Portillo Urrisola. A large contingent of Comanches had come to Taos Pueblo to barter captives taken in the 1760 raid and resume trade. Rick Hendricks, "The 1761 Comanche Massacre," in *Massacre, Murder and Mayhem in the Rocky Mountains*, ed. Tim Blevins et al. (Colorado Springs: Pikes Peak Library District, 2016), 14–37.

12. Eleanor B. Adams, ed., "Bishop Tamarón's Visitation of New Mexico 1760," *New Mexico Historical Review* 28 (July 1953): 217. María Rosa's first husband was named Juan José Jáquez. Her mother's family name has been given as Martine, which could have been Martín or Martínez, both common names in the Taos settlements, and as Valdez, also common in the Taos area. In fact, she could have been a member of both families in the small community of Taos.

13. A league is computed as 2.5999 miles in Thomas C. Barnes, Thomas H. Naylor, and Charles W. Polzer, *Northern New Spain: A Research Guide* (Tucson: University of Arizona Press, 1981), 68.

14. "Report of the Reverend Father Provincial, Fray Pedro Serrano, to the Most Excellent Señor Viceroy, the Marquis of Cruillas, in Regard to the Custodia of New Mexico, in the Year 1761," in Charles Wilson Hackett, *Historical Documents Relating to New Mexico, Nueva Vizcaya, and Approaches Thereto, to 1773*, vol. 3 (Washington, DC: Carnegie Institution of Washington, 1937), 486–487.

15. Adams, "Bishop Tamarón's Visitation," 217–222.

16. Hämäläinen, *Comanche Empire*, 46–54. Barr, *Peace Came in the Form of a Woman*, traces the practice of using women as peacemakers between the small Spanish-held colony and the wide-ranging Comanches and other Native groups in Texas. In part because kinship was key to peacemaking and the foundation of the political economy, women were necessary to literally birth intercultural families and intercultural interactions.

17. Hämäläinen, *Comanche Empire*, 8, refers to Richard White's formative study of the evolution of Native political economies and his use of "middle ground" to describe the place where Native peoples and colonial powers negotiated their relationships through fictive kinship, diplomacy, and gifting, as well as more defensive or even militaristic strategies.

18. Many narratives were collected from men and women who observed Comanche captives in the nineteenth century, when the lucrative horse and fur trade made slave labor more valuable. Hämäläinen, *Comanche Empire*, 230–259, provides an extensive overview of the demographic, economic, and social importance of taking captives, drawn largely from nineteenth-century source materials. Brooks, *Captives*

and Cousins, 180–197, discusses the importance of capture as a means for the Comanches to replenish their groups following epidemics and warfare and as a source of wealth measured by enslaved women.

19. Pekka Hämäläinen, "The Western Comanche Trade Center: Rethinking the Plains Indian Trade System," *Western Historical Quarterly* 29, 4 (Winter 1998): 490–491, http://www.jstor.org/stable/970405.

20. The letter is among a series of documents from the Archivo General de Indias (AGI) in Seville, Spain, that were compiled, copied, and summarized in translation by researcher Anna Price in 1990 for a project on the Spanish presence in Upper Louisiana. Price identifies the document's location as Papers of Cuba 109–1171, microfilm on file, Missouri Historical Society, St. Louis. Carl J. Ekberg and Sharon Person, "The 1767 Dufossat Maps of St. Louis," *Gateway: The Magazine of the Missouri History Museum* 32 (2012): 8–25, identify this document as AGI, Papeles de Cuba Legajo 109. Jerry Gurulé, a skilled paleographer and colleague from Albuquerque, prepared a full transcription and translation of the document for this chapter. Antonio de Ulloa (the first governor of Louisiana, 1762–69) sent military official Francisco Ríu to construct forts at the confluence of the Missouri and Mississippi Rivers in 1767. The forts were intended to keep the British east of the confluence area and prevent them from entering the rich fur trade with Indigenous groups as well as with Taos and Santa Fe. Noel M. Loomis and Abraham P. Nasatir, *Pedro Vial and the Roads to Santa Fe* (Norman: University of Oklahoma Press, 1967), claim that Ríu was maladroit and incompetent and disliked by his troops and the citizens of the region. He was removed from the post by Pedro Piernas, lieutenant governor of Upper Louisiana (1770–75), who established a stable, effective Spanish presence in the confluence area. Ulloa and Piernas inspired loyalty from Osage, Kansa, Pawnee, Jumano, and Comanche groups through trade and diplomatic gifts.

21. This letter is the only mention of María Rosa's "sister," and it raises the question of whether it refers to a biological sister, another woman taken in the raid, or some other woman she encountered in the Comanche or Pawnee camp. A family record for Juan Rosalio Villalpando and María Rosa Valdez, prepared by genealogist Henrietta Christmas, shows sisters María Madalena, María Hilaria, María Rosa, and Ana María. With the exception of María Rosa, there are no marriage records for these women, although such records are notoriously fragmentary. Perhaps some of these sisters were among the women killed or kidnapped during the 1760 raid.

22. Fausz, *Founding St. Louis*, 97, identifies Saintous, France, as the birthplace of Jean Baptiste Salé dit Lajoie. This may be a variant spelling of Saintes, in the southwestern department of Charente-Maritime, where others place his birth. William Clark Breckenridge, "Biographical Sketch of Judge Wilson Primm," *Missouri Historical Society Collections* 4, 2 (1913): 134. Saintes is about forty-five miles from La Rochelle, a seacoast town with strong trade ties to New Orleans. Fausz, 42.

23. María Rosa's age and the year she was born are listed or calculated differently in various sources. She appears in the 1750 census of Taos, but no age is stated. See Virginia Langham Olmsted, comp., *Spanish and Mexican Census of New Mexico,*

1750 to 1830 (Albuquerque: New Mexico Genealogical Society, 1981), 47. Brooks ("'This Evil Extends'"; *Captives and Cousins*, 66–67, 131–132) states that she was twenty-one years old when she was taken captive in 1760. According to Jack B. Tykal, "Taos to St. Louis: The Journey of María Rosa Villalpando," *New Mexico Historical Review* 65, 2 (1990): 161–174, she was a good deal older, perhaps in her thirties or even as old as forty-four, when she was taken captive. Henrietta Christmas, a skilled genealogist, cites 1726 as the year of her birth but does not list a specific reference. It seems reasonable to assume that she was in her twenties or early thirties when she met Lajoie, as she had four more children after partnering with him: Pierre born in 1771, twin girls Hélène and Marie Josèphe born in 1773, and another son named Antoine Xavier born in 1776 (not to be confused with her half-Comanche son Antoine), according to Christmas's research. Some fascinating details of Lajoie's early years in St. Louis and eventual abandonment of his family are contained in the testimony of neighbors in the case of *Salle dit La Joie v. Peter Primm*, April 23, 1833. In the 1787 census of St. Louis, Lajoie is listed as forty-seven and María Rosa as forty-six. This would have made her about nineteen at the time of the raid.

24. Brooks, "'This Evil Extends,'" 279. Breckenridge, "Biographical Sketch," traces the genealogy of the prominent Primm family of St. Louis. Hélène Salé dit Lajoie, María Rosa and Jean Baptiste's daughter, is the link in this interesting family history. Hélène married Benjamin Leroux in January 1792, and their daughter Marie Angélique married Peter Primm, a tailor, in 1809 in St. Louis. Breckenridge, 134, also briefly relates the story of "Marie Rose's" captivity in his reckoning of the Primm family history and in his account of family members' lawsuits over title to María Rosa's properties.

25. Ekberg and Person, "1767 Dufossat Maps of St. Louis," 8–25, trace the broad outlines of María Rosa and Lajoie's life, and their work led me to several other sources. The detailed 1767 maps published in their article come from the Biblioteca Nacional de España in Madrid. Their work is an important contribution to the cartographic history of colonial St. Louis. The map and catalog information can be viewed online at Rélevé d'une Partie du Missisipi et du Missouri Depuis le Vilage de Pain-Court Iusquau Rocher de l'Eau Froide Fait aux Illinois Provaince de la Louisiane le 15 Octubre 1767 [Material cartográfico], www.bdhrd.bne.es/viewer.vm?id=0000143583. Ekberg and Person suggest that since Lajoie was the only settler named on any of these maps, it raises the question of whether he enjoyed some status among the founders and was, perhaps, recognized for his specific knowledge of the area.

26. "Case of *Salée dit Lajoye* [sic] *v. Primm*, Case 368, St. Louis District, October Term," in *Reports of the Cases Argued and Determined in the Supreme Court of the State of Missouri from 1827 to 1830*, ed. Louis Houck (St. Louis: Gilbert Book Co., 1834), 280. Lajoie bought and sold other property in the town, including a portion of block 40 in the area known as Laclede's Landing and a portion of block 3.

27. Archaeological excavations conducted by the Missouri Department of Transportation between 2013 and 2107 were some of the first systematic excavations of the

original site of the French colonial town. Four city blocks, located immediately south of the Gateway Arch, were sampled, revealing the remains of several eighteenth- and nineteenth-century house foundations and associated domestic structures. The excavations uncovered several seventeenth-century Creole-style vertical post (*poteaux-en-terre*) houses, fragments of French-made faience, and an assortment of utilitarian earthenware as well as British delftware sherds. Animal bones and some grain seeds yield a more complete picture of the French colonial settlers' diet. Although later settlements disturbed much of the French colonial town site, some archaeological remains might include a portion of Lajoie's holdings as shown on the 1767 Dufossat map. Michael J. Meyer, "The French of St. Louis: Archaeological Excavation of the Madame Haycraft, Fifi and Berger Sites," *Missouri Archaeologist* 79 (2018): 18–43. The deed from John Delage to Lajoie for lot 57 dated August 8, 1767, is part of a later ejectment lawsuit between María Rosa's heirs. *Salle dit La Joie v. Peter Primm*, April 23, 1833, St. Louis Circuit Case 93.

28. I am following Fausz's broad use of *French* to describe the cultural milieu of St. Louis. In an extended opening note on terminology in *Founding St. Louis*, Fausz addresses the heart of the cultural mix that was colonial St. Louis. Eschewing the terms *French-speaking* and *Francophone*, he uses the term *French* to refer to people who came to St. Louis from France, as well as those from French colonial settings in the Western Hemisphere—Canadians, Creoles, and Caribbean islanders, all of whom spoke variants of French, practiced Catholicism, and followed cultural practices originating in France.

29. Patricia Cleary, *The World, the Flesh and the Devil: A History of Colonial St. Louis* (Columbia: University of Missouri Press, 2011).

30. In this document, María Rosa is referred to as Marie Rosa Videlpane, widow of Jean Joseph Jacques, who was killed about ten years ago by the "Laitanes," a reference to Comanches. Her father is listed as "Paul Vidalpane," but only her mother's last name, Martine, is listed—both of Taos. Jean Baptiste is identified as Jean Sallé—twenty-nine years old, a native of Saintes, France, and a voyageur living in St. Louis. He was the son of Jacques Paul Sallé and Jeanne Lupeau. Old St. Louis Archives Document Instrument 2023, Missouri Historical Society.

31. Baptismal record of Lembert [Lambert] Lajoie, July 4, 1770, signed by Father Pierre Gibault, who served the church in St. Louis from June 1770 to January 1772. Basilica of St. Louis, King of France (St. Louis, Mo.), Parish Register of Baptisms, Marriages, Burials, 1766–81, https://www.familysearch.org/ark:/61903/3:1:3Q9M-CS79-1365-F?i=467&cat=707913.

32. A transcribed and published list of the men who swore their allegiance to Spain on this day raises more questions than it answers. Jean Baptiste is not one of the thirty-one men who signed their names to the oath. Among the forty men who signed the oath with an *X* is a man whose name is transcribed as "J. Bte Savois." This is likely a transcription error for Jean Baptiste Lajoie, but that still does not answer the question of whether María Rosa and their sons were in St. Louis at that time. Harry P. Dart, ed., "The Oath of Allegiance to Spain, from the Cabildo Records,

New Orleans," *Louisiana Historical Quarterly* 4 (1921): 205–215, HathiTrust Digital Library.

33. "Census of St. Louis and Its Districts, 1791," certified as a true and exact copy from the Archivo Nacional, Havana, 1905, Missouri Historical Society, St. Louis, identifier a0254–00069.

34. Hèléne's twin sister Marie Josèphe and a brother Pierre may not have survived, as they are not mentioned in any census, settlement, or probate records in which Lambert and Hèléne are mentioned. Lajoie seems to have been in St. Louis at the beginning of 1792, as he is listed in the record of the January 17, 1792, marriage of Benjamin Leroux, legitimate son of Germain Leroux and Catherine Vallé of Quebec, to Hèléne Salé dit Lajoie, daughter of Jean Baptiste Salé dit Lajoie and Marie Rose De Vialpande (*sic*) in the parish of St. Louis in Illinois. Breckenridge, "Biographical Sketch," 132. In a later case, when Lambert sued for a portion of his mother's estate, he mentions spending eighteen months in France with his father and his father's abandonment of his mother in 1792 or 1793. Lambert also references a December 29, 1817, letter from Lajoie to María Rosa in which he states that he will remain in France and has abandoned his family. *Salée dit Lajoye* [sic] *v. Primm* was filed in 1834.

35. Testimony in *Salle dit La Joye* [sic] *v. Peter Primm*, April 23, 1833, St. Louis Circuit Case 93. This suit of ejectment lasted several years and contains extensive testimony of Lambert Lajoie and Peter Primm and the witnesses they each called as they fought over the title to properties owned by María Rosa. Peter Primm was married to Marie Angelique Leroux, who was Hèléne's daughter, making Lambert and Primm uncle and nephew by marriage, respectively. The trial transcript also includes the contents of a letter dated December 29, 1817, that Jean Baptiste sent from France in response to María Rosa's request for support in a letter dated August 18, 1816. I am grateful to Robert Moore, former historian at Gateway Arch National Park in St. Louis, who provided transcriptions of that case and a digest of the more than thirty cases filed by María Rosa beginning in 1805 and continuing among her heirs until 1834. Indeed, this series of lawsuits documents her life in St. Louis and offers some insight into her tenacious character.

36. Robert Moore has researched and traced the titles to properties in colonial St. Louis. He located four tracts, now within Gateway Arch National Park, that were held by Jean Baptiste and María Rosa from 1770 to 1804. I am grateful to Bob for allowing me to use the maps that he and Mike Venso produced. They aided my understanding of the French colonial settlement of St. Louis and the location of the Lajoie and Primm properties.

37. Instrument 895, June 9, 1802, St. Louis Recorded Archives Index, WPA-NPS Transcription Project vol. 2, book 3, 515–516. A bill of sale from Lieutenant Governor Francisco Cruzate to August Chouteau dated August 24, 1783, conveys an unborn child of a *métis* woman named Marie, confirming the practice of breeding enslaved children for sale. Document in the collections of the Missouri Historical Society and reproduced in Ekberg, *Stealing Indian Women*, 85, fig. 8.

38. Instrument 896, St. Louis Recorded Archives Index, WPA-NPS Transcription Project vol. 2, book 3, 516.

39. Between August 7, 1806, and November 4, 1807, María Rosa pressed the courts to summons witnesses in her case against Francois Reed. She had filed the suit as the mother and representative of her deceased son Antoine for payments due. Witness summons issued for Antoine Roy in the case of Marie Rose LeJoy [sic], plaintiff vs. Francois Reed, defendant, June 19, 1807; witness summons issued for August Chouteau and Baptist Poidras in the case of Marie Rose LeJoy [sic], plaintiff vs. Francois Reed, defendant, November 4, 1807, St. Louis District, Common Pleas, cause 25, Missouri Historical Society. She also had to defend a claim to the land in block 57 that she had lived on since arriving in St. Louis in about 1769. Her son Lambert asserted his right to the tract as Jean Baptiste's heir. An 1812 act of Congress perfected the title in the names of Marie Rose (María Rosa) and her son-in-law Benjamin Leroux, husband of Hèléne. The case argued that the conveyance of the lot from the plaintiff and his mother to Peter Primm (grandson of Hèléne) estopped Lambert's current case against his great-nephew Primm. Additional conveyances of this property were made to Peter Primm from María Rosa, Lambert, and Hèléne in October 1816 and were more precisely defined in the 1834 settlement of María Rosa's estate.

40. Instrument 1445, August 3, 1803, St. Louis Recorded Archives Index, WPA-NPS Transcription Project, vol. 4, book 2, 232, Missouri Historical Society. Although Jáquez testified that he needed his inheritance to support his family, he may not have returned to New Mexico immediately. His family was living near San Juan (now Ohkay Owinge) Pueblo at the confluence of the Río Grande and Río Chama north of Santa Fe. At the end of July 1809 the governor of New Mexico, in a demand sent to the governor of Texas, ordered Jáquez to give up the woman he was keeping in San Antonio, Texas, and return to his wife in New Mexico. Spanish Archives of New Mexico II:2239, July 27, 1809. María Rosa would outlive her son, who died in 1820. His death is recorded on a New Mexico Genealogical Society Family Search pedigree, which shows the death of Josae Julian Jaquez (sic) at Plaza de San Francisco del San Juan Pueblo and lists his birth in about 1758.

41. Brooks, *Captives and Cousins*, 229–230.

42. *State of Missouri vs. William Kell*, June term, 1823, microfilm, Missouri Historical Society.

43. Susan Calafate Boyle, "Did She Generally Decide? Women in Ste. Genevieve, 1750–1805," *William and Mary Quarterly* 44, 4 (1987): 775–789.

44. John C. Ewers, "The Indian Trade of the Upper Missouri before Lewis and Clark," in *Indian Life on the Upper Missouri* (1954; reprint, Norman: University of Oklahoma Press, 1968), 14–33. Ewers argues that in the eighteenth and early nineteenth centuries a number of tribes operated thriving trade centers in villages along the banks of the upper Missouri River, dealing in agricultural products, horses, manufactured goods, and luxuries. This hub was thought to be unique among Natives in North America, but Hämäläinen argues in *Comanche Empire* that the upper Arkansas was also a critical trading ground dominated by Comanche bands.

45. Gregg, *Commerce of the Prairies*, 17–21, 19n21; Fred S. Perrine, "Military Escorts on the Santa Fe Trail," *New Mexico Historical Review* 2 (April 1927): 175–291, 269–304; 3 (July 1928): 265–300.

46. Caroline Harris is typically referred to as Mrs. Harris in reports of her ordeal, while Sarah Ann Horn is usually referred to as Sarah Ann. I am not sure of the reason for this differentiation, but even Sarah Ann refers to Caroline as Mrs. Harris in her account of their trials.

47. Margaret Schmidt Hacker and Cynthia Ann Parker, *Handbook of Texas Online*, Texas State Historical Association. There are many fictionalized accounts of Parker's life as she chose to live it among the Comanches.

48. Mrs. Caroline Harris, *History of the Captivity and Providential Release Therefrom of Mrs. Caroline Harris* (New York: G. Cunningham, 1838); E. House, *A Narrative of the Captivity of Mrs. Horn and Her Two Children with Mrs. Harris by the Camanche Indians* (St. Louis: C. Keemle, 1839); Rachael Loften, Susie Hendrix, and Jane Kennedy, "The Rachel Plummer Narrative," ms., 1926, Everett D. Graff Collection of Western Americana, Newberry Library, Chicago.

49. House, *Narrative of the Captivity*, 156–157. Sarah Ann met briefly with her two sons while she was being held. They were adopted by Comanche families.

50. Miguel Gandert and Enrique R. Lamadrid have long collaborated on documenting the folk traditions of New Mexico, focusing on what Lamadrid calls the Indo-Hispano rituals of captivity and redemption. Gandert's powerful photographs capture the pathos, energy, and immediacy of this history, which, though centuries old, is still celebrated in Río Grande communities from Taos south to El Paso, Texas. See Gandert and Lamadrid, *Nuevo Mexico Profundo*; Lamadrid, *Hermanitos Comanchitos*. Lamadrid notes that tribal rolls and the US census do not allow for "hybrids"; residents of Los Ranchos do not claim tribal status, nor does the US census recognize their Native American–Hispanic mixtures. Through oral traditions and the dance cycles, residents assert and sustain their complex cultural and racial identities. Lamadrid, *Hermanitos Comanchitos*, 135.

51. Hoover, *Adventures and Sufferings*, vi–vii.

52. Brooks, "'This Evil Extends,'" 292.

2. On the Trail of Carmel Benavides Robidoux

1. David J. Weber, *The Taos Trappers: The Fur Trade in the Far Southwest, 1540–1846* (Norman: University of Oklahoma Press, 1968), places many French and Euro-American fur traders in the Taos area and occasionally in Santa Fe well before the official trade was established in 1821.

2. There appears to be no record of their marriage in any New Mexico or Missouri church, but legal documents indicate they *were* married, including Antoine's application for citizenship in New Mexico and his last will and testament.

3. Gitlin, *Bourgeois Frontier*, 120–123, 187–188.

4. Both Clara Sue Kidwell and Rebecca K. Jager trace the important role Indian woman played in advancing the frontier. Jager explores how Malinche occupies a similar place in Mexican history to that of Pocahontas and Sacagawea in North American histories. With a more nuanced analysis of colonialism and of their respective roles, all these women now occupy a more fraught historical perch. Clara Sue Kidwell, "Indian Women as Cultural Intermediaries," *Ethnohistory* 39 (Spring 1992): 97–107; Rebecca K. Jager, *Malinche, Pocahontas, and Sacagawea: Indian Women as Cultural Intermediaries and National Symbols* (Norman: University of Oklahoma Press, 2015).

5. Mary Jean Cook, "Carmel Benavides, an Early Santa Fe Trail Woman," *Wagon Tracks: Santa Fe Trail Association Quarterly* 13, 1 (1998): 9–15, attempts to establish Carmel's first eastward crossing. She states that Carmel may have been living in St. Louis or at the Robidoux family's Blacksnake Hills Trading Post on the Missouri River when she gave birth to a daughter in the early 1830s. According to Cook, that child, Carmen, was listed in the 1841 Santa Fe census, but I found no mention of Carmel or Antoine in either the 1830 census records or the church baptismal records from St. Louis, Florissant, or the immediate area in 1829–39. The child listed in the 1841 census might be the Ute girl Carmel and Antoine had baptized in 1841. The race and ethnicity of citizens were as no longer listed in civil records during the Mexican period.

6. Cook, "Carmel Benavides," 11, lists this baptism as occurring in Santa Fe on December 13, 1841, but incorrectly identifies the child as a twelve-year-old Ute boy. She suggests that the child may have been Antoine's offspring with a Ute woman—not an uncommon occurrence among his brothers and other fur trappers and traders. However, in addition to capturing and enslaving Ute, Navajo, and Apache children, New Mexico required them to be baptized. So this baptism may have been Antoine fulfilling his societal obligation or perhaps even his Christian duty rather than being an admission of paternity. See Brooks, *Captives and Cousins*.

7. Jay Feldman, *When the Mississippi Ran Backwards: Empire Intrigue, Murder and the New Madrid Earthquakes* (New York: Free Press, 2005), 3–7.

8. Ibid., 10–14.

9. Robert Willoughby's history of the brothers, *The Brothers Robidoux and the Opening of the American West* (Columbia: University of Missouri Press, 2012), is the best single source for a comprehensive overview of the wide-ranging travels, trade networks, and business interests of several generations of the family.

10. James Neal Primm, *Lion of the Valley: St. Louis, Missouri, 1764–1980*, 3rd ed. (St. Louis: Missouri Historical Society Press, 1998), 62, 129–132.

11. There are many examples of this inheritance practice. The other owners of the house were Carmel's step-siblings Nepomuceno Alarid and Rosario Alarid de Sena, the children María Guadalupe had with her second husband, according to the deeds traced by John Ruminer in *109 East Palace Avenue: A Microcosm of Santa Fe's Four Hundred Year History*, Los Alamos Historical Society Nutshell Series No. 4 (Los Alamos, NM: Bathtub Row Press, 2013), 11–12. Currently, the property includes

Trujillo Plaza (at the west end of the block containing Carmel's property) and Sena Plaza, housing many shops and a restaurant. Prince Plaza, named for Governor L. Bradford Prince, who bought the property from Carmel, has been incorporated into Trujillo and Sena Plazas. When Carmel and Antoine lived in this house during their years in Santa Fe (roughly 1828–44), they had a commanding view of the plaza and the Santa Fe Trail, which ended at the Palace of the Governors.

12. Lansing B. Bloom, "Early Vaccination in New Mexico," *Historical Society of New Mexico* 27 (1924): 3–12. Enrique Lamadrid, eminent New Mexican linguist and folklorist, has written a children's book about this famous inoculation. *Amadito and the Hero Children/Amadito y los Niños Héroes* (Albuquerque: University of New Mexico Press, 2011) could not be a more timely read for children who grew up during the COVID-19 pandemic.

13. Albert J. Gallegos and José Antonio Esquibel, "*Alcaldes* and Mayors of Santa Fe, 1613–2008," in *All Trails Lead to Santa Fe* (Santa Fe: Sunstone Press, 2010), 403–428.

14. Adrian Bustamante and Marc Simmons, trans. and eds., *The Exposition on the Province of New Mexico, 1812 by Don Pedro Baptisto Pino* (Santa Fe and Albuquerque: Rancho de las Golondrinas and University of New Mexico Press, 1995). Originally published in Cadiz, Spain, at the time Pino presented the list to the government, it has gone through several translations that were incomplete or flawed.

15. Thomas Maitland Marshall, ed., "The Journals of Jules De Mun," trans. Nettie H. Beauregard, *Missouri Historical Society Collections* 5, 3 (1928): 167–208. The original journals were donated to the Missouri Historical Society, along with DeMun's desk, by his great-great-granddaughter in 1923. The journals were written in French and translated by the historical society's capable curator Marie Antoinette Harney (Nettie H.) Beauregard (1868–1940).

16. Ibid., 172.

17. Ibid., 174.

18. Ibid.

19. Ibid., 181.

20. Weber, "Unforgettable Day," 36.

21. Ibid., 33.

22. Blackhawk, *Violence, Warfare, Terror and Colonialism*, 127. Blackhawk may be one of the authors who attributes too much to Antoine. Antoine inscribed his name on a cliff face near Uintah, but he was not the only Robidoux brother to live and trade in the Great Basin.

23. Thomas James, *Three Years among the Indians and Mexicans* [1846], ed. Walter B. Douglas, 117–118, Kindle.

24. At least four suits were filed against Antoine and his brothers or business partners between 1820 and 1823. Debt note filed by William Rector, plaintiff, and Antoine Robidoux, defendant, St. Louis Circuit Court Case 134, December 1820, Missouri Judicial Records Historical Database, box 66, folder 2, microfilm C 50456; assumpsit (breach of promise), John Graham and John McKee, plaintiffs, vs. Antoine

and Francoise Robidoux, St. Louis Circuit Court Case 55, August 1821, ibid., box 72, folder 34, microfilm C 50461; trespass suit filed by John Graham and John McKee, plaintiffs, vs. Antoine and Francoise Robidoux, St. Louis Circuit Court Case 64, June 1822, ibid., box 80, folder 5, microfilm C 50467; debt note filed by William McGuine, plaintiff, against Antoine Robidoux, Case 10, October 1822, ibid., box 81, folder 38, microfilm C 50468. Antoine Robidoux was also cited as being delinquent in state and county taxes in St. Louis County. *Missouri Republican*, September 17, 1823, 3.

25. Pass to Antoine Robidoux, File: Extranjeros, Anglo Traders, February 19, 1824, State Records Center and Archives, Santa Fe.

26. Several authors have referred to Carmel as the common-law wife of Antoine Robidoux, but he refers to her in his will as his wife and names her as his executor. The records of marriages occurring in Santa Fe in 1828 are now located in the Archives of the Archdiocese of Santa Fe, State Records Center and Archives, but they may be incomplete.

27. Pass to Antoine Robidoux.

28. Willoughby, *Brothers Robidoux*.

29. Trial of Dionisio Moya, José Sena, and Antonio Garcia for robbery of Antonio Robidoux, December 4, 1829–March 8, 1830, Mexican Archives of New Mexico, reel 10, fr. 45, State Records Center and Archives; Antonio Robidoux testimony in the case of José Sena for robbery of William Connors, Robidoux, and Juan Langame, January–August 1830, ibid. reel 11, fr. 402.

30. Amanda Taylor-Montoya, "There Is No There There: Women and Intermarriage in the Southwestern Borderlands," *Common Place: The Journal of Early American Life* 13, 3 (2013), https://commonplace.online/article/there-is-no-there-there/.

31. Janet Lecompte compares the legal and social status of women in New Mexico and the United States before the region's American conquest. See Janet Lecompte, "The Independent Women of Hispanic New Mexico, 1821–1846," in *New Mexico Women: Intercultural Perspectives*, ed. Joan M. Jensen and Darlis A. Miller (Albuquerque: University of New Mexico Press, 1986), 71–93. María E. Montoya explores the disruption of New Mexican customs, property rights, and social structures when the American legal system was imposed on centuries of Spanish laws and customs in *Translating Property: The Maxwell Land Grant and the Conflict over Land in the American West, 1840–1900* (Lawrence: University Press of Kansas, 2005).

32. John E. Sunder, ed., *Matt Field on the Santa Fe Trail* (Norman: University of Oklahoma Press, 1960), 204–205.

33. Hyde, *Empires, Nations and Families*, describes in some detail the practice of frontier polygamy—short-term or long-term relationships of convenience that were widely reported among mountain men and traders. Cook, "Carmel Benavides," suggests that Antoine did not formally marry Carmel because he might have already been married to a Ute woman, although she cites no documented source.

34. Weber, *Taos Trappers*, 85.

35. The internet is filled with rubbings and enhanced images of the inscription and

interpretations of which direction Antoine was traveling at the time. I refer readers to Willoughby, *Brothers Robidoux*, 126–128, for his cogent deciphering of the message and what it says about Antoine's intended destination and meaning.

36. Sra. A. Robidoux account with Gittings and Gentry, July 1841, Alvarez Papers, folder 12, State Records Center and Archives; "Efectos a la Sra. de A. Robidux por cuenta de Juan Manuel Baca," ibid. The latter may have been a charge made on Carmel's behalf. See Willoughby, *Brothers Robidoux*, 152, regarding Antoine being in Missouri in late autumn 1841.

37. Willoughby, *Brothers Robidoux*, 164.

38. Weber, *Taos Trappers*, 216–217. On September 5, 1844, six Ute leaders and 108 "warriors" came to Santa Fe to complain about the compensation. Antoine Robidoux described this event in the *Missouri Democrat* on September 17, 1845, quoting the *St. Joseph Gazette*, which in turn seems to be quoting Robidoux directly. However, there is some evidence that Antoine was at Fort Uintah at the time and was not an eyewitness to the actions. Weber points out that after this incident, given the worsening relations with the Utes, Antoine abruptly left New Mexico and returned to Missouri, perhaps because he was implicated in the sale of guns and ammunition to the Utes.

39. Willoughby, *Brothers Robidoux*, 170–172.

40. Ibid., 172–173. At Fort Leavenworth, Kearny offered Antoine, now living in St. Joseph, the job of interpreter for the Army of the West. Interestingly, Kearny addresses Robidoux as Anthony and refers to a letter he received from Robidoux on June 2, 1846, offering his services to the troops. Kearny to Antoine Robidoux, June 4, 1846, in Kearny Letter Book, Library and Research Center Collections, Missouri Historical Society. The Army of the West consisted of 856 men in eight companies of foot and mounted soldiers recruited from the six troops of First Dragoon Regiment, First Missouri Volunteers, and Laclede Rangers from St. Louis, who traveled west at different times. Kearny's chief scout was mountain man Tom Fitzpatrick.

41. Willoughby, *Brothers Robidoux*, 172–173.

42. According to Antoine's obituary, reprinted in the *Liberty Tribune* on September 7, 1860, he then traveled to California, perhaps with other gold seekers. As early as 1841, he had described California as an earthly paradise. Other sources place him in California in April or May 1847, where he was discharged from the army. He sailed from there in November 1847 and circled South America before making it back to St. Joseph. Willoughby, *Brothers Robidoux*, 174–175.

43. Willoughby, *Brothers Robidoux*, 205–208.

44. Martine lived with Antoine and Carmel Robidoux in Santa Fe when the 1841 census was compiled. At the time, she was listed (likely in error) as twenty years old. On the 1850 census in Missouri, her age was given as twenty-one. Twelve people were living in Isadore's household. He is listed as the head of household, forty-two years old, born in Missouri; his occupation is listed as confectioner. The other Barada family members listed in the census and born in New Mexico were eighteen-year-old Antoine, thirteen-year-old Adolph, eleven-year-old Julius, and nine-year-old Mary. E. Barada, a forty-seven-year-old woman who was born in Missouri, also lived in

the home, but her relationship to Isadore is not clear. Also residing there was Victoria Robidoux, age forty-two and born in New Jersey. It is difficult to determine the family structure of this multigenerational and multicultural household. In addition to family members, others listed in this entry include Rufus Willet, a bookkeeper, age sixteen and born in Canada; a laborer by the name (or profession) of Baker (no first name listed), age twenty-three; and a twenty-three-year-old painter named Alexander Southard from Missouri.

45. While in Santa Fe, Carmel was likely living in the home of her parents and maternal grandmother, which had been bequeathed to her. Ruminer, *109 East Palace Avenue*. For the recent history of the property, see Jennet Conant, *109 East Palace: Robert Oppenheimer and the Secret City of Los Alamos* (New York: Simon & Schuster, 2005).

46. Robert S. Stollsteimer, *Christian and Amanda: The Life and Times of a Colorado Pioneer Family* (self-published, F.E.R.S. Books, 1996). Robert was very generous while I prepared this chapter. Like all families, their history is one of happiness and sadness, incomplete information and wonderful memories.

3. Schoolgirls on the Trail: Adaline, Marian, and Francisca

1. Bustamante and Simmons, *Exposition on the Province of New Mexico*, 22–23.

2. Joseph P. Sanchez, "It Happened in Old Santa Fe, the Death of Governor Albino Pérez, 1835–1837," in *All Trails Lead to Santa Fe: An Anthology Commemorating the 400th Anniversary of the Founding of Santa Fe, New Mexico in 1610* (Santa Fe: Sunstone Press, 2010), 271.

3. Mary Jean Straw Cook, *Loretto, the Sisters and Their Chapel* (Santa Fe: Museum of New Mexico Press, 2002); Patricia Jean Manion, *Beyond the Adobe Wall: The Sisters of Loretto in New Mexico, 1852–1894* (Independence: Two Trails Publishing Press, 2002). Sister Magdalen Hayden was among the first group of nuns to arrive and remained in Santa Fe until her death in 1894. Sisters Catherine Mahoney, Rosanna Dant, and Roberta Brown also made the crossing to Santa Fe. Mother Superior Matilda Mills died of cholera en route; Sister Monica Bailey also contracted cholera, but she recuperated in Florissant, Missouri, until the next group of nuns crossed in 1855. Sister Roberta Brown left the order in February 1855, crossing the Santa Fe Trail and returning to St. Louis in the company of Vicar Machebeauf, artist William James Hinchey, and a young girl identified only as a Mexican servant.

4. Robert L. Spude, "Progressive Santa Fe, 1880–1912," in *All Trails Lead to Santa Fe*, 355. For St. Michael's High School (El Colegio de San Miguel), see https://www.stmichaelssf.org/apps/pages/index.jsp?uREC_ID=346686&type=d&pREC_ID=755200. For the Sisters of Loretto in Santa Fe, see https://www.lorettochapel.com/info/our-story.

5. Doyle Daves, "Education and the New Mexico Elite during Santa Fe Trail Days," *Wagon Tracks: Santa Fe Trail Association Quarterly* 33, 4 (2019): 11.

6. Harvey Lewis Carter, *"Dear Old Kit": The Historical Christopher Carson* (Norman: University of Oklahoma Press, 1968), provides a comprehensive, annotated timeline of Carson's life, as well as an annotated version of Carson's memoirs. It is a useful resource, but the details of Carson's travels and domestic arrangements are still not known with certainty. Marc Simmons, *Kit Carson and His Three Wives: A Family History* (Albuquerque: University of New Mexico Press, 2003), specifically examines Carson's domestic life. David Remley's *Kit Carson: The Life of an American Border Man* (Norman: University of Oklahoma Press, 2011) is a readable biography, but he too struggles to separate the legend from the actual yet elusive details of Carson's life. Carson's autobiography was most likely dictated to John Mostin, a clerk and interpreter at the Indian agency in Taos in 1856. It was published, after some emendations and what Simmons characterizes as "padding and artful decoration" by editor DeWitt Clinton Peters, as *The Life of Kit Carson, the Nestor of the Rocky Mountains* (New York: W. R. C. Clark, 1858).

7. Susan Lee Johnson, *Writing Kit Carson: Fallen Heroes in a Changing West* (Chapel Hill: University of North Carolina Press, 2020).

8. Because I relied on Simmons's research on Carson's domestic life, I followed his preference of referring to Carson's first wife as Waa-nibe rather than Singing Grass. Johnson uses the name Singing Grass.

9. Johnson, *Writing Kit Carson*, 44–45.

10. Simmons, *Kit Carson and His Three Wives*, 41–42. While acknowledging that there is no way to know how Carson and Making Out Road dissolved their marriage, Simmons bases his depiction of their divorce on what he describes as the "unreliable" biography by Stanley Vestel, *Kit Carson, the Happy Warrior of the Old West: A Biography* (Boston: Houghton Mifflin, 1928). Placing a man's belongings outside the tipi or lodge was well documented in the ethnographic literature as the way Plains Indian women initiated the dissolution of a marriage.

11. Simmons, *Kit Carson and His Three Wives*, 7–9.

12. Ibid., 10–14.

13. Ibid., 23.

14. Ibid., 18–20. See also a statistical analysis of the marriage practices of some 312 men involved in the fur trade between 1810 and 1845 by William R. Swagerty, "Marriage and Settlement Patterns of Rocky Mountain Trappers and Traders," *Western Historical Quarterly* 11, 2 (April 1980): 159–180.

15. Michael Lansing, "Plains Indian Women and Interracial Marriage in the Upper Missouri Trade, 1804–1868," *Western Historical Quarterly* 31, 4 (Winter 2000): 413–433.

16. Thorne, *Many Hands of My Relations*, traces the history of the many mixtures and names applied to the intermarriage of French Creoles, French Canadians, French Americans, Americans of other heritages, and the Central Siouan tribes of the American Midwest.

17. Simmons, *Kit Carson and His Three Wives*, 22–24.

18. E. G. Cattermole's exuberant *Famous Frontiersmen, Pioneers and Scouts:*

The Romance of American History; Thrilling Narratives of Renowned Adventurers, Explorers, Heroes, Trappers, Scouts and Indian Fighters, new and enlarged ed. (Tarrytown, NY: William Abbott, 1926), 362–363, includes lithographs of Waa-nibe and Adaline. The illustrations' source and authenticity are highly conjectural. Each illustration shows a woman of delicate beauty with the romantic accoutrements of the "Indian princess" genre of western fiction.

19. Simmons, *Kit Carson and His Three Wives*, 25–28.

20. Lewis H. Garrard's description of Taos was originally published in 1850 in *Wah-to-yah and the Taos Trail* (reprint, Norman: University of Oklahoma Press, 1955). Wah-to-yah was the name for the Spanish peaks of the Sangre de Cristo Mountains. Garrard did not arrive in Taos until 1846, by which time Josefa was already married to Kit Carson.

21. Doyle Daves, "Cross-Cultural Marriages in New Mexico: Six Jaramillo Women of Taos and the Husbands Who Came to Them across the Santa Fe Trail," *Wagon Tracks: Santa Fe Trail Association Quarterly* 35, 2 (February 2021): 13–19, provides a short biography of the six Jaramillo sisters. Interestingly, each of them married French or American men who were part of the first generation of traders and merchants to come to New Mexico. They were exceptional in this regard, since the majority of New Mexican women married within the Hispanic community, thus maintaining their social and cultural norms.

22. Simmons, *Kit Carson and His Three Wives*, 46–50, reviews the relevant literature and concludes that Adaline first stayed with the Rubeys and then spent time with the Amicks. Timothy L. Carson, a descendant of Kit Carson's line, has traced the local history regarding where Adaline resided and was educated when she lived in the beautiful farmlands between Fayette and Glasgow, Missouri.

23. Hampton Sides, *Blood and Thunder: The Epic Story of Kit Carson and the Conquest of the American West* (New York: Anchor Books, 2006), presents a sweeping overview of the US takeover of the Southwest. It is surprising that such a small cadre of men was responsible for the commercial and military conquest of the region.

24. Steve Inskeep's biography *Imperfect Union: How Jessie and John Frémont Mapped the West, Invented Celebrity and Helped Cause the Civil War* (New York: Penguin Press, 2020), examines this sweep of history and how the press, new technology, and the combustible mix of politics and propaganda propelled western expansion. Kit Carson was certainly a player at the time, and he was not the only historical figure with a troubling legacy.

25. Simmons, *Kit Carson and His Three Wives*, 88–89.

26. Ibid., 75–79; Sides, *Blood and Thunder*, 237–245; Carter, *"Dear Old Kit,"* 132–134.

27. Marian's account of her five crossings of the trail was published in serial form in *Colorado Magazine* in 1943 and 1944. She dictated her memoir, *Land of Enchantment* (Evanston, IL: Branding Iron Press, 1954), to her daughter-in-law Winnie McGuire Russell, wife of Harold. See Marc Simmons, "Afterword," in Marian Russell, *Land of Enchantment: Memoirs along the Santa Fe Trail* (reprint, Albuquerque:

University of New Mexico Press, 1993), 158–159. Subsequent cites are to the 1993 edition.

28. Bonita and Leo Oliva speculate that Eliza and Sloan were divorced or separated before the Mexican War and that Eliza chose not to reveal how or when their marriage "unraveled." Bonita Oliva and Leo Oliva, "A Few Things Marian Sloan Russell Never Told about Her Mother and Father," *Wagon Tracks: Santa Fe Trail Association Quarterly* 7, 3 (February 1993): 1, 6–8.

29. Russell, *Land of Enchantment*, 3–4.

30. Jeremiah Mahoney and Eliza St. Clair were married by a justice of the peace on September 14, 1848, in St. Louis County. *St. Louis County Index of Marriages*, vol. 4, 171. There was a quartermaster sergeant by the name of Jeremiah Mahoney listed in the records of Fort Snelling, but this appears to be a different person. Marian recalled that Jeremiah was killed while serving at Fort Snelling before the end of the 1850 school year. But this seems unlikely, as the 1850 census showed them residing at the fort at the end of September 1850. The other man, Quartermaster Jeremiah Mahoney, was discharged from the fort and moved to a farm in Minnesota in 1858; he later served in the First Minnesota Regiment as commissary sergeant. J. Fletcher Williams, Edward D. Neill, C. M. Foote, and George E. Warner, *History of Hennepin County and the City of Minneapolis: Including the Explorers and Pioneers of Minnesota, by Rev. Edward D. Neill, and Outlines of the History of Minnesota, by J. Fletcher Williams* (Minneapolis: North Star Publishing Company, 1881).

31. Register of ordinance sergeants, US Army, enlisted Fort Snelling, August 1, 1849, discharged April 1852, reenlisted July 15, 1855, and July 1858. Jeremiah Mahoney's military record is complicated. It appears that he was under arrest from May 30, 1854, until he reenlisted in July 1855; his court-martial record indicates that he was involved in the questionable pricing of military uniforms. He evidently married another woman, Anna Nevin, in 1853.

32. Russell, *Land of Enchantment*, 6–7.

33. Ibid., 10–11. Working out the timeline requires some arithmetic and chronological ordering of Russell's narrative. She was born in 1845 and moved to St. Louis when she was three; then the family spent a very short time at Fort Snelling. She states that after Mahoney's death they spent two years waiting in Kansas City for her Sloan grandfather to return from the California goldfields to help them move across the country. It seems that they were at Fort Snelling sometime in 1848 or 1849 and left in 1850, since she is very precise about the two years spent waiting for her grandfather.

34. The census taken on September 28, 1850, at Fort Snelling, Dakota County, Minnesota, lists Jeremiah Mahoney, a soldier age thirty-three and born in Ireland, living with his wife Eliza Mahoney, age thirty-one and born in Pennsylvania, with children William age seven born in Arkansas and Maryon (*sic*) age five born in Illinois. Ancestry.com.

35. Aubry, variously referred to as Francis or Françoise, was French Canadian. Marian's memoir implies that Eliza and Aubry were romantically involved; she refers

to him as her mother's "ardent admirer." Aubry was celebrated in 1848 for his feat of crossing the Santa Fe Trail from Santa Fe to Independence in five days and sixteen hours. He was killed in a senseless fight in Santa Fe in August 1854 when Colonel Richard Weighman challenged his record-breaking trail crossing. Russell, *Land of Enchantment*, 30, 145n2.

36. Ibid., 14, 22.

37. The other American girls were Barbara Price, Lizzie Enders, and the two daughters of a Captain Lewis. Ibid., 42.

38. Ibid., 37.

39. Ibid., 60–64; Oliva and Oliva, "A Few Things Marian Sloan Russell Never Told," 6.

40. Russell, *Land of Enchantment*, 66–74.

41. Ibid., 85.

42. Ibid., 85–89.

43. 1870 Federal Census of Fort Hays, Kansas, ancestry.com.

44. Russell, *Land of Enchantment*, 137, 140–143.

45. Montoya, *Translating Property*, 216–219, concludes her study of the Maxwell Land Grant litigation with the observation that much of the conflict surrounding the building of the American West was attributable to the courts' mistaken assumption that open land was available for appropriation and commercial use.

46. Montoya, *Translating Property*, 194–201, summarizes the factions and events of the Stonewall Valley War from a witness deposition in the case filed against the settlers in Las Animas County, Colorado, in 1888. As might be expected, the details in the contemporaneous deposition differ from Marian's recollections many years after the events.

47. Ibid., 199–202, 255–256n25. The case before the Supreme Court, *Russell v. Maxwell Land Grant Company*, 158 U.S. 253 (1895), concerned the boundaries of the grant, not the deaths that occurred during the Stonewall Valley War.

48. Much of the research regarding Francisca López de Kimball was published by Doyle Daves in a series of *Wagon Tracks* articles. Additional information was provided by Francisca's great-great-granddaughter Mary Kimball Outten, which she compiled in an extensive PowerPoint presentation titled "Francisca Lopez Kimball, 1841–1907: From Chihuahua to Santa Fe to St. Louis in Her Own Words." Both Daves and Outten give Dámaso's name as Damaso Lopez. Genealogist Henrietta Christmas suggests that the name Dámaso is of Basque origin and may refer to Pope Damasus.

49. List of purchases from Lorenzo López by José Francisco Ortiz, Ortiz Family Papers, folder 16, box 2, State Records Center and Archives, Santa Fe, cited in Doyle Daves, "Damaso Lopez: He Traveled El Camino Real and the Santa Fe Trail," *Wagon Tracks: Santa Fe Trail Association Quarterly* 29, 4 (2015): 26.

50. John O. Baxter, *Las Carneradas: Sheep Trade in New Mexico, 1700–1860* (Albuquerque: University of New Mexico Press, 1987), 117–118.

51. Thomas E. Chávez, *Manuel Alvarez, 1794–1856: A Southwestern Biography* (Niwot: University Press of Colorado, 1990).

52. Dámaso López to Manuel Alvarez, August 10, 1840, cited by Mary Outten as being in the Jerome Cahill and Sandy López Cahill Family Papers, in the possession of the Cahill family.

53. Daves, "Damaso Lopez," 28; *New Mexico Burials: Santo Tomás Apóstol de Abiquiú, 1777–1861* (Albuquerque: New Mexico Genealogical Society, 2018), 144. Daves writes that María Carmen was living with her widowed mother, Josefa Angulo de Esparza, at the time of this child's birth. When José Fernando married in 1863, however, his mother is referred to as Carmen Leyva. Although this could have been a scrivener's error, Carmen Leyba (Levia) is named in other documents associated with Dámaso, including serving as *padrinos* with his son José Melaquides at the August 1842 baptism of one of the Ute children at Abiquiú. The other *padrinos* for a Ute girl baptized the same day were Dámaso's son José Trinidad and infant daughter María Francisca. María Carmen de López gave priest Don José Francisco Leyva power of attorney to act for Dámaso in a real estate sale in 1845. Daves, "Damaso Lopez," 30, thinks María Carmen de López and Carmen Leyva are the same person and notes that María Carmen's brother started to use the surname Leyba at about the same time; he attributes this to their connection to priest José Francisco Leyva, who was somehow related to the family. Carmen Leyva is identified as Dámaso's wife at the time he created his will. The December 1850 census shows Dámaso living in Santa Fe with Conrad Ekert, age thirty-five from Germany, and twenty-four-year-old New Mexico–born Juana Garcia, although the relationships among the three are not apparent. Thanks to Henrietta Christmas for helping to trace, if not always unravel, this complicated family history.

54. Abiquiú and San Miguel del Vado have fascinating histories that began in the Spanish colonial period. They were settlements intended for *genízaros*, detribalized Native American people who were encouraged to settle in these outposts in exchange for land and community rights. In the nineteenth century Abiquiú continued to serve as a point of embarkation for traders and stockmen on the Spanish Trail to California. San Miguel del Vado was the westernmost river ford for Santa Fe Trail travelers. The identity and place of *genízaros* are important elements of New Mexico history. See Brooks, *Captives and Cousins*; Moises Gonzales, "The Genízaro Land Grant Settlements of New Mexico," *Journal of the Southwest* 56, 4 (Winter 2014): 583; Ramón A. Gutiérrez, *When Jesus Came, the Corn Mothers Went Away* (Palo Alto, CA: Stanford University Press, 1991).

55. Chávez, *Manuel Alvarez*, 120–128.

56. Dámaso López to Manuel Alvarez, May 17, 1850, Jerome Cahill and Sandy López Cahill Family Papers.

57. History of Chapel Hill College, Chapel Hill, Lafayette County, Missouri (http://www.cumberland.org/hfcpc/schools/ChaHilMO.htm), citing Report of the Committee on Education, in Minutes of the General Assembly of the Cumberland Presbyterian Church, 1851, 37.

58. Chávez, *Manuel Alvarez*, 162–169.

59. Inventory and Ledger: Student Accounts, 1833–1847, box 1, entry 76, Visitation Academy Archives, St. Louis.

60. Prospectus of the Menard Young Ladies Academy of the Visitation, Kaskaskia, Illinois, ca. 1840–42, Visitation Academy Archives, St. Louis.

61. Letter from Francisca, Academy of the Visitation, St. Louis, to My Dear Father, April 22, 1852, private collection of Mary Outten, St. Louis.

62. Baxter, *Las Carneradas*, 116–124.

63. Ibid., 122–125; Daves, "Damaso Lopez," 29.

64. Chávez, *Manuel Alvarez*, 184–191; Daves, "Damaso Lopez," 29.

65. The other young women were Kate Clemens, Helen Clemens, Annie Ewing, Alice Mosley, Mary Soulard, Blanche Soulard, and Adele Sarpy, all members of upper-class families from St. Louis and environs. Probate records for Dámaso López's estate include a payment made by Anastacio Sandoval on December 17, 1859, for Visitation Convent in Georgetown. Francisca was a student at Georgetown Academy of the Visitation in 1858–59. The payment was made on her behalf and is reflected in the Santa Fe County Probate Records, reel 1, 238.

66. Glasgow Brothers to Anastacio Sandoval, June 19, 1860, Santa Fe County Probate Records, reel 1, 238–239.

4. Seeking Health on the Santa Fe Trail

1. Much of the material concerning Kate Kingsbury's life and death on the trail was published in an article I wrote: Frances Levine, "A Beautiful Death on the Santa Fe Trail," *El Palacio* 125, 1 (Spring 2020): 64–78. A sidebar by Alysia L. Abbott, entitled "Kate's Final Journey," appeared on page 79. *Santa Fe New Mexican* reporter Robert Nott interviewed Abbott in December 2021 about the recently discovered coffin at an archaeological site in downtown Santa Fe that may have marked the approximate location of Kate's grave. Kate's story has been published in several other sources, including Conevery Bolton Valenčius, "Gender and the Economy of Health on the Santa Fe Trail," *Osiris*, 2nd ser., 19 (2004): 79–92.

2. Valenčius, "Gender and the Economy of Health"; Conevery Bolton Valenčius, "The Geography of Health and the Making of the American West: Arkansas and Missouri, 1800–1860," in *The Health of the Country* (New York: Basic Books, 2002), 121–145.

3. Gregg, *Commerce of the Prairies*, 23.

4. Randolph B. Marcy, *The Prairie Traveler* (1859; reprint, Bedford, MA: Applewood Books, 1993).

5. Esmond R. Long, "Weak Lungs on the Santa Fe Trail," *Bulletin of the History of Medicine* 8, 7 (1940): 1040–1054, quoting Dr. Samuel George Morton, *Illustrations of Pulmonary Consumption* (Philadelphia: Key & Biddle, 1834).

6. Barton H. Barbour, ed., *Reluctant Frontiersman: James Ross Larkin on the Santa Fe Trail, 1856–1857* (Albuquerque: University of New Mexico Press, 1990). Larkin's journal does not specifically contrast how he felt on his return trip to St. Louis, but his health was evidently not restored, and he continued to suffer from

lifelong neuralgia and stomach issues. He lived in St. Louis with his wife and children until he died of pneumonia on January 14, 1875, at age forty-three. Ibid., 25–27.

7. Jane Lenz Elder and David J. Weber, *Trading in Santa Fe: John M. Kingsbury's Correspondence with James Josiah Webb, 1853–1861* (Dallas: Southern Methodist University Press, 1996), is an impressive compilation of letters between Kingsbury and Webb. Elder and Weber annotated the 44 letters in the DeGolyer Library at Southern Methodist University (SMU) and the 150 letters held by the Library and Research Center of the Missouri Historical Society in St. Louis. The SMU letters were part of a collection Mr. DeGolyer purchased in 1945 from Edward Eberstadt, according to Elder and Weber's acknowledgments. The Missouri Historical Society purchased 1,100 letters and letter books from Paul Webb, a descendant of James Josiah Webb, in 1965. Paul Webb was a resident of Branford, Connecticut, not far from the estate J. J. Webb built in the mid-nineteenth century. Larkin's unpaid debt caused Kingsbury some trouble, as he reported to Webb in a letter dated May 31, 1858.

8. W. W. H. Davis, *El Gringo; or New Mexico and Her People* (New York: Harper Brothers, 1857), 24.

9. J. D. B. DeBow, *Mortality Statistics of the Seventh Census of the United States, 1850*, House of Representatives, 33rd Congress, 2nd session, Executive Document No. 98 (Washington, DC: A. O. P. Nicholson, 1855), tabulated the mortality rates for all reported causes of deaths in the United States and its territories. For the year ending July 1, 1850, deaths totaled 328,023, and those attributed to acute epidemic or "zymotic diseases" totaled 131,818, or 40 percent. Consumption accounted for 33,516, or 10 percent, of the deaths, but the disease was concentrated in urban areas and specific geographic regions. Deaths caused not by epidemics but by "sporadic disease," including those who died of diseases of the respiratory organs, totaled 54,800, or 17 percent, of all deaths. These cases could have included deaths not attributed to a specific diagnosis of consumption. Ibid., 17–20.

10. Samuel Sheldon Fitch, *Six Discourses on the Functions of the Lungs; and Causes, Prevention and Cure of Pulmonary Consumption, Asthma, and Diseases of the Heart; on the Lawes of Life; and on the Mode of Preserving Male and Female Health to an Hundred Years* (New York: S. S. Fitch, 1853), Becker Medical Library, Washington University Medical School, St. Louis.

11. Professor C. B. Coventry, "Tuberculosis," *St. Louis Medical Journal* (1856): 466–468, Missouri Historical Society Library and Research Center, St. Louis.

12. James Clark, *A Treatise on Pulmonary Consumption: Comprehending an Inquiry into the Causes, Nature, Presentation and Treatment of Tuberculosis and Scrofulous Diseases in General* (Philadelphia: Carey, Lea & Blanchard, 1835).

13. Ibid., 33–34.

14. Messervy entered the Santa Fe trade and prospered along with other Americans in advance of (and after) the 1846 conquest of the region. Messervy and Webb entered New Mexico politics in the territorial period. Messervy served as secretary of the territory in 1853 and as acting governor during the short term of William Carr Lane (1852–53). Webb served in the New Mexico legislature, as did other Santa Fe

Trail traders, such as the Robidoux brothers. Webb was also active in civic life in other ways and sought to improve the educational system in New Mexico by selling, at low cost, Spanish-language books for elementary students. Elder and Weber, *Trading in Santa Fe*, xxiii–xxiv.

15. Messervy was anxious to return to his family in Salem, Massachusetts. Correspondence between Messervy and Webb during this period, held in the Webb Papers at the Missouri Historical Society, show that Messervy urged Webb to convince Kingsbury to marry Kate and buy out Messervy's share of the business. Messervy also wrote to Kingsbury, suggesting that Kate accompany him to New Mexico if her health was up to it. William S. Messervy to James J. Webb, Santa Fe, October 1, 1853, and James J. Webb to John M. Kingsbury, Cornwall, CT, October 5, 1853, Webb Correspondence, Missouri Historical Society, St. Louis.

16. Elder and Weber, *Trading in Santa Fe*, xii.

17. J. J. Webb to John [Kingsbury], Cornwall Bridge, CT, October 5, 1853, Webb Correspondence.

18. J. J. Webb to John [Kingsbury], Cornwall Bridge, CT, November 5, 1853, Webb Correspondence. Webb and Lillie married on December 1, 1853, in Cornwall Bridge.

19. W. S. Messervy to John M. Kingsbury, Santa Fe, February 28, 1854, Webb Correspondence.

20. Wm. S. Messervy to James J. Webb, Santa Fe, March 28, 1854, Webb Correspondence. It seems likely that Messervy wrote this letter over the course of a few days. Although it is dated March 28, it contains news of a battle that took place between US dragoons and the Jicarilla near Taos two days later. Ronald K. Wetherington and Frances Levine, *Battles and Massacres on the Southwestern Frontier: Historical and Archaeological Perspectives* (Norman: University of Oklahoma Press, 2014).

21. Davis, *El Gringo*, 248–251. The full report, "Narrative of the Sufferings of Mrs. Jane Adeline Wilson during her Captivity among the Camanche Indians," which Davis received from the Reverend Louis Smith, was published on the front page of the *St. Joseph Gazette* on Wednesday, February 15, 1854. Mrs. Wilson and three of her brothers-in law were turned over to authorities in El Paso after her husband and his father were killed attempting to steal cattle from the Ysleta del Sur Pueblo in retaliation for the Ysleta allegedly stealing the Wilsons' cattle. Mrs. Wilson and two of her brothers-in-law were being taken back to Paris, Texas, when their wagon was attacked by Comanches. She managed to escape after a month in captivity and hid on the plains until the New Mexico hunting party rescued her. Gary Wilson, "Hostage among the Comanches: The Ordeal of Jane Wilson," *Red River Historical Review* 5, 2 (Spring 1980): 4–12.

22. Bills of lading, Webb Correspondence.

23. W. S. Messervy to John M. Kingsbury, Santa Fe, April 29, 1854, Webb Correspondence.

24. Kingsbury to Webb, Santa Fe, October 29, 1855, letter 16, in Elder and Weber, *Trading in Santa Fe*, 24n24.

25. Davis, *El Gringo*, 163–164.

26. Thomas B. Hall, *Medicine on the Santa Fe Trail* (Arrow Rock, MO: Morningside Bookshop, 1987), 56–73; Mark L. Gardner and Marc Simmons, eds., *The Mexican War Correspondence of Richard Smith Elliott* (Norman: University of Oklahoma Press, 1997), 47, 108, 190–191.

27. Elder and Weber, *Trading in Santa Fe*, xxvii–xxix.

28. Ibid., 23n22. Perhaps it was a birthday cake, as Davis's birthday was July 20. The letter quoted by Elder and Weber is dated August 26, 1854, and is held in Papers of W. H. Davis, WA, MSS 1323, Beinecke Library, Yale University, New Haven, CT.

29. W. S. Messervy to John M. Kingsbury, Salem, March 13, 1855, Webb Correspondence.

30. James J. Webb to John [Kingsbury], Fort Union, September 4, 1855; W. S. Messervy to John M. Kingsbury, Salem, October 15, 1855; John M. Kingsbury to James J. Webb, Santa Fe, October 29, 1855, Webb Correspondence.

31. William S. Messervy to John M. Kingsbury, Salem, December 11, 1855, Webb Correspondence. Messervy was responding to a letter from Kingsbury dated September 30, but a robbery of the mail delayed its delivery until November 30.

32. John M. Kingsbury, Westport Crossing, KS, to James J. Webb, Santa Fe, September 22, 1856, in Elder and Weber, *Trading in Santa Fe*, 39–42, n. 7.

33. Kingsbury to Webb, Salem, October 13, 1856, in Elder and Weber, *Trading in Santa Fe*, 43n23.

34. Kingsbury to Webb, November 12, 1856; Messervy to Webb, Salem, November 12, 1856; John M. Kingsbury to James J. Webb, Salem, December 11, 1856, Webb Correspondence.

35. John M. Kingsbury to James Webb, Salem, February 15, 1857, letter 33, in Elder and Weber, *Trading in Santa Fe*, 54.

36. Wm. S. Messervy, New York, to James J. Webb, Santa Fe, March 15, 1857, Webb Correspondence.

37. J. M. Kingsbury to James J. Webb, Westport, April 29, 1857, Webb Correspondence.

38. Wm. S. Messervy to J. J. Webb, Salem, May 16, 1857, Webb Correspondence.

39. Elder and Weber, *Trading in Santa Fe*, 57. See also James Webb to Lillie, June 18, 1857, and obituary, *Santa Fe Gazette*, June 20, 1857, ibid., 58–60. Kate Kingsbury's obituary was also included in Marian Meyer, "Death on the Santa Fe Trail," *Wagon Tracks: Santa Fe Trail Association Quarterly* 4, 4 (August 1990): 8–9.

40. For a discussion of nineteenth-century beliefs about death, see Harvey Green, *The Light of the Home: An Intimate View of the Lives of Women in Victorian America* (New York: Pantheon Books, 1983), 165–179.

41. Kingsbury's order for the headstone is found in J. M. Kingsbury to James J. Webb, Santa Fe, February 28, 1858, Webb Correspondence. Archaeologist Alysia L. Abbott has been recording the graves in the cemetery but has not determined whether the remains were moved or just the headstones. Alysia L. Abbott, "'A Little Earth for

Charity': Cultural Resources Investigations at the International Order of Odd Fellows Cemetery, Santa Fe, 2018," cited with permission of the author. The cemetery's archaeological record number is LA 175664, and the report is cataloged as NMCRIS 126928.

42. Alysia L. Abbott, "Kate's Final Journey," *El Palacio* 125, 1 (Spring 2020): 73; *Santa Fe New Mexican*, December 26, 2021. Kate's gravestone was removed for preservation by private parties from the unkempt Odd Fellows Cemetery in the summer of 2023. There is still some dispute over who authorized this removal and where the stone will be placed after it is cleaned. Since I completed this manuscript, the stone has been cleaned, mounted in a protective metal frame, and reinstalled in the Odd Fellows Cemetery. *Santa Fe New Mexican*, November 8, 2023.

43. Elder and Weber, *Trading in Santa Fe*, 285–290.

44. Nancy Owen Lewis, *Chasing the Cure in New Mexico: Tuberculosis and the Quest for Health* (Santa Fe: Museum of New Mexico Press, 2016); Jordana Rosenfeld, "How White People Used Tuberculosis to Settle the Southwest," *OG History, Teen Vogue* ser., July 28, 2020, https://www.teenvogue.com/story/southwest-settlers-tuberculosis/amp. Rosenfeld draws parallels between nineteenth-century health seekers' social impact on New Mexico and the rise of COVID-19 among Native American and Hispanic populations in New Mexico in 2020. She concludes this discussion by reminding readers that the COVID-19 pandemic had the greatest impact on marginalized people and that systemic racism still exists in the delivery of health care in the United States.

5. Unequal Companions: African American Women on the Santa Fe Trail

1. Dedra McDonald, "Intimacy and Empire: Indian-African Interaction in Spanish Colonial New Mexico, 1500–1800," *American Indian Quarterly* 22, 1–2 (Winter–Spring 1998): 134–156.

2. Dedra McDonald, "To Be Black and Female in the Spanish Southwest: Toward a History of African Women on New Spain's Far Northern Frontier," in *African American Women Confront the West, 1600–2000*, ed. Shirley Ann Wilson Moore and Qunitard Taylor (Norman: University of Oklahoma Press, 2003), 32–52; George P. Hammond and Agapito Rey, *Don Juan de Oñate, Colonizer of New Mexico 1595–1628* (Albuquerque: University of New Mexico Press, 1953), 560–562.

3. Frances Levine, *Doña Teresa Confronts the Spanish Inquisition: A Seventeenth-Century New Mexican Drama* (Norman: University of Oklahoma Press, 2016), contains the trial transcript of the proceedings against Doña Teresa. The inventory of her property in Santa Fe at the time of her arrest contains a detailed, if not utterly voyeuristic, description of the clothing she put on while the guards watched her dressing in her bedroom. There is also an exhaustive list of the items the Inquisition would hold as evidence and to support her imprisonment. Ibid., 167–175.

4. Ibid., 139–140, 181–182. The inventory listed five Indian women in Doña Teresa's possession at the time of her imprisonment, including two women of the Quivira nation, two Apache women, and another Indian woman from Mexico. Unlike Clara and Diego, they apparently did not stay with her in prison. Doña Teresa claimed that she had been accompanied by four other Indian women on the road from Santa Fe to the Mexican prison and that these Indian women were sold as slaves or died of maltreatment on the road, though she does not say who was responsible for their sale or maltreatment.

5. McDonald, "Intimacy and Empire," 140–141, reviews some of the literature that evaluates the extent to which Blacks, or any outsiders, would have been given the authority to lead the rebellion. It seems more reasonable to assume that the conditions that gave *castas* the opportunity to live in Pueblo communities also gave them common cause to participate in the rebellion against oppressive conditions.

6. Jacque Lafaye, "La Sociedad de Castas en la Nueva España: La Pintura de Castas," *Artes de Mexico* 8 (1998): 25–35.

7. Alicia V. Tjarks, "Demographic, Ethnic and Occupational Structure of New Mexico, 1790," *Americas* 35, 1 (July 1978): 45–88.

8. McDonald, "Intimacy and Empire," 148–150.

9. Alice L. Baumgartner, *South to Freedom: Runaway Slaves to Mexico and the Road to the Civil War* (New York: Basic Books, 2020), 43–67.

10. William P. O'Brien, "Hiram Young: Black Entrepreneur on the Sata Fe Trail," *Wagon Tracks: Santa Fe Trail Association Quarterly* 33, 4 (August 2019): 22–25.

11. Elizabeth Keckley, *Behind the Scenes; or, Thirty Years a Slave, and Four Years in the White House* (New York: G. W. Carleton,1868); Lucy Delaney, *From the Darkness Cometh the Light; or, Struggles for Freedom* (St. Louis: J. T. Smith, 1891), Kindle.

12. Drumm, *Down the Old Santa Fe Trail*. Drumm was the stalwart librarian for the Missouri Historical Society from 1913 to 1944. She was also a well-regarded, even fierce, researcher of western expansion. Miss Drumm, as she evidently preferred to be called, as indicated by her correspondence files at the Missouri Historical Society, persuaded Susan Shelby Magoffin's daughter, Jane Magoffin Taylor, to permit publication of the journal. The original journal is housed at the Beinecke Library at Yale University and can be viewed online at https://brbl-dl.library.yale.edu/vufind/Record/3791455. The book is labeled the second volume of her diary; the first, which covered her journey from Kentucky to New York, is presumed lost.

13. Virginia Scharff, "The Hearth of Darkness: Susan Magoffin on Suspect Terrain," in *Twenty Thousand Roads: Women, Movement and the West* (Berkeley: University of California Press, 2003), 35–63.

14. Howard R. Lamar, foreword in Drumm, *Down the Old Santa Fe Trail*, ix.

15. Drumm, *Down the Old Santa Fe Trail*, 62, 133. Based on a dispatch from the *Vicksburg (MS) Daily World*, they reportedly joined the caravan on June 30, 1846. Jane is not mentioned in this short article, nor are any of the attendants who may have traveled with the Leitensdorfers. Dr. Leitensdorfer and Solidad Abreu had been married

in Santa Fe in December 1845, so the crossing from Missouri back to Santa Fe was evidently her second trip across the trail. Eliza Michaud married Thomas Leitensdorfer in Carondelet, Missouri, just south of St. Louis, in May 1845. This may have been her first crossing of the trail. The women were also at Bent's Fort at the same time as the Magoffins, and they visited Susan at the Magoffins' temporary home in Santa Fe.

16. Drumm, *Down the Old Santa Fe Trail*, 4, 11–12.

17. Ibid., 20–21.

18. Ibid., 28, 34, 54–55.

19. Ibid., 66.

20. Susan lost another child during a second pregnancy in Chihuahua. Drumm tends to gloss over these deeply personal remarks, providing no information about the different cultural and medical practices. Instead, she turns to the genealogy and connections of Susan's attending physician, Dr. Masure, whom Susan describes as a delicate and polite Frenchman and an excellent doctor in the realm of "female cases." Ibid., 53, 66.

21. Ibid., 111.

22. Ibid., 130.

23. William Elsey Connelly, *War with Mexico, 1846–1847: Doniphan's Expedition and the Conquest of New Mexico and California* (Topeka, KS: published by the author, 1907), 215–216, devotes a considerable number of words and observations to the women of New Mexico, focusing on their clothing, jewelry, and graceful movements. For her part, Susan Magoffin was scandalized by New Mexican women's uncorseted movements and the garishness of their jewelry and makeup. Drumm, *Down the Old Santa Fe Trail*, 119, 142–145. Janet Lecompte, "La Tules and the Americans," *Arizona and the West* 20, 3 (1978): 215–230, and Mary Jean Straw Cook, *Doña Tules: Santa Fe's Courtesan and Gambler* (Albuquerque: University of New Mexico Press, 2007), provide scholarly considerations of Doña Tules's life and importance during the early years of American control of Santa Fe.

24. Drumm, *Down the Old Santa Fe Trail*, 174–175.

25. Thavolia Glymph, *Out of the House of Bondage: The Transformation of the Plantation Household* (Cambridge: Cambridge University Press, 2008), 18–62, analyzes the power and violence that slave-owning women exerted on their enslaved house staff. In some cases, the violence inside the home exceeded that of the whippings inflicted by slaveholding men.

26. Drumm, *Down the Old Santa Fe Trail*, 182. Earlier, they had "rescued" an orphaned child just south of Albuquerque. On Wednesday, October 28, a young boy came into the camp and asked Samuel to buy him and rescue him from his misery. He had been kidnapped by Apaches some three years ago, and his mother and father were dead. He had been held captive until he managed to escape and found refuge with an old man in a miserable hut by the river. If Samuel could pay $7 for his release—the sum the boy owed the old man for his protection—the boy could go with the Magoffins. The money was paid, and Francisco, a boy of nine or ten, became one of their servants.

27. Drumm, *Down the Old Santa Fe Trail*, 205–207.

28. Marian Meyer, *Mary Donoho: New First Lady of the Santa Fe Trail* (Santa Fe: Ancient City Press, 1991), 117n1, suggests that Jane was not the first woman of her race to travel the Santa Fe Trail. She cites David Lavender's *Bent's Fort* (Garden City, NY: Doubleday, 1954), 160, and assumes that the first might have been "Black Charlotte."

29. Hyde, *Empires, Nations and Families*, 147–168, cites the Bents as one of several extended families in the West that used marriage with Native American women and a deep understanding of Native customs, rituals, and language to build a successful fur trade in the period before the Mexican War. The Bents were among the families that migrated from Kentucky to Missouri and then expanded their interests through tribal trade networks.

30. Shirley Ann Wilson Moore, *Sweet Freedom's Plains: African Americans on the Overland Trails, 1841–1869* (Norman: University of Oklahoma Press, 2016).

31. Simmons, *Kit Carson and His Three Wives*, 33.

32. Drumm, *Down the Old Santa Fe Trail*, 60–63.

33. Sunder, *Matt Field on the Santa Fe Trail*, 73, 144. Matthew C. Field, of Irish and English descent, came to the United States from London as a child after the War of 1812. He was trained as a jeweler in New York and as a Shakespearean actor who toured a circuit that included Mobile, Alabama, New Orleans, and St. Louis. He took to the Santa Fe Trail in the summer of 1839 to restore his physical health and leave behind two women who had spurned his marriage proposals. He performed for the last time on June 11, 1839, to some critical acclaim but departed St. Louis soon after and made his way on a steamer to Independence, Missouri. He joined a small group of wagons with a total of eighteen travelers. His journal entries and verbal sketches of this trip and a subsequent one in 1843 are some of the most literary trail writings we have from before the American annexation. Field's health did not improve, and after his second trip to the West, he died and was buried at sea on November 15, 1844, as he attempted to sail from Boston back to New Orleans. Sunder's introduction (xvii–xxix) and editor's notes are kind to Field's memory and literary aspirations.

34. Garrard, *Wah-to-yah*, 73. A. B. Guthrie Jr. wrote the introduction (ix–xvi) to the 1955 edition of Garrard's book. Hector Lewis Garrard published under the name Lewis H. Garrard. Young Garrard began his journey in the caravan led by Céran St. Vrain, traveling from Westport Landing to Bent's Fort. He traveled several times from Bent's Fort to Taos and back. Garrard had an eye for details and an ear for the speech patterns of the many different cultures he encountered during his year of travels, contrasting the family roles, clothing, and customs of Native American and New Mexican women with those he knew from his life in Cincinnati.

35. Garrard, *Wah-to-yah*, 74.

36. George F. Ruxton, *Adventures in Mexico and the Rocky Mountains* (London: John Marks, 1849). Ruxton's writings were collected by Clyde and Mae Reed Porter and published in Leroy R. Hafen, ed., *Ruxton of the Rockies* (Norman: University of Oklahoma Press, 1950). Garrard and Ruxton would meet by chance in Buffalo in

1848 while Ruxton was en route back west. He would never make it; he died a few weeks later of "epidemic dysentery" he contracted in St. Louis, which was ravaged by the disease that summer. Hafen, *Ruxton of the Rockies*, 310–312.

37. William W. Gwaltney, "Black Fur Traders and Frontiersmen: Beyond the Pale; African Americans in the Fur Trade West," in *Lest We Forget: African-American Military History*, 1994, http://lestweforget.hamptonu.edu/page.cfm?uuid=9FEC4006-CDFF-44A2-E3D69CC34C3AE4FE.

38. Garrard, *Wah-to-yah*, 262.

39. Gardner and Simmons, *Mexican War Correspondence of Richard Smith Elliott*, 149, 154. There are several dramatic secondary accounts of Green rushing into battle at the siege of Taos Pueblo. Elliott's contemporary account of those wounded or killed in the various battles surrounding the insurrection at Taos lists Dick, a Black servant of Governor Bent, as being severely wounded at Embudo. It is therefore unlikely that he took part in the siege of Taos Pueblo on February 3 or 4.

40. Leo E. Oliva, "A Faithful Account of Everything: Letters from Katie Bowen on the Santa Fe Trail, 1851," *Kansas History* 19, 4 (1996): 265, 281. The Bowen letters cover the period 1845–58 and have been edited and annotated by Oliva. They are particularly detailed about Katie's life on military posts before the Civil War.

41. Barbour, *Reluctant Frontiersman*, 81–83.

42. Seth Hays was a great-grandson of Daniel Boone and a cousin of Kit Carson. He established a trading post at Council Grove in 1847 to trade with the Kaw Indians. Sally Taylor (1807–72) was an enslaved woman he brought with him to serve as housekeeper and attend to his adopted daughter, Kittie Parker Robbins, whose father abandoned her after the death of her mother. Sally Taylor stayed with Hays after she was freed in 1861. She is buried near him in Greenwood Cemetery in Council Grove. "Miss Kittie," as she is referred to at the Hays Historic Site, made her own crossing of the Santa Fe Tail to live near Las Vegas, New Mexico. Historical Marker Database, Seth Hays Home, https://www.hmdb.org/m.asp?m=45142; Find a Grave https://www.findagrave.com/memorial/11575844/seth-millington-hays. Hezekiah Brake's narrative is in Marc Simmons, *On the Santa Fe Trail* (Lawrence: University Press of Kansas, 1986), 37–51.

43. Simmons, On the Santa Fe Trail, 77. In this slim volume, Simmons published several original journals and letters of importance to Santa Fe Trail historians, including the translation of Ernestine's complete trail journal, written in German and now in the Huning-Ferguson Papers at the Zimmerman Library, University of New Mexico. Simmons repeats some details that came from the Huning family. Although family members said the young couple crossed the trail in 1863, the Missouri Compiled Marriage Index lists the date of their marriage as March 5, 1864. Ernestine's journal covers the period from April 4, when they left St. Louis, to May 30, when they were camped just outside Las Vegas, New Mexico. She lists the dates of travel but not the year. I assume it was 1864, following their wedding a month earlier.

44. Simmons, *On the Santa Fe Trail*, 8; Franz Huning and Lina Fergusson Browne,

Trader on the Santa Fe Trail: Memoirs of Franz Huning with Notes by His Granddaughter (Albuquerque: Calvin Horn, 1973), 72–75.

45. Huning and Browne, *Trader on the Santa Fe Trail*, 88–96.

46. Simmons, *On the Santa Fe Trail*, 106–119. Simmons includes Huning's memoir of this horrible tragedy, edited by his granddaughter Lina Fergusson Browne, sister of the well-regarded authors of New Mexico history Erna and Harvey Fergusson and of Francis. Franz Huning came to New Mexico with four of his brothers and established a profitable mercantile business in Los Lunas, just south of Albuquerque. Franz and his younger brother Charles came to the United States from Bremen, Germany, in the summer of 1848. They arrived in St. Louis in January 1849 and were there during a historic cholera epidemic and massive fire on the riverfront. Christopher Alan Gordon, *Fire, Pestilence and Death: St. Louis 1849* (St. Louis: Missouri Historical Society Press, 2018), focuses on this year of historic events that shaped the region and beyond. The brothers headed west to California but settled in Albuquerque and prospered in the Santa Fe trade. Huning began his memoir in October 1894, noting that he would have preferred to write in German but knew his children would understand it better if he wrote in English.

47. The portion of Christy's memoir cited is reprinted in Simmons, *On the Santa Fe Trail*, 106–119.

48. Huning and Browne, *Trader on the Santa Fe Trail*, 96.

49. Hämäläinen, *Comanche Empire*, 321–326; Sides, *Blood and Thunder.*

50. William H. Leckie, *The Buffalo Soldiers: A Narrative of the Negro Cavalry in the West* (Norman: University of Oklahoma Press, 1967), 21–23.

51. Simmons, *On the Santa Fe Trail*, 120–133. Gurulé returned to Las Placitas, where he outlived his first wife, married again, and raised a family on his *rancho* (farm), where he likely pastured animals in the nearby mountains.

52. Darlis A. Miller, "Foragers, Army Women and Prostitutes," in *New Mexico Women: Intercultural Perspectives*, ed. Joan M. Jensen and Darlis A. Miller (Albuquerque: University of New Mexico Press, 1986), 141–168.

53. Ibid., 155–157, citing Carvallo to the Post Adjutant, March 15 and 18, 1879, and Quartermaster's Notice of Death, March 12, 1879, Fort Union Post Records, LR, RG 393, National Archives.

54. Ruxton, *Adventures in Mexico*, 317; Hafen, *Ruxton of the Rockies*, 294.

55. Ruxton, *Adventures in Mexico*, 20; Hafen, *Ruxton of the Rockies*, 296.

6. THE END OF THE TRAIL

1. Gardner and Simmons, *Mexican War Correspondence of Richard Smith Elliott.* Elliott has a newsman's eye and the ability to describe events from several points of view. His dispatches are sometimes touchingly empathetic as he writes about the captured people and property in New Mexico, yet carefully couched to preserve the US position.

2. Timothy L. Kimball, "Most Beautiful Are the Evenings: Fischer's German-American Artillery Volunteers on the Santa Fe Trail, 1846–1847," *Wagon Tracks: Santa Fe Trail Association Quarterly* 26, 1 (2011): 21–24. At Fort Leavenworth they joined other Missouri volunteer companies.

3. Letter dated July 29, 1846, "In Camp Near Bent's Fort," *Daily Reveille*, September 6, 1846, in Gardner and Simmons, *Mexican War Correspondence of Richard Smith Elliott*, 54.

4. Letter dated July 31, 1846, "In Camp Near Bent's Fort," *Daily Reveille*, September 8, 1846, in Gardner and Simmons, *Mexican War Correspondence of Richard Smith Elliott*, 56.

5. Calvin Ross, ed., *Lieutenant Emory Reports: Notes of a Military Reconnaissance* (Albuquerque: University of New Mexico Press, 1951), 50. Emory was an astute observer of the geography of the route of conquest. Ross argues in the introduction that Emory's report is still relevant to modern readers, even though Ross omitted the lieutenant's scientific field illustrations and detailed notes on the astronomical readings and maps that guided the expedition, in addition to "dated" ethnographic descriptions of the Native peoples. Even without these sections, Emory's report remains a valuable resource, as do many other journals and diaries that recorded both the momentous and the inconsequential events on the front lines of the Mexican-American War.

6. Matthew Saionz, "Governor, Trader and Scapegoat for the American Conquest: The Career and Legacy of Manuel Armijo," *Wagon Tracks: Santa Fe Trail Association Quarterly* 34, 4 (2020): 14–21. Saionz reconsiders the historiography surrounding Armijo's surrender of New Mexico to the Americans and takes a longer view of Armijo's service to New Mexico, the difficulties of his position, and choices he faced when confronted by the strength of the US Army and no support from the central government or Mexican troops. Saionz concludes that historians' interpretations of Armijo's alleged cowardice and the possibility that he accepted bribes to leave New Mexico undefended are based on speculation and judgments of Armijo's character that do not square with his leadership in the 1837 revolt or his ability to negotiate the complex relationships among Texan, American, and Mexican traders after Texans' failed invasion of New Mexico in 1841. The anticipated battle at Apache Canyon did not take place, but the US annexation of the Southwest was certainly not a "bloodless conquest." Saionz suggests that Armijo may have calculated the risks differently in his assessment of the chances of success in that encounter.

7. Gardner and Simmons, *Mexican War Correspondence of Richard Smith Elliott*, 17; Richard Smith Elliott, *Notes Taken in Sixty Years* (St. Louis: R. P. Studley, 1883), 218, https://archive.org/search.php?query=external-identifier%3A%22urn%3Aoclc%3Arecord%3A1049958725%22.

8. Connelly, *War with Mexico*, 206. The quotation is from Connelly's reprint of the campaign diary kept by Colonel John Taylor Hughes. Hughes enlisted and served with the Clay County, Missouri, volunteers and was a sympathetic believer in the American cause. In Connelly's preface (v) he calls the Missourians' service in the

Mexican War heroic and notes that they were not appropriately credited for "marching . . . footsore and weary over desert wastes, as they bivouacked shelterless on the frozen ground under the cold and silent stars, as they starved and their hair and beards ran riot and their clothing fell to pieces, as they appeared on the battlefield fighting like demons for their country which neglected them, and as citizens of a great State returning to the pursuits of please and pleasures of home." He prayed that one day their service would be recognized in a great painting.

9. The Jaramillo sisters were members of elite New Mexican families. Rumalda was Ignacia's daughter with her first husband, José Rafael Luna, and the stepdaughter of Charles Bent. Rumalda was newly married to Thomas Oliver Boggs in May 1846. He was a descendant of Daniel Boone and the prominent Lilburn Boggs family of Missouri. He was a teamster for the Bents and married Rumalda when she was about fourteen years old. All were part of the intersection of American frontiersmen and elite Hispanic families. Hyde, *Empires, Nations and Families*, 351–354, 385–388.

10. Letter dated August 23, 1846, "In Camp at Galasted [sic], New Mexico," *Daily Reveille*, September 25, 1846, in Gardner and Simmons, *Mexican War Correspondence of Richard Smith Elliott*, 74–76.

11. Connelly, *War with Mexico*, 211–214.

12. Robert W. Frazer, ed., *Over the Chihuahua and Santa Fe Trail, 1847–1848: George Rutledge Gibson's Journal* (Albuquerque: University of New Mexico Press, 1981).

13. Deena González, "Gertrudis Barceló: La Tules of Image and Reality," in *Latina Legacies*, ed. Vicki L. Ruiz and Virginia Sanchez Korrol (London: Oxford University Press, 2005), 39–58; Anna M. Nogar and Enrique R. Lamadrid, "Nuevomexicano Cultural Memory and the Indo-Hispana *Mujerota*," *Journal of the Southwest* 58, 4 (2016): 751–779.

14. Lecompte, "Independent Women of Hispanic New Mexico," 73–82.

15. Montoya, *Translating Property*, 53–63, discusses the property losses suffered by several women who had inherited portions of land grants in northern New Mexico, particularly the heirs of tracts within the Maxwell Land Grant.

16. Letter dated April 29, 1847, Santa Fe, *Daily Reveille,* June 3, 1847, in Gardner and Simmons, *Mexican War Correspondence of Richard Smith Elliott*, 186.

17. William Carson, with an introduction by Frances Levine, "William Carr Lane: First Mayor of St. Louis, Second Governor of New Mexico Territory," *Gateway: The Magazine of the Missouri History Museum* 36 (2016): 8–17.

18. Gordon, *Fire, Pestilence and Death*, 5–11, traces the changing demographics of St. Louis and the rapid growth of the region.

19. Julius Froebel, "Western Travels, Part I," *Wagon Tracks*: *Santa Fe Trail Association Quarterly* 22, 3 (2008): 114–119, and "Western Travels, Part II," *Wagon Tracks*: *Santa Fe Trail Association Quarterly* 22, 4 (2008): 18–21. Froebel's travel articles were originally published in London in 1859.

20. Julius Froebel, "Western Travels, Part VI," *Wagon Tracks*: *Santa Fe Trail Association Quarterly* 26, 4 (2012): 21–23.

21. Joy Poole, "Henry and Rebecca Mayer's 1852 Honeymoon with 50 Men and 500 Mules," *Wagon Tracks: Santa Fe Trail Association Quarterly* 37, 2 (2023): 16–21; 37, 3 (2023): 14–20.

22. Henry Tobias, *A History of the Jews in New Mexico* (Albuquerque: University of New Mexico Press, 1990), 27–28. The quotation is from a letter written from Las Cruces by Phoebus Freudenthal to his German family on July 11, 1869. Ibid., 30.

23. Albert Speyer is an example of someone who was identified by others as Jewish, but his biography does not confirm this. Tobias, *History of the Jews in New Mexico*, 23–24, examines the facts of Speyer's identity—as he lived his life and as others characterized him. Speyer may have been on the Santa Fe Trail as early as 1843, and he was implicated in smuggling arms during the Mexican-American War. He was also accused of being an agent for Jay Gould and James Fish in the gold speculation that sparked the stock market crash of 1869 and of engaging in questionable trading activities in 1840. Speyer took his own life; his funeral was held at St. Mark's Church in New York, and his obituary was published in the *New York Times* on December 24, 1880. *James Josiah Webb's Adventures in the Santa Fe Trade*, 29, 189, identifies Speyer as a Prussian Jew but expresses disappointment at his inability to spot a painting that was clearly not as valuable as the sellers believed. Speyer was identified as a Jew when he failed to display the stereotypical mercantile acumen attributed to Jews and was accused of participating in other unsavory situations.

24. William Patrick O'Brien, "'Olam Katan' (Small World): Jewish Traders on the Santa Fe Trail," *Journal of the Southwest* 48, 2 (2006): 211–231.

25. Not all the early traders from Missouri were German, however. Doyle Daves, "George and Louis: Golds of Territorial New Mexico," *Wagon Tracks*: *Santa Fe Trail Association Quarterly* 25, 3 (2011): 17–21, traces the complicated migration that brought George and Louis Gold to New Mexico. Whether they were Jewish is open to question, given how they self-identified in the absence of a Jewish community. George Gold was born in Scotland, immigrated to Quebec, and then presumably followed the fur trade to St. Louis. He arrived in New Mexico in the 1820s, the earliest years of the trade. He married or established families with several Hispanic women. He was wounded in the Taos Revolt of 1847 and lived for the remainder of his life near Mora, New Mexico. Louis Gold was of Polish descent. He came to New Mexico with his wife Mary, but she left after 1858 and returned to New York City.

26. Flora wrote about her travels on the Santa Fe Trail when she was in her eighties, and her reminiscences were first published in the *Jewish Spectator* in 1937. They have been reprinted and abstracted in several publications. I used the version annotated and introduced by Mary Jean Straw Cook, "Flora Spiegelberg: 'Tenderfoot Bride of the Santa Fe Trail,'" *Wagon Tracks*: *Santa Fe Trail Association Quarterly* 15, 1 (2000): 11–16.

27. Lew Wallace served as governor of New Mexico from August 1878 to March 1881. *Ben Hur*, published in 1880, was the best selling American novel of the nineteenth century, surpassing even Harriet Beecher Stowe's *Uncle Tom's Cabin*, a work with a profound and timeless resonance.

28. Flora remained a committed voice for public health and was known in New York as "Garbage Can Flora" for her advocacy on behalf of sanitation workers and for the sanitary disposal of garbage. Lawrence Bush, "Garbage Can Flora," 2014, https://archive.jewishcurrents.org/september-10-garbage-can-flora. Flora also published a children's fairy tale in 1915 titled *Princess Goldenhair and the Wonderful Flower.* Her circular, which she distributed from her residence at 67 Riverside Drive in Manhattan, urged all who received it to share it with their friends and neighbors "until the masses of our citizens shall raise their voices and demand a sanitary and dustless removal of refuse in covered noiseless wagons." Address by Mrs. Flora Spiegelberg, "A Dustless and Sanitary Collection of Ashes and Garbage," collection of the New York Historical Society.

29. Sandra L. Myers, "Romance and Reality on the American Frontier: Views of Army Wives," *Western Historical Quarterly* 13, 4 (1982): 409–427, and Simmons, "Women on the Santa Fe Trail," 233–243, remain useful surveys of the literature produced by women on the trail. An updated bibliography would certainly provide a larger social and political context.

30. Kenneth L. Holmes, comp. and ed., "A Military Wife on the Santa Fe Trail: Anna Maria Morris," in *Covered Wagon Women: Diaries & Letters from the Western Trails, 1840–1890*, vol. 2 (Glendale, CA: Arthur H. Clark, 1983), 15–43. The 1850 census of New Mexico shows Anna Maria Morris living with twenty-one-year-old Louisa Morris, who was born in Missouri, and sixteen-year-old Alvino Lopez from New Mexico.

31. Ibid., 41.

32. Samuel E. Sisneros, "'She Was Our Mother': New Mexico's Changes of National Sovereignty" and "Juan Bautista Vigil y Alarid: The Last New Mexico Governor," in *All Trails Lead to Santa Fe: An Anthology Commemorating the 400th Anniversary of the Founding of Santa Fe, Mexico in 1610* (Santa Fe: Ancient City Press, 2010), 279–299.

33. John P. Hays carefully parses the legal language of the deed of trust by which Carleton assigned Hannah and Benjamin to Governor Lane. He makes it clear that Lane would not have derived any personal benefit from this arrangement. However, others claim that Lane purchased the two enslaved people from Carleton for his personal use. See John P. Hays, "The Curious Case of New Mexico's Pre–Civil War Slave Code," *New Mexico Historical Review* 92, 3 (2017): 251–283.

34. Leo Oliva provides an excellent overview of domestic life at Fort Union and the frontier army in "Fort Union NM: Fort Union and the Frontier Army in the Southwest," chap. 4 in *A Historic Resource Study, Fort Union National Monument, New Mexico*, Southwest Cultural Resources Center Professional Papers No. 41 (Santa Fe: Southwest Cultural Resources Center, 1993), 49–59. Bonita and Leo Oliva published a series of Katie Bowen's letters to her parents in *Wagon Tracks: Santa Fe Trail Association Quarterly.*

35. C. Francis Clarke to sister Mary Anne, June 22, 1850, and to his father, July 18, 1850, in *Above a Common Soldier: Frank and Mary Clarke in the American West*

and Civil War, rev. ed., ed. Darlis A. Miller (Albuquerque: University of New Mexico Press, 1997), 32–33. Forty-four of forty-six letters were published in Darlis A. Miller, ed., *To Form a More Perfect Union: The Lives of Charles Francis and Mary Clarke from Their Letters, 1847–1871* (Albuquerque: University of New Mexico Press, 1997). These letters were originally published in 1941. In the 1997 edition of *To Form a More Perfect Union*, Miller expands the context of the letters and notes their importance for expressing the point of view of an enlisted man and his wife. The letters that cover Mary and Frank's marriage and move to New Mexico and then back to St. Louis were all written by Frank. After Frank's death from scarlet fever on December 10, 1862, while he fought for the Union near Memphis, Tennessee, Mary wrote letters to his mother in England about her life in Kansas. Miller, 95.

36. Gordon, *Fire, Pestilence and Death*. The title captures the devastation that gripped St. Louis in 1849.

37. Clarke to his father, September 29, 1852, in Miller, *Above a Common Soldier*, 42–43.

38. In Wetherington and Levine, *Battles and Massacres on the Southwestern Frontier*, William Gorenfeld analyzes the historical records, including the US Military Court of Inquiry and other contemporaneous accounts of the battle, and David Johnson interprets the artifacts found at the site of the Battle of Cieneguilla as evidence of the tactics used by the Jicarilla and the US Dragoons and Davidson's failure of command.

39. Clarke to his father and mother, May 25, 1854, in Miller, *Above a Common Soldier*, 48–49.

40. Lydia Spencer Lane, *I Married a Soldier* (Albuquerque: University of New Mexico Press, 1987), 91. Lydia did not have kind memories of St. Louis because she believed one of her children contracted scarlet fever while staying in a St. Louis hotel.

41. Lydia Spencer Lane, *A Frontier Officer: Stories of a Wandering Family* (n.p.: Big Byte Books, 2014), 102–104, Kindle. Lane's memoir *I Married a Soldier*, written in 1892, published in 1893, and annotated, edited, and published by the University of New Mexico Press in 1987, is a well-told account of the life of an officer's wife in the crucial years 1854–70, as she accompanied and supported her husband as they moved their family from fort to fort across the country and back, primarily in a wagon.

42. Miller, "Foragers, Army Women and Prostitutes," 141–168. Miller summarizes many of the experiences of women living on New Mexico's isolated frontier posts and a few cases of the larger posts offering opportunities to socialize at balls, teas, and picnics.

43. Ibid., 145. A more complete but unsourced biography of Martin Koslowski is Kathy Weiser-Alexander, "Legends of the West," 2018, https://www.legendsofamerica.com/kozlowski-trading-post/#. Koslowski was tried and jailed in Las Vegas, New Mexico, for murdering a man in 1878. He and Ellen apparently lived separately for the remainder of their lives.

44. Kenneth L. Holmes, "To Pike's Peak and New Mexico, 1858: Julia Archibald (Holmes)," in *Covered Wagon Women*, vol. 2, 191–215. She addresses her letter to the

Sibyl as "Dear Sister Sayer"; this is Lydia Sayer Hasbrouck, who published the feminist newsletter, with her husband, from 1861 to 1864. Hasbrouck encouraged writers to address their readers with familial terms, which she called "the sisterly editorial voice." The reform movement aligned with suffrage and embraced the abolition of slavery. See Laura J. Ping, "'He May Sneer at the Course We Are Pursuing to Gain Justice': Lydia Sayer Hasbrouck, *The Sibyl* and Corresponding about Women's Suffrage," *New York History* 98, 3–4 (2017): 317–328. Hasbrouck promoted comfort over fashion for women and believed that women should not pay taxes if they did not have the vote. Her civil disobedience resulted in serval run-ins with the law in New York.

45. Holmes, "To Pike's Peak and New Mexico," 195.

46. Agnes Wright Spring, ed., *A Bloomer Girl on Pike's Peak, 1858: Julia Archibald Holmes, First White Woman to Climb Pike's Peak* (Denver: Denver Public Library, Western History Department, 1949), 33.

47. Ibid., 51–54.

48. Mark J. Stegmaier, "A Law that Would Make Caligula Blush? New Mexico Territory's Unique Slave Code, 1859–1861," *New Mexico Historical Review* 87, 2 (2012): 209–243; Hays, "Curious Case of New Mexico's Pre–Civil War Slave Code." Both Stegmaier and Hays discuss the political machinations that led Congressman Otero and others in New Mexico to support this act. Since New Mexico did not have plantations, the Slave Code was not tied to an existing economic system, but it was clearly aligned with southern politicians. Stegmaier refers to more sinister reasons for New Mexican support for the act. The March 5, 1859, issue of the *St. Louis Daily Missouri Republican* sarcastically called it an invitation to the South to bring Blacks to the gold-producing states, which could serve as breeding grounds for slaves for Mississippi and Louisiana.

49. Spring, *Bloomer Girl on Pike's Peak*, 55.

50. Primm, *Lion of the Valley*, 200–226, provides an overview of the negotiations, machinations, and politics surrounding the development of railroads in St. Louis and across Missouri. He dismisses the myth that St. Louisans were content with river-based commerce or unwilling to invest in railroads.

51. Susan E. Wallace, *The Land of the Pueblos* (New York: John B. Alden, 1888; commemorative ed., Crawfordsville, IN: Lew Wallace Study Preservation Society, 2015), 111–120, 175, Kindle.

Conclusion: The Legacy of the Santa Fe Trail

1. Deena J. González, *Refusing the Favor: The Spanish-Mexican Women of Santa Fe, 1820–1880* (Oxford: Oxford University Press, 1999), 40–41.

2. Ibid., 70–71.

3. Susan Lee Johnson, "'A Memory Sweet to Soldiers': The Significance of Gender in the History of the 'American West,'" in *Women and Gender in the American West: Jensen-Miller Prize Essays from the Coalition for Western Women's History*,

ed. Mary Ann Irwin and James F. Brooks (Albuquerque: University of New Mexico Press, 2004), 89–109.

BIBLIOGRAPHY

Abbott, Alysia L. "Kate's Final Journey." *El Palacio* 125, 1 (Spring 2020): 73.
———. "'A Little Earth for Charity': Cultural Resources Investigations at the International Order of Odd Fellows Cemetery, Santa Fe, 2018."
Adams, Eleanor B., ed. "Bishop Tamarón's Visitation of New Mexico, 1760." *New Mexico Historical Review* 28, 2–4 (1953): 81–114, 192–221, 291–315.
Alonso, Ana María. "Reconsidering Violence: Warfare, Terror and Colonialism in the Making of the United States." *American Quarterly* 60, 4 (2008): 1089–1097.
Aron, Stephen. *American Confluence: The Missouri Frontier from Borderlands to Border State*. Bloomington: Indiana University Press, 2006.
Barbour, Barton H., ed. *Reluctant Frontiersman: James Ross Larkin on the Santa Fe Trail, 1856–1857*. Albuquerque: University of New Mexico Press, 1990.
Barnes, Thomas C., Thomas H. Naylor, and Charles W. Polzer. *Northern New Spain: A Research Guide*. Tucson: University of Arizona Press, 1981.
Barr, Juliana. *Peace Came in the Form of a Woman: Indians and Spaniards in the Texas Borderlands*. Chapel Hill: University of North Carolina Press, 2007.
Barr, Juliana, and Edward Countryman, eds. *Contested Spaces of Early America*. Philadelphia: University of Pennsylvania Press, 2014.
Baumgartner, Alice L. *South to Freedom: Runaway Slaves to Mexico and the Road to the Civil War*. New York: Basic Books, 2020.
Baxter, John O. *Las Carneradas: Sheep Trade in New Mexico, 1700–1860*. Albuquerque: University of New Mexico Press, 1987.
Beauregard, Mrs. Nettie H., trans. "The Journals of Jules De Mun, Edited by Thomas Maitland Marshall." *Missouri Historical Society Collections* 5, 3 (1928): 167–208.
Beyreis, David C. *Blood in the Borderlands: Conflict, Kinship and the Bent Family, 1821–1920*. Lincoln: University of Nebraska Press, 2020.
———. "Business, Politics, and Power: The Transcontinental World of Bent, St. Vrain and Company, 1829–1849." *Wagon Tracks: Santa Fe Trail Association Quarterly* 36, 2 (2022): 17–23.
Bieber, Ralph P., ed. *Adventures in the Santa Fe Trade, 1844–1847*. Lincoln: University of Nebraska Press, 1995. Originally published Glendale, CA: A. H. Clark, 1931.

Blackhawk, Ned. *Violence, Warfare, Terror and Colonialism in the Making of the United States.* Cambridge, MA: Harvard University Press, 2006.

Bloom, Lansing B. "Early Vaccination in New Mexico." *Historical Society of New Mexico* 27 (1924): 3–12.

Boyle, Susan Calafate. "Did She Generally Decide? Women in Ste. Genevieve, 1750–1805." *William and Mary Quarterly* 44, 4 (1987): 775–789.

———. *Los Capitalistas: Hispano Merchants and the Santa Fe Trade.* Albuquerque: University of New Mexico Press, 1997.

Breckenridge, William Clark. "Biographical Sketch of Judge Wilson Primm." *Missouri Historical Society Collections* 4, 2 (1913): 127–140.

Brooks, James F. *Captives and Cousins: Slavery, Kinship and Community in the Southwest Borderlands.* Chapel Hill: University of North Carolina Press, 2002.

———. "'This Evil Extends Especially . . . to the Feminine Sex': Negotiating Captivity in the New Mexico Borderlands." *Feminist Studies* 22, 2 (1996): 279–309.

Burholt, Eleanor. "1863—Elizabeth Keckley, Striped Evening Dress for Mary Todd Lincoln." Fashion Institute of Technology, New York, NY. Posted June 11, 2020. https://fashionhistory.fitnyc.edu/1863-keckley-striped-evening-dress/.

Bustamante, Adrian, and Marc Simmons, trans. and eds. *The Exposition on the Province of New Mexico, 1812 by Don Pedro Bautista Pino.* Santa Fe and Albuquerque: El Rancho de las Golondrinas and University of New Mexico Press, 1995.

Carson, Kit. *The Life of Kit Carson, the Nestor of the Rocky Mountains.* Edited by DeWitt Clinton Peters. New York: W. R. C. Clark, 1858.

Carson, Timothy. "The Enduring Legacy of Hiram Young." *Missouri Life* (January–February 2022): 40–45.

———. "'Go East, Young Woman!' How Kit Carson's Daughter of the West Was Raised in Missouri." *Boone's Lick Heritage Quarterly* 19, 3 (2020): 10–11.

———. "If This Cemetery Could Talk (Oh, but It Does)." *Boone's Lick Heritage Quarterly* 20, 1 (2021): 7.

Carson, William, with an introduction by Frances Levine. "William Carr Lane, First Mayor of St. Louis, Second Governor of New Mexico Territory." *Gateway: The Magazine of the Missouri History Museum* 36 (2016): 8–17.

Carter, Harvey Lewis. *"Dear Old Kit": The Historical Christopher Carson.* Norman: University of Oklahoma Press, 1968.

Castañeda, Antonia I. "Women of Color and the Rewriting of Western History: The Discourse, Politics and Decolonization of History." In *Women and Gender in the American West: Jensen-Miller Prize Essays from the Coalition for Western Women's History,* ed. Mary Ann Irwin and James F. Brooks, 66–88. Albuquerque: University of New Mexico Press, 2004.

Cattermole, E. G. *Famous Frontiersmen, Pioneers and Scouts: The Romance of American History; Thrilling Narratives of Renowned Adventurers, Explorers, Heroes, Trappers, Scouts and Indian Fighters.* New and enlarged ed. Tarrytown, NY: William Abbott, 1926.

Chávez, Thomas E. "Don Manuel Alvares (de las Abelgas): Multi-Talented Merchant of New Mexico." *Journal of the West* 18, 1 (1979): 22–31.

———. *Manuel Alvarez, 1794–1856: A Southwestern Biography.* Niwot: University Press of Colorado, 1990.

Chouteau, Auguste. *Fragment of Col. Auguste Chouteau's Narrative of the Settlement of St. Louis: A Literal Translation from the Original French Ms., in Possession of the St. Louis Mercantile Library Association.* St. Louis: George Knapp, 1858. http://www.americanjourneys.org/aj-126.

Clapsaddle, David C. "Negro Slaves on the Santa Fe Trail." *Wagon Tracks: Santa Fe Trail Association Quarterly* 28, 2 (2014): 10–11.

Clark, James. *A Treatise on Pulmonary Consumption: Comprehending an Inquiry into the Causes, Nature, Presentation and Treatment of Tuberculosis and Scrofulous Diseases in General.* Philadelphia: Carey, Lea & Blanchard, 1835.

Cleary, Patricia. "Fashioning Identities on the Frontier: Clothing, Culture and Choice in Early St. Louis." In *French St. Louis: Landscape, Contexts and Legacy*, ed. Jay Gitlin, Robert Michael Morrissey, and Peter J. Kastor, 93–128. Lincoln: University of Nebraska Press, 2021.

———. *The World, the Flesh and the Devil: A History of Colonial St. Louis.* Columbia: University of Missouri Press, 2011.

Cleland, Robert Glass. *This Reckless Breed of Men: The Trappers and Fur Traders of the Southwest.* Albuquerque: University of New Mexico Press, 1950.

Conant, Jennet. *109 East Palace: Robert Oppenheimer and the Secret City of Los Alamos.* New York: Simon & Schuster, 2005.

Connelley, William Elsey. *War with Mexico, 1846–1847: Doniphan's Expedition and the Conquest of New Mexico and California.* Topeka, KS: published by the author, 1907.

Cook, Mary Jean Straw. "Carmel Benavides, an Early Santa Fe Trail Woman." *Wagon Tracks: Santa Fe Trail Association Quarterly* 13, 1 (1998): 9–15.

———. *Doña Tules: Santa Fe's Courtesan and Gambler.* Albuquerque: University of New Mexico Press, 2007.

———. "Flora Spiegelberg: 'Tenderfoot Bride of the Santa Fe Trail.'" *Wagon Tracks: Santa Fe Trail Association Quarterly* 15, 1 (2000): 11–16.

———. *Loretto, the Sisters and Their Chapel.* Santa Fe: Museum of New Mexico Press, 2002.

Coventry, Professor C. B. "Tuberculosis." *St. Louis Medical Journal* (1856): 466–468. Missouri Historical Society Library and Research Center, St. Louis.

Culmer, Frederic A. "Marking the Santa Fe Trail." *New Mexico Historical Review* 9, 1 (1934): 78–97.

Danisi, Thomas C. "Reconstructing the Founding of St. Louis." *Missouri Historical Review* 115, 2 (2021): 134–156.

Dart, Harry P., ed. "The Oath of Allegiance to Spain, from the Cabildo Records, New Orleans." *Louisiana Historical Quarterly* 4 (1921): 205–215. HathiTrust Digital Library.

Daves, Doyle. "Cross-Cultural Marriages in New Mexico: Six Jaramillo Women of Taos and the Husbands Who Came to Them across the Santa Fe Trail." *Wagon Tracks: Santa Fe Trail Association Quarterly* 35, 2 (February 2021): 13–19.

———. "Damaso López: He Traveled El Camino Real and the Santa Fe Trail." *Wagon Tracks: Santa Fe Trail Association Quarterly* 29, 4 (2015): 26–30.

———. "Education and the New Mexico Elite during Santa Fe Trail Days." *Wagon Tracks: Santa Fe Trail Association Quarterly* 33, 4 (2019): 19–24.

———. "Francisca López Kimball: Across the Santa Fe Trail to Missouri." *Wagon Tracks: Santa Fe Trail Association Quarterly* 31, 2 (2017): 16–20.

———. "George and Louis: Golds of Territorial New Mexico." *Wagon Tracks: Santa Fe Trail Association Quarterly* 25, 3 (2011): 17–21.

———. "New Mexico Daughters Sent to School in St. Louis." *Wagon Tracks: Santa Fe Trail Association Quarterly* 33, 3 (2019): 15–20.

———. "Teodoro Ruiz de Esparza and Maria Josefa Angulo: Their New Mexico Legacy." *Herencia Journal* 28, 1 (2020): 12–21.

———. "Trinidad López, College Boy on the Santa Fe Trail." *Wagon Tracks: Santa Fe Trail Association Quarterly* 24, 2 (2010): 1, 16–19.

Davis, W. W. H. *El Gringo; or New Mexico and Her People.* New York: Harper Brothers, 1857.

———. Papers. Beinecke Library, Yale University, New Haven, CT.

DeBow, J. D. B. *Mortality Statistics of the Seventh Census of the United States, 1850.* House of Representatives, 33rd Congress, 2nd session, Executive Document No. 98. Washington, DC: A. O. P. Nicholson, 1855.

Delaney, Lucy. *From the Darkness Cometh the Light; or, Struggles for Freedom.* St. Louis: J. T. Smith, 1891.

DeLay, Brian. *War of a Thousand Deserts: Indian Raids and the U.S.-Mexican War.* New Haven, CT: Yale University Press, 2008.

Deutsch, Sarah. *No Separate Refuge: Culture, Class, and Gender on an Anglo Hispanic Frontier in the American Southwest, 1880–1940.* New York: Oxford University Press, 1987.

Drumm, Stella M., ed. *Down the Old Santa Fe Trail and into Mexico: The Diary of Susan Shelby Magoffin, 1846–1847.* New Haven, CT: Yale University Press, 1926; reissued 1962. Lincoln: Bison Books, University of Nebraska Press, 1982.

———. Papers, 1913–1943. Missouri Historical Society, Library and Research Center, St. Louis.

Dufossat Map of St. Louis. *Relevé d'une Partie du Missisipi et du Missouri Depuis le Vilage de Pain-Court Iusquau Rocher de l'Eau Froide Fait aux Illinois Provaince de la Louisiane le 15 Octubre 1767 [Material cartográfico].* www.bdhrd.bne.es/viewer.vm?id=0000143583.

Early, Gerald. *"Ain't but a Place:" An Anthology of African American Writings about St. Louis.* St. Louis: Missouri Historical Society Press, 1998.

Ekberg, Carl J. *Stealing Indian Women: Native Slavery in the Illinois Country.* Urbana: University of Illinois Press, 2007.

Ekberg, Carl J., and Sharon Person. "The Making (and Perpetuating) of a Myth: Pierre Laclède and the Founding of St. Louis." *Missouri Historical Review* 111, 2 (2017): 87–103.

———. "The 1767 Dufossat Maps of St. Louis." *Gateway: The Magazine of the Missouri History Museum* 32 (2012): 8–25.

Elder, Jane Lenz, and David J. Weber. *Trading in Santa Fe: John M. Kingsbury's Correspondence with James Josiah Webb, 1853–1861.* Dallas: Southern Methodist University Press, 1996.

Epstein, Daniel Mark. *The Lincolns: Portrait of a Marriage.* New York: Ballantine Books, 2009.

Ewers, John C. "The Indian Trade of the Upper Missouri before Lewis and Clark." In *Indian Life on the Upper Missouri.* 1954. Reprint, Norman: University of Oklahoma Press, 1968.

Fausz, J. Frederick. "The Capital of St. Louis: From Indian Trade to American Territory, 1764–1825." In *French St. Louis: Landscape, Contexts and Legacy*, ed. Jay Gitlin, Robert Michael Morrissey, and Peter J. Kastor, 67–91. Lincoln: University of Nebraska Press, 2021.

———. *Founding St. Louis: First City of the New West.* Charleston, SC: History Press, 2011.

———. *Historic St. Louis: 250 Years Exploring New Frontiers.* San Antonio, TX: HPN Books and University of Missouri–St. Louis, 2014.

Feldman, Jay. *When the Mississippi Ran Backwards: Empire Intrigue, Murder and the New Madrid Earthquakes.* New York: Free Press, 2005.

Felton, Hattie. *"More Than Ordinary": Early St. Louis Artist Anna Maria Von Phul.* St. Louis: Missouri Historical Society, 2021.

Fitch, Samuel Sheldon. *Six Discourses on the Functions of the Lungs; and Causes, Prevention and Cure of Pulmonary Consumption, Asthma, and Diseases of the Heart; on the Lawes of Life; and on the Mode of Preserving Male and Female Health to an Hundred Years.* New York: S. S. Fitch, 1853.

Franzwa, Gregory. *Images of the Santa Fe Trail.* St. Louis: Patrice Press, 1988.

———. *Impressions of the Santa Fe Trail: A Contemporary Diary.* St. Louis: Patrice Press, 1988.

———. *Maps of the Santa Fe Trail.* St. Louis: Patrice Press, 1989.

Frazer, Robert W., ed. *Over the Chihuahua and Santa Fe Trail, 1847–1848: George Rutledge Gibson's Journal.* Albuquerque: University of New Mexico Press, 1981.

Froebel, Julius. "Western Travels, Part I." *Wagon Tracks: Santa Fe Trail Association Quarterly* 22, 3 (2008): 114–119. Originally published 1859, London.

———. "Western Travels, Part II." *Wagon Tracks: Santa Fe Trail Association Quarterly* 22, 4 (2008): 18–21. Originally published 1859, London.

———. "Western Travels, Part VI." *Wagon Tracks: Santa Fe Trail Association Quarterly* 26, 4 (2012): 21–23. Originally published 1859, London.

Gallegos, Albert J., and José Antonio Esquibel. "*Alcaldes* and Mayors of Santa Fe, 1613–2008." In *All Trails Lead to Santa Fe*, 403–428. Santa Fe: Sunstone Press, 2010.

Gandert, Miguel, and Enrique R. Lamadrid. *Nuevo Mexico Profundo: Rituals of the Indo-Hispano Homelands.* Santa Fe: Museum of New Mexico Press, 2000.

Gardner, Mark L., ed. *Edward James Glasgow and William Henry Glasgow: Brothers on the Santa Fe and Chihuahua Trails.* Niwot: University Press of Colorado, 1993.

———. Introduction to *Adventures in the Santa Fe Trade, 1844–1847*, ed. Ralph P. Bieber. Lincoln: University of Nebraska Press, 1995.

Gardner, Mark L., and Marc Simmons, eds. *The Mexican War Correspondence of Richard Smith Elliott.* Norman: University of Oklahoma Press, 1997.

Garrard, Lewis H. *Wah-to-yah and the Taos Trail.* Norman: University of Oklahoma Press, 1955.

Gianini, Charles A. "Manuel Lisa: One of the Earliest Traders on the Missouri River." *New Mexico Historical Review* 2, 4 (1927): 323–333.

Gitlin, Jay. *The Bourgeois Frontier: French Towns, French Traders and American Expansion.* New Haven, CT: Yale University Press, 2010.

Gitlin, Jay, Robert Michael Morrissey, and Peter J. Kastor, eds. *French St. Louis: Landscape, Contexts and Legacy.* Lincoln: University of Nebraska Press, 2021.

Glymph, Thavolia. *Out of the House of Bondage: The Transformation of the Plantation Household.* Cambridge: Cambridge University Press, 2008.

Gonzales, Moises. "The Genízaro Land Grant Settlements of New Mexico." *Journal of the Southwest* 56, 4 (Winter 2014): 583–602.

González, Deena. "Gertrudis Barceló: La Tules of Image and Reality." In *Latina Legacies*, ed. Vicki L. Ruiz and Virginia Sanchez Korrol, 39–58. London: Oxford University Press, 2005.

———. *Refusing the Favor: The Spanish-Mexican Women of Santa Fe, 1821–1880.* New York: Oxford University Press, 1999.

Gordon, Christopher Alan. *Fire, Pestilence and Death: St. Louis 1849.* St. Louis: Missouri Historical Society Press, 2018.

———. "St. Louis, the Santa Fe Trade and the Great Flood of 1844." *Wagon Tracks: Santa Fe Trail Association Quarterly* 33, 3 (2019): 20–26.

Gray, Annette. *Journey of the Heart: A True Story of Mamie Aguirre (1844–1906), a Southern Belle in the "Wild West."* Self-published, Graytwest Books, 2004.

Green, Harvey. *The Light of the Home: An Intimate View of the Lives of Women in Victorian America.* New York: Pantheon Books, 1983.

Gregg, Josiah. *Commerce of the Prairies.* 1844. Reprinted and edited by Max L. Moorhead, Norman: University of Oklahoma Press, 1954.

———. *Diary & Letters of Josiah Gregg . . . Excursions in Mexico & California, 1847–1850.* Edited by Maurice Fulton. Norman: University of Oklahoma Press, 1944.

Gutiérrez, Ramón A. *When Jesus Came, the Corn Mothers Went Away.* Palo Alto, CA: Stanford University Press, 1991.

Gwaltney, William W. "Black Fur Traders and Frontiersmen: Beyond the Pale; African Americans in the Fur Trade West." In *Lest We Forget: African-American Military History*, 1994. http://lestweforget.hamptonu.edu/page.cfm?uuid=9FEC4006-CDFF-44A2-E3D69CC34C3AE4FE.

Hacker, Margaret Schmidt, and Cynthia Ann Parker. *Handbook of Texas On-line.* Texas State Historical Association.
Hackett, Charles Wilson. *Historical Documents Relating to New Mexico, Nueva Vizcaya, and Approaches Thereto, to 1773.* Vol. 3. Washington, DC: Carnegie Institution of Washington, 1937.
Hafen, Leroy R., ed. *Ruxton of the Rockies.* Norman: University of Oklahoma Press, 1950.
Hall, Thomas B. *Medicine on the Santa Fe Trail.* Arrow Rock, MO: Morningside Bookshop, 1987.
Hämäläinen, Pekka. *The Comanche Empire.* New Haven, CT: Yale University Press, 2008.
———. "The Western Comanche Trade Center: Rethinking the Plains Indian Trade System." *Western Historical Quarterly* 29, 4 (Winter 1998): 485–513. http://www.jstor.org/stable/970405.
Hammond, George P., and Agapito Rey. *Don Juan de Oñate, Colonizer of New Mexico 1595–1628.* Albuquerque: University of New Mexico Press, 1953.
Harris, Mrs. Caroline. *History of the Captivity and Providential Release Therefrom of Mrs. Caroline Harris.* New York: G. Cunningham, 1838.
Hays, John P. "The Curious Case of New Mexico's Pre–Civil War Slave Code." *New Mexico Historical Review* 92, 3 (2017): 251–283.
Hendricks, Rick. "The 1761 Comanche Massacre." In *Massacre, Murder and Mayhem in the Rocky Mountains,* ed. Tim Blevins, Dennis Dany, Sydne Dean, Chris Nicholl, William G. Thomas, Michael L. Olsen, and Katherine Scott Sturdevant, 14–37. Colorado Springs: Pikes Peak Library District, 2016.
Holmes, Kenneth L., comp. and ed. "A Military Wife on the Santa Fe Trail: Anna Maria Morris." In *Covered Wagon Women: Diaries & Letters from the Western Trails, 1840–1890,* vol. 2, 15–43. Glendale, CA: Arthur H. Clark, 1983.
———. "To Pike's Peak and New Mexico, 1858: Julia Archibald (Holmes)." In *Covered Wagon Women: Diaries & Letters from the Western Trails, 1840–1890,* vol. 2, 191–215. Glendale, CA: Arthur H. Clark, 1983.
Hoover, John Neal. *Adventures and Sufferings: The American Indian Captivity Narrative through the Centuries.* 2nd rev. ed. St. Louis: St. Louis Mercantile Library, 2002.
Houck, Louis, ed. "Case of *Salée dit Lajoye v. Primm,* Case 368, St. Louis District, October Term." In *Reports of the Cases Argued and Determined in the Supreme Court of the State of Missouri from 1827 to 1830,* 280–285. St. Louis: Gilbert Book Co., 1834.
———. *The Spanish Regimen in Missouri.* Chicago: R. R. Donnelley, 1909.
House, E. *A Narrative of the Captivity of Mrs. Horn and Her Two Children with Mrs. Harris by the Camanche Indians.* St. Louis: C. Keemle, 1839.
Huning, Franz, and Lina Fergusson Browne. *Trader on the Santa Fe Trail: Memoirs of Franz Huning with Notes by His Granddaughter.* Albuquerque: Calvin Horn, 1973.
Hyde, Anne F. *Born of Lakes and Plains: Mixed-Descent Peoples and the Making of the American West.* New York: W. W. Norton, 2022.
———. *Empires, Nations and Families: A New History of the North American West, 1800–1860.* New York: Ecco Paperbacks, 2012.

Inskeep, Steve. *Imperfect Union: How Jessie and John Frémont Mapped the West, Invented Celebrity and Helped Cause the Civil War.* New York: Penguin Press, 2020.

Irwin, Mary Ann, and James F. Brooks, eds. *Women and Gender in the American West: Jensen-Miller Prize Essays from the Coalition for Western Women's History.* Albuquerque: University of New Mexico Press, 2004.

Jacobs, Margaret. "Out of a Rut: Decolonizing Western Women's History." *Pacific Historical Review* 79, 4 (2010): 585–604.

———. "What's Gender Got to Do with It?" *Western Historical Quarterly* 42, 3 (2011): 297–304.

Jager, Rebecca K. *Malinche, Pocahontas, and Sacagawea: Indian Women as Cultural Intermediaries and National Symbols.* Norman: University of Oklahoma Press, 2015.

James, Thomas. *Three Years among the Indians and Mexicans* [1846]. Edited by Walter B. Douglas. Kindle.

Jensen, Joan M., and Darlis A. Miller. "The Gentle Tamers Revisited: New Approaches to the History of Women in the American West." *Pacific Historical Review* 49, 2 (1980): 173–213.

———. *New Mexico Women: Intercultural Perspectives.* Albuquerque: University of New Mexico Press, 1986.

John, Elizabeth A. H. "Nurturing the Peace: Spanish and Comanche Cooperation in the Early Nineteenth Century." *New Mexico Historical Review* 59 (1984): 345–369.

———. *Storms Brewed in Other Men's Worlds.* College Station: Texas A&M Press, 1975.

Johnson, Susan Lee. "'A Memory Sweet to Soldiers': The Significance of Gender in the History of the 'American West.'" In *Women and Gender in the American West: Jensen-Miller Prize Essays from the Coalition for Western Women's History*, ed. Mary Ann Irwin and James F. Brooks, 89–109. Albuquerque: University of New Mexico Press, 2004.

———. *Writing Kit Carson: Fallen Heroes in a Changing West.* Chapel Hill: University of North Carolina Press, 2020.

Johnson, Walter. *The Broken Heart of America: St. Louis and the Violent History of the United States.* New York: Basic Books, 2020.

Kavanagh, Thomas. *The Comanches: A History, 1706–1875.* Lincoln: University of Nebraska Press, 1999.

Keckley, Elizabeth. *Behind the Scenes; or, Thirty Years a Slave, and Four Years in the White House.* New York: G. W. Carleton, 1868.

Kessell, John L. *Kiva, Cross and Crown: The Pecos Indians and New Mexico, 1540–1840.* Washington, DC: National Park Service, 1979.

———. *Miera y Pacheco: A Renaissance Spaniard in Eighteenth Century New Mexico.* Norman: University of Oklahoma Press, 2013.

Kidwell, Clara Sue. "Indian Women as Cultural Intermediaries." *Ethnohistory* 39 (Spring 1992): 97–107.

Kimball, Timothy L. "Most Beautiful Are the Evenings: Fischer's German-American Artillery Volunteers on the Santa Fe Trail, 1846–1847." *Wagon Tracks: Santa Fe Trail Association Quarterly* 26, 1 (2011): 21–24.

Lafaye, Jacque. "La Sociedad de Castas en la Nueva España: La Pintura de Castas." *Artes de Mexico* 8 (1998): 25–35.

Lamadrid, Enrique R. *Amadito and the Hero Children/Amadito y los Niños Héroes.* Albuquerque: University of New Mexico Press, 2011.

———, with photos by Miguel Gandert. *Hermanitos Comanchitos: Indo-Hispano Rituals of Captivity and Redemption.* Albuquerque: University of New Mexico Press, 2003.

Lamar, Howard R. *The Far Southwest, 1846–1912.* New York: W. W. Norton, 1970. Originally published New Haven, CT: Yale University Press, 1966.

———. Foreword to *Down the Old Santa Fe Trail and into Mexico*, ed. Stella Drumm. Lincoln: Bison Books, University of Nebraska Press, 1982.

Lane, Lydia Spencer. *A Frontier Officer: Stories of a Wandering Family.* N.p.: Big Byte Books, 2014.

———. *I Married a Soldier.* 1893. Reprint, with an introduction by Darlis A. Miller. Albuquerque: University of New Mexico Press, 1987.

Lansing, Michael. "Plains Indian Women and Interracial Marriage in the Upper Missouri Trade, 1804–1868." *Western Historical Quarterly* 31, 4 (Winter 2000): 413–433.

Laughlin, Ruth. *The Wind Leaves No Shadow.* Caldwell, ID: Caxton Press, 1986.

Lavender, David. *Bent's Fort.* Garden City, NY: Doubleday, 1954.

Leckie, William H. *The Buffalo Soldiers: A Narrative of the Negro Cavalry in the West.* Norman: University of Oklahoma Press, 1967.

Lecompte, Janet. "The Independent Women of Hispanic New Mexico, 1821–1846." In *New Mexico Women: Intercultural Perspectives*, ed. Joan M. Jensen and Darlis A. Miller, 71–93. Albuquerque: University of New Mexico Press, 1986.

———. "La Tules and the Americans." *Arizona and the West* 20, 3 (1978): 215–230.

Lemann, Nicholas. "Is Capitalism Racist?" Review of Walter Johnson's *The Broken Heart of America: St. Louis and the Violent History of the United States* (Basic Books). *New Yorker*, May 25, 2020. https://www.newyorker.com/magazine/2020/05/25/is-capitalism-racist.

Levine, Frances. "A Beautiful Death on the Santa Fe Trail." *El Palacio* 125, 1 (Spring 2020): 64–78.

———. "Desperately Seeking Carmel." *El Palacio* 124, 2 (2019): 52–59.

———. *Doña Teresa Confronts the Spanish Inquisition: A Seventeenth-Century New Mexican Drama.* Norman: University of Oklahoma Press, 2016.

———. "From Captive to Creole: María Rosa Villalpando." *Gateway: The Magazine of the Missouri History Museum* 39, 2 (2019): 6–15.

———. Introduction to "William Carr Lane: First Mayor of St. Louis, Second Governor of the New Mexico Territory," by William Carson. *Gateway: The Magazine of the Missouri History Museum* 36 (2016): 9–12.

———. *Our Prayers Are in This Place: Pecos Pueblo Identity through the Centuries.* Albuquerque: University of New Mexico Press, 1999.

———. "Palace of the Governors, a Witness to History." In *Santa Fe: History of an Ancient City*, ed. David Noble, 109–121. Santa Fe: School of American Research Press, 2008.

———. "Stella Drumm, the Not-so-Quiet Librarian." *Gateway: The Magazine of the Missouri History Museum* 37, 2 (2017): 44–49.

———. "Trading Places: Seeing the Santa Fe Trail from the Flip Side." *El Palacio* 122, 1 (2017): 56–63.

———. "What Is the Significance of a Road? Culture Change and Cultural Exchange along El Camino Real." In *El Camino Real de Tierra Adentro*, vol. 2, ed. Gabrielle Palmer, 1–13. Santa Fe: Bureau of Land Management, 1996.

Lewis, Nancy Owen. *Chasing the Cure in New Mexico: Tuberculosis and the Quest for Health*. Santa Fe: Museum of New Mexico Press, 2016.

Limerick, Patricia Nelson. *The Legacy of Conquest: The Unbroken Past of the American West*. New York: W. W. Norton, 1987.

Loften, Rachael, Susie Hendrix, and Jane Kennedy. "The Rachel Plummer Narrative." Ms., 1926. Everett D. Graff Collection of Western Americana, Newberry Library, Chicago.

Long, Esmond R. "Weak Lungs on the Santa Fe Trail." *Bulletin of the History of Medicine* 8, 7 (1940): 1040–1054.

Loomis, Noel M., and Abraham P. Nasatir. *Pedro Vial and the Roads to Santa Fe*. Norman: University of Oklahoma Press, 1967.

Magoffin, Susan Shelby. *Down the Old Santa Fe Trail and into Mexico*. 1846. Beinecke Library, Yale University, New Haven, CT.

Manion, Patricia Jean. *Beyond the Adobe Wall: The Sisters of Loretto in New Mexico, 1852–1894*. Independence: Two Trails Publishing Press, 2002.

Marcy, Randolph B. *The Prairie Traveler*. 1859. Reprint, Bedford, MA: Applewood Books, 1993.

Mariotti, Anna. "1861—Elizabeth Keckley, Purple Velvet Day and Evening Dress." Fashion Institute of Technology, New York, NY. Posted June 12, 2020. https://fashionhistory.fitnyc.edu/1861-keckley-purple-velvet-dress/.

Marshall, Thomas Maitland, ed. "The Journals of Jules De Mun." Translated by Nettie H. Beauregard. *Missouri Historical Society Collections* 5, 3 (1928): 167–208.

McDonald, Dedra. "Intimacy and Empire: Indian-African Interaction in Spanish Colonial New Mexico, 1500–1800." *American Indian Quarterly* 22, 1–2 (Winter–Spring 1998): 134–156.

———. "To Be Black and Female in the Spanish Southwest: Toward a History of African Women on New Spain's Far Northern Frontier." In *African American Women Confront the West, 1600–2000*, ed. Shirley Ann Wilson Moore and Qunitard Taylor, 32–52. Norman: University of Oklahoma Press, 2003.

Meyer, Marian. "Death on the Santa Fe Trail." *Wagon Tracks: Santa Fe Trail Association Quarterly* 4, 4 (August 1990): 8–9.

———. *Mary Donoho: New First Lady of the Santa Fe Trail*. Santa Fe: Ancient City Press, 1991.

Meyer, Michael J. "The French of St. Louis: Archaeological Excavation of the Madame Haycraft, Fifi and Berger Sites." *Missouri Archaeologist* 79 (2018): 18–43.

Miller, Darlis A., ed. *Above a Common Soldier: Frank and Mary Clarke in the American West and Civil War.* Rev. ed. Albuquerque: University of New Mexico Press, 1997.

———. "Cross-Cultural Marriages in the Southwest: The New Mexico Experience, 1846–1900." *New Mexico Historical Review* 57, 4 (1982): 335–359. Reprinted in *New Mexico Women: Intercultural Perspectives*, ed. Joan M. Jensen and Darlis A. Miller, 95–119. Albuquerque: University of New Mexico Press, 1986.

———. "Foragers, Army Women and Prostitutes." In *New Mexico Women: Intercultural Perspectives*, ed. Joan M. Jensen and Darlis A. Miller, 141–168. Albuquerque: University of New Mexico Press, 1986.

———, ed. *To Form a More Perfect Union: The Lives of Charles Francis and Mary Clarke from Their Letters, 1847–1871.* Albuquerque: University of New Mexico Press, 1997.

Montoya, María E. *Translating Property: The Maxwell Land Grant and the Conflict over Land in the American West, 1840–1900.* Lawrence: University Press of Kansas, 2005.

Moore, Shirley Ann Wilson. *Sweet Freedom's Plains: African Americans on the Overland Trails, 1841–1869.* Norman: University of Oklahoma Press, 2016.

Moore, Shirley Ann Wilson, and Qunitard Taylor. *African American Women Confront the West, 1600–2000.* Norman: University of Oklahoma Press, 2003.

Moorhead, Max L. *New Mexico's Royal Road: Trade and Travel on the Chihuahua Trail.* Norman: University of Oklahoma Press, 1958.

Myers, Joan, and Marc Simmons. *Along the Santa Fe Trail.* Albuquerque: University of New Mexico Press, 1986.

Myers, Sandra L. "Mexican Americans and Westering Anglos: A Feminine Perspective." *New Mexico Historical Review* 57, 4 (1982): 314–333.

———. "Romance and Reality on the American Frontier: Views of Army Wives." *Western Historical Quarterly* 13, 4 (1982): 409–427.

———. "Women on the Santa Fe Trail." In *The Santa Fe Trail, New Perspectives*, ed. Marc Simmons, 27–45. Denver: Colorado Historical Society, University Press of Colorado, 1992.

"Narrative of the Sufferings of Mrs. Jane Adeline Wilson during Her Captivity among the Camanche [sic] Indians." Sent by Rev. Louis Smith. *St. Joseph Gazette*, February 15, 1854, 1.

New Mexico Burials: Santo Tomás Apóstol de Abiquiú, 1777–1861. Albuquerque: New Mexico Genealogical Society, 2018.

Noble, David Grant, ed. *Santa Fe: History of an Ancient City.* Rev. and expanded ed. Santa Fe: School for Advanced Research, 2008.

Nogar, Anna M., and Enrique R. Lamadrid. "Nuevomexicano Cultural Memory and the Indo-Hispana *Mujerota*." *Journal of the Southwest* 58, 4 (2016): 751–779.

O'Brien, William Patrick. "Hiram Young: Black Entrepreneur on the Sata Fe Trail." *Wagon Tracks: Santa Fe Trail Association Quarterly* 33, 4 (August 2019): 23–25.

———. "'Olam Katan' (Small World): Jewish Traders on the Santa Fe Trail." *Journal of the Southwest* 48, 2 (2006): 211–231.

Oliva, Bonita, and Leo Oliva. "A Few Things Marian Sloan Russell Never Told about Her Mother and Father." *Wagon Tracks: Santa Fe Trail Association Quarterly* 7, 3 (February 1993): 1, 6–8.

———, eds. "Katie Bowen Letters, Parts 1–4." *Wagon Tracks: Santa Fe Trail Association Quarterly* 16, 2 (2002): 1, 26–28; 16, 4 (2002): 22–25; 17, 4 (2003): 14–17; 18, 2 (2004): 15–20.

Oliva, Leo E. *Confrontation on the Santa Fe Trail*. Selected papers from the Santa Fe Trail Symposia, La Junta, CO, 1993, and Larned and Great Bend, KS, 1995. Santa Fe Trail Association, 1996.

———. "A Faithful Account of Everything: Letters from Katie Bowen on the Santa Fe Trail, 1851." *Kansas History* 19, 4 (1996): 260–281.

———. "Fort Union NM: Fort Union and the Frontier Army in the Southwest." Chapter 4 in *A Historic Resource Study, Fort Union National Monument, New Mexico*. Southwest Cultural Resources Center Professional Papers No. 41. Santa Fe: Southwest Cultural Resources Center, 1993. santafetrailresearch.com.

Olmsted, Virginia Langham, comp. *Spanish and Mexican Census of New Mexico, 1750 to 1830*. Albuquerque: New Mexico Genealogical Society, 1981.

Paredes, Raymund A. "The Mexican Image in American Travel Literature, 1831–1869." *New Mexico Historical Review* 52 (1977): 139–165.

Parkhill, Forbes. *The Blazed Trail of Antoine Leroux*. Los Angeles: Westlore Press, 1965.

Parkinson, Jami. *Path to Glory: A Pictorial Celebration of the Santa Fe Trail*. Kansas City: Highwater Editions, 1996. Published by the First Business Bank of Kansas City, N.A., in support of the Jackson County Historical Society.

Parkman, Francis, Jr. "Across the Great Plains." In *In Their Own Words: Warriors and Pioneers*, ed. T. J. Stiles, 8–22. New York: Perigee Books, 1996.

Pascoe, Peggy. "Race, Gender, and Intercultural Relations: The Case of Interracial Marriage." In *Women and Gender in the American West: Jensen-Miller Prize Essays from the Coalition for Western Women's History*, ed. Mary Ann Irwin and James F. Brooks, 53–65. Albuquerque: University of New Mexico Press, 2004.

Pearson, Thomas A. "Free Men and Women of Color in St. Louis, 1821–1860." Ms., n.d., St. Louis Public Library Rare Books and Special Collections.

Perrine, Fred S. "Military Escorts on the Santa Fe Trail." *New Mexico Historical Review* 2 (April 1927): 175–291, 269–304; 3 (July 1928): 265–300.

Peterson, Charles E. *Colonial St. Louis: Building a Creole Capital*. Tucson, AZ: Patrice Press, 1993.

Ping, Laura J. "'He May Sneer at the Course We Are Pursuing to Gain Justice': Lydia Sayer Hasbrouck, *The Sibyl* and Corresponding about Women's Suffrage." *New York History* 98, 3–4 (2017): 317–328.

———. "A Tale of Two Bloomer Costumes: What Mary Stickney's and Meriva Carpenter's Bloomers Reveal about Nineteenth-Century Dress Reform." *Costume Society of America* 47, 2 (2021): 139–153.

Poole, Joy. "Henry and Rebecca Mayer's 1852 Honeymoon with 50 Men and 500 Mules."

Wagon Tracks: Santa Fe Trail Association Quarterly 37, 2 (2023): 16–21; 37, 3 (2023): 14–20.
Poole, Joy L., and Dr. Rowland Willard. *Over the Santa Fe Trail to New Mexico: The Travel Diaries and Autobiography of Dr. Rowland Willard.* Norman, OK: Arthur H. Clark, 2015.
Prescott, Cynthia Culver. *Pioneer Mothers Monuments: Creating Cultural Memory.* Norman: University of Oklahoma Press, 2019.
Primm, James Neal. *Lion of the Valley: St. Louis, Missouri, 1764–1980.* 3rd ed. St. Louis: Missouri Historical Society Press, 1998.
Remley, David. *Kit Carson: The Life of an American Border Man.* Norman: University of Oklahoma Press, 2011.
Riding In, James. "American Indians and the Santa Fe Trail." *Wagon Tracks: Santa Fe Trail Association Quarterly* 35, 4 (2021): 17–24.
Rittenhouse, Jack D. *Trail of Commerce and Conquest: A Brief History of the Road to Santa Fe.* Albuquerque: University of New Mexico Press, 2000. Originally published 1971, Santa Fe Trail Association.
Rock, Rosalind Z. "*Pido y Suplico*: Women and the Law in Spanish New Mexico." *New Mexico Historical Review* 65, 2 (1990): 145–159.
Roland, Aulton E. "Bob." *The Ballad of Plácida Romero: A Woman's Captivity & Redemption.* Santa Fe: Museum of New Mexico Press, 2022.
Rosenfeld, Jordana. "How White People Used Tuberculosis to Settle the Southwest." *OG History, Teen Vogue* ser., July 28, 2020. https://www.teenvogue.com/story/southwest-settlers-tuberculosis/amp.
Ross, Calvin, ed. *Lieutenant Emory Reports: Notes of a Military Reconnaissance.* Albuquerque: University of New Mexico Press, 1951.
Ruminer, John. *109 East Palace Avenue: A Microcosm of Santa Fe's Four Hundred Year History.* Los Alamos Historical Society Nutshell Series No. 4. Los Alamos, NM: Bathtub Row Press, 2013.
Russell, Marian. *Land of Enchantment: Memoirs of Marian Russell along the Santa Fe Trail.* Edited by Garnet M. Brayer. Evanston, IL: Branding Iron Press, 1954. Reprint, Albuquerque: University of New Mexico Press, 1993, with an afterword by Marc Simmons.
Ruxton, George F. *Adventures in Mexico and the Rocky Mountains.* London: John Marks, 1849.
———. *Life in the Far West.* 1849. Reprint, Glorieta, NM: Rio Grande Press, 1972.
Saionz, Matthew. "Governor, Trader and Scapegoat for the American Conquest: The Career and Legacy of Manuel Armijo." *Wagon Tracks: Santa Fe Trail Association Quarterly* 34, 4 (2020): 14–21.
Sanchez, Joseph P. "It Happened in Old Santa Fe: The Death of Governor Albino Pérez, 1835–1837." In *All Trails Lead to Santa Fe: An Anthology Commemorating the 400th Anniversary of the Founding of Santa Fe, New Mexico in 1610*, 267–278. Santa Fe: Sunstone Press, 2010.
Saunt, Claudio. "A Review of *Violence, Warfare, Terror and Colonialism in the Making of the United States.*" *William and Mary Quarterly* 65, 1 (2008): 197–199.

Scharff, Virginia. *Twenty Thousand Roads: Women, Movement and the West.* Berkeley: University of California Press, 2003.

Schlissel, Lillian. *Women's Diaries of the Westward Journey.* New York: Schocken Books, 2004.

Segale, Sister Blandina. *At the End of the Santa Fe Trail.* 1932. Reprint, Albuquerque: University of New Mexico Press, 1999.

Shane, Karen. "New Mexico: Salubrious El Dorado." *New Mexico Historical Review* 56, 4 (1981): 61–73.

Sides, Hampton. *Blood and Thunder: The Epic Story of Kit Carson and the Conquest of the American West.* New York: Anchor Books, 2006. Paperback ed., New York: Random House, 2007.

Simmons, Marc. *Following the Santa Fe Trail: A Guide for Modern Travelers.* 2nd ed. Santa Fe: Ancient City Press, 1986.

———. *Kit Carson and His Three Wives: A Family History.* Albuquerque: University of New Mexico Press, 2003.

———. *Murder on the Santa Fe Trail: An International Incident, 1843.* El Paso: Texas Western Press, 1987.

———. *New Mexico: An Interpretive History.* Albuquerque: University of New Mexico Press, 1988.

———. *The Old Trail to Santa Fe: Collected Essays.* Albuquerque: University of New Mexico Press, 1996.

———. *On the Santa Fe Trail.* Lawrence: University Press of Kansas, 1986.

———. "Report of Manuel Alvarez, 1842." In *On the Santa Fe Trail*, 6–17. Lawrence: University Press of Kansas, 1986.

———. *The Santa Fe Trail: New Perspectives.* Denver: Colorado Historical Society, University Press of Colorado, 1992.

———. "Women on the Santa Fe Trail: Diaries, Journals, Memoirs; an Annotated Bibliography." *New Mexico Historical Review* 61, 3 (July 1986): 233–243.

Sisneros, Samuel E. "'She Was Our Mother': New Mexico's Changes of National Sovereignty" and "Juan Bautista Vigil y Alarid; the Last New Mexico Governor." In *All Trails Lead to Santa Fe: An Anthology Commemorating the 400th Anniversary of the Founding of Santa Fe, Mexico in 1610*, 279–299. Santa Fe: Ancient City Press, 2010.

Sneed, David. "The Remarkable St. Louis Wagon Builders." *Wagon Tracks: Santa Fe Trail Association Quarterly* 32, 2 (2018): 10–11.

Spidle, Jake W., Jr. "'An Army of Tubercular Invalids': New Mexico and the Birth of a Tuberculosis Industry." *New Mexico Historical Review* 56, 4 (1986): 179–201.

Spivak, Emily. "The Story of Elizabeth Keckley, Former Slave Turned Mrs. Lincoln's Dressmaker." *Smithsonian Magazine*, April 24, 2013. https://www.smithsonianmag.com/arts-culture/the-story-of-elizabeth-keckley-former-slave-turned-mrs-lincolns-dressmaker-41112782/.

Spring, Agnes Wright, ed. *A Bloomer Girl on Pike's Peak, 1858: Julia Archibald Holmes, First White Woman to Climb Pike's Peak.* Denver: Denver Public Library, Western History Department, 1949.

Spude, Robert L. "Progressive Santa Fe, 1880–1912." In *All Trails Lead to Santa Fe: An Anthology Commemorating the 400th Anniversary of the Founding of Santa Fe, New Mexico in 1610*, 339–360. Santa Fe: Sunstone Press, 2010.

Stegmaier, Mark J. "A Law that Would Make Caligula Blush? New Mexico Territory's Unique Slave Code, 1859–1861." *New Mexico Historical Review* 87, 2 (2012): 209–243.

Stiles, T. J., ed. *In Their Own Words: Warriors and Pioneers*. New York: Perigee Books, 1996.

Stoddard, Amos. *Sketches, Historical and Descriptive, of Louisiana*. Philadelphia: Mathew Carey, 1812.

Stollsteimer, Robert S. *Christian and Amanda: The Life and Times of a Colorado Pioneer Family.* Self-published, F.E.R.S. Books, 1996.

Sunder, John E., ed. *Matt Field on the Santa Fe Trail*. Norman: University of Oklahoma Press, 1960.

Swagerty, William R. "Marriage and Settlement Patterns of Rocky Mountain Trappers and Traders." *Western Historical Quarterly* 11, 2 (April 1980): 159–180.

Taylor, Quintard. *In Search of the Racial Frontier: African Americans in the American West, 1528–1990*. New York: W. W. Norton, 1998.

Taylor-Montoya, Amanda. "There Is No There There: Women and Intermarriage in the Southwestern Borderlands." *Common Place: The Journal of Early American Life* 13, 3 (2013). https://commonplace.online/article/there-is-no-there-there/.

Thorne, Tanis C. *The Many Hands of My Relations: French and Indians on the Lower Missouri.* Columbia: University of Missouri Press, 1996.

Tjarks, Alicia V. "Demographic, Ethnic and Occupational Structure of New Mexico, 1790." *Americas* 35, 1 (July 1978): 45–88.

Tobias, Henry. *A History of the Jews in New Mexico*. Albuquerque: University of New Mexico Press, 1990.

Trigg, Heather B. *From Household to Empire: Society and Economy in Early Colonial New Mexico*. Tucson: University of Arizona Press, 2005.

Tykal, Jack B. "Taos to St. Louis: The Journey of María Rosa Villalpando." *New Mexico Historical Review* 65, 2 (1990): 161–174.

Ulibarri, George S. "The Chouteau-DeMun Expedition to New Mexico, 1816–1817." *New Mexico Historical Review* 36, 4 (1961): 263–273.

Utley, Robert. *Fort Union and the Santa Fe Trail*. El Paso: Texas Western Press, 1989.

Valenčius, Conevery Bolton. "Gender and the Economy of Health on the Santa Fe Trail." *Osiris*, 2nd ser., 19 (2004): 79–92.

———. "The Geography of Health and the Making of the American West: Arkansas and Missouri, 1800–1860." In *The Health of the Country*, 121–145. New York: Basic Books, 2002.

Van Ravenswaay, Charles. *St. Louis: An Informal History of the City and Its People, 1764–1865.* Edited by Candace O'Connor. St. Louis: Missouri Historical Society Press, 1991.

Vestel, Stanley. *Kit Carson, the Happy Warrior of the Old West: A Biography*. Boston: Houghton Mifflin, 1928.

Wallace, Susan E. *The Land of the Pueblos.* New York: John E. Alden, 1888. Commemorative ed., Crawfordsville, IN: Lew Wallace Study Preservation Society, 2015.

Warner George W., and Edward Duffield Neill. *History of Hennepin County and the City of Minneapolis: Including the Explorers and Pioneers of Minnesota.* Outlines of Minnesota History. Minneapolis: North Star, 1881. https://archive.org/details/cu31924006600484.

Webb, James Josiah. *James Josiah Webb's Adventures in the Santa Fe Trade, 1844–1847.* Edited by Ralph Bieber. Glendale, CA: A. H. Clark, 1931. Reprint, Lincoln: University of Nebraska Press, 1995, with an introduction by Mark L. Gardner.

———. Papers, 1839–1889. Missouri Historical Society, Library and Research Center, St. Louis.

Weber, David J. *The Extranjeros: Selected Documents from the Mexican Side of the Santa Fe Trail, 1825–1828.* Santa Fe: Stagecoach Press, 1967.

———. *The Taos Trappers: The Fur Trade in the Far Southwest, 1540–1846.* Norman: University of Oklahoma Press, 1968.

———, ed. "An Unforgettable Day: Facundo Melgares on Independence." *New Mexico Historical Review* 48, 1 (1973): 27–44.

Wegmann, Andrew N. "The Creole Frontier: Free People of Color in St. Louis and along the French Mississippi Corridor, 1800–1870." In *French St. Louis: Landscape, Contexts and Legacy,* ed. Jay Gitlin, Robert Michael Morrissey, and Peter J. Kastor, 157–184. Lincoln: University of Nebraska Press, 2021.

Weiser-Alexander, Kathy. "Legends of the West." 2018. https://www.legendsofamerica.com/kozlowski-trading-post/#.

Wetherington, Ronald K., and Frances Levine. *Battles and Massacres on the Southwestern Frontier: Historical and Archaeological Perspectives.* Norman: University of Oklahoma Press, 2014.

White, David A., comp. and annotator. *News of the Plains and Rockies 1803–1865.* Vol. 2C, *Santa Fe Adventurers, 1818–1843.* Spokane, WA: Arthur H. Clark, 1996.

White, Richard. *"It's Your Misfortune and None of My Own": A History of the American West.* Norman: University of Oklahoma Press, 1991.

Williams, J. Fletcher, Edward D. Neill, C. M. Foote, and George E. Warner. *History of Hennepin County and the City of Minneapolis: Including the Explorers and Pioneers of Minnesota, by Rev. Edward D. Neill, and Outlines of the History of Minnesota, by J. Fletcher Williams.* Minneapolis: North Star Publishing Company, 1881.

Willoughby, Robert J. *The Brothers Robidoux and the Opening of the American West.* Columbia: University of Missouri Press, 2012.

Wilson, Chris. *The Myth of Santa Fe.* Albuquerque: University of New Mexico Press, 1998.

Wilson, Gary. "Hostage among the Comanches: The Ordeal of Jane Wilson." *Red River Historical Review* 5, 2 (Spring 1980): 4–12.

INDEX

Abbott, Alysia L., 113, 116, 211n41
abolition, 141–142, 162–170, 180, 223n44
abortion, 140–141
Abreu Leitensdorfer, Solidad, 126, 145, 213–214n15
activism, 162–170
African Americans
   casta paintings of, 120–121
   cross-cultural marriages of, 14, 15
   as enslaved, 31, 38–39, 47, 118–121, 176–177, 180, 195n37, 196n38
   legal limitations of, 119, 121–122
   at Mississippi and Missouri Rivers communities, 7, 15–16, 31, 77, 118–124
   mixed-race terms regarding, 38, 121
   photos, 123, 128
   population mid-19th century New Mexico, 141
   on the Santa Fe Trail, 23–24, 122–124, 140–142, 157, 160–161
   as soldiers, 137–138, 161
African American women, 118–124, 136–41. *See also specific persons*; women
Agapito, Don, 132
Aguila, Refugio, 154
Aguilera y Roche, Doña Teresa, 119–120, 212n3, 212–213n4
Alexander, Edmund B., 157
Alonso, Ana María, 12
Alvarez, Manuel, 63, 89, 90, 93, 94
American Midwest, historical connection with Hispanic Southwest and, 6–7, 77, 175
Amick, Mrs. Leander, 79
Anglo-Americans, 152, 186n1
Anza, Juan Bautista de, 207n53–54
Apache tribe, 10, 20, 45
Arapaho tribe, 138, 139

Archibald, Jane, 169–170
Archibald Holmes, Julia Anna
   as abolitionist, 162, 166–169
   children of, 169
   divorce and scandal of, 169–170
   family history of, 167–169
   legacy of, 162, 180, 182
   New Mexico troubles of, 167–169
   photo, 163
   on Pike's Peak, 162, 166
   Santa Fe Trail clothing of, 162, 164–166
   as suffragist, 162–170, 222–223n44
   as writer, 163, 169–170, 222–223n44
Arias de Quiros, Diego, 54
Arizona, statehood of, 141
Arkansas River
   Bent's Fort on, 133, 136
   Comanche settlements and, 34
   contested Spanish boundary and, 55–57
   Ernestine Franke murder near, 136–139
   Kate Kingsbury's death near, 110–113
   trading on, 56
Armijo, Antonio, 124
Armijo, Manuel, 64, 89, 218n6
Army of the West, 64–65, 79, 90, 145, 148–149, 153, 201n40
Army wives in the West, 157–162
Aron, Stephen, 10, 187n3
Arrow Rock, Missouri, 7
Atchison, Topeka, and Santa Fe railroad, 171
Aubry, Francis Xavier, 82, 83, 94, 96, 147, 205–206n35

Baca, María Guadalupe, 54, 55
Barada, Adolph, 201n44
Barada, Amanda, 65, 66
Barada, Antoine, 201n44

Barada, Isadore, 65
Barada, Julius, 201n44
Barada, Martine, 65, 201n44
Barada, Mary E., 201n44
Barceló, María Gertrudes, 130, 179. *See also* Tules, Doña
Barclay, Alexander, 167
Barclay's Fort, 167
Barr, Juliana, 26, 190n7, 191n16
Barrere, Madame, 39
Battle of Cieneguilla, 107, 159, 222n38
Battle of Glorieta, 168
Battle of Monterey, 81
Battle of San Pasqual, 64, 65, 147
Battle of Valverde, 95, 168
Beales, Dolores, 43
Beales, John, 43
Becknell, William, 3, 7
Becks, Emma, 140–141
Benavides, José Pablo, 55
Benavides Robidoux, Carmel (María Carmen de la Cruz Benavides)
  childhood of, 3
  Colorado and, 50, 52, 63, 66–68, 178
  cross-cultural marriage of, 60–62, 177–178
  death of, 67
  family of origin of, 3, 52–53, 54–55, 62
  lack of written documents of, 50–52
  overview of, 48, 67–68
  Santa Fe home of, 54, 67, 198–199n11
  trail crossings of, 62–67
Bent, Charles
  assassination of, 80, 90, 135, 147–148
  caravan of, 78
  family of origin of, 219n9
  Kit Carson and, 73–74
  networks of, 177
  trading post of, 133
  travels of, 78
Bent, George, 133
Bent, Ignacia Jaramillo Luna, 148
Bent, María Ignacia, 78
Bent, Robert, 133
Bent, William, 133, 136
Bent family, 15, 73–74, 215n29
Benton, Jessie, 79–80, 170
Benton, Thomas Hart, 79, 170
Bent's Fort, 133–135, 136, 145–146
Berry, Margaret, 140–141
Berthold, Pelagie, 95
Beyreis, David C., 13

Black
  casta paintings of, 120–121
  cross-cultural marriages of, 14, 15, 77
  as enslaved, 31, 38–39, 47, 118–121, 176–177, 180, 195n37, 196n38
  legal limitations on, 119, 121–122
  at Mississippi and Missouri River communities, 7, 15–16, 31, 77, 118–124
  mixed-race terms regarding, 38, 121
  photos, 123, 128
  population mid-19th century New Mexico, 141
  on the Santa Fe Trail, 23–24, 122–124, 140–142, 157, 160–161
  as soldiers, 137–138, 161
Blackhawk, Ned, 10, 12, 31, 59, 187n9
Blackwelder, Bernice Fowler, 73
Blackwood, Mary Josephine, 168
Boggs, Lilburn, 219n9
Boggs, Rumalda, 219n9
Boggs, Rumalda Luna, 148
Boggs, Thomas Oliver, 219n9
Boone, Daniel, 216n42, 219n9
Boone's Lick, Missouri, 7
Bowen, Captain Isaac, 136, 157
Bowen, Catherine Cary "Katie," 136, 157–159, 216n40
Bowler, Tom, 112
Boyle, Susan, 20, 41
Brake, Hezekiah, 137
Brooks, James, 28, 190n7, 191–192n18
Brown, Roberta, 84, 202n3
Browne, Lina Fergusson, 217n46

Cachupín, Vélez, 32–33
California, 63, 80, 141
Camino Real de Tierra Adentro, 89
Camp Morris, Anna Maria De, 156–157
captivity
  children taken in, 28, 31, 32, 34
  narratives of, 45–47, 197n50
  women captives rescued from, 42–47, 210n20, 214n26
Carleton, Captain James H., 157, 159, 221n33
Carleton, Sophia W., 157
Carson, Adaline "Prairie Flower"
  behavior clothing of, 78–81
  birth and childhood of, 77–79
  death of, 80
  education of, 72, 78–81, 179
  lithograph of, 75
  marriage of, 80

INDEX

overview of, 22–23, 69, 72–74, 96
school girls on the trial and, 22–23
Carson, Christopher "Kit"
   Adaline and, 77–81 (*See also* Carson, Adaline "Prairie Flower")
   Antoine Robidoux and, 146
   in California, 80
   expeditions of, 79–80
   family background of, 69, 73, 216n42
   at Green River rendezvous, 75–76, 78
   historiography of, 72–74, 79, 203n10
   marriages of, 23, 73, 76, 78
   meeting John C. Frémont by, 78–81
   moving Adaline to Missouri by, 77–81
   networks of, 177
   renown of, 78
   as scout, 64, 95
Carson, Josefa Jaramillo, 77, 78, 80, 148
Carson, Timothy L., 204n22
Carson Rubey, Mary Anne, 79
Carter, Harvey Lewis, 72
Carvallo, Carlos, 140
castas
   color quebrado (casta), 121
   limpieza de sangre, 121
   paintings, 120–121
   Pino's 1812 report on, 121–122
   racial purity, 14, 121
   system defined, 47, 118
Chapel Hill Academy, 91
Cheyenne tribe, 136, 138, 139
cholera, 82–83
Chouinard (Shunar), Joseph, 76
Chouteau, Auguste P., 35, 56
Christian Brothers Academy, 71
Christy, Charles, 138
Civil War
   impact on the Santa Fe Trail, 24, 68, 137–138, 141–142, 156, 170, 179
   monuments and memorials, 181, 188n21
   in New Mexico, 138, 156, 160–161, 179
Clark, Dr. James, 101, 103
Clark, William, 2–3, 56–57, 176
Clarke, Charles Francis (Frank), 157–158, 222n35
Clarke, Charley, 158
Clarke, Mary Gowan, 157–158
Cleary, Patricia, 16
Clemens, Helen, 208n65
Clemens, Kate, 208n65
clothing, 16–17, 162–170
Colegio de San Miguel, 71

Collins, James L., 168
Colorado
   Antoine Robidoux and, 47, 49, 63
   Carmel Benavides Robidoux and, 50, 52, 63, 66–68, 178
   Flora Langerman Spiegelberg and, 24
   Julia Anna Archibald Holmes and, 162, 166–168
   Marian Sloan Russell and, 86, 88, 204n27, 206n46
   Santa Fe Trail and, 6, 154, 161, 171
Comanche tribe
   abduction by, 1–2, 26, 27–28, 43–44
   and attacks in New Mexico, 31–32, 66, 210n21
   captives taken by, 30, 31–32, 42–47, 197n50
   changes to economy and, 42–43, 191–192n18
   cultural aspects of, 45–46
   dominance in trade of, 30
   horses and, 30, 43
   Josiah Gregg describes Ranchos De Taos raid regarding, 27–28
   Kotsotekas (Buffalo-Eater) band, 190–191n9
   Kwahada band, 191n9
   massacre of, 191n11
   New Mexico relationship with, 28–33, 54
   prostitution and, 152
   Santa Fe Trail crosses territory of, 20
   trade fairs in New Mexico and, 30–33, 43, 48
   Treaty of Medicine Lodge and, 139
   Treaty of 1786 with, 54
Comanchita, La, 46
Comet of 1811, 52–53
Company A, St. Louis Horse Artillery, 145
Company B, Missouri Light Artillery Battalion, 145
Confederates, 66, 160–161, 167–168
confluence Mississippi and Missouri rivers
   French settlement of, 14–15, 35, 53, 192n20
   Native American settlement in, 35
   significance for US history, 6–7, 187n8
   significance of, 10
   trade and, 4, 174, 176
Connelly, Henry, 168
consumption, 100–103, 116, 209n9. *See also* disease
cooks, African American women as, 136–141

Coventry, C. B., 101
COVID-19 pandemic, 97–98, 182, 212n44
Creole culture
    French in St. Louis and, 2, 14–16, 22, 27–28, 40–41, 45–47, 60, 62, 170–177, 194n27, 194n28
    metis identity and, 16, 34–35, 47, 77, 187n9, 195n37
    Upper Louisiana French colonists, 14–17
cross-cultural marriages
    advantages for Santa Fe Trail traders, 13, 22, 60–62, 204n21
    with Indigenous women, 15–16, 187n9, 191n16, 203n16
    in New Mexico, 177–179, 204n21
    in St. Louis French colony, 2–4, 13–14, 22, 35–37, 176–179

Daily National Republican (newspaper), 169
Dant, Sister of Loretto Rosanna, 202n3
Daughters of the American Revolution (DAR), 18
Davidson, John W., 107, 159
Davis, William Watts Hart, 99–100, 108
Day McClung, Quantrille, 73
DeMun, Jules, 55–57
disease
    consumption or tuberculosis, 100–103, 209n9
    19th century ideas about, 109
    Santa Fe Trail travel as cure for, 97–100, 136–137
Dodge, Henry, 134
Dolores, Texas, 43
domestic workers, African American women as, 136–141
Doniphan, Alexander, 147, 148
Donoho, Mary, 44
Donoho, William, 44
Drumm, Stella, 125–127, 188–189n23, 213n12, 214n20
Duchesne, Rose Philippine, 79
Dufossat, Guy, 35, 36, 192n20, 193n25

education
    convent education for women, 79, 91–93
    history of in New Mexico, 70–72
    in St. Louis, 179, 208n65
Elliott, Richard Smith
    Army of the West occupies Santa Fe and, 148–149, 151
    battle at Taos Pueblo and, 216n39
    Laclede Rangers in St. Louis and, 145–146
    Reveille reports from the war front, 143–144, 146–147, 178–179, 217n1
Emory, Lieutenant William Hensley, 64–65, 131, 146, 218n5
environment, and health in the 19th century, 97–100. *See also* disease
Esparza, Josefa Angulo de, 207n53
Espenschied Wagon Co., 7
Esteban, Black Moor, 118–119
ethnicity, expansion of the American West and, 141–142
Eurocentric American historiography, 14, 20–21

families, changes to through Santa Fe Trail, 13–14. *See also specific persons*
fandangos, 149–150
fashion, 16–17, 162–170
Fausz, Fred, 14, 192n22, 194n28
Feast of Saint Emmanuel, 45–46
Fergusson, Erna, 217n46
Fergusson, Harvey, 217n46
Fergusson Browne, Lina, 217n46
Field, Martha, 67
Field, Matthew C., 61, 134, 215n33
First US Dragoons, 159
Fort Fillmore, 160, 168
Fort Leavenworth, 85, 158, 201n40
forts, purpose of, 192n20. *See also specific forts*
Fort Snelling, 82, 205n31, 205n33, 205n34
Fort Union, 157, 158
Fort William, 133
Fort Zarah, 137–138
Fowler Blackwelder, Bernice, 73
Franke, Ernestine, 137, 138
Franklin, Missouri, 7, 78–79
Frémont, Jessie Benton, 79–80, 170
Frémont, John C., 79, 170
French American settlements, 14–17, 48, 49, 55–56, 61, 178
French colonial women, 179. *See also* women
Froebel, Julius, 152–153
frontier, defined, 9–10
Frontier Guard, 167
fur trade
    decline of, 63–64
    Missouri economy and, 35, 38–39, 53, 60, 63, 67
    Missouri families and, 15–16, 35, 50, 215n29

INDEX 245

Native American women in, 15–16, 50, 76–77
New Mexico and, 35, 53–54, 220n25
Spanish regulation of, 192n20, 197n1
women and, 16, 18, 26, 43, 50, 74–77, 203n14
See also trade

Garcia, Guadalupe, 60
Garrard, Lewis Hector, 78, 134–135, 204n20, 215n34, 215–216n36
Georgetown Academy of the Visitation, 95
German immigrants, 152, 153–154
Gitlin, Jay, 15
Glasgow Brothers Trading Company, 95, 99, 107
Gold, George, 220n25
Gold, Louis, 154, 220n25
Gold, Mary, 154
González, Deena J., 150, 177
Gould, Jay, 220n23
Great Basin trade centers, 51–52, 59–61, 63, 75, 78–79, 187n9, 199n22
Green, Charlotte "Black Charlotte," 133–135
Green, Dick, 133, 147, 216n39
Green River rendezvous, 75–76
Gregg, James Josiah
    biography, 189n3
    as collector of botanical specimens, 189n2
    on healthy effects of trail travel, 98, 99
    story of María Rosa by, 27–28, 46–47, 176
    on trade, 43
    trading center of, 23
Gurulé, José Librado, 139, 140
Guthrie, A. B., Jr., 215n34
Gwaltney, William, 135

Hancock, Winfield Scott, 138
Harris, Caroline, 43–45, 47
Harris, Richard, 43–44
Hayden, Sister of Loretto Magdalen, 202n3
Hays, Seth, 137, 216n42
Hayward, H. E., 128
health, 97–100, 116–117
Hersch, Joseph, 154
Hinchey, William James, 202n3
Hispanic/Hispanic women, 22, 49, 150, 170, 212n44. *See also* women
Hispanic Southwest, historical connection with American Midwest and, 6–7
Holmes, James, 166–167, 168–169, 180
Holmes, Julia Anna Archibald. *See* Archibald Holmes, Julia Anna

Holmes, June, 169
Holmes, Phoebe, 169
Horn, John, 43–44
Horn, Sarah Ann, 43–44, 45, 47
hospital, in Santa Fe, 108–9
human trafficking, 31, 176
Huning, Charles, 139, 217n46
Huning, Franz, 137–138, 217n46
Hyde, Anne, 14, 200n33, 215n29, 219n9

Immigrants on the Santa Fe Trail, 151–155
Indian Peace Commission, 139
influenza epidemic, 98, 182
Iturbide, Agustín de, 57

Jacobs, Margaret, 17
James, Thomas, 3, 58, 59
Jane (enslaved maid of Magoffins), 23–24, 124, 127–129, 130–131
Jáquez, José Julián, 33, 40, 196n40
Jáquez, Juan José, 191n12
Jaramillo, María Ignacia, 177, 219n9
Jaramillo, María Josefa, 78, 80, 148, 177–178, 204n8, 219n9
Jefferson Barracks, 9, 157–158, 159–160
Jewish people, 153–154, 220n23
Jicarilla Apache tribe, 20, 107, 158–159, 210n20, 222n38
J. Murphy & Sons, 7, 9
Johnson, Susan Lee, 73
Johnson, Walter, 10, 187n8
Josepha (enslaved Black woman), 40
Judaism, outlawed in colonial New Mexico, 119–120

Kansa (Kaw) tribe, 20
Kansas, factions of, 85
Kansas tribe, 15
Kastor, Peter J., 15
Kearny, Stephen Watts
    Army of the West enters Santa Fe and, 147–149
    character and comportment of, 129–130, 145
    hosts a ball in Santa Fe, 149–150
    promotion to Brigadier General of, 129
    recruits Antoine Robidoux, 64, 201n40
    as taking possession of New Mexico, 90, 129–130, 146
Kearny Code (Organic Law of the Territory of New Mexico), 147–148
Kellogg, Elizabeth, 44

Kimball, Pierre Benjamin, 95, 179
Kingsbury, Eliza Ann, 106, 110, 111
Kingsbury, John M.
  competitors of, 154
  concerns of, 99–100, 109
  Kate's death and, 110–116
  marriage of, 105–106, 209n7, 210n15
  overview of, 23, 97
  in Santa Fe, 108–110
  travels of, to Santa Fe, 103–108
  work of, 103, 104–105
Kingsbury, Kate Messervy
  as chastised by her brother William, 104, 109
  crossings on the Santa Fe Trail by, 23, 97, 99, 103–104, 111–112
  death on the Santa Fe Trail of, 112
  declining health of, 98, 104–105, 110–111
  grave and gravestone of, 113–116, 208n1
  home in Santa Fe of, 107–109
  marriage of, 105–106, 209n7, 210n15
  short life of son George of, 109–110
Kiowa-Apache tribe, 139
Kiowa tribe, 20, 133, 136, 138–139, 152
Koslowski, Ellen, 162
Koslowski, Martin, 162

Laclède, Pierre Liquest, 105–6, 209n7, 210n15
Laclede Rangers, 145
Lamadrid, Enrique, 150, 186n2, 197n50, 199n12
Lamar, Howard, 126
Lamy, Jean-Baptiste, 71, 108, 155
Lane, Lt. William Bartlett, 159–161
Lane, Lydia Spencer, 24, 159–161, 179
Lane, William Carr, 104, 151, 157, 159, 209, 221n33
Langerman Spiegelberg, Florence "Flora," 24, 154–155, 172, 180, 220n26, 221n28
Larkin, James Ross, 99, 136–137, 208–209n6
laundresses, African American women as, 136–141
Lechat (Ute chief), 59
Leitensdorfer, Dr. Eugene, 126, 153–154, 213–214n15
Leitensdorfer, Eliza Michaud, 126
Leitensdorfer, Solidad Abreu, 126, 145, 213–214n15
Leitensdorfer, Thomas, 126, 214n15
Leroux, Benjamin, 193n24, 195n34
Leroux, Hèléne. *See* Salé dit Lajoie, Hèléne
Leroux, María. *See* Salé dit Lajoie, Hèléne

Leroux, Marie Angelique, 193n24, 195n35
Liguest, Pierre Laclède, 35
Limerick, Patricia, 17
Linstroth Wagon Co., 9
Little Jerusalem neighborhood Santa Fe, 154
López, Dámaso
  Basque family history of, 88
  business in Mexico and New Mexico of, 88–90
  children of, 88–91, 95, 207n53
  death in California of, 93–94
  death of wife María Carmen, 90
  as east on the Santa Fe Trail, 91
  as guardian of López children, 94–95
López, Jesus María, 89
López, José Francisco, 90, 91, 95
López, José Melaquides, 89, 91, 95
López, José Trinidad, 89, 91, 95
López, Lorenzo, 88
López, María del Carmen (Serefina Ruiz de Esperza), 89, 90, 207n53
López de Mendizábal, Bernardo, 119–120
López Kimball, Francisca "Fanny"
  death in St. Louis of, 95
  family history of, 88–95, 207n53
  marriage to Benjamin Kimball by, 95
  schoolgirls on the trail and, 22–23
  at Visitation Academy St. Louis, 91–94
  at Visitation Academy Washington, DC, 95, 208n65
Los Angeles Star (newspaper), 94
Louisa (enslaved nurse of Hayward family), 128
Louisiana Purchase, 2, 55–56, 176
Luedinghaus Wagon Co., 7, 9
Luna, José Rafael, 219n9

Magoffin, James Wiley, 124, 132, 146
Magoffin, Jane, 132–133
Magoffin, Samuel, 124, 130, 132, 146, 147
Magoffin, Susan Shelby
  diary edited by Stella Drumm of, 125–126, 188–189n23, 213n12
  observations on New Mexico culture by, 126–127, 129–130, 214n23, 214n26
  photo, 125
  pregnancies and miscarriages of, 132, 147, 214n20
  relationship with enslaved servant June by, 118, 127–131
  returns to Kentucky and Missouri, 132–133
  war in Mexico by, 132

Magoffin, William, 130, 132
Magoffin family, 124–33. *See also specific persons*
Magoffin Taylor, Jane, 213n12
Mahoney, Eliza St. Clair Sloan
　marriage to Jeremiah Mahoney by, 81–82, 205n30, 205n34
　on the Santa Fe Trail, 69, 81–86, 158, 162
Mahoney, Jeremiah, 81–82, 205n30, 205n31
Mahoney, Sister of Loretto Catherine, 202n3
Making Out Road, 73, 78, 203n10
Manifest Destiny, 19, 64, 126–127, 129
Marcy, Randolph B., 98–99
Margaret (servant of Bowens), 136, 157
Maxwell Land Grant, 80, 86, 206n45
Mayer, Henry, 152–153
Mayer, Rebecca, 152–153
Maynez, Alberto, 56
McClung, Quantrille Day, 73
McDonald, Dedra, 119
Melgares, Facundo, 2–3, 57–58
Menard Young Ladies' Academy of the Visitation, 92–93
Messervy, William S., 23, 103, 104, 105, 106, 107–8, 209n14, 210n15
Messervy Kingsbury, Kate. *See* Kingsbury, Kate Messervy
métis, 15–16, 34–35, 47, 77
Mexican-American War, 143–145
Mexico
　education in, 70–72
　independence of, 2, 53, 57, 177
　occupation and annexation by US of, 129, 143, 146
　slavery laws in, 121–122
　trade with, 3, 6–7
Michaud, Eliza, 214n15
Miera y Pacheco, Bernardo, map of New Mexico, 1760, 29
Miller, Darlis, 140, 161
Mills, Mother Superior Matilda, 202n3
Mississippi River, 7, 9, 36, 48–49, 53, 122
Missouri, 2, 3, 22, 53, 69, 85
Missouri Daily Republican (newspaper), 94
Missouri River, 7, 9, 48–49, 122
mixed-race
　importance in Western history, 15–16, 203n16
　mestizo, 77
　métis, 15–16, 35, 47, 77
　mulattos, 120–121, 141
　negro(a), 38

pardo, 38
　terms regarding, 15–16, 121, 203n16
monuments, 18, 180–181, 188n21
Moorhead, Max, 12
Morris, Anna Maria De Camp, 156–157
Morris, Gouverneur, 156–157
Mosley, Alice, 208n65

National American Woman Suffrage Association, 169–170
Native Americans
　conflicts with, 12, 138–139, 158–159
　cross-cultural marriages with, 13–14, 34–35, 61, 73–77, 200n33, 215n29
　displacement of, 45–46, 141, 170
　enslavement of, 31, 34–37, 76–77, 185n1
　French and, 14–17, 48, 49–50, 55–56, 61, 178
　fur trade and, 16
　legacy conquests of, 6, 170–172
　painting of, 38
　peace with, 12, 33–36
　pottery of, 175, 185n1
　as romanticized in western writings, 122, 215n34
　Santa Fe Trail and, 12, 43–45, 180–181
　and slave trade, 33–35, 191–192n1, 192n21
　Spanish interaction with, 10, 30–33, 185n1, 207n54
　terminology defined, 186n1
　See also specific tribes
Native American women, 38, 50, 76–77
Navajo peoples, 10, 45, 90, 198n6
New Mexican women
　accommodating American dominance by, 150, 177
　cross-cultural marriages with Santa Fe Trail traders, 13, 22, 60–62, 204n21
　culture of, 61, 149–150
　domestic partnerships of, 177
　domestic spheres of, 150–151
　family of origin of, 150
　French American attraction to, 61
　property and legal rights of, 148, 150–152, 167, 176, 179, 200n31
New Mexico
　African Americans in, 118–124, 141
　American *entrada* into, 23–24, 129
　conditions of, 156, 160
　description of, 84
　domestic life in, 175
　economic reports of, 55

New Mexico, *continued*
  folk history and folklore of, 1
  fur trade and trapping in, 35, 53–54, 56, 192n20, 197n1, 220n25
  healthy climate and, 99, 116–117
  immigrants on the Santa Fe Trail in, 151–155
  Jewish community 19th century in, 24, 152–155, 174, 220n23, 220n25, 220n26
  map of trails in, 29
  into Ninth Military Department, 143
  population of at time of US seizure, 149
  statehood delayed of, 141, 148, 168, 170, 180
  US military families in, 156–162
  US seizure of, 23, 129, 143–148
New Spain, African American women in, 118–124
Nogar, Anna, 150
Nott, Robert, 208n1

Odd Fellows Cemetery, Santa Fe, 113, 115, 212n42
Oliva, Bonita, 205n28
Oliva, Leo, 205n28, 216n40, 221n34
Omaha tribe, 15
Onacama, Comanche leader, 32
Organic Law of the Territory of New Mexico (Kearny Code), 147–148
Ortiz, Ana Gertrudis, 54
Osage tribe
  cross-cultural marriages of, 15, 38
  French and Spanish relations with, 35, 192n20
  painting of, 38
  removal from ancestral lands of, 187n8
  Santa Fe Trail impacts on, 10, 20
  trade goods of, 38

Palace of the Governors
  Confederate takeover of, 66, 168–169
  fandango description of, 130
  photo of, 13
  US occupation and, 148–149, 151
  Ute visits and raid on, 59, 63
  women selling products and, 150
Parker, Cynthia Ann, 44
Parker, James Pratt, 44
Parker, John, 44
Parker, Quanah, 44
Parker Robbins, Kittie, 216n42
Parkman, Francis, Jr., 7

Pawnee tribe
  María Rosa captive of, 2, 26, 34, 192n21
  peace with Spanish and, 192n20
  Santa Fe Trail and, 20, 43
Pecos Pueblo tribe, 20, 54, 162
Peñalosa, Francisco de Sosa, 119
Perea, José Leandro, 139–140
Piernas, Pedro, 36–37, 192n20
Pike, Zebulon Montgomery, 2–3, 162
Pike's Peak, 162, 166, 170, 222–223n44
Pino, Pedro Bautista, report to Spanish *cortes*, 1812, 55, 57, 70–71, 121–122, 199n14
Plains Apache tribe, 20
Plains Indians, 1, 28, 32, 46, 48, 190n7
Platte River, 56–57
Plum Buttes, Kansas, 138
Plummer, James Pratt, 44
Plummer, Rachel Parker, 43–44, 47
Polk, James K., 80, 143, 145
Ponca tribe, 15
Portillo Urrisola, Manuel de, 32, 191n11
Presbyterian Young Ladies Seminary, 85
Primm, Peter
  family history of, 195n34, 195n35, 196n39
  lawsuits with Salé dit Lajoie family, 193–194n27, 193n26, 195n23, 196n39
  marriage with Marie Angélique Salé dit LaJoie by, 193n23
Prince, L. Bradford, 67, 198–199n11
Prince Plaza, 67, 198–199n11
Pueblo Revolt, 120

race, expansion of the American West and, 25, 141–142
railroads
  advertisement for, 170–171
  changing demographics of New Mexico and, 9–10, 12, 116
  and immigration and the American West, 161–162, 170–172
  and the Santa Fe Trail, 12, 161
  travelers' comfort on, 155, 170–172
Ranchos de Taos
  abduction of María Rosa from, 1–2, 26–28, 189–190n4
  Comanche raids on, 30, 31–32, 34, 45, 176
  Los Comanches dance and folklore and, 45–46
  multicultural history of, 28–30
  photo, La Comanchita, 46
Reed, Francois, vs. María Rosa LeJoy, 196n39
Riding In, James, 20

roads, significance of, 4
Robbins, Kittie Parker, 216n42
Robidoux, Antoine
  background of, 53
  brothers
    Robidoux, Isadore, 60
    Robidoux, Joseph, 53, 60
    Robidoux, Joseph, Jr., 60
    Robidoux, Louis, 60, 61, 63, 177
    Robidoux, Michel, 60
  death of, 65–66
  family history of, 48, 60, 67–68
    parents: Robidoux, Catherine Rolet and Robidoux, Francois, 60
  injuries at Battle of San Pascual of, 64–65
  lawsuits against, 61, 199–200n24, 201n38
  Mexican naturalization of, 60–62
  military pension of, 65
  portrait of, 51
  records of, 51, 52
  relationships and marriage of, 60–62, 177, 178
  Santa Fe politics and, 62–64
  trading posts of, 59
  as trapper and trader, 49, 58–59, 60, 62
  as US translator, 129, 146, 149
  in War of 1812, 53
  western travels of, 62–67, 201n42
Robidoux, Carmel. *See* Benavides Robidoux, Carmel (María Carmen de la Cruz Benavides)
Robidoux, Catherine Rolet, 60
Robidoux, Guadalupe Garcia, 60, 177
Robidoux, María Carmel. *See* Benavides Robidoux, Carmel (María Carmen de la Cruz Benavides)
Robidoux family, 15, 49–50, 59, 60. *See also specific persons*
Rubey, Mary Anne Carson, 79, 204n22
Russell, Marian Sloan
  childhood of, 81–86
  in Kansas, 84–85
  marriage to Richard Russell by, 86, 88
  on Maxwell Land Grant and Stonewall Ranch, 206nn45–47
  memories of trail beauty by, 83–84
  mother Eliza of, 179–180, 205n28, 205n30, 206n35
  murder and death of husband Richard of, 87–88, 206n46
  photo, 88

publication of memoir of, 188–189n23, 204–5n27
  in Santa Fe, 83–84, 86–87
  schoolgirls on the trail and, 22–23
  violence on the Santa Fe Trail and, 179
  See also Mahoney, Eliza St. Clair Sloan
Russell, Richard, 86–88, 206nn45–47
Ruxton, George Augustus Frederick
  death of, 215–216n36
  disease in St. Louis and, 215–216n36
  inhumanity of US slavery and, 141–142
  travels in the West and Mexico by, 135
  US reckoning with slavery and white supremacy and, 180

Sacred Heart Academy, 71
Saionz, Matthew, 218n6
Salé dit Lajoie, Hèléne
  children of, 192–193n23, 194
  as entrusted with title to enslaved child, 40
  lawsuits with Primm family and, 193–194n27, 193n23, 193n26, 195n34, 196n39
  lawsuit with half-brother José Julián Jáquez, 33, 40, 196n40
  marriage of, 39, 193n24
  portrait of, 42
  property in St. Louis of, 41
  on 1791 census, 37–38
Salé dit Lajoie, Jean Baptiste
  brings María Rosa to St. Louis, 35, 176
  children of, 36, 193n23, 193n24, 195n34, 195n36
  family of origin of, 26, 37–38
  first settlers of St. Louis and, 2, 35
  map of St. Louis property, 36
  marriage to María Rosa by, 2, 26–27, 35–36, 194n30
  oath of allegiance to Spain, 194–195n32
  reports Spanish women in Pawnee camp, 34
  return to France by, 39
  St. Louis property of, 35, 36, 39, 195n36
Salé dit Lajoie, Lambert
  as baptized in St. Louis, 194n31
  as born in Pawnee camp, 34, 36
  children of, 39–40
  as entrusted with title to enslaved child, 39–40
  in France with his father Jean Baptiste, 38–39

Salé dit Lajoie, Lambert, *continued*
   lawsuits with Primm family and, 193–194n27, 193n23, 196n26, 196n39
   on 1791 census, 37–38
Salé dit Lajoie, María Rosa Villalpando
   as abandoned by Jean Baptiste Salé dit Lajoie, 39
   abduction of, 1–2, 26, 27–28, 31–32
   age of, 192–193n23
   arrival in creole St. Louis of, 26, 35, 177
   children of, 36, 195n34, 195n36
   citizenship of, 1
   as Comanche captive, 33–34
   Comanche raid on family compound of, 30–31
   death of, 41–42
   family of origin of, 2, 35, 37–38, 192n21, 193n23
   household, 1791 census of, 36–38
   legacy of, 35, 182–183
   legal actions of, 39–41, 47, 196n39
   living in Pawnee camp, 34, 192n21
   map of St. Louis property of, 41
   marriage to Jean Baptiste by, 2, 26–27, 35–36, 194n30
   overview of, 22, 28, 46–47, 176–177, 189–190n4
   as owner enslaved Black women and children, 39–40
   property/property rights of, 40, 143, 150–151, 167–168, 170
   as purchased by Jean Baptiste Salé dit Lajoie, 34
   spelling of family name of, 27, 190n4
Salé dit Lajoie, Marie Josèphe, 193n23, 195n34
Salé dit Lajoie, Pierre, 193n23, 195n34
Sandoval, Anastacio, 94–95, 208n65
Sangre de Cristo Mountains, 28, 30, 204n20
San Miguel Church, 83
San Miguel del Vado, 90, 146, 207n54
Santa Fe, New Mexico
   Army of the West arrival to, 12, 145–150
   Camino Real and, 12, 59, 89
   Confederate takeover of, 168–169
   demographic change by the trail to, 9, 149–150, 170–172
   first impressions of, 86, 108, 156–157
   illegal French and American traders in, 2–3, 53, 54–57
   lithograph of, 49, 58
   map of 1846 of, 131

   Mexican independence celebrated in, 3, 58
   nexus of historic trails in, 12
   railroad impacts on, 12–13, 170–172
   romantic myths of, 12–13, 24, 172
   Sisters of Loretto and, 71, 83–85, 202n3
Santa Fe Republican (newspaper), 168–169
Santa Fe Trail
   camps along, 98
   embarkation points of, 7, 11
   expanding the legacy of, 4, 6, 17, 141, 173–183
   handbook for travelers on, 98–99
   hostilities on, 138–139
   location and map of, 5, 11, 131
   monuments on, 18–19, 180–181, 188n21
   profits of, 3, 12, 30, 175–176
   racialized capitalism and, 175, 187n8
   railroad impact on, 12–13, 170–172
   as route of US conquest, 12, 143
Sarah "Aunt Sally Taylor," 137
Scharff, Virginia, 125, 126
Seligman Spiegelberg, Bertha "Betty," 154
Serrano, Fray Pedro, 32
Shunar, 76
Sibley, Charlotte, 157
Sibley, Ebenezer S., 157
Sibyl (magazine), 166
Simmons, Louis (Louy) W., 80
Simmons, Marc, 72–73, 76, 78, 133, 137, 189n2, 189n23, 199n14, 203n6, 204–205n27
Sisters of Loretto, 71, 83–85, 202n3
Sisters of the Visitation, 93
Slave Code (An Act to Provide for the Protection of Property of Slaves in This Territory), 167–168, 180, 223n48
slavery, 23–24, 31, 121–122, 152, 167–169, 180, 185n1, 214n25
Sloan, Eliza St. Clair (Mahoney)
   marriage to Jeremiah Mahoney by, 81–82, 205n30, 205n34
   on the Santa Fe Trail, 69, 81–86, 158, 162
Sloan, Marian. *See* Russell, Marian Sloan
Sloan, William James "Will," 69, 81, 83–85, 96, 158
Soulard, Blanche, 208n65
Soulard, Mary, 208n65
Spain, 2, 54, 55
Speyer, Albert, 220n23
Spiegelberg, Bertha "Betty" Seligman, 154
Spiegelberg, Elias, 154
Spiegelberg, Emanuel, 154

INDEX

Spiegelberg, Florence "Flora" Langerman, 24, 154–155, 172, 180, 220n26, 221n28
Spiegelberg Brothers
    Spiegelberg, Lehman, 154
    Spiegelberg, Levi, 154
    Spiegelberg, Solomon Jacob, 154
    Spiegelberg, Willi, 154–155
    Spiegelberg, Willie, 24
St. Clair Mahoney, Eliza. *See* Mahoney, Eliza St. Clair Sloan
Steamboat Arabia Museum, Kansas City, 174–175
Stearns, Charles Luther, 169
Stearns, George Luther, 168
Stilts, George, 80
St. Joesph Gazette (newspaper), 64, 65
St. Louis, Kansas City and Northern Short Line Railroad, 171
St. Louis, Missouri
    archaeology and mounds of, 35, 193–194n27
    cross-cultural marriages in, 14–15, 22
    demographics of, 35, 152
    education in, 70–72
    French colonial history of, 13–17, 22, 35–37, 193–194n27, 194n28
    human trafficking in, 31
    immigrants in, 153
    indigenous settlements of, 9–10, 12–13, 34–35, 192n20
    lithograph of, 8, 38
    map of, 36, 41
    Native peoples of, 9–10, 12–13, 34–35, 38, 192n20
    property owners in 1823, 41
    strategic importance of, 7–8, 10–11, 12
    wagon manufacturers in, 7–9
    waterfront and wharves in, 7–8
St. Louis Daily Missouri Republican (newspaper), 223n48
St. Louis Enquirer (newspaper), 60
St. Louis University, 71, 91
St. Louis Weekly Reveille (newspaper), 144, 145
Stollsteimer, Christian Frederick, 66–67
Stonewall Valley Ranch and War, 206nn45–47
suffrage, 155, 162–170, 222–223n44
Sukey, Aunt, portrait, 123

Taos, town of, 73–74, 78, 80–81
Taos Pueblo
    captives ransomed at, 32–33
    trade fair at, 30–32
    traders and, 48, 56–57, 197n1
    US battle at, 135, 147–148, 170, 216n39, 220n25
Taos Revolt, against US, 147–148, 216n39, 220n25
Taos Valley, 28–30, 35
Taylor, "Aunt Sally," 137, 216n42
Taylor, Jane Magoffin, 213n12
Taylor-Montoya, Amanda, 61
Tecumseh, prophecy, 52–53
trade
    alliances in, 22
    expansion of, 60
    fairs and rendezvous for, 30, 32
    goods for, 7, 12, 175
    human trafficking, 26, 31, 34, 176
    legality of, 48–49, 59
    market conditions of, 12
    Native Americans and, 10, 12
    partnerships of, 3, 6–8
    profits from, 175–176
    waterways supporting, 7, 9
    See also fur trade
travel, 19th-century, 97–100
Treaty of Guadalupe Hidalgo, 148, 151–152, 170
Treaty of Medicine Lodge, 139
tuberculosis, 97, 100–103, 116. *See also* consumption
Tules, Doña, 130, 150, 179, 213n23

United States, conquest of the Southwest, 2, 5. *See also specific locations*
Upper Louisiana, 14, 36, 41, 60, 192n20
Ute tribe
    Antoine Robidoux and, 198nn5–6, 200n22, 201n38
    attacks on New Mexico and, 31, 32, 90, 158, 179
    Carmel Benavides Robidoux as living near, 66–67, 178
    leader Lechat invites traders to Great Basin, 59–63
    peace with New Mexico and, 54, 59
    pressure on Ute lands, 20, 63
    raid on Santa Fe of, 63
    trade of captives and children by, 63, 198nn5–6, 207n53
    trade with, 10, 12, 59–63

Valenčius, Conevery Bolton, 98, 208n1
Vallé, Catherine, 195n34

Vélez Cachupín, Tomás, 31
Villalpando, Antoine, 36
Villalpando, María Rosa. *See* Salé dit Lajoie, María Rosa Villalpando
Villalpando compound, 30–32
Visitation Academy
   Georgetown, Washington, DC, 95, 208n65
   St. Louis, 71, 91–93, 207n59
von Phul, Anna Maria, 37, 38

Waa-nibe (Singing Grass)
   biography of, 22–23, 69, 73, 76–78, 133
   children of, 69, 73, 77–78, 133
   marriage to Kit Carson, 76–77
   portrait of, 74
Wagon Mound, attack on mail train by Ute and Jicarilla Apaches, 158
Waldo, David, 91–92
Waldo, Donaciana, 92, 94
Wallace, Lew, 24, 155, 220n27
Wallace, Susan Elston, 24, 171–172, 180
Webb, Florilla "Lillie" Mansfield Slade, 106, 108–110
Webb, James Josiah
   child with Flora and, 109
   competition among merchants and, 154
   descendant sells letters of, 209n7
   marriage to Flora by, 105–106
   progression of Kate Kingsbury's health and, 104–105, 110–111
   repositories of letters of, 209n7
   Santa Fe politics and, 108–109, 209–210n14
   Santa Fe store and, 103–104, 107
Weber, David, 62, 197n1, 201, 201n38, 209n7
Weightman, Richard Hanson, 145, 206n35
Willoughby, Robert, 68
Wilson, Jane Adeline, 107, 210n21

women
   abduction of, 31
   African American and Black, 118–124, 136–141 (*See also specific persons*)
   authority of, 41, 47
   as commodities of fur trade, 26, 32
   cross-cultural marriages and, 14, 15, 22, 49, 60–62, 77, 177–178
   as culture brokers and peacemakers, 32–34, 50, 191n16
   description of, 214n23
   French colonial women, 179
   in fur trade, 16, 26, 43, 50, 74–75, 76–77
   Hispanic, 22, 49, 150, 170, 212n44
   historical significance of, 182–183
   illustration of, 37, 38
   influence of, 41
   labor importance of, 185n1
   monuments and memorials to, 18, 181, 188n21
   property rights loss of, 143, 148, 150–151, 170, 200n31
   public rape of, 32
   railroad travels of, 172
   as rendezvous participants, 73, 75–78
   rights of, 179
   and slavery, 24n25, 127
   Spanish colonial rights of, 179
   trafficking of, 26, 30–32, 34, 176
   on US military posts, 161
   white women and the trail, 18–19, 126, 167, 181
   See also specific women

Yoacham, Daniel, 78–81
Yoacham, Susannah, 78–81
Young, Hiram, 122
Young, Matilda, 122
Ysleta del Sur Pueblo, 210n21

Zuni tribe, 118–119

www.ingramcontent.com/pod-product-compliance
Lightning Source LLC
Chambersburg PA
CBHW050611200525
26969CB00008B/94/J